Group Consensus and Minority Influence

𝕁𝔹

Group Consensus and Minority Influence
Implications for Innovation

Edited by

Carsten K. W. De Dreu and Nanne K. De Vries

BLACKWELL
Publishers

Copyright © Blackwell Publishers Ltd 2001

First published 2001

2 4 6 8 10 9 7 5 3 1

Blackwell Publishers Ltd
108 Cowley Road
Oxford OX4 1JF
UK

Blackwell Publishers Inc.
350 Main Street
Malden, Massachusetts 02148
USA

British Library Cataloguing in Publication Data

A CIP catalogue record for this book is available from the British Library.

Library of Congress Cataloging-in-Publication Data

Group consensus and minority influence : implications for innovation / editors, Carsten K. W. De Dreu and Nanne K. De Vries.
    p. cm.
  Includes bibliographical references and index.
  ISBN 0-631-21232-9 (alk. paper) – ISBN 0-631-21233-7 (pb. : alk. paper)
  1. Social influence. 2. Social groups. 3. Majorities. 4. Minorities. 5. Consensus (Social sciences) I. Dreu, Carsten K. W. de. II. Vries, Nanne K. de.
  HM1176 .G76 2001

                                                                                    00-050769

Typeset in 10½ on 12½ pt Bembo
by Best-set Typesetter Ltd., Hong Kong
Printed in Great Britain by MPG Books, Ltd., Bodmin

This book is printed on acid-free paper

Contents

Notes on Contributors

The Editors

Carsten K.W. De Dreu is Professor of Organizational Psychology at the University of Amsterdam, The Netherlands. He received his PhD in social psychology from the University of Groningen, The Netherlands, and was visiting researcher at the University of Geneva in Switzerland, the University of Illinois at Champaign-Urbana, and Yale University. He is program director of the Work and Organizational Psychology program at the University of Amsterdam, and research director of the Kurt Lewin Graduate School for Social Psychology and its applications. He received the Best Dissertation Award from the International Association for Conflict Management in 1994, and the Early Career Award (Jaspars Lecture) from the European Association of Experimental Social Psychology in 1996. Carsten De Dreu was elected President of the International Association for Conflict Management, and he serves on the editorial board of the *European Journal of Social Psychology*, *Journal of Organizational Behavior*, and the *International Journal of Conflict Management*. He is coeditor of *Using conflict in organizations* (1997) and has published over 50 journal articles and book chapters on interpersonal and group negotiation, minority–majority influence, and team innovation.

Nanne De Vries is Professor of Health Education and Promotion at Maastricht University, The Netherlands. He studied social psychology at the University of Groningen where he obtained his PhD in 1988 and was Associate Professor of Social Psychology at the University of Amsterdam from 1989 to 2000. He has been Chair of the Dutch Association for Social Psychology and served on the reviewing board of the Dutch National Science Foundation (NWO). He is the coauthor of two Dutch textbooks on social cognition and on attitude change and persuasion, and has published numerous articles on social comparison and social identity theory and on attitude structure, persuasion, and attitude change.

The Authors

Elizabeth M. Anderson is a study director for Calder LaTour Inc., a consumer research firm located in Evanston, IL. She is currently completing her PhD. in applied social psychology at Loyola University, Chicago, where she received the 2000 Sujack Award for excellence in graduate student teaching. Her research interests include academic procrastination, self-regulation theories of motivation, and the effects of violence in the media.

Bianca Beersma received her MA in social psychology from the Free University of Amsterdam and is currently a PhD student in organizational psychology at the University of Amsterdam. Her research concerns the motivational, cognitive, and structural aspects of group negotiations. Her work is forthcoming in the *International Journal of Conflict Management* and has been presented at several conferences.

Gerd Bohner is Senior Lecturer in Psychology at the University of Kent, Canterbury, UK, where he teaches social psychology, statistics, and research methods. After graduating in psychology at the University of Heidelberg in 1986, he received his Dr. Phil. at Heidelberg in 1990, and his *Habilitation* at the University of Mannheim, Germany, in 1997. In addition to posts at Heidelberg and Mannheim, he was a Feodor Lynen Research Fellow at New York University (1991–2) and held a temporary professorship at the University of Würzburg, Germany (1998), until he moved to Canterbury in 1998. His research interests include social influence and persuasion, gender-related attitudes and behavior, and the interplay of affect and cognition in social judgments. He is consulting editor of the *British Journal of Social Psychology*, the *European Journal of Social Psychology*, and *Group Processes and Intergroup Relations*.

Fabrizio Butera is professor of social psychology at the Université Pierre-Mendes France in Grenoble, France. He received his Ph.D in social psychology from the University of Geneva. He is interested in majority and minority influence, and in judgment and decision making. His publications include articles in the *European Journal of Social Psychology* and the *British Journal of Social Psychology*.

Shelly Chaiken received her PhD in 1978 from the University of Massachusetts at Amherst before teaching at the University of Toronto and then Vanderbilt University. She has been professor of Psychology at New York University since 1985. She has published *The Psychology of Attitudes* with Alice H. Eagly (1993) and is also the author of numerous theoretical, review, and empirical articles on attitude structure, formation, and change.

William D. Crano is Professor of Psychology at Claremont Graduate University. He received his A.B. from Princeton in 1964. His MS (1966) and PhD (1968) from Northwestern University were directed by Donald Campbell. He has served on the faculties of Michigan State University, Texas A&M University, and the University of Arizona. He served as the Program Director in Social Psychology for the National Science Foundation, as Liaison Scientist for the Office of Naval Research, London, as NATO Senior Scientist, University of Southampton, and was a Fulbright Fellow to the Federal University–Rio Grande do Sul, Porto Alegre, Brazil. He was founder/director of the Center for Evaluation and Assessment, Michigan State University, and directed the Public Policy Resources Laboratory of Texas A&M. Crano's research is currently funded by the National Institute on Drug Abuse and the National Institute for Child Health and Human Development. He has written eight books, more than 30 book chapters, and over 300 scholarly articles and scientific presentations. He is the past President of the Society for Experimental Social Psychology, and is a Fellow of the American Psychological Association, the American Psychological Society, and the Society for Personality and Social Psychology. He serves on two review panels for the National Institutes of Health, and is on the editorial boards of three journals in social psychology and communication.

Barbara David is a Lecturer in Psychology at The Australian National University, Canberra. She attended Macquarie University, was awarded the APS Honours Prize, an Australian Postgraduate Research Award, and attained her doctorate in behavioral sciences. She moved to Canberra in 1991 and since then has lectured in psychology at the ANU. In her PhD thesis, "Self-categorization and minority conversion," she was supervised by John Turner and has continued this collaboration in influence research since. Her interest and involvement in the women's movement has been an impetus for understanding the ways in which members of social movements, frequently negatively stereotyped, and with little power, are able to be a force for change in society. Her other area of research interest, the social psychology of gender, springs from the same source.

Hans-Peter Erb is currently working as a Postdoctoral Fellow at the University of Maryland, College Park. He graduated in psychology at the University of Mannheim in 1993 and earned his doctoral degree at the University of Heidelberg in 1996. Before he moved to Maryland he worked as an assistant professor at the University of Würzburg. His primary interests focus on social influence, persuasion, and human judgment in general.

Ernestine Gordijn received her PhD from the University of Amsterdam in 1998, where she is currently a Postdoctoral Research Associate. Her research interests are minority influence and attitude change, automatic and controlled processes in stereotyping, and emotions in intergroup processes.

Miles Hewstone studied psychology at the University of Bristol, and obtained his D.Phil from Oxford University in 1981, and his *Habilitation* from the University of Tübingen in 1986. He then undertook postdoctoral work with Serge Moscovici in Paris and Wolfgang Stroebe in Tübingen. He has held chairs in social psychology at the universities of Bristol and Mannheim, and is now Professor of Psychology at Cardiff University. He has published widely on the topics of attribution theory, social cognition, stereotyping, and intergroup relations. His books include *Causal attribution: From cognitive processes to collective beliefs* (Blackwell, 1989), *Contact and conflict in intergroup encounters* (edited with R. Brown, Blackwell, 1986), *Stereotypes and stereotyping* (edited with C.N. Macrae and C. Stangor, 1996), and *Introduction to social psychology* (edited with W. Stroebe; 3rd edn., Blackwell, 2000). His current work centers on the reduction of intergroup conflict, via intergroup contact, stereotype change, and crossed categorization. He is a former editor of the *British Journal of Social Psychology*, and cofounding editor of the *European Review of Social Psychology*. He is a past recipient of the British Psychological Society's Spearman Medal, and has twice been a Fellow at the Center for Advanced Study in the Behavioral Sciences, Stanford (1987–8, 1999–2000).

Juliet Kaarbo received her PhD in 1993 from The Ohio State University where she was awarded a dissertation fellowship from the United States National Science Foundation Research Training Group on Cognition and Collective Political Decision Making. She is currently as Associate Professor of Political Science at the University of Kansas. Her research focuses on comparative foreign policy, political leadership and personality, group dynamics, the comparative case study method, international relations theory, and international negotiations. She has recently contributed articles to *International Studies Quarterly, Political Psychology, European Journal of International Relations,*

Leadership Quarterly, Cooperation and Conflict, and *Mershon International Studies Review*. She currently serves as coeditor of the International Society of Political Psychology newsletter and as an officer in the Foreign Policy Analysis section of the International Studies Association.

Norbert L. Kerr is Professor of Psychology at Michigan State University. After receiving his BA in physics in 1970 from Washington University, St. Louis, he completed his graduatework in social psychology in 1974 at the University of Illinois, Champaign–Urbana. He is a Fellow of the American Psychological Society, the Society of Personality and Social Psychology, and the Society for the Psychological Study of Social Issues. Besides serving on several journal's editorial boards, he is a past Associate Editor of the *Journal of Personality and Social Psychology-Interpersonal Relations and Group Processes* and the *Personality and Social Psychology Review*. His research interests center on several aspects of small group behavior, including group decision making (particularly developing and applying mathematical models), group performance (particularly the study of group member task motivation), cooperation in groups (particularly within social dilemmas), and jury decision making. In addition, he does work on juror decision making and scientific hypothesis development. Besides authoring many scientific articles, he is the coeditor of *The psychology of the courtroom* (1982) and coauthor of *Group process, group decision, group action* (1992).

John M. Levine did his undergraduate work at Northwestern University and received his PhD in 1969 from the University of Wisconsin at Madison. He is currently Professor of Psychology and Senior Scientist in the Learning Research and Development Center at the University of Pittsburgh. His research focuses on small group processes, particularly group socialization, majority and minority influence, and team performance. Dr. Levine has served as associate editor of the *Journal of Research in Personality* and as both associate editor and editor of the *Journal of Experimental Social Psychology*. He has also been a member of several editorial boards, including *Social Psychology Quarterly, Journal of Personality and Social Psychology, Personality and Social Psychology Review, Basic and Applied Social Psychology, Personality and Social Psychology Bulletin, Social Cognition,* and *Group Processes and Intergroup Relations*. He has served on the NSF Advisory Panel for Social and Developmental Psychology and the NIMH Social and Group Processes Review Committee. He is a fellow of the American Psychological Association and the American Psychological Society, an affiliate member of the European Association of Experimental Social Psychology, and a member (and Chair of the Executive Committee) of the Society of Experimental Social Psychology.

Robin Martin has research interests in both social and organizational psychology. He obtained his doctorate from The Open University in 1986 with a thesis examining the effects of social categorization on minority influence. Following this he spent five years as a research fellow at the MRC/ESRC Social and Applied Psychology Unit at Sheffield University. During that time he was involved in a project examining the psychological and organizational implications of computer-controlled technology in manufacturing organizations. After leaving Sheffield, he held lecturing positions at the University of Wales Swansea and Cardiff University. He is currently an Associate Professor of Psychology and Director of the Centre for Organizational Psychology at the University of Queensland in Brisbane, Australia. In addition to his academic work, he has acted as a management consultant to a large number of public and private organizations. His current research interests are in attitude change, social influence processes (especially majority and minority influence), psychological effects of job relocation, and workplace leadership.

Gordon Moskowitz received his PhD from New York University in 1993. While at NYU, he developed interests in impression formation, automaticity, minority influence, accessibility effects, stereotypes, and the effects of goals on each of these processes. Following graduate training he went to Munich to do postdoctoral research with Peter Gollwitzer on the preconscious operation of goals. After one year as a faculty member at the University of Konstanz, he moved to Princeton University, where he has been an Assistant Professor in the Psychology department since 1994. In addition to his research presented in psychology journals, he has edited *Cognitive social psychology* (in press) and is writing a textbook on person perception.

Gabriel Mugny is professor of social psychology at the Université de Geneva. He is interested in sociocognitive development of intelligence, and in majority–minority influence. He has published several books and edited volumes, including *The Power of Minorities* (1982). In addition, he has written numerous research papers that have appeared in such journals as the *European Journal of Social Psychology* and the *British Journal of Social Psychology*, and has edited the *Swiss Journal of Psychology*.

K. Yee Ng is a doctoral student in Organizational Behavior at Michigan State University. She received her Bachelor's degree (1995) from Nanyang

Business School in Singapore, and was awarded a scholarship by the school in 1997 to pursue a PhD at Michigan State. Her primary research interests include cultural influences in minority influence, negotiation, and psychological contracts, as well as the role of individual differences in motivation under dual tasks. Her publications include articles in the *Journal of Applied Psychology* and *Organizational Behavior and Human Decision Processes* as well as a chapter on psychological contracts in Singapore in *Psychological Contracts in Employment: Cross-national Perspectives* (2000).

Tom Postmes has a PhD from the University of Amsterdam and holds a fellowship of the Royal Netherlands Academy of Arts and Sciences at the Amsterdam School of Communications Research, University of Amsterdam. His research focuses on social influence and social identity in groups, examining both fundamental aspects and applications in fields such as computer-mediated communication, collective behavior, and organizational contexts. His research has been published in various journals, such as *Psychological Bulletin, Journal of Personality and Social Psychology*, and *Personality and Social Psychology Bulletin*.

Christine M. Smith is an associate professor of Psychology at Grand Valley State University, Allendale, MI. Her research interests include minority influence in small interacting groups and group decision making. She is a consulting editor for *Group Processes and Intergroup Relations*.

R. Scott Tindale is a Professor and the Director of the Applied Social Psychology program at Loyola University Chicago. He is a coeditor for the *Social Psychological Applications to Social Issues* series sponsored by the Society for the Psychological Study of Social Issues and has recently coedited the *Group Processes* volume for the *Blackwell Handbook of Social Psychology*. He is also an associate editor for *Group Processes and Intergroup Relations*. His research interests include small group decision making, group information processing, and majority–minority influence in small interacting groups.

John C. Turner is Professor of Psychology at the Australian National University, Canberra. He obtained his BA (1971) and PhD (1975) degrees in social psychology in England at the Universities of Sussex and Bristol respectively. He is a past Visiting Member of the Institute for Advanced Study, Princeton, NJ (1982–3) and has also held appointments at the University of Bristol (1974–83) and Macquarie University in Sydney (1983–90). He is the co-originator of social identity theory with Henri Tajfel, with whom he worked closely on social identity and intergroup relations in the early 1970s at Bristol, and he is also the author of self-categorization theory, a theory of the relationship between self, cognition, and the group. His work on social influence began in 1978 in the context of his self-categorical analysis of group processes. His research interests are in the role of social identity and self-categorization processes in intergroup relations; group processes, particularly social influence; social cognition; and the self-concept. In 1999 he gave the Tajfel Memorial Lecture of the European Association of Experimental Social Psychology on "The prejudiced personality and social change: A self-categorization perspective," and he is currently working on a book on prejudice.

Linn Van Dyne is Associate Professor in the department of Management at Michigan State University. She received her PhD from the University of Minnesota in Strategic Management and Organizations. Her primary research interest is proactive employee behaviors involving initiative, including affiliative and challenging extrarole behavior and minority influence. Additional interests include international organizational behavior and the effects of work context, roles, and groups on employee attachment and behavior. Her research has been published in *Academy of Management Journal, Academy of Managment Review, Journal of Applied Psychology, British Journal of Social Psychology, Journal of Organizational Behavior,* and *Research in Organizational Behavior.* She is on the editorial board of *Academy of Management Review* and is Consulting Editor for *Journal of Organizational Behavior.*

Acknowledgements

This book is born out of a small group meeting we organized in Amsterdam, in the fall of 1998. The meeting was made possible through the generous funding of several organizations. We are grateful to the Netherlands Organization for Scientific Research (NWO), to the Royal Netherlands Academy of Sciences (KNAW), to the Dutch Association of Social Psychologists (ASPO), to the European Association for Experimental Social Psychology (EAESP), and to the Department of Psychology of the University of Amsterdam.

Without a wonderful editorial team at Blackwell this book would not exist. We very much appreciate Martin Davis for his confidence and early initiatives, and thank Siobhan Pattinson, Alison Dunnett, and their colleagues for their patience and constructive guidance throughout.

1

Group Consensus and Minority Influence: Introduction and Overview

Nanne K. De Vries and
Carsten K. W. De Dreu

Since the beginnings of social psychology, social influence has been at the core of the discipline. Most theory and research has been directed at understanding the way in which people come to share opinions, attitudes, norms, and behavior. All levels of analysis have been applied: intraindividual cognitive processes, interaction between persons, processes within and between groups. Given this focus on conformity, compliance, and the way that groups come to function as norms emerge, relatively little attention has been given to the processes by which groups change and innovate. Anecdotes from political and jury decision making, as well as from revolutionary movements, suggest that sometimes small factions within a group or society can influence the larger majority. Sometimes minorities convince the majority (i.e., direct influence), and sometimes they inspire the majority to come to new and previously unconsidered points of view (indirect influence).

These everyday observations inspire a broad and diverse set of interrelated questions, including: How do people respond to majority or minority opposition? When do minority factions impact the beliefs and opinions of members of the majority? Is there a general tendency towards group consensus based on the majority point of view, or can minority opposition change the way groups "think"? Can minority opposition influence innovation? How does majority and minority influence affect individual judgment and group decision making? These are questions that have long been of interest in social psychology and related disciplines, and it is these questions that were pursued in the seminal and original theorizing and empirical work of Serge Moscovici (1976, 1980).

Moscovici's original and groundbreaking work will be discussed in greater detail in the next section. His thinking inspired many researchers to conduct experimental and observational studies that have resulted in a variety of theoretical positions and conceptual models. Although the field has moved forward tremendously in the past several decades, there has also been a tendency to put forward rather idiosyncratic theories, including different labels for similar (if not identical) processes. This may result in a "Babel-like confusion of tongues" (De Vries, De Dreu, Gordijn, & Schuurman, 1996, p. 146) which obscures the debate and limits scientific progress. To counteract this, and to further our understanding of majority and minority influence, we organized a small-group meeting in Amsterdam in October 1998. With an aim toward integration and improved comparability, social psychologists from Europe, Australia, and the United States with an interest in majority and minority influence presented their views on the topic and discussed recent empirical work.

This book is a product of that conference. It presents 13 state-of-the-art literature reviews on the impact of majority and minority influence on attitude change and persuasion, on individual and group problem solving, and on group performance and innovation. To set the stage, this chapter first introduces Moscovici's original conversion theory, that still inspires much of the recent work, and summarizes some of his original experiments. Second, we describe a few important developments of Moscovici's theory. We conclude with an overview of the chapters in this book, and highlight implications for practice and avenues for future research.

Conversion Theory

Recognizing that the dominant tendency in social psychological theorizing was on how majorities in groups influence smaller factions, the question was how and when minorities affect the larger group they belong to. The starting point of Moscovici's conversion theory (1976) is, accordingly, the distinction between majority and minority influence, which is conceived of as a dual process theory since it assumes that there is a qualitative difference between the two. The theory focuses on the reactions of group members when they realize that their opinions and judgments deviate from those of some of the other members. When these others constitute a majority, a comparison process is started (perhaps best represented by the question: "What are they saying?"). When these others represent a minority, a validation process is set off (perhaps best represented by the question "Why would they say that?"). The influence of majorities via the comparison process is portrayed as compliance, as in Asch's (1955) work on conformity: The power of a majority resides in its ability to punish and reward group members. Deviance is punished in subtle or not so subtle ways; group members therefore are inclined to comply to group norms of appropriate behavior and opinions. Compliance does not necessarily imply that this conformity is internalized; rather, it is a superficial process in which one's own judgments and opinions are compared to those that are prevalent within the group and adapted accordingly. This is how Moscovici conceived of majority influence: There is change, albeit without any adaptation of the cognitive system on which the original opinion, judgment, or behavior was based; it is unconflicted change. Often, the process of social comparison does not result in any real, persistent changes in the cognitive structure.

Minority influence is based on a more involving process, called validation. A minority lacks the power to reward or punish; it cannot exert influence by sheer force. But when a minority expresses its ideas repeatedly (resisting the conformity pressures from the group) and with confidence, majority members will come to consider exactly what is being said, and why. In other words, when a minority expresses a deviant view using a behavioral style that expresses confidence and consistency, the majority group member wants to understand why they (dare) do this. In trying to understand what the minority apparently understands, a cognitive conflict is brought about and the group member, in trying to comprehend the deviant position, validates it.

Often, this validation process will not lead to direct, immediate, or publicly announced change. Because of the power of the majority, group members are reluctant to align publicly with the minority. Rather, the process of reconsidering one's own point of view, and the thoughtful consideration of alternative views, results in changing the (cognitive) basis of the original opinion: "real" change, not contingent upon the power of the group and its presence, but based on new ideas and cognitions. This "real" influence will be indirect rather than direct, delayed rather than immediate. As such, minority influence has two different components: resistance to immediate influence, but conversion to other views in the long run.

Original Empirical Evidence

To demonstrate minority influence, Moscovici and his associates conducted several experiments using a reversed Asch paradigm. In the first of these studies (Moscovici, Lage, & Naffrechoux, 1969), six-person groups judged the color of slides. The slides were clearly blue as was corroborated in a control condition where virtually all participants called the color blue after seeing the slide. However, in the experimental conditions, two confederates publicly and consistently announced that they saw a green slide. Consistent with a minority influence effect, 8% of the four "naive" participants in these conditions called the color "green" after they saw the slide. In follow-up studies, conditions promoting or inhibiting minority influence were studied. For instance, when the confederates deviated inconsistently (two-thirds of all trials), their influence dropped to nonsignificant levels (Moscovici & Lage, 1976). Thus, these experiments support conversion theory's proposition that as long as a minority remains consistent, it may influence judgment and attitudes.

Conversion theory, however, predicts that the influence of minorities is indirect rather than direct, and private rather than public. Moscovici and Personnaz (1980) conducted a study on the judgment of afterimages of colors rather than of the color itself. A blue slide should evoke an orange/yellow afterimage, whereas a green slide should evoke a red/purple afterimage. Moscovici and Personnaz (1980) reasoned that majority influence should affect judgments of the color of the slides, but minority influence should affect judgments of the afterimage (since this reflects how people "really" judge the slide). Groups of two, a genuine participant and a confederate, judged the color of slides and of the afterimage they perceived. In a pretesting phase, both the naive participant and the confederate made private judgments of slide and afterimage. Then the experimenter announced that either a majority or a minority of previously tested subjects saw this slide to be green (wrong answer), whereupon the confederate announced her response to be green as well. Finally the participant privately wrote down his or her own answers. Results revealed no differences in private judgments of the color of the slide between the majority and the minority conditions. But analysis of afterimage judgments revealed that in the minority conditions more than in the majority conditions, participants' judgments of afterimages suggested they really saw green (rather than blue) slides. Moscovici and Personnaz (1980) concluded that private judgments of color may be influenced by minority viewpoints, but not by majority ones, and that this will become apparent in indirect measures.

Many more variations of the color perception studies and the afterimage paradigm have been reported, by Moscovici and colleagues and by others. The evidence from these studies has not remained uncriticized (see Martin and Hewstone in this volume). More importantly for the present purposes, the original empirical work by Moscovici inspired a multitude of studies both in the domain of individual and group problem solving and in the domain of persuasion and attitude change. We briefly review these research traditions in the next sections.

Divergent Thinking

Research on simple problem-solving tasks has brought more clarity about what happens when a minority in a group dissents from the majority. Nemeth (1986; Nemeth & Kwan, 1987) suggests that the way people react to a minority differs qualitatively from the response to a majority. When a group member discovers that there is a discrepancy between their own opinion and that of a majority in the group, attention will be focused on those two points of view. The group member considers only these two alternatives, in order to decide whether to stick to their own position (and ignore the power of the group) or to conform to the majority. Nemeth calls this process *convergent thinking*.

When confronted with a dissenting minority, the pressure to conform to that particular view is rather low, and direct change of opinion towards the minority is unlikely. However, given a consistent and persistent behavioral style, the minority will trigger the consideration of alternatives, not necessarily the one suggested by the minority itself. This creative thought process is called *divergent thinking*. To test this differential effect of majority versus minority influence Nemeth and Kwan (1987) asked participants in groups of four to note the first three-letter word they discovered in a string of six letters (e.g., tNOWap). The obvious answer is *NOW*. The participants subsequently received feedback indicating that either one or three of the other group members had noted a different word (e.g., *WON*). The experimenters were particularly interested in the effect this feedback had on the solution of the next problems. When confronted with the dissenting majority, participants often adopted the strategy of the majority (backward reading). Those exposed to a dissenting minority, however, used wider variety of strategies such as mixing up all the letters, reading forward, and reading backward. The strategy of the minority therefore was not "blindly" followed, but rather the minority led to a consideration of all possible strategies.

An interesting application of these ideas on minority influence on attitudes is reported by Pérez and Mugny (1987), who have shown that divergent processing of dissenting minority messages leads to change on attitude issues related to the message itself. In particular, they were able to show that a counterattitudinal message concerning abortion, supposedly originating from a minority, affected abortion attitudes on a posttest. In addition they measured attitudes towards contraception: These were not affected by the majority message concerning abortion. When the proabortion message came from a minority source, however, hardly any direct influence on the abortion attitude was observed but attitude change on birth control attitudes was observed. Indirect influence of minorities in the realm of attitudes therefore apparently can mean diffusion to issues related but not identical to the attitude targeted in a persuasive message.

Dual Process Theories of Persuasion

Maass and Clark tested conversion theory in the realm of attitude change (Maass & Clark, 1983, 1986; Clark & Maass, 1988). In their typical study, they provided participants with written transcripts of group discussions on gay rights. In these group discussions, a minority of one group member gave eight arguments favoring gay rights, while the majority of four also gave a total of eight arguments which opposed gay rights (or vice versa). Thus, participants read eight minority-supported arguments for one position, and eight majority-supported arguments for the opposing position. Subsequently, participants were asked to give their opinions about gay rights. In one condition, these opinions would be publicly disclosed in anticipation of group discussion, whereas in another condition these opinions would remain private and anonymous. Results repeatedly revealed that in the public disclosure conditions, attitudes agreed more with the majority rather than the minority viewpoint, whereas in the private attitude conditions, the reverse pattern was found. Moreover, especially in the private opinion conditions, attitude change could be successfully predicted from thought listings that participants provided afterwards (Maass & Clark, 1983).

This latter result can be understood by applying dual process theories of persuasion (the elaboration likelihood model; Petty & Cacioppo, 1986; the heuristic-systematic model; Eagly & Chaiken, 1993). In terms of these models, conversion theory predicts that majorities who enforce conformity instigate superficial processing of their position: it is heuristically adopted. The validation process that minorities cause is a systematic thought process. In systematic processing, the thoughts that come up should be related to attitude change.

Dual process theories have been applied to minority influence by several authors (see, e.g., Moskowitz & Chaiken in this volume). In our own work (see De Vries et al., 1996) we combined the dual processing view with

Nemeth's work on convergent and divergent thought. Assuming that majority dissent is more motivating than minority dissent, we predict that (other things being equal) systematic processing of majority messages is more likely. Minorities thus have a double disadvantage: (a) their messages are at risk of being heuristically processed; and, if so, (b) the "consensus implies correctness" heuristic (Axsom, Yates, & Chaiken, 1987) implies small effects of their persuasive attempts. This double disadvantage may, however, be counteracted by a variety of factors, rendering minority messages motivating and more likely to be processed systematically. Provided the minority message contains solid and valid arguments, such systematic processing should result in attitude change toward the minority position. For example, when the minority employs a consistent behavioral style it increases the majority members' motivation to process systematically the minority message. Or when the minority message cannot be attributed to the minorities' self-interest, majority members are expected to become more motivated to engage in systematic processing of the minority message.

Following Nemeth's work, we suggested that the systematic processing of majority messages will be mostly convergent by nature, leading to direct influence on the attitude that is the focus of the majority message. Minority messages will predominantly lead to divergent processing, promoting change on issues related to the focus of the persuasive message. Direct change in this case will be absent due to a fear of being identified with the minority. Consistent with this reasoning, the many factors outlined by De Vries et al. (1996) as leading to an increase in majority members' motivation to engage in systematic processing of the minority message are associated with more indirect minority influence (Wood, Lundgren, Ouellette, Busceme, & Blackstone, 1994). Many of the elements of our theoretical analysis return in the work of Crano (see Chapter 6), who describes how groups have an implicit agreement (the *leniency contract*) to at least listen respectfully to minorities, provided the minority members understand that consensus cannot be disrupted. Therefore it is not expected that minorities will have direct influence. The influence of the minority message will, however, be apparent on attitudes related to the focal issue because the message and arguments have received attention.

Overview of the Chapters

The following five chapters (chapters 2–6) in this volume all deal, in one way or another, with the influence of majority and minority messages on individual perceptions, attitudes, and judgments. The next seven chapters (chapters 7–13) consider the influence of majority and minority influence on group problem solving, group decision making, and group judgment. This section gives a brief summary of each of the chapters in an effort to highlight some of the important similarities and discrepancies. Gradually, we move up from the intrapersonal level of perception and cognitive processes to group levels, including small groups, organizations, and culture.

In chapter 2, Martin and Hewstone review the literature on color perception and afterimage effects, as used in the original studies by Moscovici and colleagues. They report their own experiments in which new procedures and dependent measures are used, and draw theoretical conclusions. Chapter 3 is based on the idea that the only real essential difference between a majority and a minority is the numerical size. In most experiments, much more information than just sheer numbers is provided to participants when majority or minority messages are delivered to them. Erb and Bohner investigate the effects of this variable in isolation, or, in their own words, "mere consensus."

In the next three chapters an old discussion is revived: Are there qualitative differences between the processes by which majorities and minorities persuade their audiences? In chapter 4, Moskowitz and Chaiken analyze minority influence in terms of the heuristic-systematic model and point at important mediators of the impact of minorities. In chapter 5, David and Turner question the assumptions underlying dual process models and suggest that both minority and majority influence can be understood in terms of the same single process. Self-categorization, in their view, provides a sufficient and simple account for their data, based on processes of identification with the group one feels one belongs to and of differentiation from outgroups. In chapter 6, Crano describes his model of minority influence as described in the previous section, based on the leniency contract, and reports data supporting this model. Importantly, he relates the existence of this leniency contract to social identity processes, thereby bridging the gap with self-categorization theory as reported in the chapter by David and Turner.

In chapter 7, Gordijn, De Vries, and Postmes describe a number of studies about self-persuasion: Participants are requested to empathize with the views expressed by either a minority or a majority, and subsequently effects of this cognitive exercise on attitudes and underlying beliefs are measured. These effects are related to identification and cognitive processes. The concept of conflict, the core of conversion theory, is central to chapter 8 by Butera and Mugny. They analyze this concept in the realm of hypothesis testing, a lay epistemological process, showing that information from minorities is treated differently than majority information.

In the previous chapters, experiments mostly employ a method in which information is provided to participants without them actually interacting with sources of influence. In chapter 9, Smith, Tindale, and Anderson analyze the interactions within groups, showing that minority influence is mediated by the extent to which other group members can recognize themselves in the representation of issues forwarded by that minority. In chapter 10, Kerr makes the important observation that groups face different types of problems, and contrasts judgment tasks with intellective tasks for which one single correct answer exists. He carefully analyzes the consequences of task type for majority and minority influence and offers interesting avenues for future research. Levine and Kaarbo, in chapter 11, offer a theoretical analysis of decision making in politics and more specifically of minority influence within this context. They focus on the potentials of minority influence within political decision-making systems.

Chapter 12 extends the analysis of minority influence to groups in organizations. De Dreu and Beersma describe performance effects, based on the idea that divergent thought increases creativity and innovation, and furthermore analyze the effects of minority dissent on cooperative relations within organizations. In the final chapter, Ng and Van Dyne place minority influence in a cultural context. Using Hofstede's classification system of cultural variations, they predict the potential for minorities to exert influence.

Emerging Issues

To conclude this introduction, we would like to discuss some of the main topics that are discussed in the book, drawing upon the different chapters. We hope this will help the reader to put the different chapters into context. Furthermore, it draws the outline of a research agenda for future years. We have organized them in three sections: contextual factors, processing motivations, and dependent variables.

Contextual factors

Early work on the influence of majority and minority factions was relatively context free. Moscovici's conversion theory (Moscovici, 1980) was strongly influenced by intelligent observation of tendencies in society, but was otherwise presented as a generic theory. Similarly, the innovative work by Nemeth (1986) has considered the impact of minority dissent on divergent thinking and group innovation to be relatively independent of specific contextual variation. Likewise, many of the chapters in this book are based on the same assumption. The authors analyze the influence of majority and minority factions in terms of, for instance, the faction's behavioral style and resultant attribution processes (Moskowitz & Chaiken, chapter 4), in terms of self-categorization processes (David & Turner, chapter 5; Gordijn, De Vries, & Postmes, chapter 7), and in terms of within-group psychological contracts (Crano, chapter 6).

Although assuming context-free processes have a number of advantages, several authors have taken issue with contextual factors as key in understanding the influence of majority and minority influence. Levine and Kaarbo (chapter 11; see also De Dreu & Beersma, chapter 12) suggest four different types of minority factions, based on the kind of change advocated by the minority (forward, or backward) and the minorities' impact on change (promotion or blockage). They argue that different types of minority factions have important implications for their effectiveness in political decision-making groups, and De Dreu and Beersma (chapter 12) use this typology to analyze minority dissent in organizational teams and work groups. Both chapters present theoretical analyses, and research is needed to test the authors' propositions.

Another important contextual factor that emerges in several chapters is the nature of the issue under debate (i.e., Smith, Tindale, & Anderson, chapter 9; Butera & Mugny, chapter 8; and Kerr, chapter 10). Building upon a theoretical analysis of group decision making (Baron, Kerr, & Miller, 1993), Kerr analyzes minority influence in terms of the issue under debate. He distinguishes between intellective, partially intellective, and evaluative (or judgmental) issues. Intellective issues have correct solutions according to commonly accepted standards. Examples are what is the shortest way from A to B, and which procedure is most efficient. Evaluative issues, however, have no correct solution and are a matter of taste. Examples are the question of how to get from A to B, and whether efficiency should be the prevailing criterion in selecting a procedure. Intellective issues are associated with being influenced to accept information from another person about reality (informational influence), while evaluative issues are associated with being influenced to conform with the positive expectations of another person (normative influence; Deutsch & Gerard, 1955).

Kerr's analysis is important in that it provides a bridge between currently distinct and isolated lines of research, that is, those on group decision making and those on majority and minority influence on attitudes and attitude change. The analysis also allows us to connect these diverse literatures to research and theory on social conflict (De Dreu, Harinck, & Van Vianen, 1999; Levine & Thompson, 1996). Generally speaking, social conflict is defined as the process that starts when someone perceives a difference with someone else about something that he or she cares about (Thomas, 1992; Pruitt, 1998). This difference may relate to the allocation and distribution of both tangible and intangible resources such as time, money, power, status, and responsibility (i.e., conflict of interests). Alternatively, differences may relate to opposing views on intellective and evaluative issues (conflict of understanding; see, e.g., De Dreu et al., 1999; Kelley & Thibaut, 1969; Levine & Thompson, 1996; Thomas, 1992). Recent research has begun to unravel the effects of different conflict issues on motivation, cognition, and behavioral interaction (Druckman, 1994; Harinck, De Dreu, & Van Vianen, 2000) and suggests that conflict of interest is more easily resolved through mutual give and take than is conflict of understanding. Interestingly, research and theory on majority and minority influence has focused primarily on conflict of understanding and confuses intellective and evaluative issues. Future work is needed to unravel the consequences of minority dissent regarding the allocation and distribution of resources, or regarding views with regard to intellective or evaluative issues.

A final contextual factor that needs future work is the culture in which minority dissent occurs. Ng and Van Dyne (chapter 13) analyze culture in terms of Hofstede's typology including collectivism–individualism, power distance, masculinity–femininity, and uncertainty orientation (Hosftede, 1980). Most of the work on majority and minority influence has been conducted in Western societies characterized by individualistic values, and research is needed to examine minority influence in collectivist culture characterized by greater interdependence, need for harmony, and conflict avoidance. Interestingly, however, majority–minority influence research has been conducted in several countries that differ in terms of power distance (high in the UK, in France, and in Spain, but low in the USA and in The Netherlands) and that differ in terms of masculinity and femininity (high in France, Spain, the USA and the UK, but low in The Netherlands). To some extent the results obtained in these countries converge, suggesting limited influence of power distance and masculinity–femininity. Obviously, research is needed to examine this in a more controlled manner and Ng and Van Dyne provide a careful analysis of how to do this.

Processing motivations

The majority of the chapters in this volume, and most of the research concerned with majority and minority influence, recognizes that variation in the motivation to engage in effortful systematic processing of information may have important consequences for attitude change towards majority or minority positions. Contemporary theories of motives for information processing and attitude change appear to converge on a tripartite distinction. Wood (2000, p. 541) notes that a social influence:

> can be motivated by normative concerns for (a) ensuring the coherence and favorable evaluation of the self, and (b) ensuring satisfactory relations with others . . . along with an informational concern for (c) understanding the entity or issue featured in the influence appeal.

Wood reviews recent evidence for the differential influence of these distinct motivations and relates it to recent work by Bohner (cf. chapter 3) and Crano (cf. chapter 6) on majority and minority influence, suggesting that different motivational goals influence the processing and effects of majority and minority appeals. Future research is needed to consider these various motivational influences more systematically and in greater detail.

Dependent variables

The authors of the chapters in this book focus on a diverse set of dependent variables. Martin and Hewstone (chapter 2) analyze change in (color) perceptions as a function of majority and minority influence. Others focus on attitude change but either concentrate on direct influence only (Erb & Bohner, chapter 3; Moskowitz & Chaiken, chapter 4; David & Turner, chapter 5; Gordijn, De Vries, & Postmes, chapter 7) or on direct and indirect influence (Crano, chapter 6; De Dreu & Beersma, chapter 12). Other chapters are less concerned with attitude change per se, and consider information processing (e.g., divergent thinking; Erb & Bohner; De Dreu & Beersma) and group decision making (Levine & Kaarbo, chapter 11; Butera & Mugny, chapter 8; Smith et al., chapter 9; and Kerr, chapter 10).

To obtain a full understanding of the influence of majority and minority factions in groups and societies, research needs to consider multiple processes simultaneously. That is, future research would benefit from the specific insights provided by the current chapters by incorporating measures of attitude change on both focal and related topics, of convergent and divergent information processing, and of the quality of group decision making including group innovation. In addition, future research needs to take issue with something no single study has done, that is, to examine the consequences of minority dissent for individual well-being and stress. Although research and theory tends to deliver advice for practice, that is, for ways to improve group decision making and foster innovation, we need to know more about the potential downside of minority dissent in terms of its affective consequences for both the dissenter and the receiving majority faction.

REFERENCES

Asch, S. E. (1955). Opinions and social pressure. *Scientific American, 193*, 31–35.

Axsom, D., Yates, S., & Chaiken, S. (1987). Audience response as a heuristic cue in persuasion. *Journal of Personality and Social Psychology, 53*, 30–40.

Baron, R. S., Kerr, N., & Miller, N. (1993). *Group process, group decision, group action.* Buckingham: Open University Press.

Clark, R. D. III, & Maass, A. (1988). The role of social categorization and perceived source credibility in minority influence. *European Journal of Social Psychology, 18*, 381–394.

De Dreu, C. K. W., Harinck, F., & Van Vianen, A. E. M. (1999). Conflict and performance in groups and organizations. In C. L. Cooper and I. Robertson (Eds.), *International review of industrial and organizational psychology* (Vol. 14, pp. 369–414). Chichester: Wiley.

Deutsch, M., & Gerard, H. (1955). A study of normative and informational social influences upon individual judgment. *Journal of Abnormal and Social Psychology, 51*, 629–636.

De Vries, N. K., De Dreu, C. K. W, Gordijn, E. & Schuurman, M. (1996). Majority and minority influence: A dual role interpretation. In W. Stroebe & M. Hewstone (Eds.), *European review of social psychology* (Vol. 7, pp. 145–172). Chichester, UK: Wiley.

Druckman, D. (1994). Determinants of compromising behavior in negotiation. *Journal of Conflict Resolution, 38*, 507–556.

Eagly, A., & Chaiken S. (1993). *The psychology of attitudes.* New York: Hartcourt Brace Jovanovich.

Harinck, F., De Dreu, C. K. W., & Van Vianen, A. E. M. (2000). Assumed conflict in negotiation. The importance of interests, facts and values. *Organizational Behavior and Human Decision Processes, 81*, 359–382.

Hofstede, G. (1980). *Culture's consequences.* London: Sage.

Kelley, H. H., & Thibaut, J. (1969). Group problem solving. In G. Lindzey & E. Aronson (Eds.), *The handbook of social psychology* (2nd ed., Vol. 4, pp. 367–418). Reading, MA: Addison-Wesley.

Levine, J. M., & Thompson, L. L. (1996). Conflict in groups. In E. T. Higgins, and A. W. Kruglanski (Eds.), *Social psychology: Handbook of basic principles* (pp. 745–776). New York: Guilford.

Maass, A., & Clark, R. D. III (1983). Internalization versus compliance: Differential processes underlying minority influence and conformity. *European Journal of Social Psychology, 13*, 197–215.

Maass, A., & Clark, R. D., III (1986). Conversion theory and simultaneous majority/minority influence: Can reactance offer an alternative explanation? *European Journal of Social Psychology, 16*, 305–309.

Moscovici, S. (1976). *Social influence and social change.* London: Academic Press.

Moscovici, S. (1980). Toward a theory of conversion behavior. In L. Berkowitz (Ed.), *Advances in experimental social psychology* (Vol. 13, pp. 209–239). New York: Academic Press.

Moscovici, S., & Lage, E. (1976). Studies in social influence III: Majority versus minority influence in a group. *European Journal of Social Psychology, 6*, 149–174.

Moscovici, S., Lage, E., & Naffrechoux, M. (1969). Influence of a consistent minority on the responses of a majority in a color perception task. *Sociometry, 32*, 365–380.

Moscovici, S., & Personnaz, B. (1980). Studies in social influence V: Minority influence and conversion behavior in a perceptual task. *Journal of Experimental Social Psychology, 10*, 270–282.

Nemeth, C. (1986). Differential contributions of majority and minority influence processes. *Psychological Review, 93*, 10–20.

Nemeth, C., & Kwan, J. (1987). Minority influence, divergent thinking and detection of correct solutions. *Journal of Applied Social Psychology, 17*, 786–797.

Pérez, J. A., & Mugny, G. (1987). Paradoxical effects of categorization in minority influence: When being an outgroup is an advantage. *European Journal of Social Psychology, 17*, 157–169.

Petty, R. E., Cacioppo, J. T. (1986). The elaboration likelihood model of persuasion. In L. Berkowitz (Ed.), *Advances in experimental social psychology* (Vol.19, pp. 123–205). New York: Academic Press.

Pruitt, D. G. (1998). Social conflict. In D. Gilbert, S. T. Fiske, & G. Lindzey (Eds.), *Handbook of social psychology* (4th ed., Vol. 2, pp. 89–150). New York: McGraw-Hill.

Thomas, K. W. (1992). Conflict and negotiation processes in organizations. In M. D. Dunnette & L. M. Hough (Eds.), *Handbook of industrial and organizational psychology* (2nd ed., pp. 651–717). Palo Alto, CA: Consulting Psychologists Press.

Wood, W. (2000). Attitude change: Persuasion and social influence. *Annual Review of Psychology, 51*, 539–570.

Wood, W., Lundgren, S., Ouellette, J. A., Busceme, S., & Blackstone, T. (1994). Minority influence: A meta-analytical review of social influence processes. *Psychological Bulletin, 115*, 323–345.

2

Afterthoughts on Afterimages: A Review of the Afterimage Paradigm in Majority and Minority Influence Research

Robin Martin and Miles Hewstone

Do my eyes deceive me earsight? (*Artemus Ward 1834–67*)

Introduction

This chapter reviews and evaluates a group of studies that examines how a numerical majority or minority can influence participants' color perception. These studies were developed by Serge Moscovici and his colleagues. The basic design is relatively simple and involved participants naming the color of a slide which, based on prior responding, is known to be unambiguously blue. In the experimental conditions the naive participant hears another participant (in fact, a confederate) name the unambiguously blue slide "green." The confederate's response, which is obviously incorrect, is presented as either a majority or minority position by supplying the participant with (false) feedback concerning previous participants' judgments. In these experiments naive participants experience a situation similar to that described in the Artemus Ward quote above, namely a conflict between what they hear the confederate say and what they see with their eyes. The situation has some parallels with the famous Asch studies, except in this case participants are exposed to an erroneous response which they believe is shared by either the numerical majority or minority. While there are two groups of color judgment studies – those concerning the blue–green paradigm (e.g., Moscovici, Lage, & Naffrechoux, 1969) – and those that have developed this initial paradigm to include a measure of perceptual afterimages (e.g., Moscovici & Personnaz, 1980, 1991), this chapter reviews the latter group which are often referred to as the *afterimage studies*.

The fact that these studies were intended to examine true perceptual change, as opposed to verbal compliance, is made clear by Moscovici's (1996) entertaining discussion of the development of the paradigm. He recalls that the idea for the experiments arose out of a discussion with Leon Festinger on the effects of innovation:

> Pointing to the carpet in Claude Faucheux's living room, he [Festinger] asked us: "Do you want to say that if someone declares that this white carpet is pink or blue, I will begin to see it pink or blue?" What else could we answer than "theoretically, yes!"? (p. 10)

Thus the color perception research had two main research questions: First, does the numerical support (majority versus minority) of an incorrect judgment affect its impact upon the naive participant; second, and perhaps more importantly, can the source of influence bring about a true change in perception beyond the public level to a more private level?[1] In other words, can the majority or minority change the way people perceive colors? The answers to these research questions have many implications for understanding the psychological processes involved in majority and minority influence.

It would be reasonable at this stage for the reader to ask, "Why are we devoting an entire review to just one series of studies?". Indeed, we asked ourselves the same question! To answer this, our first thoughts concerned the impact of the afterimage studies in the majority and minority influence literature. A search of citation counts for psychology articles confirmed our impression, and that of other researchers we had talked to, that the Moscovici and Personnaz (1980) paper is the most cited empirical article in the minority influence literature. We believe this to be the case for several reasons. First, the results of these studies are counterintuitive and they challenge many pre-existing concepts of social influence. Indeed, Baron, Kerr, and Miller (1992) describe the results of the afterimage studies as "Astounding! Astonishing! Implausible?" (p. 81). Second, the methodology which these studies developed, and particularly the distinction between influence levels, was ingenious and the afterimage studies have been the catalyst for other researchers to examine conversion effects. Third, as noted by Brewer and Crano (1994), the results of replications of the Moscovici and Personnaz (1980) study "are as interesting as they are controversial" (p. 395). Fourth, the paper was published in the same year as Moscovici's (1980) highly influential conversion theory, and the results of the afterimage studies are often cited as one of the main supporting pieces of evidence for that theory. It is for these reasons, and probably others, that the afterimage studies continue to amaze and puzzle researchers, and that we believe a review and evaluation of them is pertinent.

The chapter is divided into three parts. The first part considers how the color perception studies are important for testing theoretical models of the majority and minority area. The second part contains a narrative review of studies employing the afterimage paradigm. Finally, in the third part we provide an evaluation of the afterimage paradigm and raise a number of methodological and theoretical issues.

Theoretical Issues

While a full review of the theoretical models of majority and minority influence is beyond the scope of the present chapter (see Martin & Hewstone, in press) it is important to note that the afterimage studies were designed to test a set of hypotheses derived from Moscovici's (1980) conversion theory (see chapter 1). Moscovici proposes that majority and minority influence is determined by two separate processes which result in different levels of public and private influence. In the case of majority influence, individuals engage in a *comparison process* whereby they compare their own response with that of the majority without considering, in detail, the majority's message. The result of this process is that majorities lead to public compliance with little private change. On the other hand, minorities are unlikely to have public influence, as individuals wish to avoid directly identifying with minority groups. However, because of their distinctiveness, minorities cause a *validation process* where individuals engage in cognitive processing of the message in order to understand the minority's position. This can lead to conversion behavior which, according to Moscovici and Personnaz (1980), is ". . . a subtle process of perceptual or cognitive modification by which a person gives up his/her usual response in order to adopt another view or response, without necessarily being aware of the change or forced to make it" (p. 271).

Evidence in favor of Moscovici's dual process model relies heavily upon the demonstration that majority and minority influence have a differential impact upon different levels of influence. Moscovici and Personnaz (1980) refer to two levels of influence, namely the manifest or public and the latent or private levels. The main difference between the manifest (public) and latent (private) levels of influence is the degree to which the participants are consciously aware of the change in their responses, with the former being at the conscious level and the latter at the unconscious level. The unique contribution of conversion theory is that it goes beyond the manifest or public level, which had been the focus of previous research, and predicts that minority influence is likely to be greater at the latent or private level and, furthermore, that this change will be unconscious to the individual. This leads to the intriguing situation that exposure to a minority can lead to change without conscious awareness. How influence on the latent level becomes transferred to the manifest level is not specified by conversion theory (but see Alvaro & Crano, 1997; Personnaz, 1981).

A critical consideration in designing research that addresses the issue of manifest and latent influence is the techniques that are used to measure these responses (see Alvaro & Crano, 1997 and chapter 6, this volume). In designing responses to measure the manifest–latent levels of influence three important criteria need to be satisfied. First, there needs to be a link between the manifest and latent response dimension such that change on the manifest response results in a corresponding change in the latent response (manifest–latent correspondence). Ideally, the relationship between manifest–latent response should be known and preferably linear. If the relationship between manifest and latent responses is not known or is unstable, then manifest–latent correspondence cannot be assumed and it becomes difficult to extrapolate findings from the manifest level to the latent level. Second, the relationship between the manifest and latent response should be consistent and insensitive to situational factors (manifest–latent consistency). If, for example, the relationship between manifest and latent responses is sensitive to changes over time, then it is difficult to interpret differences between source conditions, especially in pretest–posttest research designs. In other words, changes between pretest and posttest may reflect a change in the consistency of the manifest–latent responses rather than an effect due to the source conditions. Third, participants should not be aware of the link between the manifest and latent responses and ideally they should use different response codes (manifest–latent perceived independence). Clearly, perceived response independence is essential to overcome the potential problem of response generalization and response inhibition.[2]

Narrative Review

Afterimage studies

The afterimage paradigm. The afterimage paradigm concerns color perception and, like the original blue–green experiment, exposes participants to blue slides that a confederate calls "green." The number of occasions on which the naive participant also calls these slides "green" represents the manifest response. However, the latent measure of influence employs a well-known perceptual effect, namely the perception of afterimages. When a person stares at a colored stimulus and then looks at a white background, the person will briefly perceive a different color to that of the original stimulus (termed the "afterimage"). There is a predictable relationship between the color of the stimulus and that of the afterimage which is due to the physiological properties of the eyes' rods and cones. The afterimage tends to be the chromatic complementary color of the original stimulus. If one stares at a blue object on a white background and then casts one's eyes onto another homogeneous white surface, the same object will be seen briefly as yellow. There are several lines of evidence that suggest that afterimages are attributable to peripheral processes in the visual system, such as photochemical changes or receptor adaptation (e.g., Brindley, 1962; Craik, 1940).

In the afterimage paradigm, if the confederate who calls the blue slide "green" has no influence, then one would expect participants to perceive afterimages toward the complementary color of blue (i.e., yellow). However, if the confederate does succeed in changing participants' perception then they should perceive an afterimage towards the complementary color of green (i.e., red/purple). Moscovici and Personnaz (1980) argue that since the afterimage responses are directly related to slide perception, they are recorded using a different response dimension from the manifest responses, and participants are presumably unaware of the afterimage effect, then these responses can be considered to represent the latent level of influence. Indeed, afterimage responses represent latent influence par excellence and for this reason alone the first afterimage experiment stimulated great interest (and controversy).

The experiment involved two participants (both of whom were female) who were shown a series of blue slides. For each slide the participants were required to make two responses (a) color of slide (either blue or green) and (b) a judgment of the afterimage of the slide. An afterimage judgment was obtained by participants viewing a white screen after looking at the blue

Table 2.1 *Description of the Four Phases in Moscovici and Personnaz (1980) Study 1*

Phase	Trials	Description of phase
Phase 1 Preinfluence	5	Slide and afterimage responses given in private In source conditions (false) feedback was given concerning prior participants' responses
Phase 2 Influence	15	Slide judgment given aloud, no afterimage judgment made. In source conditions confederate responded first and called the slide "green"
Phase 3 Postinfluence I: Confederate present	15	Same as phase 1 In source conditions confederate makes excuse to leave laboratory due to a prior appointment
Phase 4 Postinfluence II: Confederate absent	5	Naive participant alone gives slide and afterimage responses in private

Notes: All the participants and the confederate were female. The same slide was used throughout the study. The false feedback indicated that either 81.2% of participants had seen the slide as "blue" and 18.8% as "green" (minority condition) or vice versa (majority condition). Afterimages were formed by the experimenter turning off the projector and the participant gazing onto a white screen. Afterimages were rated on a 9-point scale. In study 2 of Moscovici and Personnaz (1980) there were five trials in phase 3.

slide. Under these circumstances an afterimage develops which is the complementary color of the stimulus. Afterimage responses were recorded on a 9-point scale (1 = yellow, yellow/orange, orange, orange/red, red, red/pink, pink, pink/purple, 9 = purple). In fact, the same slide, which was unambiguously blue, was used throughout the experiment.

Before the experiment commenced, participants were required to take a color blindness test to eliminate participants with faulty color perception. The experiment had four phases with each phase consisting of a number of trials (see Table 2.1). The first phase (preinfluence phase) consisted of five trials where the slide and afterimage judgment were recorded in private upon a response form. Before phase 2 (influence phase) commenced, the participants were informed of the responses of previous participants in the experiment. The feedback was, in fact, fictitious with the aim of portraying a "green" response as being either a majority or a minority response. In the majority condition, participants were given the feedback that 81.2% previous participants saw the slide as green and 18.2% saw it as blue (the percentages were reversed in the minority condition). Phase 2 consisted of 15 trials where the participants gave their judgment of the slide color aloud and no afterimage judgments were made. In the experimental conditions the confederate always gave her response aloud first and responded "green" to every slide. The role of the confederate was to express a response clearly different from the initial perception of the participant. It should be noted that the only occasion the participant was aware of the confederate's responses was during the second phase and that was only in relation to the slide color and not to the afterimage. Phase 3 (postinfluence phase I: confederate present) consisted of 15 trials where both the slide and afterimage judgments were recorded in private. Before commencing the final phase, the confederate informed the experimenter that she had an important appointment and therefore would have to leave. Therefore, phase 4 (postinfluence phase II: confederate absent) consisted of the naive participant completing a further five trials alone with responses made in private. Phase 4, where the confederate was absent, was included because it has been shown that social influence is more likely to occur when the source of change is not present (Moscovici & Nève, 1971).

Results of the Moscovici and Personnaz (1980) experiments. The design of the first study by Moscovici and Personnaz (1980) was one factor, consisting of majority or minority source and a control condition (without confederate). The results for the perceived color of the slide (manifest response) showed that in the first phase (preinfluence) all the participants reported the slide as being blue, confirming the unambiguous nature of the stimulus. In the second phase (influence), the number of "green" responses rose slightly to 5% but there was not a reliable difference between the experimental conditions. These results do not support Moscovici's (1980) conversion theory, as this would predict a majority to exert compliance and therefore cause a greater number of "green" responses than in the minority condition.

Turning to the afterimage scores, which represent the latent response, the key comparisons are between (a) phase 1 (preinfluence) and phase 3 (postinfluence I: confederate present) and (b) phase 1 and phase 4 (postinfluence II: confederate absent) (see Table 2.2). The results were consistent with conversion theory and showed a significant shift in afterimage judgments towards the complementary color of green in the minority condition between preinfluence and both postinfluence phases. Furthermore, there were no reliable shifts in the perceived afterimage in either the majority or the control con-

Table 2.2 *Mean Afterimage Scores for Moscovici and Personnaz (1980), Doms and Van Avermaet (1980), and Sorrentino, King, and Leo (1980)*

	Phase 1 Preinfluence	Phase 3 Postinfluence: Confederate Present	Phase 4 Postinfluence: Confederate Absent
Moscovici and Personnaz (1980) Study 1			
Majority ($n = 18$)	5.90	5.56	5.54
Minority ($n = 18$)	5.47	6.17	6.22
Control ($n = 10$)	5.70	5.45	5.45
Doms and Van Avermaet (1980) Study 1			
Majority ($n = 12$)	5.55	5.77	6.35
Minority ($n = 12$)	6.08	6.56	6.47
Control ($n = 12$)	6.05	6.05	5.55
No-information Group ($n = 12$)	5.15	5.33	5.17
Sorrentino, King and Leo (1980)			
Minority ($n = 20$)	4.89	4.69	4.53

Notes: Scores on 9-point scale with higher score indicating a judgment closer to the complement of green (red/purple). Moscovici and Personnaz (1980) report mean standardized scores; these raw means were obtained from Moscovici (1980). The "no information" condition in Doms and Van Avermaet (1980) included a confederate who responded "green" to the slides but without feedback concerning numerical support. Sorrentino et al. (1980) did not report mean afterimage judgments. These means were obtained from the raw data provided by Richard Sorrentino (see note 3). This study also included two conditions which used a different method to measure afterimage judgments and, because direct comparisons cannot be made with the other studies, the data are not included.

ditions. The findings were replicated in a second study that only differed from the first in that it consisted of five trials per phase and that it did not include a control condition; once again there was a significant change in afterimages towards the complement of green for those in the minority condition and not for those in the majority condition.

In summary, both studies described in Moscovici and Personnaz (1980) suggest that a numerical minority was able to produce a genuine change in perception, as evidenced by changes in afterimage scores, whilst a numerical majority was not able to produce a perceptual conversion. The authors noted that there were a number of potential problems with their paradigm and concluded that "the phenomenon we describe is more suggestive than it is firmly established" (p. 274). The next section reviews a number of direct replications of the Moscovici and Personnaz (1980) studies.

Immediate direct replications. Two direct replications of Moscovici and Personnaz's (1980) experiment appeared immediately following their own article in the same issue of the *Journal of Experimental Social Psychology* (see Table 2.2). Doms and Van Avermaet (1980) conducted two studies that included the three conditions of the Moscovici and Personnaz (1980) study (majority, minority, and control) and a no information condition (this was the same as the influence conditions except no details of the prior response survey were given and therefore the confederate's deviant response was not labeled as being a majority or minority position). The aim of the no information condition was to determine whether a deviant response alone, without numerical information, could produce afterimage shifts. As with the Moscovici and Personnaz (1980) studies, there was no evidence that compliance had taken place as there were very few "green" responses (in fact, only three participants in the majority condition gave any "green" responses). Turning to the afterimage judgments (see Table 2.2), significant afterimage shifts towards the complementary color of green were found for both a majority and minority source, though the latter results were only reached with a post hoc one-tailed test. Interestingly, the pattern of afterimage shifts varied between source conditions. In the majority condition the afterimage shift only reached significance between phase 1 (preinfluence) and phase 4 (postinfluence: confederate absent). In the minority influence condition, by contrast, the afterimage shift was significant only between phase 1 (preinfluence) and phase 3 (postinfluence: confederate present). There were no significant changes in afterimages in either the control or no information conditions.

Doms and Van Avermaet's explanation for these findings was based upon Upmeyer's (1971) observation that participants exposed to discrepant information given by a majority performed better in a discrimination task than control participants who had not been exposed to this information. Upmeyer's interpretation of these results was made on the basis that social motivation leads to heightened attention to the object of judgment under social influence conditions and hence to more accurate perception, although no operational definition of accuracy was specified. Using this interpretation, Doms and Van Avermaet (1980) proposed that afterimage shifts were "a direct result of increased attention to the object of judgment" (p. 290). If afterimage shifts were due to exposure to a deviant response why did they not occur in the no information condition which also had the confederate? Doms and Van Avermaet's answer for this is that in the no information condition the single confederate's deviant responses may have been seen as "idiosyncratic" and perhaps not valid. Indeed, it appears that the deviant response "green" needs to be located within a social framework in order for it to be taken seriously and not as a quirk of eyesight of a particular individual.

Doms and Van Avermaet (1980) proposed that a possible explanation for why their results differed from those of Moscovici and Personnaz (1980) was due to the weakness of their source manipulation. Indeed, one does wonder how successfully one can convince participants that over 80% of people see slides that are unambiguously blue as green! Doms and Van Avermaet explored this issue in a second study that was identical to their first, except that participants were asked to indicate the percentage of people they thought would agree with their own response and that of their partner (the confederate). The authors do not state the point during the study at which these questions were asked. Participants believed that 54% and 24.5% would agree with the confederate when they held a majority or minority position respectively. Since this difference is significant, the authors concluded that the source manipulation was successful and eliminated this as a factor that might explain the difference between their results and those of Moscovici and Personnaz (1980).

Doms and Van Avermaet report no results for manifest influence (number of "green" responses) for the second study. With respect to the afterimage scores, the authors state they are "very similar" (p. 288) to those found in the first study, but closer examination shows important differences. First, the overall influence source by phases interaction was not significant and the difference between the pretest and postinfluence phases was only just significant on one-tailed a priori tests and, though not stated, the difference appears between phase 1 (pretest) and phase 4 (posttest: confederate absent). The degree of change in afterimage scores is extremely small compared to that found in the Moscovici and Personnaz (1980) study. In addition, to add confusion to the interpretation, the mean afterimage scores in the two experimental conditions were lower than that observed in the control group. Thus, there is not unequivocal evidence from both these studies to show reliable afterimage shifts for both source conditions.

Doms and Van Avermaet (1980) interpret their findings of a significant afterimage shift for both a majority and minority source as suggesting that a universal process may be in operation rather than the dual process model proposed by conversion theory. Moscovici and Personnaz (1980) comment upon the results of Doms and Van Avermaet in a "Note added in proof" in their 1980 paper. They argue that the results of Doms and Van Avermaet do in fact show that differential processes may be operating in majority and minority influence because each had a different pattern of afterimage shifts. In the case of minority influence the afterimage shift was prominent at posttest I when the confederate was present, whilst for a majority it appeared at posttest II when the confederate was absent. If this afterimage pattern does indicate different process then it also indicates, contrary to conversion theory, that a majority too can induce a validation processes leading to conversion.

The second replication to be published at the same time as Moscovici and Personnaz's original study was by Sorrentino, King, and Leo (1980). Sorrentino et al. (1980) raised some concerns about the 9-point scale used by Moscovici and Personnaz (1980) to measure perception of the afterimage (this issue is discussed in more detail in a later section). In an attempt to improve the measurement of the afterimage, Sorrentino et al. (1980) showed participants a range of different colored chips and asked them to point to the one that most accurately matched the color of their afterimage. The study consisted of three conditions: two minority influence conditions (one using Moscovici and Personnaz's 9-point scale, see Table 2.2, and the other using an array of color chips to indicate afterimage color) and a no influence control condition. The results reported by Sorrentino et al. (1980) failed to replicate the Moscovici and Personnaz (1980) study in the minority condition except for those participants who were highly suspicious of the experiment (as determined by a postexperimental questionnaire). In their explanation, Sorrentino et al. suggested that highly suspicious participants may conceivably stare more intensely at the stimulus than do unsuspicious participants, and the shift in their afterimages over time may be a result of this greater attention to the stimulus.

Later direct replications. Martin (1995) notes that many explanations for the afterimage shifts share the common view that the causal process centers on increased attention to the slide and, since the slide contains green hues, this leads to the perception of afterimages which are the complementary color of green. In fact, the slide used in the original Moscovici and Personnaz (1980) study is termed "blue-green" by the manufacturers and has a large portion of its wavelength within the green spectrum. Martin (1995) reasoned that if increased attention is the causal mechanism of afterimage shifts, then the resulting afterimage should reflect the wavelength composition of the stimulus. What would happen if the stimulus was pure blue and virtually none of its wavelength was in the green spectrum? Under this situation increased attention to the slide should result in afterimages more in the direction of the complementary color of blue (as virtually none of the slide's color spectrum was in the green zone). Social influence, in this study, would be represented by afterimages shifting towards the complement of blue and not green as in the original Moscovici and Personnaz (1980) experiment. Martin's (1995) study followed the same procedure as the Moscovici and Personnaz (1980) experiment except that it used a slide which the manufacturers termed "deep blue" (i.e., one that contained a very small proportion of green hues). The results showed that afterimages shifted towards the complementary color of blue for both a majority and minority source but not in a no influence control condition. This pattern of results is consistent with Doms and Van Avermaet's hypothesis that a deviant response, irrespective of numerical support, leads to afterimage shifts.

An interesting methodological point noted by Martin (1998) was that all the afterimage studies had analyzed the mean score for each phase and had not examined within-phase effects (see also Martin, 1995). Martin (1998) examined this issue and found that across five studies there was a significant within-phase afterimage shift in all the phases (preinfluence and postinfluence) and for phases that contained either five or 15 trials. This showed that participants' afterimage judgments shifted towards the complementary color of green (that is, red) over progressive trials.

The reason for the within-phase effect is unknown, but Martin (1998) has suggested that it may be due to a perceptual phenomenon that arises from repeated exposure to the same stimulus. Afterimage studies are conducted in semidarkness, where the brightest source is usually the stimulus. During the study the participants shift their gaze from the slide to less bright aspects of the room, such as when the participants receive instructions for the next phase. It is possible that between phases the participants' eyes adapt to the less bright environment and that when they first look at the bright slide they subsequently perceive fainter (and lighter) afterimages which, in the case of a blue stimulus, would lead to afterimages closer to the complement of green (yellow). Thus, this perceptual artefact may lead to afterimage shifts consistent with those one would expect following influence.

The within-phase effect has implications for the observed findings, especially as the afterimage studies differ in the number of trials employed in each of the phases. The original Moscovici and Personnaz (1980) study employed more trials postinfluence (15) than preinfluence (five). If a within-phase effect does result in afterimage scores shifting progressively to the complementary color of green (indicating greater influence), then one should expect the mean of a 15-trial phase to be more toward the complementary color of green than the mean of a five-trial phase. If this were true, then studies with more postinfluence than preinfluence trials would show a tendency toward finding afterimage shifts. Indeed, in two of the studies reported

Table 2.3 *Mean Afterimage Scores for Martin (1998) Study 4*

Trials	Phase 1 Preinfluence	Phase 3 Postinfluence: Confederate Present		
	1–5	1–5	6–10	11–15
Source conditions ($n = 32$)	4.29	4.61	4.85	5.09
Control ($n = 16$)	3.71	4.07	4.05	3.99

Note: Scores on 9-point scale with higher score indicating a judgment closer to the complement of green (red/purple).

by Martin (1998, studies 1 and 2) which had the same number of trials preinfluence and postinfluence, there was no significant afterimage shifts for either source, while two studies (4 and 5) which had more postinfluence (15) than preinfluence (five) trials found reliable afterimage shifts for both a majority and minority source. More importantly, in the studies with 15 trials in the postinfluence phase, there was no difference in the afterimage scores between the preinfluence phase (five trials) and the first five trials of the postinfluence phase (see Table 2.3 for means for study 4). However, significant afterimage shifts, for both source conditions, were observed when comparing the preinfluence phase (five trials) and later trials in the 15 trial postinfluence phase (i.e., trials 6–10 and 11–15). Interestingly, participants in the control condition did not show a difference in afterimage judgments between the pretest phase and any of the blocks of trials in the postinfluence phase. These results reinforce the claim that results resembling afterimage shifts can occur in situations where there is a deviant confederate and where there are more postinfluence trials than preinfluence trials.

Another factor explored by Martin (1998) was the role of participant suspicion. As with Sorrentino et al. (1980), those participants who were high in suspicion reported higher afterimage scores, indicating influence, than those who were low in suspicion, independent of source condition. Furthermore, the effects of suspicion interacted with the trial order effect discussed above. Those who were high in suspicion showed a consistent level of afterimage score across the trials while those who were low in suspicion showed a linear trend but did not reach the level of those in the high suspicion group.[3] We return to the implications of these findings later.

To summarize, replications of Moscovici and Personnaz's (1980) experiment have resulted in inconsistent findings and there are a number of potential explanations for afterimage shifts. A number of researchers have been critical of the use of the 9-point scale to measure afterimages and the next section considers three studies that have attempted to improve the measurement of the perception of both the slide and the afterimage by use of a spectrometer.

Methodological issues concerning the measurement of afterimages

In an attempt to deal with some of the criticisms of the self-report scale for measuring afterimages, Personnaz (1981) employed a spectrometer to measure participants' responses. A spectrometer is a device that permits the perceiver to match colors with their corresponding wavelengths (measured in nanometers). After perceiving the afterimage, the participant looks into the spectrometer which contains the color scheme of the visual spectrum. By adjusting the color in the spectrometer, via a dial, the participant can identify the color that matches the afterimage. When the participant indicates the color that matches that of the stimulus, the experimenter is able to record the wavelength of that color. The participant is unaware of the reading taken from the spectrometer. One of the main advantages of using the spectrometer is that the participant does not have to name the color verbally, and therefore this reduces the possibility of response generalization between the different measurements. In this respect, the spectrometer technique is similar to that used in Sorrentino's et al.'s (1980) "random minority" condition discussed earlier, where participants pointed to a color chip that matched their perception of the afterimage. The advantage of the spectrometer is that the participant has a much wider range of colors from which to choose and that the exact wavelength of each color can be recorded.

The materials and procedure of the Personnaz (1981) experiment were similar to those used by Moscovici and Personnaz (1980) and had two experimental conditions, majority and minority influence. The main difference was that three measures were taken for each presentation of the slide: (a) a verbal report of the slide color (blue or green), (b) spectrometer score for slide color, and (c) spectrometer score for afterimage color.[4] The first measure is the same as that used in previous studies and corresponds to the manifest level. As with previous studies, very few participants gave a "green" response. Although the total number of "green" responses in the minority condition in phase 4 (confederate absent) was greater in the majority than the minority condition, the

Table 2.4 *Mean Spectrometer Scores of Afterimage Judgment for Personnaz (1981)*

	Phase 1 Preinfluence	Phase 3 Postinfluence: Confederate Present	Phase 4 Postinfluence: Confederate Absent
Majority (*n* = 10)	624.11	625.63	619.47
Minority (*n* = 10)	622.12	633.00	635.10

Note: Scores correspond to wavelength in nanometers with higher scores indicating a judgment closer to the complement of green.

number was extremely low and, as the author correctly noted, the number of participants who responded "green" did not differ between the conditions (one in the majority and two in the minority conditions).

The results for the spectrometer scores for slide perception showed that participants modified their perception when they were exposed to a minority. More specifically, the spectrometer scores for the slide moved toward green between phase 1 (pretest) and phase 4 (postinfluence II: confederate absent) but that there was no differences between these phases and phase 3 (postinfluence I: confederate present). There were no differences across the phases for participants in the majority condition. For the afterimage spectrometer scores, there was a reliable difference across the phases in the minority condition (see Table 2.4). Spectrometer scores for the afterimage moved towards the complement of green between phases 1 (preinfluence) and phase 3 (postinfluence I: confederate present) and between phases 1 and phase 4 (postinfluence II: confederate present). There was no difference in spectrometer scores for the afterimage judgments in the majority conditions. This pattern of results for the afterimage judgments is very similar to that of Moscovici and Personnaz (1980) and suggests that a numerical minority was able to produce a perceptual conversion, as measured by the spectrometer scores, while a numerical majority was not able to produce such an effect. A similar set of results was obtained by Personnaz (1988), which also included a control (no influence) condition which did not show any changes over the phases.

The use of different measurement techniques in the spectrometer studies offers an interesting insight into the conversion process (see also Moscovici and Personnaz, 1991). It appears that the change in the minority condition occurred in two stages which varied over time and was on different levels. The first stage of the change occurred on the perception of the afterimage, a dimension unrelated to the source's response, in phase 3 (postinfluence I: confederate present), while the second stage of the change occurred later in time (postinfluence II: confederate absent) on the slide color which is a dimension indirectly related to the source's response. This suggests that conversion initially occurs on latent dimensions where influence is not explicitly linked to the source and then transfers onto a more manifest dimension.

Moscovici and Personnaz (1986) used the spectrometer technique in a study of majority and minority influence which examined the effects of psychologization, that is, the process of attributing a deviant response to an internal disposition (Mugny & Papastamou, 1980). The study used the same procedure as the Personnaz (1981) study except that four dependent measures were taken: three were identical to the first study (verbal name of slide, spectrometer measures of slide, and afterimage) and the fourth was a measure of the afterimage on the 9-point scale used in Moscovici and Personnaz (1980). The psychologization variable was manipulated before phase 2 (interaction). In the psychologization condition, participants were informed that the study concerned the relationship between personality and color perception which, according to the researchers, should lead participants to attribute the deviant response to an internal disposition. By contrast, in the nonpsychologization condition, participants were informed that the study was concerned with the aesthetic values of colors (which should highlight the fact that perception is linked to external criteria). It should be noted, however, that no supporting evidence is given to show that participants actually make these attributions in these conditions.

As expected, when the minority was psychologized (i.e., the relationship between the deviant response and personality was emphasized), it did not result in changes across the phases for any of the dependent measures. However, when the minority was not psychologized, and therefore in a situation similar to the previous experiment, there were reliable changes across the phases. These changes were very similar to Personnaz (1981) and showed modification of (a) spectrometer score of the slide towards green in phase 4 (postinfluence II: confederate absent) and (b) both spectrometer score and scale score of afterimage towards the complement of green for both postinfluence phases. With respect to the majority condition, psychologization of the source led to latent influence on all three measures in an almost identical fashion to the nonpsychologized minority. In the nonpsychologized majority condition, there were no reliable changes across the phases.

The results for the minority influence condition can be easily interpreted with reference to prior research. In the psychologization condition, the participants link the deviant response to a (presumably negative) personality disposition and therefore resist influence. In the nonpsychologization condition, where the aesthetic value of judgments is emphasized and the need to consider perception against external criteria, the usual pattern of conversion is found. The results for the majority condition are less easily reconciled by conversion theory. Unlike Moscovici's original formulation of conversion theory (1980), which states two distinct and separate processes for majority and minority influence, Moscovici and Personnaz (1986) suggest that both processes can operate for each source. They suggest that normally the conflict caused by a majority leads to a social comparison which results in public compliance and little private change. However, when the majority is psychologized, individuals are

> inclined to seek to validate, to examine to what extent this response corresponds to the object, for now one is less sure that the four eyes of the majority see better than one's own two eyes. It becomes necessary to investigate to what extent the majority's opinion or perception is reasonable. (p. 356)

Implying that the majority's response is due to a personal bias weakens its credibility and this might motivate individuals to analyze why this has occurred (cf. Personnaz & Personnaz, 1994).

The use of the spectrometer in these studies overcame many of the methodological problems associated with the afterimage studies discussed above and it provided new insights into the process of conversion. One of the main contributions has been to show that conversion effects are sensitive to the salient group norms. Indeed, conversion effects can be found for both a majority and minority depending on the prevailing norm and this might help to understand different findings between studies. The second major contribution of these studies is the use of multimethod multilevel measures of influence and the attempt to understand the process of change from a latent to a manifest level.

Related studies. The afterimage paradigm has been employed in a number of studies to examine the limiting conditions for afterimage shifts to occur (e.g., Moscovici & Doms, 1982). Many of these studies did not explicitly manipulate source status and therefore they were not considered in the above sections. However, in the absence of numerical support (i.e., fictitious feedback concerning prior responding), one can assume that participants believed the confederate to be giving a minority response and therefore they address minority influence (but see the earlier discussion of Doms & Van Avermaet's 1980 interpretation of their no information control condition for a differing view). These studies showed that afterimage shifts towards the complement of green were more likely when (a) the confederate was from an outgroup (determined by sex, Personnaz & Personnaz, 1992, or nationality, Personnaz & Orii's 1989 study as cited in Personnaz & Personnaz 1994, see also Personnaz & Personnaz, 1987), (b) was physically unattractive (Personnaz & Personnaz's 1989 study as cited in Personnaz & Personnaz 1994), and (c) dissimilar to the source (Kozakaï, Moscovici, & Personnaz, 1994). These studies show that afterimage shifts are more likely with a source that is categorized as "different" from the participant and this is in keeping with Personnaz and Personnaz's (1994) conclusion that ". . . any factor that stirs conflict will induce conversion to the minority's point of view" (p. 180).

Summary and Conclusions

The final part of this chapter is divided into four subsections. First, we briefly review the results of the afterimage studies. In the second subsection we consider whether the afterimage paradigm is able to satisfy the criteria described at the beginning of this chapter as being necessary for the measurement of manifest and latent influence. In the third subsection we consider whether the afterimage paradigm is able to test Moscovici's conversion theory, and in the last subsection of the chapter we make some final remarks about the research.

Summary of findings

The review of the afterimage studies shows little consistency in the findings. With the exception of the spectrometer studies by Personnaz (1981, 1988), no other published study has replicated the original Moscovici and Personnaz (1980) findings of afterimage shifts for a minority but not for a majority source. There is stronger support, in terms of number of studies, for the claim that afterimage shifts can occur for both majority and minority sources (Doms & Van Avermaet, 1980, studies 1 and 2; Martin, 1995; Martin, 1998 studies 4 and 5). The latter findings support Doms and Van Avermaet's (1980) hypothesis that afterimage shifts are due to increased attention to the stimulus arising from exposure to discrepant information. Interestingly, the only pattern of findings which has not been reported in the literature is for after-image shifts only for a majority source.[5] The spectrometer studies have introduced clever ways to measure social influence which vary along the manifest–latent continuum and thereby offered interesting insights into the process of change from the latent to the manifest level (see also the Lenin studies, Moscovici & Personnaz, 1991). Three potential moderators have been proposed for afterimage shifts (psychologization, participant suspicion, and within-phase effects) but it is noted that neither alone nor in combination can any of these fully explain the observed findings.

Assessing the afterimage paradigm against the manifest–latent response criteria

As outlined at the beginning of this chapter, three main criteria were iden-tified with respect to the measurement of manifest and latent responses which need to be fulfilled in order to overcome problems associated with response generalization and inhibition. In the light of this review it is possible to examine whether the afterimage studies have successfully met these criteria.

The first criterion concerned the manifest–latent relationship and stated that the association between the two measures should be known. No after-image study has reported the relationship between the slide (manifest) and afterimage (latent) scores. Since measurement of the perception of the slide was effectively nominal (blue or green) with extremely low variance (as very few participants gave a "green" response), it is not, however, possible to cal-culate the relationship between this and the afterimage scores. The only studies in which such a relationship could be calculated were those using the spectrometer method (and potentially the Lenin study, Moscovici and Personnaz, 1991) where both the slide and afterimage was measured in nanometers. This relationship was not, however, reported in these studies.[6]

The second criterion refers to the manifest–latent consistency and states that the relationship between these measures should be insensitive to a range of situational factors. It is unlikely that afterimage perception is stable over time as it can be affected by a number of factors such as light intensity (Abramov & Gordon, 1994). As discussed earlier, afterimage perception varies as a function of repeated exposure, with scores moving towards the comple-mentary color of green over successive trials. Such problems make it difficult to disentangle changes in afterimage scores due to the independent variables from those due to situational factors.

The third criterion concerns perceived independence between the manifest and latent measures. Although manifest and latent responses are linked, it is essential that participants are not aware of that link in order to avoid the potential problems of response generalization and/or inhibition. Moscovici and Personnaz (1980) state that the afterimage shifts:

> cannot be considered as an instance of response generalization given that: (a) the response to the stimulus and the response to the chromatic afterimage were different . . . ; (b) only the response to the stimulus was given in public, the response to the afterimage was always private and thus, the subject never heard the words yellow, orange, purple etc., uttered; and (c) the subject was not aware of the relationship between a color and its complement. (p. 280)

These assumptions have been challenged. For example, Kakavelakis (1996) comments that many of the authors of afterimage studies, like Moscovici and Personnaz, report that their participants were unaware of the relationship between the slide and afterimage color, but these studies do not report how this was ascertained. This general assumption was explored by Kakavelakis who tested his participants' knowledge of afterimages using an extensive questionnaire. He found that the participants, who were nonpsychology students, had a good understanding of the afterimage effect, and because of this he had to eliminate a large number of potential participants from his study.

Even if participants were unaware of the afterimage effect before the study began they could not fail to become aware of the link between slide and afterimage during the course of the study because of the methodology employed. Afterimages were formed by the experimenter turning off the projector and asking participants to stare at a white screen. The afterimage appears on the screen and lasts for a short period of time before it fades. Given the short time between slide presentation and afterimage perception it is clear that the former causes the latter (in fact there is nothing else that could cause the afterimage). If participants make the link between slide and afterimage it is also highly likely that they assume that changes in slide perception would result in changes in afterimage perception. Thus, although participants might not be aware of the afterimage effect (in terms of knowing the complementary colors of blue and green), it is highly likely that they believe the afterimage score is caused by the color of the slide, and that if the confederate publicly states a different slide color to the participant then they also perceive a different afterimage.

From the above discussion we can conclude that the afterimage paradigm has failed to meet the three criteria necessary for manifest and latent responses. In particular, one cannot rule out that participants were aware of the link between manifest and latent responses and therefore a number of response biases cannot be eliminated as competing explanations for the observed findings.

The utility of the afterimage paradigm in testing conversion theory

According to Moscovici's (1980) conversion theory, majority influence evokes a comparison process where individuals comply with the majority group without considering the issues which the majority proposed. This leads to public compliance with little change on a private or latent level (public greater than private influence). On the other hand, minority influence motivates individuals to engage in a validation process whereby they consider the minority position in detail. While individuals may not publicly agree with the minority, in order to avoid minority group membership and associated stigma, the validation process can lead to a private or latent attitude change (private greater than public influence). It is important to note that the predictions of majority versus minority influence are made *between* response modalities (public versus private or manifest versus latent) and not *across* source conditions (majority versus minority). Although conversion theory implies that a majority should have more public influence than a minority, and the reverse for private change, such a pattern by itself does not support the theory (indeed these could occur without the differences predicted by conversion theory on both public and private responses).

To test conversion theory using the afterimage paradigm one would, then, need to compare between response modalities (i.e., manifest and latent response) which, of course, was not possible due to the different response formats. Instead, the afterimage studies compared latent responses before and after influence which indicates change *within* response modality and not, as predicted by conversion theory, *between* response modality. The afterimage paradigm was designed to examine changes in latent responses, as represented by afterimage scores, in isolation from public attitude change. For this reason it has limited utility in testing hypotheses derived from theories of social influence such as conversion theory which compare source effects between levels of influence.

Final remarks

When we began this chapter we stated that the afterimage studies have had a profound impact upon the majority and minority influence literature and because of this they deserved a critical review. Although we are unable to concur with Moscovici and Personnaz's (1980) claim that a minority is able to cause a perceptual conversion, we believe that the afterimage studies nonetheless represent an extremely important series of studies that have shaped the development of this research area. They are important for two reasons. First, they were the first studies to examine the influence of a minority beyond the public level to a latent and unconscious level, and second, by measuring influence on multiple levels, they have focused attention on the psychological processes involved in change from the latent to the manifest level.

NOTES

The writing of this chapter was facilitated by a grant from the Economic and Social Research Council (R000236149). It was completed while Miles Hewstone was a Fellow at the Center for Advanced Study in the Behavioral Sciences, Stanford, for which he gratefully acknowledges financial support provided by the William and Flora Hewlett Foundation. We are most grateful to Mark Georgeson, Tom Troscianko, and Ioannis Kakavelakis for discussions concerning methodological and theoretical issues associated with this research.

1   In their meta-analytic review of the majority and minority influence literature, Wood, Lundgren, Ouellette, Buscerne, and Blackstone (1994) categorized studies according to the response mode employed. The main distinction was whether the target of influence's response was made in public (i.e., "under the surveillance of the source," p. 328) or in private (i.e., "without the surveillance of the influence source, although they are public to the experimenter," p. 328). The private response category was further divided. First, there were studies that measured direct responses (i.e., influence on the same dimension as proposed by the source) and second, there were studies that measured indirect responses (i.e., influence on a different, but related, dimension than proposed by the source). Wood et al. (1994) placed the afterimage studies in the "indirect private category."

2   Of course, response facilitation may occur in the case of majority influence where individuals want to agree publicly with the majority group.

3   The original data sets for both the Moscovici and Personnaz (1980) and Doms and Van Avermaet (1980) are now not available (personal communication, Serge Moscovici and Eddy Van Avermaet). However, the authors are grateful to Richard

Sorrentino who was able to provide a copy of his data. Interestingly, and consistent with Martin's (1998) studies, there was a significant interaction between participant suspicion and trial order in the minority condition. Although the pattern of the interaction is not identical to that of Martin (1998), they do show that those high in suspicion give higher afterimage scores and that the difference between those low and high in suspicion increased over trial order. In addition, Sorrentino et al. (1980) report an "informal study" where they presented participants with 10 trials using the same slide as Moscovici and Personnaz (1980). The 10 trials were divided into two blocks of five trials with each block being either low or high in light intensity (block order was counterbalanced). The afterimage scores for the second block of five trials was more towards the complement of green (that is, red) than that for the first block of five trials.

4   The order of measurement was not counterbalanced. Since afterimages fade very quickly, and probably before the participants made their afterimage judgments, participants most likely relied upon memory rather than judging the afterimage itself.

5   Note that Doms and Van Avermaet (1980) found a significant afterimage shift for the majority, but only for the minority using a one-tailed post hoc test.

6   Although the relationship between slide and afterimage scores could be calculated, there would be the additional problem that they were measured on the same scales, which would violate the manifest–latent perceived independence criterion.

REFERENCES

Abramov, I., & Gordon, J. (1994). Color appearance: On seeing red – or yellow, or blue. *Annual Review of Psychology*, *45*, 451–85.

Alvaro, E. M., & Crano, W. D. (1997). Indirect minority influence: Evidence for leniency in source evaluation and counter argumentation. *Journal of Personality and Social Psychology*, *72*, 949–64.

Baron, R. S., Kerr, N., & Miller, N. (1992). *Group process. Group decision. Group action.* Buckingham, UK: Open University Press.

Brewer, M. D., & Crano, W. D. (1994). *Social psychology.* St Paul, MN: West Publishing.

Brindley, S. G. (1962). Two new properties of foveal afterimages and a photochemical hypothesis to explain them. *Journal of Physiology*, *164*, 168–79.

Craik, K. J. W. (1940). Origin of visual after-images. *Nature*, *145*, 512.

Doms, M., & Van Avermaet, E. (1980). Majority influence, minority influence and conversion behavior: A replication. *Journal of Experimental Social Psychology*, *16*, 283–92.

Kakavelakis, I. (1996). *Cognitive processes in majority and minority influence.* Unpublished doctoral dissertation, University of Bristol, UK.

Kozakaï, T., Moscovici, S., & Personnaz, B. (1994). Contrary effects of group cohesiveness in minority influence: Intergroup categorization of the source and levels of influence. *European Journal of Social Psychology, 24*, 713–8.

Martin, R. (1995). Majority and minority influence using the afterimage paradigm: A replication with an unambiguous blue slide. *European Journal of Social Psychology, 25*, 373–81.

Martin, R. (1998). Majority and minority influence using the afterimage paradigm: A series of attempted replications. *Journal of Experimental Social Psychology, 34*, 1–26.

Martin, R., & Hewstone, M. (in press). Conformity and independence in groups; majorities and minorities. In M. A. Hogg & R. S. Tindale (Eds.), *The Blackwell handbook of social psychology: Group processes.* Oxford: Blackwell.

Moscovici, S. (1980). Towards a theory of conversion behavior. In L. Berkowitz (Ed.), *Advances in experimental social psychology* (Vol. 13, pp. 209–39). London: Academic Press.

Moscovici, S. (1996). Foreword: Just remembering. *British Journal of Social Psychology, 35*, 5–14.

Moscovici, S., & Doms, M. (1982). Compliance and conversion in a situation of sensory deprivation. *Basic and Applied Social Psychology, 3*, 81–94.

Moscovici, S., Lage, E., & Naffrechoux, M. (1969). Influence of a consistent minority on the response of a majority in a color perception task. *Sociometry, 32*, 365–80.

Moscovici, S., & Nève, P. (1971). Studies in social influence: I. Those absent are in the right: Convergence and polarization of answers in the course of a social interaction. *European Journal of Social Psychology, 1*, 201–14.

Moscovici, S., & Personnaz, B. (1980). Studies in social influence V. Minority influence and conversion behavior in a perceptual task. *Journal of Experimental Social Psychology, 16*, 270–82.

Moscovici, S., & Personnaz, B. (1986). Studies on latent influence using the spectrometer method I: Psychologization effect upon conversion by a minority and majority. *European Journal of Social Psychology, 16*, 345–60.

Moscovici, S., & Personnaz, B. (1991). Studies in social influence VI: Is Lenin orange or red? Imagery and social influence. *European Journal of Social Psychology, 21*, 101–18.

Mugny, G., & Papastamou, S. (1980). When rigidity does not fail: Individualization and psychologization as resistances to the diffusion of minority innovations. *European Journal of Social Psychology, 10*, 43–61.

Personnaz, B. (1981). Study in social influence using the spectrometer method: Dynamics of the phenomena of conversion and covertness in perceptual responses. *European Journal of Social Psychology, 11*, 431–8.

Personnaz, B. (1988). Zmiany normatywne I percepcyne jako stutky wplywu spolecznego I diferencjacji [Normative and perceptive changes on the effects of social influence and differentiation]. *Przglzad Psychologiczny, 31*, 167–83.

Personnaz, B., & Personnaz, M. (1987). Un paradigme pour l'étude experimentale de la conversion [An experimental paradigm for the study of conversion]. In

S. Moscovici & G. Mugny (Eds.), *Psychologie de la conversion: Etudies sur l'influence inconsciente* (pp. 35–68). Cousset, Switzerland: Del Val.

Personnaz, B., & Personnaz, M. (1992). Contextes intergroupes et niveaux d'influence. *Bulletin de Psychologie, 45,* 173–82.

Personnaz, M., & Personnaz, B. (1994). Perception and conversion. In S. Moscovici, A. Mucchi-Faina, & A. Maass (Eds.), *Minority influence* (pp. 165–83). Chicago: Nelson-Hall.

Sorrentino, R. M., King, G., & Leo, G. (1980). The influence of the minority on perception: A note on a possible alternative explanation. *Journal of Experimental Social Psychology, 16,* 293–301.

Upmeyer, A. (1971). A social perception and signal detectability theory: Group influence on discrimination and usage of scale. *Psychologische Forschung, 34,* 283–94.

Wood, W., Lundgren, S., Ouellette, J. A., Buscerne, S., & Blackstone, T. (1994). Minority influence: A meta analytic review of social influence processes. *Psychological Bulletin, 115,* 323–45.

3

Mere Consensus Effects in Minority and Majority Influence

Hans–Peter Erb and Gerd Bohner

Introducing the Notion of Mere Consensus

Information about what most other people do or think is a pervasive element of everyday social life (e.g., Festinger, 1954; Hardin & Higgins, 1996). Consensus determines what is expected, normal, and fashionable. Democratic political systems are built on majority rule. People are interested in the results of opinion polls concerning a diversity of social issues that are frequently reported in the mass media. Many advertisements try to persuade on the basis of consensus, by suggesting that a majority of people hold favorable attitudes toward a certain product or brand (Erb, 1998). Consensus determines attributional judgments and makes people "know that they know" (Kelley, 1967). Thus, consensus seems to be a most basic variable to which the human mind may be specifically tuned.

It seems hardly surprising then, that the role of consensus information has been of longstanding interest to social psychologists. Specifically, research in social influence has long been concerned with conformity as the psychological process to explain majority influence (e.g., Asch, 1956; Mackie, 1987). Since the seminal work of Moscovici (1976, 1980) it has also become obvious that minorities can exert considerable influence. However, even after many years of extensive research on the topic, it seems difficult to talk about a uniform minority or majority psychology (see Kruglanski and Mackie, 1990, p. 230). By contrast, the tendency to theorize in multiple ways about thinking and judging in minority and majority influence settings has resulted in a fragmentation of assumed underlying processes and the development of a diversity of theories. Some theorists have aligned minority and majority influence with qualitatively different processes (e.g., Maass & Clark, 1984;

Moscovici, 1980), others have proposed unitary (mathematical) models to account for both minority and majority influence (Latané & Wolf, 1981; Tanford & Penrod, 1984). Minorities and majorities have been defined using various criteria, such as numerical size (e.g., Latané & Wolf, 1981; Tanford & Penrod, 1984), social power and status (e.g., Moscovici, 1976; Mugny, 1982) or (counter)normative positions (e.g., Moscovici, 1980). Their influence has been studied within small groups with face-to-face interactions (e.g., Levine & Russo, 1987; Smith, Tindale, & Dugoni, 1996; Van Dyne & Saavedra, 1996) or in highly structured settings with (written) persuasive messages (e.g., Bohner, Frank, & Erb, 1998; De Dreu & De Vries, 1993; Mackie, 1987). The number of studies is large, but comparisons between them appear to be difficult (see Wood, Lundgren, Oulette, Busceme, & Blackstone, 1994). This is because the potential effects of minorities and majorities have been studied with multiple independent and dependent variables.

In an influential review, Kruglanski and Mackie (1990) discussed the effects of a number of variables previously examined in research on social influence. These authors found only one variable that necessarily covaries with minority and majority status, namely *consensus*. In our own theorizing, we used this analysis to propose that consensus has to be regarded as the key concept to understanding minority and majority influence: A minority necessarily reflects lower consensus than does a majority. In this chapter we want to direct attention to the operation of consensus in social information processing and judgment. Our aim is to show that studying consensus effects is a fruitful approach to learning about processes in minority and majority influence. In order to do so, we demonstrate that *mere consensus* has evaluative implications and can evoke differential information processing strategies.

The idea behind the notion of "mere consensus" refers to the most basic information that group status as a minority or majority can provide: numerical information about socially shared agreement over a certain attitude object. Importantly, mere consensus also refers to the exclusion of a number of variables that we believe have not been sufficiently dissociated from group status in previous research, both theoretically and empirically.

We cannot review here all such variables as Zeitgeist effects (e.g., Maass & Clark, 1984), the ingroup–outgroup distinction (e.g., Mackie, Gastardo-Conaco, & Skelly, 1992), social power (Mugny, 1982), double minorities (Maass, Clark, & Haberkorn, 1982), normative contexts (e.g., Paicheler, 1977), opinion discrepancy (e.g., Nemeth & Endicott, 1976) and so forth (see Kruglanski & Mackie, 1990; Wood et al., 1994). As an example, let us direct attention to one variable among these which we believe has profound consequences in social influence, namely prior attitudes as a prerequisite of attitude discrepancy and social conflict with a minority or majority of others.

When we started researching consensus effects on attitudes, we had to realize that many explanatory approaches account for situations in which social influence opposes respondents' prior attitudes. For example, within Moscovici's (1980) work, the amount of issue-related conflict introduced by a minority is directly related to processes of conversion. Similarly, Mackie (1987) and Baker and Petty (1994) attributed systematic processing of attitude-relevant information within the realm of minority and majority influence to violations of expectancies derived from prior attitudes and the false-consensus effect (Ross, Greene, & House, 1977). De Vries, De Dreu, Gordijn, and Schuurman (1996) have explicitly shaped their "differential processing model" to situations in which individuals receive a message of counterattitudinal content. Nemeth's (1986) studies on creativity within social influence through minorities have demonstrated that individuals, when confronted with a minority solution in a given task, generate more creative solutions to that task relative to those generated in response to a majority source. Again, according to Nemeth (1986), the key to understanding these effects is dissent and conflict (pp. 25–6).

However, researchers within these approaches did not ever discuss the idea that prior attitudes quite likely affect the perception of an attitude object and the processing of attitude-relevant information, independent of any differences evoked by consensus. Prior attitudes call to mind attitude-relevant information (e.g., Houston & Fazio, 1989). They can induce motivated information processing strategies via ego involvement (Petty & Cacioppo, 1981), personal relevance (Trost, Maass, & Kenrick, 1992), and tendencies to defend a prior attitude (Chaiken, Giner-Sorolla, & Chen, 1996). Even more importantly, prior attitudes can introduce conflict with a socially valued influence source (e.g., Mackie, 1987). Prior attitudes may interact with group status, as Baker and Petty (1994) found for the initiation of extensive content processing, or may even offset any use of consensus information (e.g., Maheswaran & Chaiken, 1991). However, neither cognitive nor motivational consequences of prior attitudes covary necessarily with the status of an influence group as a minority or a majority. Moreover, we already know that consensus can affect responses even if no attitudes are involved or new attitudes have to be formed (e.g., Crano & Hannula-Bral, 1994; Sherif, 1958).

Following this logic, we propose that we may gain new insights into psychological processes in social influence when we study mere consensus effects relatively detached from opinion discrepancy and other variables not necessarily linked to group status (Erb, Bohner, Schmälzle, & Rank, 1998). To be clear, we do not argue that variables other than consensus (e.g., prior attitudes) should not be studied. There is no doubt that such variables can help in the understanding of minority and majority influence processes. Instead, we argue that studying mere consensus effects should take theoretical precedence, in order to establish which of the well-known effects formerly attributed to variables like social conflict, dissent with prior attitudes, identification with a highly valued influence group, and so forth, can be explained more parsimoniously by the operation of consensus alone. Based on the results of such an analysis, a more complete understanding of minority and majority influence should be possible.

Mere Consensus Effects on Attitudes

How should social influence through mere consensus become prominent? In studying consensus effects on attitudes, we developed our *biased processing* hypothesis (Erb et al., 1998). We argue that even if messages are not discrepant and influence groups are not socially relevant to individuals, consensus can have profound effects on message-related processing and subsequent attitude judgments. We derive three hypotheses regarding the cognitive effects of mere consensus. These address (a) the valence of cognitive responses, (b) the cognitive effort invested in message processing, and (c) the convergence/divergence of cognitive responses to messages that are attributed to sources of either low or high consensus.

Valence

Opinion uniformity or high consensus is positively valued. High consensus provides social support and validation (Festinger, 1954; Kelley, 1967), and may also imply correctness (Mackie, 1987). On the other hand, people respond negatively to minorities who impede consensus (Festinger, 1950; Levine, 1989), and low consensus can serve as a discounting cue to disparage a message (e.g., Watts & Holt, 1979). In short, responses to influence attempts by majorities usually are more positive than responses to influence attempts by minorities. Thus, we expect an initial positive reaction to an attitude object that is associated with high consensus and a negative initial reaction to an attitude object that is associated with low consensus. In subsequent message processing, such initial judgments should lead to positive bias in processing a message attributed to high consensus and to a negative bias in the case of low consensus. Such biases should affect the perception of the message's persuasiveness and determine subsequent attitude judgments.

Effort

The question of whether minorities (Moscovici, 1980; Hewstone, Martin, & Kakavelakis, 1997) or majorities (De Dreu & De Vries, 1993; Mackie, 1987) induce higher processing effort has been of longstanding interest to researchers. The mere consensus perspective can help to clarify this question. Despite the fact that opinion discrepancy alone, and in interaction with consensus (Baker & Petty, 1994), may moderate the initiation of effortful processing, an initial judgment about the validity of message content should reduce cognitive effort. Perceivers who can evaluate a message on the basis of consensus information that is available at the outset of message scrutiny should engage in less effortful processing than perceivers for whom consensus is not available. Thus, having access (vs. not having access) to information about either low or high consensus should reduce the overall amount of thought devoted to the issue.

Convergence/divergence

Nemeth (1986) also suggests that consensus can be conceptualized as a cue to bias in subsequent information processing. Divergent processing in response to minority influence reflects the generation of issue-related information that goes beyond the information that is readily available. On the other hand, convergent processing of a majority message focuses more narrowly on the information presented. Although dissent is conceived as a crucial antecedent of divergence/convergence effects in Nemeth's work, some findings in the literature suggest that dissent might not be a necessary condition (e.g., Volpato, Maass, Mucchi-Faina, & Vitti, 1990). Accordingly, differences in divergence/convergence may also emerge as a function of mere consensus

Empirical testing

In our experimental paradigm we attempted to study mere consensus effects in social influence relatively detached from social conflict, socially relevant influence groups, and other context variables known to moderate minority

Table 3.1 *Thought Listing Measures and Attitude Index as a Function of Consensus Information (Expt. 1 in Erb, Bohner, Schmälzle, & Rank, 1998)*

	Consensus Information		
	low	*high*	*none*
(a) Perceived persuasiveness	4.90	6.05	4.37
	(2.31)	(2.21)	(2.24)
(b) Total Number of thoughts	4.68	4.60	7.00
	(1.46)	(1.70)	(1.63)
(c) Valence of thoughts	−0.21	+0.08	−0.09
	(0.42)	(0.45)	(0.48)
(d) Novelty of thoughts	6.51	4.08	5.80
	(1.50)	(2.14)	(1.83)
(e) Attitude index	5.39	6.41	5.86
	(1.45)	(1.02)	(1.17)

Note: Standard deviations in parentheses. Number of cases per cell from left to right: 19, 20, 20 for (a), (b), (c) and (e); and 14, 14, 15 for (d). Higher numbers indicate: (a) higher perceived persuasiveness, range from 1: *not at all convincing* to 9: *very convincing*; (c) higher favorability, range from −1: *unfavorable* to +1: *favorable*; (d) higher novelty, range for (c) 1: *old idea* to 9: *new idea*; (e) higher favorability, range from 1: *unfavorable* to 9: *favorable*.

and majority influence. We chose majorities and minorities that were mostly socially irrelevant to research participants and we used fictitious attitude objects to minimize any effects of prior attitudes. For illustration here, we present a very simple test of the biased processing hypothesis. In this experiment, participants were provided with consensus information about a fictitious large-scale building project on which a public discussion meeting was said to have taken place. Participants were informed that in this meeting either a majority of 86% or a minority of 14% of attendants had expressed their agreement with the project. In a control condition participants received no consensus information. They then read a persuasive message containing arguments supposed to have been provided by those in favor of the project.[1] Later they were asked to list any thoughts they had had while reading the message. Then they indicated their perception of the message and their own attitudes towards the project on several attitude items that were later combined to form an index of general agreement.

The major results are shown in Table 3.1 (for more detailed analyses see Erb et al., 1998). We found that respondents perceived the message as more

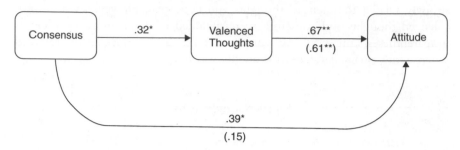

Figure 3.1 *Direct effects and effects mediated by valenced cognitive responses of consensus (0 = low, 1 = high) on postmessage attitude index. Coefficients appearing above lines are beta weights for uncorrected paths. Coefficients in parentheses appearing below lines are beta weights for corrected paths (*p < .05, **p < .01).*

persuasive when consensus was high rather than low. This indicates cognitive bias that led to a more favorable assessment of message content under high than low consensus. We further found, as predicted, that the total number of listed thoughts was lower when consensus information — either high or low — was available, compared to the condition where no consensus information was available. This indicates that participants' use of consensus information had reduced the amount of systematic processing they dedicated to the message. We also computed an index of thought valence by subtracting the proportion of disagreeing thoughts from that of agreeing thoughts. High consensus evoked more favorable thoughts than low consensus, again indicating the operation of cognitive bias. Tendencies of divergent versus convergent thinking were assessed through external ratings of thought novelty, ranging from 1 ("almost literally reproduced from the message") to 9 ("completely new idea that had not been suggested in the text at all"). Novelty scores showed that low-consensus participants generated more novel (i.e., divergent) thoughts than did high-consensus respondents. This result indicates that variations in consensus can evoke divergent and convergent thinking, independent of dissent within the influence setting. Finally, high consensus led to favorable attitudes and low consensus led to unfavorable attitudes.

To further test the biased processing assumption that thought valence mediated the effects of consensus on attitudes, we conducted a multiple regression analysis with consensus and valenced thoughts as independent variables, and attitude measures as dependent variables. As Figure 3.1 shows, consensus introduced bias into the valenced thought measure and attitudes were strongly related to valenced thoughts and consensus. However, when both valenced thoughts and consensus were included in the analysis (coefficients in parentheses), the effect of consensus on attitudes was clearly reduced whereas the effect of valenced thoughts was not.

Some Conclusions

Mere consensus affects information processing and attitude judgments

Taken together, these results indicate that perceivers can use mere consensus as a basis for subsequent information processing. When a majority introduces a previously unknown attitude object, cognitive responses are more favorable than when the same message stems from a minority. Such biases lead to favorable or unfavorable attitude judgments and help to simplify information processing. Moreover, mere consensus can trigger tendencies in information processing that can be described as divergent or convergent in Nemeth's (1986) sense. As we were able to replicate such findings (Erb et al., 1998, Expt. 2; Erb & Bohner, 1999; Erb & Weinerth, 1997), we believe that consensus itself has profound consequences regarding information processing and subsequent attitude judgment.

What can such results tell us about minority and majority influence? Moscovici (1980) and many others have argued that minorities are usually regarded as more negative than majorities. This assumption was at least partially based on the notion that minorities introduce conflict with prior attitudes and/or undermine consensus within a group of which the target of influence is a member. By contrast, mere consensus effects show that different evaluations of majority and minority positions can occur independent of social relevance and opinion discrepancy. Consensus itself has evaluative consequences that allow perceivers to assess the validity of a forwarded position. We may speculate that consensus information calls to mind a judgmental heuristic such as "high consensus implies correctness" (e.g., Mackie, 1987), but future research will have to answer the question why consensus is associated with positive versus negative evaluations even under conditions relatively detached from social conflict.

Also, mere consensus reduced cognitive effort in processing the message when compared to conditions in which consensus information was not available to bias systematic processing. This result is consistent with other research showing that the use of general knowledge structures such as stereotypes (Macrae, Milne, & Bodenhausen, 1994) or schemata (Markus & Zajonc, 1985)

can save cognitive energy (see also Bless et al., 1996). It suggests that conflicting findings that either minorities or majorities induce higher message
scrutiny are probably due to other variables than consensus. Such variables
may interact with consensus or even override consensus effects on cognitive
effort. However, we can conclude that hypotheses attributing higher effort to
either minorities or majorities per se have to be refuted (see also Baker &
Petty, 1994). We would also like to stress the importance of baseline conditions without consensus information in future studies on this question. Only
by comparing low and high consensus conditions with a baseline can we
decide whether minority or majority influence or both increase or decrease
cognitive effort within a given situation.

Moreover, mere consensus can lead to tendencies toward divergent and
convergent thinking for low and high consensus positions, respectively. These
effects occur in the absence of conflict and opinion discrepancy. This implies
that dissent, which was favored by Nemeth (1986) as an explanation for these
effects, may not be a necessary condition. By contrast, cognitive bias on the
divergence/convergence dimension may be related to a more general aspect
of minority and majority influence, namely degree of consensus.

One possible explanation of how mere consensus may influence the
divergence/convergence of processing can be derived from Nemeth's (1986)
original reasoning. Erb and Weinerth (1997) speculated that under majority
influence "the world of alternatives is reduced to two" (Nemeth, 1986, p.
25), because the individual would have to decide whether to adopt the majority's position or not. High consensus signals that there are not many other
alternatives under consideration. Accordingly, recipients should focus attention on the information provided by the majority, resulting in convergent
processing. On the other hand, exposure to a low consensus minority position may leave open a diversity of possible alternatives (Nemeth, 1986), the
processing of which should be divergent in nature. Low consensus thus may
signal that the alternative under consideration is one out of many others.
Note that such an explanation would be independent of dissent with prior
attitudes.

In the Erb and Weinerth (1997) experiment, participants received information about the (fictitious) issue of improving the infrastructure in a
German district close to the Czech border. They were informed that in a
public discussion meeting either *a minority* or *the majority* of citizens had
agreed with the construction of a road and a border checkpoint to improve
connections with the neighboring Czech Republic. In two other conditions,
no consensus information was provided. Instead, those participants received
information that the construction project was either *the only alternative* or *one*

of five alternatives discussed at the meeting. Participants then read a persuasive message in favor of the road construction project. We expected to replicate mere consensus effects on the valence of cognitive responses and attitude judgments (as described above) in the minority and majority influence conditions. This was indeed the case, indicating that the procedure in this experiment was suitable for producing mere consensus effects. For the variation in alternatives (one vs. five), we expected that in the one alternative condition participants would engage in convergent processing and that participants in the five alternatives condition would engage in divergent processing.

Results showed that indeed mentioning the number of alternatives significantly influenced divergence/convergence. Novelty of generated thoughts was higher for five alternatives ($M = 3.55$) as well as low consensus ($M = 3.34$) compared to one alternative ($M = 2.77$) and high consensus ($M = 2.54$; seven-point rating scales). In addition to novelty ratings, we used an index of originality of thoughts (see Vinokur & Burnstein, 1974) and again found the hypothesized effect ($Ms = 0.50, 0.57, 0.17,$ and 0.16, for five alternatives, low consensus, one alternative, and high consensus, respectively). These results provide first evidence that perceived diversity of alternatives can affect the divergence and convergence of message processing. However, parallel effects do not necessarily imply that perceived diversity underlies consensus effects. Thus, further research is needed on the processes that lead to divergent or convergent thinking in response to consensus information.

Cognitive bias versus heuristic effects on attitudes

Biased processing in response to consensus information requires that recipients encode consensus information before engaging in message processing. In a critical test of the biased processing hypothesis (Erb et al., 1998, Expt. 2) we replicated mere consensus effects on attitudes via biased processing when consensus information was introduced before message processing, but we did not find any effect of mere consensus when participants were provided with consensus information after encoding the message. This pattern of results would not have been obtained if the effects of mere consensus were a result of simply using consensus as a heuristic cue to come up with an attitudinal judgment (e.g., Mackie, 1987, Expt. 4). Mere consensus did not seem to provide a heuristic basis that individuals used to form attitude judgments. Rather, individuals based their judgments on issue-related information processing which was guided by a positively or negatively valenced initial reaction that mere consensus had elicited.

Do these results prove that consensus itself has no detectable effect in the absence of systematic processing? Obviously not. For example, those participants in the Erb et al. (1998) study who received consensus information after message processing could already have formed an attitude judgment via unbiased systematic processing, and may have been reluctant to change this judgment in response to the consensus information. Things might be different if respondents receive consensus information at the outset but are either unwilling or unable to engage in further systematic processing. Of course, we would expect cognitive bias only when systematic processing occurs. However, when consensus information is present but cognitive bias cannot operate during message processing, consensus could influence attitudes directly via heuristic processing. We hypothesize that such purely heuristic processing should have a lower impact on attitudes than consensus-based biased systematic processing: Systematic processing of content information often provides a basis for subsequent judgment that subjectively seems more reliable to the individual and quantitatively outweighs the information conferred by a heuristic cue (Bohner, Moskowitz, & Chaiken, 1995).

Based on this reasoning, we explored potential effects of mere consensus independent of biased processing, which may occur when systematic processing is impeded by a distractor task (Erb, Bohner, & Deutsch, 1999). Distracting respondents from systematic processing provides an even more stringent test of the cognitive bias hypothesis than introducing consensus information after message processing. This is because under distraction individuals should not be able to arrive at an attitudinal judgment on the basis of systematic processing. We utilized a 2 (consensus low vs. high) × 2 (no distraction vs. distraction) factorial design. The procedure followed very closely the one described above (Erb et al., 1998, Expt. 1). Participants assigned to the distraction condition were asked to solve a distractor task during message exposure.

Results showed that nondistracted participants engaged in biased processing of issue-relevant information on the basis of consensus information. When processing message content systematically, these participants generated favorable thoughts to the message and judged the message to be rather high in persuasiveness in response to high consensus. Low consensus, on the other hand, resulted in more negative cognitive responding and rather low ratings of persuasiveness. Biased cognitive responding, then, led to attitudes that were more favorable under high than under low consensus. Again, a multiple regression analysis provided further evidence that these attitude effects were mediated via biased cognitive responding. In the distraction conditions, however, where processing of message content was impeded, none of these effects emerged: Consensus did not bias cognitive responses and did not affect attitude judgments.

Taken together, our studies showed no indication of a direct heuristic effect of consensus on attitudes, either alone (as could have been the case in the distraction study by Erb et al., 1999) or in combination with the processing of message content (as could have emerged in Experiment 2 by Erb et al., 1998, when consensus information was presented after the message). In both studies, for mere consensus effects on attitudes to emerge it was crucial that issue-relevant information be processed in light of high or low consensus.

Thus, in two independent studies, consensus had no detectable impact on attitudes when it could not bias systematic message processing. These results imply that cognitive bias seems to be a necessary mediator of mere consensus effects on attitudes. At present, we do not know whether individuals consciously discount mere consensus as a direct basis for attitude judgments, whether they regard consensus information as insufficient or subjectively invalid for attitude judgments, or whether any other process renders the use of mere consensus for attitude judgments under such conditions unlikely. However, we would like to argue that these results closely relate to contemporary theorizing on minority and majority influence and shed new light on some effects previously discussed in the literature.

For example, Moscovici (1980) explicitly postulated compliance with a majority to occur in the absence of "validation," that is, any processing of content information. Accordingly, majority influence is assumed to follow from social conflict that evokes social comparison processes in which individuals in conflict focus on the question why their opinion may be wrong. Mackie (1987) explicitly studied heuristic-based effects of majority influence in one of her experiments. Those participants were informed that an ingroup majority agreed over a certain attitude object, but did not receive content information. Mackie (1987) found that participants moved towards the majority position, but this effect was neither long-lasting nor did it generalize to related issues, as was found when the majority argued with a persuasive message. This implies that this influence was accompanied by only shallow processing of issue-related information. Mackie (1987) attributed the attitude change observed to participants' perceptions of similarity to the source, implicating identification.

We obtained comparable effects in a study in which an ingroup majority produced attitude change under conditions of low processing effort independent of any effects on information processing (Darke et al., 1998). Thus, individuals seem to use ingroup consensus but not mere consensus as a heuristic basis for attitude judgments. Interestingly, under conditions of systematic processing, ingroup consensus affected attitude judgments only when consensus biased the valence of (self-generated) issue-relevant thoughts. When the reliability of the consensus cue was discounted (for details see Darke et al., 1998), ingroup consensus affected neither processing nor judgments. Again, biased processing appeared to be a moderator of consensus effects under conditions that promote systematic processing.

However, the mere consensus perspective sheds new light on the explanatory relevance of such findings. As far as there seem to exist prerequisites for mere consensus to affect attitudes (cf. biased systematic processing), majority influence in the absence of systematic processing, as studied by Moscovici (1980), Mackie (1987), and others, seems to require that the influence source is a socially valued group or argues against prior attitudes. Mackie (1987) herself has interpreted such agreement with a majority as a consequence of identification with the influence group (Kelman, 1961). Obviously, the motive not to be deviant (Moscovici, 1980) or identification with a highly valued influence group (Mackie, 1987) can lead to agreement with an influence source independent of any processing effects. However, from our perspective, social influence based on such motives does not necessarily covary with the status of the influence group as a minority or a majority. "In principle, both minority and majority sources could be associated with circumstances in which compliance or resistance seems desirable" (Kruglanski & Mackie, 1990, p. 254). Such variables play their roles in a wide range of social influence settings apart from minority and majority influence, as for example those reviewed by Eagly and Chaiken (1993) or Petty and Cacioppo (1986).

Regarding minority influence, the same logic holds true. Imagine a thought experiment with a minority influence source that is highly valued (e.g., imbued with positive attributions) or think of a minority that provides strong arguments for its attitudinal position under conditions of systematic processing. From our perspective it does not make sense to attribute favorable attitudes under such conditions to minority influence. Positive source characteristics such as expertise, or highly influential content information such as strong arguments, as well as many other variables, may influence processing and judgments, but may also render the operation of consensus in a given situation unlikely. When such "competing" inferences occur, the use of consensus may be offset because other information provides a more accessible or a subjectively more valid basis for subsequent attitude judgments. In order to demonstrate minority influence under a certain condition it has to be shown empirically that low consensus operates when individuals process attitude-relevant information or form their judgments. Technically, a candi-

date variable to explain minority influence processes has to produce an interaction effect with consensus information (low, high, none). Such effects have
already been obtained, for example in attitude change on related issues (De
Dreu & DeVries, 1993; Mugny, 1982; Wood et al., 1994), and hopefully future
research may find conditions under which low consensus is associated with
attitude change on focal issues.

The finding that mere consensus can have only weak direct effects on attitudes is also clearly at odds with other theorizing in the realm of persuasive
effects of heuristic cues on attitudes. We can conceptualize the biased processing assumption within a more general theory of social information processing, the heuristic-systematic model (HSM; Bohner et al., 1995; Chaiken,
Liberman, & Eagly, 1989). The HSM describes processing activities along a
continuum from a relatively effortless, top-down heuristic mode, to an effortful, bottom-up systematic mode. Within the heuristic mode, individuals
respond to heuristic cues that call to mind simple decision rules or heuristics. Such heuristics enable the individual to reach an attitude judgment
without scrutinizing any detailed information. Systematic processing, on the
other hand, includes individuals' attempts to evaluate content information
pertaining to the issue under consideration. The HSM specifies conditions
under which heuristic and systematic processing may co-occur (for a full discussion see Bohner et al., 1995). According to the HSM's bias hypothesis,
individuals who are sufficiently able and motivated to scrutinize relevant
information may use heuristics to evaluate content information. Thus, heuristic inferences bias subsequent information processing (Bohner, Chaiken, &
Hunyadi, 1994; Chaiken & Maheswaran, 1994). From the HSM perspective,
one would also predict effects on attitudes based on heuristic inferences under
conditions that impede systematic processing (Bohner et al., 1995; see also
Petty & Cacioppo, 1986). A valenced cue that can bias systematic processing should be even more likely to lead to heuristic-based attitude effects
under conditions of shallow content processing. Accordingly, manipulations
of source credibility, likability, physical attractiveness, message length, number
of arguments, and so forth have been shown to have a significant impact on
attitudes when motivation or ability for message-relevant and issue-relevant
thinking is low, but to have only little impact when motivation and ability
are high (*attenuation*; for reviews see Chaiken & Stangor, 1987, and Eagly &
Chaiken, 1993; see also Petty & Cacioppo, 1986).

Thus, according to the HSM, a persuasion cue such as consensus (a) should
lead to heuristic-based judgments when systematic processing is low, and (b)
may bias systematic processing of message content under conditions that give
rise to systematic processing. Moreover, suppressing the impact of issue-

relevant information, for example by distraction from systematic processing, is expected to increase heuristic effects on attitudes. In fact, within the HSM, Eagly and Chaiken (1993) explicitly predicted such effects of increased cue importance.

In contrast, our results suggest that there may exist heuristic cues that require biased systematic processing to affect attitude judgments. As a consequence, persuasion research has to pay closer attention to the content of heuristic-based inferences. Two heuristics that may have identical effects under conditions of extensive processing (e.g., biased systematic processing) may not necessarily have identical effects under shallow processing (e.g., heuristic processing). Such a discussion speaks to the predictive value of dual process models in persuasion. The assumption that the specific content of heuristic inferences may be decisive for a priori predictions may need to be explicitly integrated into the HSM. In a similar vein, Bohner et al. (1995) proposed that the content of heuristic inferences may constrain the types of interplay between heuristic and systematic processing. Persuasion research will have to find answers to such challenging questions.

Concluding Remarks

In this chapter we discussed mere consensus effects on information processing and attitude judgments. We started with the postulate that consensus is the only variable that necessarily covaries with the status of an influence group as a majority or a minority: Majorities reflect higher consensus than minorities. Thus, we regarded consensus to be the key concept to understanding minority and majority influence. To explain consensus effects on attitudes, we proposed the cognitive bias hypothesis. According to this model, low or high consensus causes valenced inferences that bias subsequent information processing. On the basis of such cognitive bias, individuals arrive at attitudes that are favorable for high and unfavorable for low consensus positions.

On a theoretical level, this approach allows one to re-examine the explanatory relevance of a number of variables previously studied in the realm of minority and majority influence. Variables that affect social influence independent of consensus (e.g., source characteristics, strong arguments provided in a persuasive message, identification with a socially valued influence group, social conflict, dissent with previously held attitudes, the motive not to appear socially deviant or rejecting) do not seem to be crucial for explaining minority or majority influence, because these variables are not necessarily linked to group status. Thus, the mere consensus approach sheds new light on minority and majority influence processes that we hope will prove fruitful in future research on this topic.

NOTES

The preparation of this chapter was supported by a grant from the Deutsche Forschungsgemeinschaft to the authors (ER 257/1-5). We gratefully acknowledge the thoughtful comments on a previous draft by Nanne K. De Vries, Roland Deutsch, and Carsten K. W. De Dreu, as well as stimulating discussions with the participants of the "Conference on Minority Influence," Amsterdam, October 1998. Reprints of Figure 3.1 and parts of Table 3.1 from Erb, H.-P., Bohner, G., Schmälzle, K., & Rank, S., *Personality and Social Psychology Bulletin, 24*, pp. 620–633, copyright 1998 by Sage Publications, Inc. Reprinted by Permission of Sage Publications, Inc.

1   Biased processing requires the systematic processing of message content. The message we used here makes it possible to assess systematic processing without crossing low versus high consensus with a between-subjects variation of argument strength (see discussion below). Instead, the message always contained the same six arguments. According to pretesting, four arguments were of average persuasiveness, whereas one was highly persuasive, and another was quite unpersuasive. The strong and weak argument referred to different aspects of the building project; participants later judged both the "strong" and the "weak" aspect on separate attitude scales. The analysis revealed a main effect of aspect but no interaction with consensus. This indicates that, across conditions, the message had been processed systematically (see Erb et al., 1998, for details).

REFERENCES

Asch, S. E. (1956). Studies of independence and conformity: A minority of one against a unanimous majority. *Psychological Monographs, 70* (9), pp. 1–70 (whole No. 416).

Baker, S. M., & Petty, R. E. (1994). Majority and minority influence: Source-position imbalance as a determinant of message scrutiny. *Journal of Personality and Social Psychology, 67,* 5–19.

Bless, H., Clore, G. L., Schwarz, N., Golisano, V., Rabe, C., & Wölk, M. (1996). Mood and the use of stereotypes: Does happy mood really lead to mindlessness? *Journal of Personality and Social Psychology, 71,* 665–679.

Bohner, G., Chaiken, S., & Hunyadi, P. (1994). The role of mood and message ambiguity in the interplay of heuristic and systematic processing. *European Journal of Social Psychology, 24,* 207–221.

Bohner, G., Frank, E., & Erb, H.-P. (1998). Heuristic processing of distinctiveness information in minority and majority influence. *European Journal of Social Psychology*, *28*, 855–860.

Bohner, G., Moskowitz, G., & Chaiken, S. (1995). The interplay of heuristic and systematic processing of social information. In W. Stroebe & M. Hewstone (Eds.), *European review of social psychology* (Vol. 6, pp. 33–68). Chichester, UK: Wiley.

Chaiken, S., Giner-Sorolla, R., & Chen, S. (1996). Defense and impression motives in heuristic and systematic information processing. In P. M. Gollwitzer & J. A. Bargh (Eds.), *The psychology of action: Linking cognition and motivation to behavior* (pp. 553–578). New York: Guilford.

Chaiken, S., Liberman, A., & Eagly, A. H. (1989). Heuristic and systematic information processing within and beyond the persuasion context. In J. S. Uleman & J. A. Bargh (Eds.), *Unintended thought* (pp. 212–252). New York: Guilford.

Chaiken, S., & Maheswaran, D. (1994). Heuristic processing can bias systematic processing: Effects of source credibility, argument ambiguity, and task importance on attitude judgment. *Journal of Personality and Social Psychology*, *66*, 460–473.

Chaiken, S., & Stangor, C. (1987). Attitudes and attitude change. *Annual Review of Psychology*, *38*, 575–630.

Crano, W. D., & Hannula-Bral, K. A. (1994). Context/categorization model of social influence: Minority and majority influence in the formation of a novel response norm. *Journal of Experimental Social Psychology*, *30*, 247–276.

Darke, P. R., Chaiken, S., Bohner, G., Einwiller, S., Erb, H.-P., & Hazlewood, J. D. (1998). Accuracy motivation, consensus information, and the law of large numbers: Effects on attitude judgment in the absence of argumentation. *Personality and Social Psychology Bulletin*, *24*, 1205–1215.

De Dreu, C. K. W., & De Vries, N. K. (1993). Numerical support, information processing, and attitude change. *European Journal of Social Psychology*, *23*, 647–662.

De Vries, N. K., De Dreu, C. K. W., Gordijn, E., & Schuurman, M. (1996). Majority and minority influence: A dual role interpretation. In W. Stroebe & M. Hewstone (Eds.), *European review of social psychology* (Vol. 7, pp. 145–172). Chichester: Wiley.

Eagly, A. H., & Chaiken, S. (1993). *The psychology of attitudes.* Fort Worth, TX: Harcourt Brace Jovanovich.

Erb, H.-P. (1998). Sozialer Einfluß durch Konsens: Werbung mit Meinungsüberein-stimmung [Social influence through consensus: Advertising with shared attitudes]. *Zeitschrift für Sozialpsychologie*, *29*, 156–164.

Erb, H.-P., Bohner, G., & Deutsch, R. (1999). *Conformity, compliance, and cognitive bias in minority and majority influence: What mere consensus effects on attitudes can tell.* Unpublished manuscript, University of Maryland, College Park.

Erb, H.-P., Bohner, G., Schmälzle, K., & Rank, S. (1998). Beyond conflict and discrepancy: Cognitive bias in minority and majority influence. *Personality and Social Psychology Bulletin*, *24*, 620–633.

Erb, H.-P., & Weinerth, T. (1997, March). *Effekte wahrgenommener Meinungsvielfalt auf die Verarbeitung persuasiver Kommunikation.* [*Effects of perceived diversity of attitudes on the processing of persuasive communication*]. 39. Tagung experimentell arbeitender Psychologen, Berlin, Germany.

Festinger, L. (1950). Informal social communication. *Psychological Review, 57,* 271–282.

Festinger, L. (1954). A theory of social comparison processes. *Human Relations, 7,* 117–140.

Hardin, C. D., & Higgins, E. T. (1996). Shared reality: How social verification makes the subjective objective. In R. M. Sorrentino & E. T. Higgins (Eds.), *Handbook of motivation and cognition* (Vol. 3, pp. 28–84). New York: Guilford.

Hewstone, M., Martin, R., & Kakavelakis, I. (1997). *Differential information processing in majority and minority influence.* Unpublished manuscript.

Houston, D. A., & Fazio, R. H. (1989). Biased processing as a function of attitude accessibility: Making objective judgments subjectively. *Social Cognition, 7,* 51–66.

Kelley, H. H. (1967). Attribution theory in social psychology. In D. Devine (Ed.), *Nebraska symposium on motivation.* Lincoln: University of Nebraska Press.

Kelman, H. C. (1961). Processes in opinion change. *Public Opinion Quaterly, 25,* 57–78.

Kruglanski, A. W., & Mackie, D. M. (1990). Majority and minority influence: A judgmental process analysis. In W. Stroebe & M. Hewstone (Eds.), *European review of social psychology* (Vol. 1, pp. 229–261). Chichester, UK: Wiley.

Latané, B., & Wolf, S. (1981). The social impact of majorities and minorities. *Psychological Review, 88,* 438–453.

Levine, J. M. (1989). Reaction to opinion deviance in small groups. In P. B. Paulus (Ed.), *Psychology of group influence* (2nd ed., pp. 187–231). Hillsdale, NJ: Erlbaum.

Levine, J. M., & Russo, E. M. (1987). Majority and minority influence. In C. Hendrick (Ed.), *Review of personality and social psychology* (Vol. 8, pp. 13–54). Newbury Park, CA: Sage.

Maass, A., & Clark, R. D. III (1984). Hidden impact of minorities: Fifteen years of minority influence research. *Psychological Bulletin, 95,* 428–450.

Maass, A., Clark, R. D. III, & Haberkorn, G. (1982). The effects of differential ascribed category membership and norms on minority influence. *European Journal of Social Psychology, 12,* 89–104.

Mackie, D. M. (1987). Systematic and nonsystematic processing of majority and minority persuasive communications. *Journal of Personality and Social Psychology, 53,* 41–52.

Mackie, D. M., Gastardo-Conaco, M. C., & Skelly, J. J. (1992). Knowledge of the advocated position and the processing of in-group and out-group persuasive messages. *Personality and Social Psychology Bulletin, 18,* 145–151.

Macrae, C. N., Milne, A. B., & Bodenhausen, G. V. (1994). Stereotypes as energy saving devices: A peek inside the toolbox. *Journal of Personality and Social Psychology, 66,* 37–47.

Maheswaran, D., & Chaiken, S. (1991). Promoting systematic processing in low motivation settings: The effect of incongruent information on processing and judgment. *Journal of Personality and Social Psychology, 61,* 13–25.

Markus, H., & Zajonc, R. B. (1985). The cognitive perspective in social psychology. In G. Linzey & E. Aronson (Eds.), *The handbook of social psychology* (3rd ed., Vol. 1, pp. 137–230). New York: Random House.

Moscovici, S. (1976). *Social influence and social change*. London: Academic Press.

Moscovici, S. (1980). Toward a theory of conversion behavior. In L. Berkowitz (Ed.), *Advances in experimental social psychology* (Vol. 13, pp. 209–239). New York: Academic Press.

Mugny, G. (1982). *The power of minorities*. London: Academic Press.

Nemeth, C. (1986). Differential contributions of majority and minority influence. *Psychological Review, 93*, 23–32.

Nemeth, C., & Endicott, J. (1976). The midpoint as an anchor: Another look at discrepancy of position and attitude change. *Sociometry, 39*, 11–18.

Paicheler, G. (1977). Norms and attitude change: II. The phenomenon of bipolarization. *European Journal of Social Psychology, 7*, 5–14.

Petty, R. E., & Cacioppo, J. T. (1981). Issue involvement as a moderator of the effects on attitude of advertising content and context. *Advances in Consumer Research, 8*, 20–24.

Petty, R. E., & Cacioppo, J. T. (1986). *Communication and persuasion: Central and peripheral routes to attitude change*. New York: Springer.

Ross, L., Greene, D., & House, P. (1977). The "false consensus effect": An ego-centric bias in social perception and attribution processes. *Journal of Experimental Social Psychology, 13*, 279–301.

Sherif, M. (1958). Group influences upon the formation of norms and attitudes. In E. E. Maccoby, T. M. Newcomb, & E. L. Hartley (Eds.), *Readings in social psychology*. New York: Holt.

Smith, C. M., Tindale, R. S., & Dugoni, B. L. (1996). Minority and majority influence in freely interacting groups: Qualitative versus quantitative differences. *British Journal of Social Psychology, 35*, 137–149.

Tanford, S., & Penrod, S. (1984). Social influence model: A formal integration of research on majority and minority influence processes. *Psychological Bulletin, 95*, 189–225.

Trost, M. R., Maass, A., & Kenrick, D. T. (1992). Minority influence: Personal relevance biases cognitive processes and reverses private acceptance. *Journal of Experimental Social Psychology, 28*, 234–254.

Van Dyne, L., & Saavedra, R. (1996). A naturalistic minority influence experiment: Effects on divergent thinking, conflict and originality in work-groups. *British Journal of Social Psychology, 35*, 151–167.

Vinokur, A., & Burnstein, E. (1974). Effects of partially shared persuasive arguments on group induced shifts: A group-problem-solving approach. *Journal of Personality and Social Psychology, 22*, 14–23.

Volpato, C., Maass, A., Mucchi-Faina, A., & Vitti, E. (1990). Minority influence and social categorization. *European Journal of Social Psychology, 20*, 119–132.

Watts W. A., & Holt, L. E. (1979). Persistence of opinion change induced under conditions of forewarning and distraction. *Journal of Personality and Social Psychology*, *37*, 778–789.

Wood, W., Lundgren, S., Ouellette, J. A., Busceme, S., & Blackstone, T. (1994). Minority influence: A meta-analytic review of social influence processes. *Psychological Bulletin*, *115*, 323–345.

4

Mediators of Minority Social Influence: Cognitive Processing Mechanisms Revealed Through a Persuasion Paradigm

Gordon B. Moskowitz and Shelly Chaiken

Nonviolent direct action seeks to create such a crisis and foster such a *tension* that a community which has constantly refused to negotiate is forced to *confront the issue* . . . Just as Socrates felt that it was necessary to create a tension in the mind so that individuals could rise from the bondage of myths and half-truths to the unfettered realm of *creative analysis and objective appraisal,* so must we see the need for nonviolent gadflies to create the kind of tension in society that will help men rise from the dark depths of prejudice and racism to the majestic heights of understanding and brotherhood. (*Martin Luther King Jr., 1963, emphasis added*)

The history of North American research on social influence is focused on the power of a majority: power to exert pressure to conform and power to direct judgment in both ambiguous and unambiguous stimulus environments (e.g., Asch, 1952; Deutsch & Gerard, 1955; Kelman, 1961; Sherif, 1936). In contrast, Moscovici (1976) provided a European perspective to social influence, showing that minorities determine one's subjective construal of a stimulus. This research cleverly used measures and procedures similar to those used in research on majority influence (e.g., perceptual judgments made after exposure to judgments of others) in order to highlight the unique power of minorities. Consistent with King's (1963; see above) ideology, Moscovici held that minorities are able to adopt actions (namely, consistent intransigence) that can foster tension in the mind of perceivers, a tension that motivates a careful and open-minded appraisal of the minority position. Social influence occurs when perceivers reject preconceived beliefs in favor of such an objective, often creative, analysis of an issue (e.g., Nemeth, 1986).

Although minority influence research has flourished over the past two decades, it has generally eschewed the social-cognitive methods embraced by North American researchers over this same time period. Yet there is an incongruity between this literature's lack of empirical emphasis and its theoretical emphasis on cognitive processing. For example, Moscovici's (1976, 1980, 1985) theoretical model made clear processing assumptions, positing that minorities succeed at influencing others when attributions are formed that serve to oppose the negative expectancies perceivers typically hold toward minorities. Attributions triggering this expectancy violation were said to initiate uncertainty, doubt, and tension (psychological conflict) in the mind of perceivers, creating motivation to resolve such conflict. Resolution was posited to occur through a validation process, where private beliefs toward the minority are reassessed and cognitive effort is expended to scrutinize the minority view (similar to what Chaiken, 1980, called systematic processing).

Social Cognition and Minority Influence

Attributions, tension, and creative problem solving

This disjunction between theory and research does not imply that minority influence research has been totally devoid of interest in cognitive processing. To the contrary, since Maass and Clark's (1984) and Chaiken and Stangor's (1987) review of the literature, examinations of social cognition in minority influence have steadily captured research focus.

Attributions. Clark and Maass (1988) examined the types of attributions formed toward members of minority groups, with the focus of interest on the question of whether people spontaneously attribute a minority position to negative causes such as bias or lack of credibility. It was found that positive attributions, such as deciding that a minority source is credible and influential, were capable of being formed toward a minority, but this was dependent upon whether there were prior stereotypes and biases associated with the minority. Thus, if a minority is an outgroup member (minority status is based on social group membership), it is likely that negative expectancies and stereotypes exist that will guide attributional processes (e.g., Taylor & Jaggi, 1974). In this case, negative attributions may be formed toward behavior that might otherwise be interpreted positively had such expectancies related to group membership not existed (cf., Pérez & Mugny, 1987). The stronger the outgroup stereotype, the more likely that attributions will be formed that serve to maintain the negative evaluation (reducing the possibility of influence). However, if the minority is an ingroup member (minority status defined numerically), there are unlikely to be as many negative expectancies and stereotypes that impact on attributional processes. Hence, fewer hindrances exist toward forming positive attributions, increasing the possibility that a minority's behavior is attributed to causes such as credibility, and increasing the possibility of influence.

Bohner, Erb, Reinhard, and Frank's (1996) research presents a recent example of social cognition, in the form of attributional mediators, being incorporated into examinations of minority influence. They proposed that when a minority source exhibits high distinctiveness (when their positions on the focal topic versus other topics are distinct, e.g., Kelley, 1967), influence will be promoted. In fact, a distinctive minority was viewed positively because participants attributed their position to some aspect of the particular topic under consideration. Having discarded "negative person attributions that are based on dispositions such as general deviance" (p. 30), perceivers were open to being influenced.

Tension.   Positive attributions formed in response to minority behaviors were proposed by Moscovici (1980) to trigger tension, with the desire to reduce this tension stimulating a subsequent validation process. Although relatively little research has examined whether tension states mediate minority influence, Pérez, Falomir, and Mugny (1995) addressed this issue. Participants were smokers who received an antismoking message from a minority source and were asked to memorize part of the message. The dependent variable was a question assessing the intention to stop smoking. The participants were either given the option of smoking during the experiment or not. Additionally, they were tested for their recall of the message either immediately after reading it (completed task condition) or at the end of the experiment (uncompleted task condition). This design was meant to manipulate whether participants experienced a tension state prior to answering the question that served as the dependent variable. The experience of tension was manipulated in two ways. First, participants in the "uncompleted task" condition were said to be experiencing a tension state. This assumption was based on the *Zeigarnik effect*, where disruption of a goal, such as when one is not allowed to complete a task, creates a tension state that motivates one to perseverate on the disrupted goal pursuit (Zeigarnik, 1927). Second, manipulating whether participants were allowed to smoke was included in the design because it was believed that smoking would reduce tension, whereas the inability to smoke would be tension-arousing. Thus, minority influence should be greatest when recall for the minority message is delayed and smoking is not allowed (the condition where tension should theoretically be greatest). The impact of the minority should be lowest in conditions where no source of tension exists – when the task is completed and smoking is allowed. This is precisely what was found. Although this research does not demonstrate either the role played by attributional processes in triggering tension, or that tension's effects on influence are mediated through a validation process, it establishes that the experience of tension is involved in reactions to minority messages.

The question of whether tension is necessary for minority influence to occur suggests a related question – whether misattribution of tension can interfere with influence. This mirrors issues faced by cognitive dissonance researchers. Festinger (1957) described dissonance as an arousal state originating from conflicting cognitions. To test whether dissonance is mediated by arousal, Zanna and Cooper (1974) proceeded from Schachter and Singer's (1962) claim that arousal states are differentiated only by an attributed cognitive label. Supporting the notion that dissonance findings are mediated by arousal, they found misattribution of arousal (altering the attributed cognitive label) diminished dissonance. The misattribution paradigm employed by dissonance researchers is a useful, though as yet unused, paradigm for examining the role of tension in minority influence.[1]

Creative problem solving. Finally, cognitive processes in minority influence have also been examined by Nemeth and colleagues in their work on problem solving (e.g., Nemeth & Wachtler, 1983; Nemeth & Kwan, 1985; Nemeth, Mayseless, Sherman, & Brown, 1990). Their studies demonstrate that when confronted with minority solutions to problems, the solutions generated by research participants are more creative and novel. They interpret these findings as reflecting processes such as cognitive reassessment and divergent thinking. This type of finding is consistent with the presumption by Moscovici and others that minorities trigger a validation process whereby minority positions are evaluated, objectively appraised, and one's own positions (and biases) are thus re-evaluated. Such mechanisms, however, are not directly observed, nor are they linked to either the existence of tension or attributional reasoning.

In summary, social-cognitive research of the sort just described complements traditional research questions in minority influence, such as how a minority's behavioral strategies determine whether influence occurs.

However, such research does not address the specific processing mechanisms – a validation process, systematic processing – that presumably produce influence given the formation of the appropriate attributions and the motivational force of a tension state. This chapter reviews evidence that a specific type of social influence – persuasion – provides both models and methods that allow researchers to examine such processes. In particular, recent research relying on dual process notions has provided initial evidence detailing how the behavior of a minority is transformed into influence.

Examinations of processing mechanisms: Persuasion paradigms and minority influence

Unlike majorities, which are seen as legitimate by virtue of the consensus they represent (Eagly & Chaiken, 1993; Landy, 1972), minorities are likely to be seen as illegitimate and biased (Moscovici & Lage, 1976; Kruglanski & Mackie, 1990). Consistent with this reasoning, Wood, Lundgren, Oullette, Busceme, and Blackstone's (1994) meta-analysis of minority influence research documented that normative pressures exist for individuals to publicly differentiate themselves from a minority. Tajfel and Turner (1986) have suggested that this type of differentiation from an outgroup corresponds with a tendency to denigrate the outgroup and form negative impressions and stereotypes. Minority influence is unlikely to succeed if perceivers are relying on such negative expectancies/stereotypes when evaluating the minority. Influence will be more likely to occur if the perceiver is able to move beyond a dependency on negative stereotypes and heuristics.

Dual process theories of persuasion include several principles that inform when perceivers are likely to rely on such heuristics and when they are likely to move beyond heuristic processing to engage in a more thorough analysis and appraisal when evaluating the positions espoused by and qualities possessed by others. First, relying on heuristics, stereotypes, and expectancies is simpler and requires less mental work relative to more systematic processes such as fitting inconsistencies into a unified impression, elaborating on individuating information, and accurately evaluating either one's own beliefs or others' arguments (e.g., Chaiken, Liberman, & Eagly, 1989; Petty & Cacioppo, 1986). Second, although people typically use heuristics as a default in thinking about others, they can be seduced into spending the greater effort that systematic processing entails (for a review see Chen & Chaiken, 1999). Third, this motivation to exert greater processing effort arises from the tension experienced when one lacks sufficient confidence in a judgment (e.g., Eagly &

Chaiken, 1993). Finally, greater cognitive effort expended by a message recipient is not equivalent to more objective appraisal of the message, but can be exerted in the service of defending one's biases (e.g., Chaiken, Giner-Sorolla, & Chen, 1996; Wood, Pool, Leck, and Purvis, 1996).

Trost, Maass, and Kenrick (1992) leaned on this dual process logic when it was suggested that consistent advocacy of a minority position should elicit careful scrutiny of a persuasive message. However, using thought listing as an index of systematic processing, they found no increases in message-relevant or total thoughts as a function of attending to a minority source. Thus, although this research was among the first to examine the links between processing style and minority influence, support for the notion that minority influence resulted from increased systematic processing was not strong.

Moskowitz (1992, 1996) applied these dual process notions to minority influence by examining whether messages delivered by a minority source were more persuasive when systematic rather than heuristic processing of the message occurred. Systematic processing was defined as actively attempting to evaluate the arguments (and issues related to the arguments) raised in the message.[2] The amount of systematic processing was posited to be affected by the types of attributions perceivers had formed about the minority communicator. Positive attributions were said to be opposed to the existing stereotypes and heuristics that perceivers possessed, and these positive impressions once formed would challenge pre-existing beliefs. This would undermine the confidence in relying on those expectancies and heuristics, generating the sort of motivation that Eagly and Chaiken (1993) described as being capable of triggering systematic processing. Negative impressions would not challenge these heuristics and would be less likely to trigger systematic processing. Thus, when relying on a heuristic is deemed by the perceiver to provide an insufficient basis for forming a confident evaluation of the minority position, the perceiver would be motivated to engage in further scrutiny and systematic processing of the minority message (for greater elaboration on the role of such "confidence gaps" and "sufficiency thresholds" in minority influence, see Bohner, Moskowitz, & Chaiken, 1995; De Dreu & De Vries, 1996). Attributions about the minority can determine the amount of judgmental confidence one possesses, and, in turn, affect systematic processing and minority influence.

Moskowitz (1996) manipulated attributions by telling participants either that the minority was expressing a point of view regarding an issue that the minority had a vested interest in (negative attribution) or that the minority was expressing a point of view regarding an issue on which the minority messenger held an unbiased, objective position that the messenger was certain of (positive attribution). Two methods frequently used in persuasion research that allow assessment of type and amount of cognitive processing were used – thought listing and a manipulation of argument quality. Consistent with Moscovici's model, Moskowitz (1992, 1996) found that minority influence was dependent on the degree to which attributions formed regarding the reasons for the minority's position were positively valenced, and indicated that the minority was certain and confident in their position. Additionally, this impact of attributions on attitudes toward the issue was mediated by the extent to which systematic processing had occurred. Instilling positive attributions in participants was influential because it motivated them systematically to contemplate the minority position. When the message was of high quality, influence was found; when it was of low quality, it was not. Argument quality differences were not found when negative attributions were held. Thought listing data similarly suggested that heuristic processing occurred following negative attributions and systematic processing occurred following positive attributions.

In related work, Baker and Petty (1994) found that when a minority unexpectedly agreed with participants, systematic processing was triggered. Presumably, this result was caused by the unlikely pairing of a minority source with a mainstream position, and the feelings of surprise, threat, or curiosity aroused by finding out that a minority agrees with you. Thus, a type of expectancy violation led to successful minority influence by promoting systematic processing. An important discrepancy between Moskowitz (1992, 1996) and Baker and Petty (1994) concerns the relationship between the minority and the participants. While each experiment examined processing of minority messages, Moskowitz specifically chose participants with neutral attitudes on the issue and who were impartial observers of a numerically defined minority. Baker and Petty examined the interesting case where participants already possessed strong prior opinions that the message either opposed (via a counterattitudinal message) or supported (via a proattitudinal message).

Similar to Baker and Petty (1994) Wood et al. (1996) also examined the case in which a minority message advocates a position that participants agree with. Here, however, the minority was defined as a group that most individuals would be motivated not to agree with (e.g., the Ku Klux Klan). This left participants' identities threatened, as they were now in the position of being in apparent agreement with a hated minority. Wood et al.'s message topic was specifically chosen so that construal of its main theme was ambiguous and thus open to interpretation. The research documented "minority influence," but given the intensity of negative feelings toward the minority, participants' attitudes shifted away from the position endorsed by the minority (thus rejecting one's own initial attitudes). This influence was shown to be mediated by defensive processing, as the interpretations that participants offered for their opinion shifted in order to justify their changed attitude, and did so in a manner that distanced them from the minority. Thus, given the ambiguity of the main theme in the message, participants were able to change how they interpreted the message so as to decide that the minority was communicating something altogether different from them (despite superficially seeming to endorse the same position). By altering their construal of the message, participants defended against seeing themselves as aligned with a minority opinion.

Crano and Chen (1998) reported an experiment somewhat similar in design to that of Baker and Petty (1994) and Moskowitz (1992, 1996). To test the relevance of dual process models to minority influence, they manipulated both argument quality and group status of the source. They chose as the message topic one that all students found sufficiently relevant. With all participants being sufficiently involved, they should all be motivated to process systematically. This was reflected in greater attitude change following strong (versus weak) messages, thus replicating the findings of Baker and Petty (1994) and Moskowitz (1996). Thought listing data also supported the notion that the minority initiated systematic processing. Participants hearing strong (versus weak) messages generated more positive, message-relevant thoughts.

De Dreu and De Vries (1996) also examined the mediating impact of message processing on minority influence, but rather than examining an issue that was either lacking in relevance to all participants or highly relevant to all participants, they manipulated issue involvement. The logic was derived from dual process theories of attitude change (e.g., Chaiken, 1987; Petty & Cacioppo, 1986): Involvement with an issue creates a motivation to engage in systematic processing. The motivation to engage in systematic processing promotes the likelihood that one will override (or correct for) the reliance on heuristics that typically characterizes one's analysis of a minority message (for further discussion of this research program see De Vries, De Dreu, Gordijn, & Schuurman, 1996).

Finally, Erb, Bohner, Schämlzle, and Rank (1998) suggest that a communicator's minority versus majority status conveys consensus information, and that individuals use consensus as a heuristic cue that guides and biases processing of a persuasive message. Drawing on findings that heuristic processing can co-occur with and bias systematic processing (Bohner, Chaiken, & Hunyadi, 1994; Chaiken & Maheswaran, 1994), it was predicted that consensus information would bias message processing. A minority source should lead to more unfavorable thinking as a function of the negative heuristics that surround a lack of consensus. Additionally, consensus information of any sort was predicted to decrease systematic processing relative to a control group, as the consensus information was predicted to serve as a heuristic that might be deemed as sufficient information that would not warrant detailed scrutiny of the message. As predicted, consensus information led to less systematic processing relative to a control condition and minority sources were responded to with greater numbers of negative thoughts than majority sources. Finally, although consensus information decreased the amount of systematic processing, such processing still occurred to some degree – indicated by strong arguments having a greater impact on attitudes than weak ones.

In summary, dual process persuasion paradigms have emerged as a useful tool to examine the mechanisms underlying successful minority influence. The research to date indicates that dual process theories such as the elaboration likelihood model (ELM) and the heuristic-systematic model map on nicely to theories of minority influence, and provide methodologies for exploring cognitive processes. This research suggests that minorities are successful at triggering influence when they are capable of triggering an elaborate/systematic appraisal of the minority position. The challenge remains to continue linking the question of what strategies can be taken by minorities to instigate influence with the question of how systematic processing is initiated. In the reviewed research, such processing was triggered by the message being extremely relevant to participants, by minorities surprisingly agreeing with participants, by attributions being formed that challenged one's default assumptions about minorities (and their lack of consensus), and by individuals feeling threatened by the possibility of being identified with a hated minority.

Stereotype-inconsistent information, disconfirmed expectancies, and validation processes

The research we have discussed raises the question of how to seduce people toward a validation process given the propensity to rely on heuristics, thus summarily rejecting the minority message. In the language of the heuristic-systematic model, the question is one of how to create a "confidence gap," or to make perceivers feel as if the judgments they are forming toward a minority are not sufficient (Bohner, Moskowitz, & Chaiken, 1995; Eagly & Chaiken, 1993). The tendency to rely on the default mode of heuristically rejecting the minority must be undermined and challenged in order for the tension that motivates more elaborate processing to be initiated (thus making people vulnerable to influence). What creates such a challenge to perceivers' confidence in their ability to rely on heuristic-based judgments?

The answer offered by Moscovici, and examined in several of the previously discussed experiments, is via consistent behavior – putting forward a minority position and being unwavering in one's conviction. This behavioral style produces the formation of positive attributions that serve to undermine the confidence with which one may rely on one's heuristics relevant to a minority. As Eagly and Chaiken (1993) explain, if one's confidence in a heuristic-based judgment is sufficiently undermined such that the resulting level of confidence falls below a threshold that designates a desired level of confidence (having a judgment that is deemed sufficient to capture the stimulus), then one will no longer rely predominantly on heuristic processing. As Moskowitz (1992, 1996) and Bohner et al. (1995) suggested (see also De Dreu & De Vries, 1996), minorities can generate such confidence gaps in a perceiver through their consistent behavior.

However, if influence is mediated through attributions (and the information-processing strategies they trigger), then minority influence should be possible through any minority action (not simply consistency) that can promote positive source attributions. That is, any minority behavior that can serve to undermine the confidence with which one relies on heuristics during either impression formation or attitude attribution should serve to increase the likelihood of minority influence. For example, Jones and Davis's (1965) correspondent inference theory holds that perceivers form dispositional attributions when target persons perform unexpected behavior (i.e., when an expectancy is disconfirmed by the behavior of a target person). Thus, a positive, internal attribution would be likely when a negative expectancy is disconfirmed. Kelley's (1973) augmenting rule makes a similar prediction.

Jones and Harris (1967) extend this logic to the attribution of attitudes: "a person will be perceived to hold attitudes that correspond with his opinion statements when . . . perceived choice is high and the prior probability of the act occurring is low" (pp. 1–2). Perceived choice is said to be high when there are no external constraints on the observed behavior (people freely choose to act as they do). The probability of the act occurring is low when either past behavior or normative considerations lead one to expect that the observed behavior was unlikely to have occurred. Jones and Harris (Expt. 3) illustrated this principle by showing that if perceivers have a negative expectancy about a target (that the target favors segregation), and this position is disconfirmed (the target's message expresses an antisegregation position), the position actually espoused is especially believed to be a veridical representation of the target's true feelings (i.e., augmentation). If positive attributions that challenge negative heuristics and expectancies are one way to promote minority influence, this suggests another route for instigating minority influence other than consistency in the form of stringent intransigence. Thus, rather than consistency, a type of inconsistency − the target disconfirming the perceiver's expectancy by acting in a manner inconsistent with what prior experience had led the perceiver to believe − would lead to positive attributions being formed toward a minority.

The literature on when stereotypes are or are not used in evaluating others makes a similar prediction. Allport (1954) described people as likely to rely on stereotypes when interpreting others rather than challenging these well-developed expectancies about outgroups. Indeed, perceivers observing members of stereotyped groups have been shown to exhibit the tendency to focus attention encoding and recall on information that confirms their stereotypes and to ignore information that is inconsistent with those stereotypes (Hamilton & Trolier, 1986). Information that is inconsistent with a stereotype is, in fact, information that disconfirms an expectancy, and people prefer to avoid the tension associated with doubt, uncertainty, and maintaining conflicting beliefs (e.g., Allport, 1954; Festinger, 1957). However, individuals are not always able simply to rely on stereotypes in impression formation, especially when stereotype-inconsistent information is so clear and diagnostic that it cannot be ignored (e.g., Deaux & Lewis, 1984) or when the stereotype is weak (such as when stereotypes are first being developed, e.g., Stangor & Ruble, 1989).

Stangor and Ruble (1989) demonstrated that when perceivers do utilize stereotype-inconsistent information it triggers more systematic processing that can yield a more diagnostic and veridical interpretation of events. In essence, information inconsistent with a stereotype violates an expectancy and creates a state whereby prior beliefs and current inferences stand in conflict. Thus, when one attends to (rather than ignores or suppresses) stereotype-inconsistent information, this information needs to be reconciled with prior beliefs. This is done by systematically integrating new and old information (e.g., Asch & Zukier, 1984; Hastie & Kumar, 1979). Extending this logic to minority influence, positive attributions toward a minority and systematic processing of their statements should be instigated when an initial negative expectancy (or a stereotype) is disconfirmed and information inconsistent with it is provided by the minority.

An Attributional Analysis of Persuasion Applied to Minority Influence

An attributional analysis of persuasion

In their attribution analysis of persuasion, Eagly and colleagues (e.g., Eagly, Chaiken, & Wood, 1982; Wood & Eagly, 1981) argue that if a disconfirmed expectancy makes a communicator appear unbiased (e.g., Jones & Harris, 1967), it should make that communicator persuasive. In testing this model (see Eagly, et al., 1982) information is presented to participants to induce them to form an expectancy that the communicator will be biased in favor of a particular position regarding the issue in question. Such expectancies may be established, for example, by providing information suggesting that either the messenger's knowledge about the issue is biased, or that her or his willingness to express an accurate description has been compromised, or that the messenger has a vested interest that suggests favoring one side of the issue over the other. After such expectancies are formed, a message is then presented and the position advocated in that message either disconfirms or confirms the position the research participant had expected to be advocated by the messenger. An expectancy being either confirmed or disconfirmed in this fashion was predicted to lead either to the attribution that the message is biased or to the attribution that the message is veridical. Consistent with Jones and Harris's (1967) reasoning, disconfirming a negative expectancy should be more likely to lead to a positive, internal attribution than confirming such an expectancy.

If the message disconfirms one's premessage expectancies, the recipient of the message will perceive the message to present an accurate description of external reality. In explaining this prediction Eagly et al. (1982) invoke the augmentation principle (Kelley, 1973). The presence of a plausible inhibitory cause (e.g., the expectancy that the position that will be presented will be biased in the direction that favors the messenger's vested interests) serves to strengthen the other, facilitory cause – that the messenger's position on the issue may be correct. However, if the message confirms the expectancy, the message recipient will perceive the source as biased. Here, the discounting principle is invoked. The expectancy that the messenger's vested interests will lead him or her to present a biased message serves as a sufficient cause;

participants discount the viability of the message as a reflection of external reality. Once the message is attributed to bias, its ability to persuade is reduced.

This attributional analysis of persuasion serves as an interesting foil to Moscovici's model of minority influence. Both models assert that an attribution that a message is unbiased and veridical is required for influence. However, there are key differences between them. First, Moscovici's model is explicitly in reference to a minority source of a message/judgment; the model of Eagly and colleagues, in contrast, makes no reference to the group status of a message's source.

Second, Moscovici's model maintains that the behavioral consistency of the minority is key in shaping the positive attributions that lead to influence. In contrast, the Eagly model maintains that a type of inconsistency – expectancy disconfirmation – is a central component in arriving at the same type of attributions. However, it should be pointed out that "inconsistency," as it is discussed in reference to the Eagly model (and the assumption that inconsistency may cause influence), is actually the disconfirmation of an expectancy. While it is possible to view the disconfirmation of an expectancy as a type of inconsistency, it is also possible to view the disconfirmation of an expectancy as something highly distinctive. Thus, whether or not expectancy disconfirmation is actually altering the distinctiveness or the consistency dimension described in Kelley's (1967) attribution model is dependent on how that expectancy is established and subsequently disconfirmed. If, in an experimental context, a case of expectancy disconfirmation can be made analogous to inconsistency (over time), as the term is used by both Kelley (1967) and Moscovici (1980), then based on the Moscovici model we would expect influence to be less likely to occur relative to instances of consistency, but based on the Eagly et al. model we would expect influence to be more likely.

Third, Moscovici maintained that positive attributions lead to influence through what he called a validation process. Eagly's model posits that positive attributions lead to influence through application of a simple attributional rule – augmentation – without participants needing carefully to scrutinize message content when the expectancy is disconfirmed. This last point raises the interesting issue of whether group status of the source plays a role in the relationship between expectancy confirmation, attributions, message processing, and persuasion. If an instance of expectancy disconfirmation was exhibited by a minority (as opposed to the lack of specificity as to the group status of the source in Eagly and colleagues' existing research) would the predictions of the model approximate those posited by Moscovici?

The role of group status in how expectancy confirmation is perceived

How would adding group status information affect message processing and persuasion in the attributional analysis of persuasion? Consider first the instance in which a minority group member delivers a message that either confirms or disconfirms an expectancy.

A minority source and attributions. Eagly and colleagues' experimental procedures begin by establishing an expectancy about a messenger (e.g., he or she is biased) and the messenger then delivers a message that either confirms or disconfirms this expectancy. Adding minority status information would introduce a second, negative expectancy – that the source's message is not consensual. That is, by definition a minority message is one that lacks majority support.[3] If the message confirms the premessage expectancy, the model of Eagly and colleagues suggests that negative attributions are formed (e.g., the messenger is merely serving his or her own vested interests). However, this prediction does not incorporate group status information of the messenger. If the messenger is a minority we posit that this would not challenge the predictions made by Eagly et al. (1982) regarding the type of attributions that are formed. Since in the Eagly et al. model the expectancy that the messenger is biased is said to allow message recipients to discount the possibility that the message is veridical, the alteration of this prediction would require the addition of some type of information that makes discounting less likely. However, adding the information that the messenger is a minority simply provides yet another cause to suspect that the position espoused is not a reflection of external reality, which only serves to strengthen the likelihood that discounting will occur.

If the message disconfirms the premessage expectancy, the model of Eagly and colleagues suggests that positive attributions are formed (e.g., the messenger is not serving his or her own vested interests and is likely expressing an honest, objective, and veridical judgment/opinion). If the messenger is known to be in the minority regarding their position we posit that this would not challenge the predictions made by Eagly et al. (1982) regarding the type of attributions that are formed. In the Eagly et al. model the expectancy that the messenger is biased is said to lead message recipients to augment the possibility that the message is veridical when that expectancy is disconfirmed. Augmentation occurs because an inhibitory cause (bias) is overcome. The alteration of this prediction would require the addition of some type of information that makes augmenting less likely. When minority information is added it should only strengthen the inhibitory cause (bias) and increase the likelihood of augmenting occurring and positive attributions being formed.

A minority source and information processing strategies.   Although we do not posit that adding minority source information will affect the types of attributions arising from the confirmation/disconfirmation of expectancies predicted in the model of Eagly and colleagues, information regarding the minority status of the source should affect the processing triggered by these attributions. Expectancy confirmation was posited by Eagly and colleagues to lead to negative attributions. However, Eagly et al. (1982) point out that although these negative attributions reveal the source to be biased, without consensus information one cannot fully discount the possibility that they also happen to hold the better position on this particular issue. It is for this reason that Eagly et al. suggested that expectancy confirmation is not likely to lead to a simple reliance on the discounting rule, but is more likely to invoke further analysis and systematic appraisal of the message.

However, when it is known that the source of the message is a minority, this knowledge that the messenger lacks consensus removes ambiguity. That is, any ambiguity regarding whether the position is biased but correct (the possibility that the source advocates the better position on this issue) is undermined. Being perceived as both biased (e.g., one's position serves one's vested interests) and lacking consensus (few, if any, others agree with the position advocated) leaves the source and his or her message to be responded to on the basis of simple heuristics. Thus, if ambiguity surrounding the veridicality of the advocated position is removed, the message recipient is left with little motivation to move beyond heuristic processing and a reliance on simple attributional rules such as discounting. Despite negative attributions being formed in the manner described by Eagly et al. (1982), we posit that heuristic processing would follow expectancy confirmation from a minority source.

Expectancy disconfirmation was posited by Eagly et al. (1982) to result in the formation of positive attributions which would lead to the belief that the messenger has conviction due to the message recipient following a simple attributional rule (augmentation). This prediction should be challenged by the addition of the fact that the source is a minority (the addition of information suggesting that the position advocated has low consensus). We posit that the ability to rely on simple attributional rules and heuristics in guiding one's own judgment and opinion is compromised by the fact that the position advocated in the message is less likely to be correct if the source is the only one who believes the position to be true.

Thus, the minority status of the source introduces doubt and undermines willingness to agree with the message without scrutinizing it. Despite the same type of attributions being formed as in the case where no group status information is provided, these attributions now need to be reconciled with the consensus information. We posit that this cannot be attained by relying on heuristic processing alone. A minority sources who disconfirms a negative expectancy should be responded to with positive attributions and systematic processing.

This attempt to place a persuasion paradigm in the domain of minority influence is useful as it reveals yet another possible way to attain minority influence – through expectancies being disconfirmed. Before reviewing some of our research that addresses these modifications to the Attribution Analysis of Persuasion to account for a minority source, let us first examine the case of majority sources. Do participants typically assume that if no group status information is provided then the messenger is presenting a majority view? How should presenting explicit information specifying that the messenger is a majority influence the predictions from the Attribution Analysis of Persuasion?

A majority source.   Once again, the analysis begins with the creation of a premessage expectancy (e.g., that the messenger is biased) which can be either confirmed or disconfirmed by the actual message. In this case, however, the second expectancy that is established by the addition of consensus information is that the source, by holding a majority opinion, is legitimate and his or her message is valid and correct. Several predictions can be generated given this set of circumstances. First, the data might not differ at all from the attribution model of persuasion, since people might always assume, by default, that a message being presented to them in an experiment is a consensual one. Second, consensus information might serve as a powerful heuristic, overwhelming the (in this example primarily negative) premessage expectancy so that people always heuristically agree with the majority source, regardless of message content. A third possibility is that expectancy disconfirmation will not be seen positively, as in the Attribution Analysis of Persuasion, but instead be seen as "caving in" to social pressure. Disconfirmation means that the source espouses a position that was unexpected. Since this new position is adopted by someone we know to be part of the majority, the possibility exists that the source has not overcome an initial bias at all, but has chosen to conform to the group position. This assumption that the messenger is merely conforming is unlikely to occur for a majority source who confirms the premessage expectancy: While they could be espousing their position because others in the group do, participants know this is a position that the messenger has supported in the past (due to the expectancy manipulation).

An empirical examination of the effects of expectancy disconfirmation
from a minority source

Moskowitz (1992; see also Bohner et al., 1995) examined the effects of expectancy disconfirmation on minority influence, testing the predictions outlined above. Expectancies were established by giving participants a biographical sketch describing a person. These sketches were allegedly made from comments collected during an "earlier" study the person had participated in, and participants were further led to believe that in the current experiment they would be listening to excerpts of a speech given by this same person from the same "earlier" study. The biographical sketch established an expectancy about the position the messenger would take in his speech, manipulating whether the messenger would be seen as having a vested interest in his support of a particular position regarding the topic being discussed in the message.

Participants then watched a videotape of the messenger delivering a speech to a group of five other students. The videotape began with the group's moderator saying that this speaker was the last person in the group to express his opinion and that all the other participants had felt identically about the issue under discussion. To establish that the messenger was a minority, the position taken in the speech not only was opposite to that said to be held by the other group members, but the speech began by the messenger explicitly stating his opposition to the group before outlining his positions.

Expectancy confirmation or disconfirmation was attained by the match between the expectancy that had been established for the participants in the biographical sketch and the position advocated in the message. Participants heard messages all advocating the same position, so that those who read one of the two biographical sketches had their expectancies confirmed and those who had read the other sketch had their expectancies disconfirmed. The messages differed only in terms of the strength of the arguments. Half of the participants heard messages consisting of strong arguments and half heard messages consisting of weak arguments. After the tape, participants completed a booklet containing measures of attitudes toward the topic, rating scales that assessed impressions of the messenger, and thoughts generated while watching the tape.

Argument quality was manipulated in order to serve as a means for assessing the type of information processing engaged in by the participants. If the message was heuristically processed, a message with weak arguments would be equally persuasive as one with strong arguments. If the message was systematically processed, however, differences in influence would appear for strong versus weak messages. To further assess processing, a thought listing measure was also included. If heuristic processing was engaged in then few thoughts related to the specific issues raised in the message would be generated. Systematic processing would be evidenced by greater numbers of issue-relevant thoughts.

Moskowitz (1992) predicted that expectancy confirmation/disconfirmation would affect attributions, which would influence the extent to which the minority message was systematically processed, which in turn would affect the extent to which participants were persuaded.

Attributions. Consistent with the hypotheses, a path analysis revealed that there was a direct effect of expectancy on positive attributions, with expectancy disconfirmation (vs. confirmation) more likely to lead to positive attributions. Similarly, there was a direct effect of expectancy status on negative attributions, with confirmation more likely to lead to negative attributions. In each case, expectancy status did not exert a direct effect on message processing or attitudes. Specific types of attributions formed in response to confirmed and disconfirmed expectancies were examined through an Expectancy by Argument Quality MANOVA on the rating scales. As predicted, there was a main effect for expectancy: When the communicator disconfirmed the expectancy he was seen as more unbiased, objective, and factual. Thus, as predicted, expectancy disconfirmation led to an increase in the use of positive characterizations of the communicator, whereas expectancy confirmation led to an increase in the use of negative characterizations. Moreover, positive characterizations were not merely global statements (such as liking) but were specific insofar as they dealt with the communicator's lack of bias, his confidence, and certainty – just the sort of attributions said to be triggered by consistency in Moscovici's model.

Message processing. Path analyses further revealed that positive attributions exerted a direct effect on the amount of message processing engaged in. As predicted, the more positive the attribution, the more message-related thoughts generated. In contrast, negative attributions did not influence message-relevant thinking. Another method for examining the impact of attributions on processing is through an ANOVA. When expectancies were disconfirmed, high quality messages led to more positive message-related thoughts than low quality ones, and low quality messages led to more negative message-related thoughts than high quality ones. However, when expectancies were confirmed, the difference between high versus low quality messages, on both positive and negative message-related thoughts, was not reliable. Finally, processing can be examined by looking at attitudes, with evidence for systematic processing coming from increased persuasion when exposed to high (vs low) quality messages.

Attitudes. If minority influence occurs through systematic processing, message-related thoughts should influence attitudes. In support of this prediction, positive (though not negative) message-related thoughts influenced attitudes. Thus, successful influence, reflected by attitudes moving toward those advocated by the minority, was dependent on the amount of message-related thoughts. For negative attributions the only impact on attitudes was a direct effect of attributions. The more negative the attribution, the less likely participants were to agree with the message. This, plus the lack of an influence from message-related thoughts, suggests that when negative attributions were formed about the minority, systematic processing did not follow. The argument quality manipulation revealed a similar finding: The greater the positivity of the attribution formed, the greater the differentiation in participants' responses to low and high quality messages. The more positive the attribution, the more likely that high argument quality led to influence and low quality did not.

In summary, when minority positions were attributed to positive causes, these attributions instigated systematic processing and led to minority influence. When these attributions were negative in nature they exerted little influence on message processing, and instead directly affected attitudes. This was associated with participants' outright rejection of the minority position. In demonstrating these mediational processing links in minority influence this research extends Jones and Harris' (1967) belief that disconfirmation of an expected bias can lead to influence, and that this is mediated through the attributions the perceiver forms. The degree to which a speaker's viewpoint is expected is inversely related to the inference that the message represents private beliefs. Thus, when a minority disconfirms an expectancy, the perceiver is more likely to attribute the message to the minority's true beliefs (a correspondent inference). Extending the Attributional Analysis of Persuasion to the domain of minority influence, such attributions then led participants to systematically process the message. When it was of high quality this appraisal of the information led participants to be persuaded by the minority communicator.

Examining Mediators of Minority Influence via Resource Limitations/Cognitive Load

Whether effortful, systematic appraisal and evaluation accompanies a cognitive process has been examined through another classic paradigm in the social cognition literature. In research on correspondent inference, Gilbert and colleagues (e.g., Gilbert, 1989; Gilbert & Hixon, 1991; Gilbert & Malone, 1995; Gilbert, Pelham, & Krull, 1988) have used a manipulation of cognitive load to examine whether participants are effortfully processing information when attempting to form an impression of a person. The logic is that given the limited capacity of the information-processing system, an effortful task that is performed simultaneously with other tasks will not be able to be performed as elaborately relative to when there are no parallel processing demands. Without cognitive load, effortful processing is posited to occur when forming attributions. People incorporate both heuristic processing, in the form of spontaneously generated (e.g., Uleman, Newman, & Moskowitz, 1996) trait inferences, along with systematic processing, in the form of the more effortful and consciously elaborated upon inferences about the situation, when arriving at a final attribution. When operating under cognitive load, the effortful processing needed to incorporate inferences about the situation is shown to be disabled by the existence of a simultaneous task that requires effortful processing. Thus, people rely simply on the heuristically based, less effortful inferences generated spontaneously.

This methodology allows researchers to examine whether systematic processing is occurring by examining the differences in judgments that are formed as a function of processing load. Gilbert and Hixon (1991) found that a stereotype was likely to guide responses when a perceiver was placed under cognitive load, but such tendencies to apply a stereotype heuristically when making a response were diminished when perceivers had ample cognitive resources. Macrae, Milne, and Bodenhausen (1994) found that stereotype use not only was promoted by cognitive load (thus providing evidence that stereotypes operate as a heuristic), but that performance on the effortful task that was usurping load was enhanced to the extent that stereotypes were used. Thus, less effortful processing, such as the heuristic use of stereotypes, preserved cognitive resources so that (a) multiple tasks could be completed, and (b) the savings in effort provided by use of the heuristic could be applied to the more complicated task. In summary, the ability of cognitive load to promote the use of heuristics and to undermine judgments that are presumed to require systematic processing, suggests a method for assessing whether systematic processing is occurring – the manipulation of cognitive load – that can gainfully be employed to examine the processes underlying succesful minority influence.

Disabling minority influence through depleting cognitive resources

It has already been shown that argument quality manipulations and thought listing tasks are useful tools for examining whether minority influence is mediated by systematic processing. Manipulating cognitive load suggests an alternate way to demonstrate the effects of systematic processing in minority influence. If heuristic processing of the minority message is occurring, the amount of influence should be unaffected by cognitive load. If, however, systematic processing of the message is responsible for minority influence, cognitive load should interfere with the ability of participants to engage in such processing, thus eliminating influence. It is predicted that minority messages that confirm expectancies should not be systematically processed and, therefore, should show no effect of the cognitive load manipulation. In contrast, a minority that disconfirms the expectancy that they are biased should trigger systematic processing of their message, and the ability for the minority to exert influence would be contingent on the perceiver having sufficient processing resources to exert the requisite processing effort. Minority messages heard while under cognitive load would not be persuasive, whereas those heard without a load should lead to influence.

We recently examined this question using a procedure very similar to that used by Moskowitz (1992). The procedures differed only in that half the participants were placed under cognitive load, and only strong messages were used (because weak messages would not lead to persuasion and, therefore, would reveal nothing about the effects of cognitive load). Cognitive load was manipulated by asking half of the participants to perform a computerized task while listening to the message. Each trial of this task began with a fixation cross in the center of the screen, followed immediately by a word that flashed for 200 ms on either the left-hand or right-hand side of the cross. Participants were asked to press a key, as quickly and accurately as possible, to indicate which side of the screen the word had appeared. Additionally, they were to attempt to keep track of how many words had appeared over the course of the experiment.

As was predicted, expectancies influenced attributions. A message that revealed a position that disconfirmed the perceiver's expectancy led the source to be perceived as more unbiased, certain, and concerned with being objective and fair than when a perceiver's expectancy was confirmed. More importantly, examining attitudes toward the issue following exposure to the minority message revealed a marginal main effect for cognitive load and the predicted Load by Expectancy interaction. Participants who were not under cognitive load and had their expectancies disconfirmed were compared to (a) participants whose expectancies were disconfirmed and were under load and (b) participants whose expectancies were confirmed and were not under load. If influence requires effortful processing, attitude change should be found when participants are both motivated to process systematically and when there are no limits to their cognitive capacity. No influence should be found when either attributions failed to motivate systematic processing or load prohibits participants from carrying out the effortful processes that presumably produce influence. As predicted, when expectancies were disconfirmed participants not under load showed greater change in the direction of the minority message than participants who were under a cognitive load. Additionally, participants with both motivation and capacity to process systematically (disconfirmed expectancies, no load) were more influenced than participants who similarly had no constraints on capacity but lacked the motivation to exert effort (people whose expectancies were confirmed).

Systematic processing was also assessed by the number of message-relevant thoughts listed on the thought listing task (e.g., Crano & Chen, 1998; Erb et al., 1998). As with attitudes, message-related thoughts should be affected by whether participants were under cognitive load at the time they were listening to the message, but only if expectancies had been disconfirmed. A Load by Expectancy ANOVA examining message-relevant thoughts revealed this to be the case. Participants who were not under cognitive load and had their expectancies disconfirmed were compared to (a) participants whose expectancies were disconfirmed and were under load and (b) participants whose expectancies were confirmed and were not under load. As predicted, when expectancies were disconfirmed participants not under load had more message-relevant thoughts than participants who were under a cognitive load. Additionally, the participants who had both the motivation and capacity to process systematically (disconfirmed expectancies, no load) were more influenced than participants who similarly had no constraints on capacity but lacked the motivation to exert effort (people whose expectancies were confirmed).

In summary, systematic processing is effortful, and for elaborate processing of this sort to occur it requires that one have both the motivation and cognitive capacity for it to be engaged (for a review of this principle see Moskowitz, Skurnik, & Galinsky, 1999). If minority influence is operating via such effortful processing being triggered in the mind of the perceiver, then evidence for such processing should be provided when one (a) manipulates motivation to process (such as through manipulating attributions associated with the minority) and holds processing load constant (and in abundance), and (b) manipulates the availability of cognitive capacity after having motivated a perceiver to want to engage in elaboration of the message. Our research has shown that minority influence occurs only when perceivers have both motivation and capacity to process systematically. Placing participants under cognitive load (cf., Bargh & Thein, 1985; Gilbert et al., 1988) disabled the ability to process systematically and reduced both the amount of message-relevant thoughts participants exhibited and the extent to which they were drawn toward the minority position. The motivation to process systematically was provided by attributions about the minority source's lack of bias and certainty in their position. Such attributions challenged the existing heuristic assumptions about minority positions and were triggered in the current context by a source disconfirming an expectancy that they would be biased.

Motivating Systematic Processing of Minority Messages

Our findings highlight parallels between (a) Moscovici's contrast of a validation process with the simpler propensity to assume minority positions are invalid and to reject them without scrutiny, and (b) Chaiken's contrast of systematic with heuristic processing. They also imply that behavioral consistency is not the only strategy available to minorities wishing to generate positive attributions and trigger systematic processing. This is not to minimize the role of consistency, for surely a coherent and consistent minority can motivate perceivers to attend to their position. But it represents only one possible strategy available to minorities to foster elaborate processes of appraisal in the perceiver's mind.

Two sets of circumstances that produce "confidence gaps"

Systematic processing occurs when a perceiver experiences a discrepancy (in the form of psychological tension/conflict) between the amount of confidence that a heuristic-based judgment would provide and the amount of confidence in a judgment that would be required to have a sense that one's judgment provides a sufficient explanation (Chaiken et al., 1996). Two sets of circumstances can give rise to such tension states. The first is when perceivers possess motives that require a level of confidence in the veracity of their judgments that heuristic processing alone cannot provide. For example, in both the stereotyping and persuasion literatures systematic processing is shown to be prompted by both a perceiver having a vested interest in a target person and a perceiver being held accountable for judgments (e.g., Fiske & Neuberg, 1990; Johnson & Eagly, 1989; Maheswaran & Chaiken, 1991). Motivation to be accurate, fair, deliberate, objective, defensive, self-verifying, self-enhancing, and so on, raise one's metaphorical "sufficiency threshold" to the point where the type of analysis required for a judgment to be deemed sufficient would be more effortful and elaborate than that which heuristic processing alone could provide. Trost et al. (1992) point out, however, that if perceivers have a vested interest in a topic, it could trigger negatively biased scrutiny of a stereotyped minority. In such cases, systematic processing of a stereotyped minority would decrease minority influence due to what Chaiken et al. (1996) call biased systematic processing (see also Wood et al., 1996). But more generally, increased scrutiny and effort exerted when evaluating a minority position makes one vulnerable to the possibility of rejecting one's initial biases and stereotypes. Raising one's sufficiency threshold in the manner described above can accomplish this.

The second set of circumstances that give rise to the tension state that motivates systematic processing is when one's confidence in an existing judgment is undermined. In this case, a judgment that once surpassed the metaphorical sufficiency threshold is no longer experienced as being sufficient – one's confidence in that judgment is undermined by either new evidence or reflection on old evidence. We have noted several ways in which minorities can undermine perceivers' confidence in this way. For example, Moscovici (1980) described perception as subjective, and, given this, a minority was said to need to adopt behaviors that reduce perceivers' abilities subjectively to construe minorities as illegitimate. Moscovici adopted Asch's (1952) belief that subjectivity in construal could be reduced by making stimuli less ambiguous. In the case of minority behavioral strategies this could be attained through consistent and clear action. Consistency in adhering to a position would lead to the attribution that the minority is certain and confident. Such attributions stand in conflict with existing expectancies (stereotypes), setting in motion the chain of doubt, tension, and systematic reappraisal described earlier.

Behavioral strategies that initiate influence: A preponderance of responsibility

Having a minority adopt a particular behavioral strategy in order to have their arguments attended to carefully is one way in which the minority position can potentially influence others. However, this requires that the burden be placed on the minority not only to articulate valid and engaging ideas, but to worry about presentational concerns that are quite independent of content. Therefore, aside from articulating a position, a burden is placed on the minority to act in ways that force perceivers to engage in a validation process. For example, the minority must (a) act in an unyieldingly consistent manner or (b) their behavior must disconfirm expectancies held by the perceiver. In Allport's (1954, p. 384) terms, this state of affairs places a "preponderance of responsibility" on a stereotyped group. But must the motivation to engage in systematic processing be initiated by a minority's behavioral strategy? Stereotyping research has shown that people can, of their own accord, be motivated to remove the impact of stereotypes from their judgment through engaging in systematic processing . They need not be hit over the head by a minority's attempts to alter expectancies. Additionally, they need not be seduced toward fairness through being held accountable (e.g., Erber & Fiske, 1984), being told to be accurate (e.g., Neuberg, 1989), or asked to suppress stereotypes (e.g., Macrae, Bodenhausen, Milne, & Jetten, 1994). Rather, people can adopt goals to be accurate and egalitarian without the minority having the burden of instigating them to do so; in other words, they can set such goals for themselves (e.g., Monteith, in press; Moskowitz, Gollwitzer, Wasel, & Schaal, 1999).

A cautionary note about this approach is that for such "motivated correction" of a stereotype's impact to occur, perceivers must first realize that they are either being biased or relying too extensively on heuristics in an evaluation (e.g., Moskowitz, 1996). But biases often operate in a passive and unintentional manner, and heuristics often yield judgments that are subjectively experienced as functional and sufficient, even if, objectively, they are promoting overgeneralizations or falsehoods. This failure to realize the subjective elements of one's social perception was labeled *naive realism* by Asch (1952). It is difficult for perceivers to willingly adopt the strategy of being more accurate in their evaluation of a target when they are unaware that they are biased to start with. Instead, one can assume that biased reactions to minorities are the domain of some racist outgroup to which one does not belong.[4] The effects of naive realism on minority influence are not only troublesome because people fail to see the bias in their own positions, but because people additionally exaggerate the extremity of outgroup positions. Robinson, Keltner, Ward, and Ross (1995) suggest that majority groups in particular misjudge the extent to which minority positions are divergent from the majority, making influence and negotiation between groups difficult, given the perceived gap in opinion.

Thus, adopting a goal of being less biased (either through a desire to be egalitarian, a desire to be accurate, or the fear of being held accountable for invalid opinions) should allow perceivers to be open to influence. But influence may first require recognizing that one has the potential to be biased and that the perceived gap between one's position on an issue and a minority's is in part determined by one's subjective construal of the minority.

Conclusion

A focus on the processes that underlie minority influence is essential for understanding whether minority influence attempts will or will not be successful. Persuasion following a minority presenting a message is mediated through the types of attributions formed toward the source and the message-relevant thinking that is initiated. Heuristic processing of sources of any type seems to be the default strategy taken by perceivers. To exert influence, minorities, typically saddled with negative heuristics, need to challenge those heuristics with the strategies they adopt in their influence attempt, and in so doing motivate perceivers to add systematic processing to the cognitive tools they choose to utilize. Additionally, such processing must reveal cogent arguments. The strategies used to accomplish this can operate either by the minority performing behaviors or providing information that leads perceivers to doubt the validity of their heuristic-based responses, or by the perceivers adopting the belief that their judgments must be of greater accuracy and validity. This can be accomplished through a variety of strategies, ranging from the minority acting in a consistent fashion, to the minority acting in a manner that disconfirms an expectancy, to the perceivers desiring to be fair-minded and accurate, to the perceivers being held accountable for their evaluation of the minority.

NOTES

1 Zanna and Cooper (1974), using a standard dissonance experimental paradigm known as the "counter-attitudinal essay," asked research participants to write essays, for differing degrees of reward, known to be contrary to their own beliefs.

Dissonance is evidenced by beliefs changing to a greater degree as the reward decreases. In demonstrating this effect, the misattribution tool used was a placebo (a pill) that was said to account for the heightened state of arousal participants might be experiencing.

2   Heuristics processing, in contrast, involves the superficial assessment of environmental cues (e.g., opinions of others, the length of the message) and evaluating a message's validity by applying simple decision rules (e.g., "consensus implies correctness," "length implies strength") associated with such cues.

3   Except in rare cases, such as in 20th century South Africa, where a group is considered a minority by virtue of its power and social standing despite being the majority in terms of numbers.

4   James Baldwin (1964) eloquently raises this unique problem for minority influence which arises from the fact that the majority is near impossible to define: "Presumably the society in which we live is an expression – in some way – of the majority will. But it is not so easy to locate this majority" (p. 108).

REFERENCES

Allport, G. W. (1954). *The nature of prejudice*. Cambridge, MA: Addison-Wesley.

Asch, S. E. (1952). *Social psychology*. Englewood Cliffs, NJ: Prentice Hall.

Asch, S. E., & Zukier, H. (1984). Thinking about persons. *Journal of Personality and Social Psychology, 46*, 1230–1240.

Baker, S. M., & Petty, R. E. (1994). Majority and minority influence: Source–position imbalance as a determinant of message scrutiny. *Journal of Personality and Social Psychology, 67*, 5–19.

Baldwin, J. (1964). *Nobody knows my name*. New York: Penguin Books.

Bargh, J. A., & Thein, R. D. (1985). Individual construct accessibility, person memory, and the recall–judgment link: The case of information overload. *Journal of Personality and Social Psychology, 49*, 1129–1146.

Bohner, G., Chaiken, S., & Hunyadi, P. (1994). The role of mood and message ambiguity in the interplay of heuristic and systematic processing. *European Journal of Social Psychology, 24*, 207–221.

Bohner, G., Erb, H. P., Reinhard, M. A., & Frank, E. (1996). Distinctiveness across topics in minority and majority influence: An attributional analysis and preliminary data. *British Journal of Social Psychology, 35*, 27–46.

Bohner, G., Moskowitz, G. B., & Chaiken, S. (1995). The interplay of heuristic and systematic processing of social information. In W. Stroebe & M. Hewstone (Eds.), *European review of social psychology* (Vol. 6, pp. 33–68). Chichester, UK: Wiley.

Chaiken, S. (1980). Heuristic versus systematic processing and the use of source versus message cues in persuasion. *Journal of Personality and Social Psychology, 39*, 752–766.

Chaiken, S. (1987). The heuristic model of persuasion. In M. Zanna, J. M. Olson, & C. P. Herman (Eds.), *Social influence: The Ontario symposium* (Vol. 5, pp. 3–39). Hillsdale, NJ: Erlbaum.

Chaiken, S., Giner-Sorolla, R., & Chen, S. (1996). Defense-motivated and impression-motivated heuristic and systematic processing. In P. M. Gollwitzer & J. A. Bargh (Eds.), *The psychology of action: Linking cognition and motivation to behavior* (pp. 553–578). New York: Guilford Press.

Chaiken, S., Liberman, A., & Eagly, A. H. (1989). Heuristic and systematic processing within and beyond the persuasion context. In J. S. Uleman & J. A. Bargh (Eds.), *Unintended thought* (pp. 212–252). New York: Guilford.

Chaiken, S., & Maheswaran, D. (1994). Heuristic processing can bias systematic processing: Effects of source credibility, argument ambiguity, and task importance on attitude judgement. *Journal of Personality and Social Psychology, 66,* 460–473.

Chaiken, S., & Stangor, C. (1987). Attitudes and attitude change. *Annual Review of Psychology, 38,* 575–630.

Chen, S., & Chaiken, S. (1999). The heuristic-systematic model in its broader context. In S. Chaiken & Y. Trope (Eds.), *Dual process theories in social psychology* (pp. 73–93). New York: Guilford.

Clark, R. D. III., & Maass, A. (1988). Social categorization in minority influence: The case of homosexuality. *European Journal of Social Psychology, 18,* 347–364.

Crano, W., & Chen, X. (1998). The leniency contract and persistence of majority and minority influence. Journal of Personality and Social Psychology, 74, 1437–1450.

Deaux, K., & Lewis, L. L. (1984). Structure of gender stereotypes: Interrelationships among components and gender label. *Journal of Personality and Social Psychology, 46,* 991–1004.

De Dreu, C. K. W., & De Vries, N. K. (1996). Differential processing and attitude change following majority versus minority arguments. *British Journal of Social Psychology, 35,* 77–90.

Deutsch, M., & Gerard, H. B. (1955). A study of normative and informational social influences upon individual judgment. *Journal of Abnormal and Social Psychology, 51,* 629–636.

De Vries, N. K., De Dreu, C. K. W., Gordijn, E., & Schuurman, M. K. (1996). Majority and minority influence: A dual-role interpretation. In W. Stroebe & M. Hewstone (Eds.), *European review of social psychology* (Vol. 7, pp. 145–172). Chichester, UK: Wiley.

Eagly, A. H., & Chaiken, S. (1993). The psychology of attitudes. Fort Worth, TX: Harcourt Brace Jovanovich.

Eagly, A. H., Chaiken, S., & Wood, W. (1982). An attribution analysis of persuasion. In J. H. Harvey, W. Ickes, & R. F. Kidd (Eds.), *New directions in attribution theory and research* (Vol. 3, pp. 37–62). Hillsdale, NJ: Erlbaum.

Erb, H.-P., Bohner, G., Schämlzle, K., & Rank, S. (1998). Beyond conflict and discrepancy: Cognitive bias in minority and majority influence. *Personality and Social Psychology Bulletin, 24,* 620–633.

Erber, R., & Fiske, S. T. (1984). Outcome dependency and attention to inconsistent information. Journal of *Personality and Social Psychology, 47,* 709–726.

Festinger, L. (1957). *A theory of cognitive dissonance.* Stanford, CA: Stanford University Press.

Fiske, S. T., & Neuberg, S. L. (1990). A continuum model of impression formation, from category based to individuating processes: Influences of information and motivation on attention and interpretation. In M. P. Zanna (Ed.), *Advances in experimental social psychology* (Vol. 23, pp. 1–74). New York: Academic Press.

Gilbert, D. T. (1989). Thinking lightly about others: Automatic components of the social inference process. In J. S. Uleman & J. A. Bargh (Eds.), *Unintended thought* (pp. 189–211). New York: Guilford.

Gilbert, D. T., & Hixon, J. G. (1991). The trouble of thinking: Activation and application of stereotypic beliefs. *Journal of Personality and Social Psychology, 60,* 509–517.

Gilbert, D. T., & Malone, P. S. (1995). The correspondence bias. *Psychological Bulletin, 117,* 21–38.

Gilbert, D. T., Pelham, B. W., & Krull, D. S. (1988). On cognitive business: When person perceivers meet person perceived. *Journal of Personality and Social Psychology, 54,* 733–740.

Hamilton, D. L., & Trolier, T. K. (1986). Stereotypes and stereotyping: An overview of the cognitive approach. In J. F. Dovidio & S. L. Gaertner (Eds.), *Prejudice, discrimination, and racism.* Orlando, FL: Academic Press.

Hastie, R., & Kumar, P. A. (1979). Person memory: Personality traits as organizing principles in memory for behavior. *Journal of Personality and Social Psychology, 37,* 25–38.

Johnson, B. T., & Eagly, A. H. (1989). Effects of involvement on persuasion: A meta-analysis. *Psychological Bulletin, 106,* 290–314.

Jones, E. E., & Davis, K. E. (1965). From acts to dispositions: The attribution process in person perception. In L. Berkowitz (Ed.), *Advances in experimental social psychology* (Vol. 2, pp. 219–266). New York: Academic Press.

Jones, E. E., & Harris, V. A. (1967). The attribution of attitudes. *Journal of Experimental Social Psychology, 3,* 1–24.

Kelley, H. H. (1967). Attribution theory in social psychology. In D. Levine (Ed.), *Nebraska symposium on motivation* (Vol. 15, pp. 192–238). Lincoln, NE: University of Nebraska Press.

Kelley, H. H. (1973). The processes of causal attribution. *American Psychologist, 28,* 107–128.

Kelman, H. C. (1961). Processes of opinion change. *Public Opinion Quarterly, 25,* 57–78.

Kruglanski, A. W., & Mackie, D. M. (1990). Majority and minority influence: A judgmental process analysis. In W. Stroebe & M. Hewstone (Eds.), *European review of social psychology* (Vol. 1, pp. 229–261). Chichester, UK: Wiley.

Landy, D. (1972). The effects of an overheard audience's reaction and attractiveness on opinion change. *Journal of Experimental Social Psychology, 8,* 276–288.

Maass, A., & Clark, R. D., III (1984). Hidden impact of minorities: Fifteen years of minority influence research. *Psychological Bulletin, 95,* 428–450.

Macrae, C. N., Bodenhausen, G. V., & Milne, A. B., Jetten, J. (1994). Out of mind but back in sight: Stereotypes on the rebound. *Journal of Personality and Social Psychology, 67,* 808–817.

Macrae, C. N., Milne, A. B., & Bodenhausen, G. V. (1994). Stereotypes as energy-saving devices: A peek inside the cognitive toolbox. *Journal of Personality and Social Psychology*, *66*, 37–47.

Maheswaran, D., & Chaiken, S. (1991). Promoting systematic processing in low motivation settings: The effect of incongruent infromation on processing and judgment. *Journal of Personality and Social Psychology*, *61*, 13–25.

Monteith, M. J. (in press). Exerting control over prejudiced responses. In G. B. Moskowitz (Ed.) *Cognitive social psychology: On the tenure and future of social cognition*. Hillsdale, NJ: Erlbaum.

Moscovici, S. (1976). *Social influence and social change*. London: Academic Press.

Moscovici, S. (1980). Toward a theory of conversion behavior. In L. Berkowitz (Ed.), *Advances in experimental social psychology* (Vol. 13, pp. 209–239). New York: Academic Press.

Moscovici, S. (1985). Innovation and minority influence. In S. Moscovici, G. Mugny, & E. Van Avermaet (Eds.), *Perspectives on minority influence* (pp. 9–51). Cambridge, UK: Cambridge University Press.

Moscovici, S., & Lage, E. (1976). Studies in social influence III: Majority vs. minority influence in a group. *European Journal of Social Psychology*, *6*, 149–174.

Moskowitz, G. B. (1992). *Mediators of minority social influence*. Doctoral dissertation, New York University.

Moskowitz, G. B. (1996). The mediational effects of attributions and information processing in minority social influence. *British Journal of Social Psychology*, *35*, 47–66.

Moskowitz, G. B., Gollwitzer, P. M., Wasel, W., & Schaal, B. (1999). Preconscious control of stereotype activation through chronic egalitarian goals. *Journal of Personality and Social Psychology*, *77*, 167–184.

Moskowitz, G. B., Skurnik, I., & Galinsky, A. (1999). The history of dual process notions; The future of preconscious control. In S. Chaiken and Y. Trope (Eds.), *Dual process models in social psychology* (pp. 12–36). New York: Guilford.

Nemeth, C. J. (1986). Differential contributions of majority and minority influence. *Psychological Review*, *93*, 23–32.

Nemeth, C. J., & Kwan, J. L. (1985). Originality of word associations as a function of majority vs. minority influence. *Social Psychology Quarterly*, *48*, 277–282.

Nemeth, C. J., Mayseless, O., Sherman, J., & Brown, Y. (1990). Exposure to dissent and recall of information. *Journal of Personality and Social Psychology*, *58*, 429–437.

Nemeth, C. J., & Wachtler, J. (1983). Creating problem solving as a result of majority vs minority influence. *European Journal of Social Psychology*, *13*, 45–55.

Neuberg, S. L. (1989). The goal of forming accurate impressions during social interactions: Attenuating the impact of negative expectancies. *Journal of Personality and Social Psychology*, *56*, 374–386.

Pérez, J. A., Falomir, J. M., & Mugny, G. (1995). Internalization of conflict and attitude change. *European Journal of Social Psychology*, *25*, 117–124.

Pérez, J. A., & Mugny, G. (1987). Paradoxical effects of categorization in minority influence: When being an outgroup is an advantage. *European Journal of Social Psychology, 17,* 157–169.

Petty, R. E., & Cacioppo, J. T. (1986). The elaboration likelihood model of persuasion. In L. Berkowitz (Ed.), *Advances in experimental social psychology* (Vol. 19, pp. 123–205). New York: Academic Press.

Robinson, R. J., Keltner, D., Ward, A., & Ross, L. (1995). Actual versus assumed differences in construal: "Naive realism" in intergroup perception and conflict. *Journal of Personality and Social Psychology, 68,* 404–417.

Schacter, S., & Singer, J. E. (1962). Cognitive, social, and physiological determinants of emotional state. *Psychological Review, 69,* 379–399.

Sherif, M. (1936). *The psychology of social norms.* New York: Harper & Row.

Stangor, C., & Ruble, D. (1989). Schema strength and expectancy confirmation. *Journal of Experimental Social Psychology, 25,* 18–35.

Tajfel, H., & Turner, J. C. (1986). The social identity theory of intergroup behaviour. In S. Worchel & W. G. Austin (Eds.), *Psychology of intergroup relations* (pp. 7–24). Chicago: Nelson-Hall Publishers.

Taylor, D. M., & Jaggi, V. (1974). Ethnocentrism and causal attribution in a South Indian context. *Journal of Cross-cultural Psychology, 5,* 162–171.

Trost, M. R., Maass, A., & Kenrick, D. T. (1992). Minority influence: Personal relevance biases cognitive processes and reverses private acceptance. *Journal of Experimental Social Psychology, 28,* 234–254.

Uleman, J. S., Newman, L. S., & Moskowitz, G. B. (1996). People as flexible interpreters: Evidence and issues from spontaneous trait inference. In M. Zanna (Ed.), *Advances in experimental social psychology* (Vol. 28, pp. 211–280). San Diego, CA: Academic Press.

Wood, W., & Eagly, A. H. (1981). Stages in the analysis of persuasive messages: The role of causal attributions and message comprehension. *Journal of Personality and Social Psychology, 40,* 246–259.

Wood, W., Lundgren, S., Ouellette, J. A., Busceme, S., & Blackstone, T. (1994). Minority influence: A meta-analytic review of social influence processes. *Psychological Bulletin, 115,* 323–345.

Wood, W., Pool, G. J., Leck, K., & Purvis, D. (1996). Self definition, defensive processing, and influence: The normative impact of majority and minority groups. *Journal of Personality and Social Psychology, 71,* 1181–1193.

Zanna, M. P., & Cooper, J. (1974). Dissonance and the pill: An attributional approach to studying the arousal properties of dissonance. *Journal of Personality and Social Psychology, 29,* 703–709.

Zeigarnik, B. (1927). Das Behalten von erledigten und unerledigten Handlungen. *Psychologische Forschung, 9,* 1–85.

5

Majority and Minority Influence: A Single Process Self-categorization Analysis

Barbara David and John C. Turner

In concert with Petty and Cacioppo (1986), the self-categorization under-standing of influence endorses Festinger's premise that "opinions, attitudes, and beliefs . . . must have some basis . . . for their validity" and moreover that ". . . an opinion, a belief, an attitude, is 'correct,' 'valid,' 'proper' to the extent that it is anchored in a group of people with similar beliefs, opinions and attitudes" (Festinger, 1950, pp 272–3). One of the unique contribution of self-categorization theory (Turner, 1982, 1991; Turner, Hogg, Oakes, Reicher, & Wetherell, 1987) is an understanding of the self, and therefore choice of and relationship to the reference group, as fluid and context-dependent (Oakes, Haslam, & Turner, 1998; Turner and Onorato, 1999). A concept of self as dynamic rather than fixed admits of an influence process (David & Turner, 1996, 1999; Turner, 1991; Turner and Oakes, 1989) which can result in majority and minority compliance, majority and minority conversion, and differential processing of majority and minority messages, without requiring the qualifications of an extensive list of cognitive and social variables. It requires that one knows who the targets of influence experience themselves to be in the social context of the influence attempt, and what they consider their relationship to be with the would-be source of influence.

While this is theoretically straightforward, the context-dependent nature of self-categorization makes it difficult in practice to measure such self-and-other perceptions, an issue which has been discussed at greater length elsewhere (David & Turner, 1996). In order to surmount the measurement problem, the program of studies to be described in this chapter employs sources and targets of influence from "nomic" social groups (i.e., those with

a clear, named identity), and influence messages which are directly relevant
to the identity of those groups. We do not propose that our results are blue-
prints for influence outcomes, or that studies like ours, where social identity
is clear, salient, and important for participants, represent the only "true" paradigms of "real" influence – in fact, in our conclusion we will be questioning whether any single such thing can be said to exist. Rather, our aim is to
demonstrate clearly the effects of self-categorization, addressing particularly
the contention that "shared social identity actually reduces true influence
while categorization of others as out-group may increase it" (Mugny, Pérez,
& Sanchez-Mazas, 1993, p. 10).

The first two studies in the program address the purported disadvantage
that a would-be source of influence suffers under when it is perceived as representative of like-minded others.

Is Being a Member of the Outgroup an Advantage?

In a creative and revolutionary response to the conformity, and hence majority, bias of early theories of influence (e.g., Deutsch & Gerard, 1955;
Festinger, 1954), Moscovici outlined a "genetic" model of influence, which
proposed that the powerless in society – minorities – were as capable of exerting influence as the powerful majorities (Moscovici, 1976). It was proposed
that the manner in which an influence message was presented, rather than
the numerical status of the would-be source, determines its success or failure.
Studies designed to investigate genetic theory led to observation of different
patterns of influence issuing from majority and minority sources (Moscovici
& Lage, 1976, 1978; Moscovici, Lage, & Neffrechoux, 1969; Moscovici &
Neve, 1973). Typically majorities influenced in public, in the short term, and
on direct measures, while minorities influenced in private, at a temporal delay,
and on indirect measures, and this observation led to the proposal of conversion theory (Moscovici, 1980; Moscovici & Mugny, 1983). Unlike the
genetic model, which accommodated influence from any source adopting the
correct behavioral style, conversion theory offered the converse of conformity theories, suggesting that only minorities exerted "true" influence, while
people merely complied with majorities.

Twenty subsequent years of minority influence research, while frequently
demonstrating majority compliance and minority conversion, have failed to
support an exclusive connection between the source's numerical status and
type of influence outcome: Minorities do not always convert (e.g., Clark &
Maass, 1988; David & Turner, 1996; Mackie, 1987; Sorrentino, King, & Leo,

1980), and majorities and minorities produce immediate, public influence as well as influence which is delayed and private (David & Turner, 1996; Maass & Clark, 1986; Personnaz & Personnaz, 1992; Turner, 1991). In spite of the evidence that majority compliance and minority conversion, while common, are only two of a range of connections between sources and outcome, and in spite of the fact that few contemporary researchers base their work purely on conversion theory, we suggest that Moscovici and his colleagues' original formulation can be seen to inform many current approaches.

In the following section we will address the processes of majority and minority influence as put forward in conversion theory. Here we will confine ourselves to its conceptualization of the "nature" of minorities. Moscovici assests that "a minority, *by definition*, expresses a deviant judgement" (1980, p. 211, emphasis added) and in similar words, Mugny claims "*By definition* a minority position is defined by the difference between its behaviours, judgements etc., and those dictated by the dominant norms" (1982, p. 20, emphasis added). We would suggest that it is not only the deviance of the influence message which is being described here, since the message is equally deviant when it issues from a majority source, which does not, in the writings of conversion theorists, make it deviant by definition. The minority group itself is being characterized as deviant and nonnormative: It is being proposed that there is something inherently and predictably "different" about minorities.

This a priori characterization has led to a number of theoretical refinements, as well, we would claim, as some of the contradictions and confusions in the literature. For example, Pérez and Mugny (1987) claim that failure of minorities to exert immediate, direct, or public influence results from the fact that people do not want to identify with a negatively valued source, yet it is unclear why they would be prepared to identify privately or at a delay. An understanding of minorities as inherently nonnormative is also clear in Alvaro and Crano's (1996) suggested rephrasing of Nemeth (1986). The authors suggest that Nemeth attributes to minorities the capacity for indirect informational influence, resulting in divergent thinking because "the minority – which *by its very nature* transgresses normative expectations – suggests alternative ways of thinking" (Alvaro & Crano, 1996, p. 105, emphasis added). Most clearly of all, some current researchers have emphasized the notion that the inherent deviance of a source is what allows it to convert people to its point of view, to the extent that they claim that categorizing a source as an outgroup will increase its true influence (Mugny, Pérez, & Sanchez-Mazas, 1993; Pérez & Mugny 1987; Pérez, Mugny, Butera, Kaiser, & Roux, 1994).

This assertion is of special interest to us since it conflicts directly with the unambiguous prediction of self-categorization theory that true influence (as opposed to compliance) is based on shared social identity, the social categorization of others as similar to self. Self-categorization theory is a general analysis of group processes in terms of the distinction between personal and social identity (Turner, 1982, 1988; Turner, Hogg, Oakes, Reicher, & Wetherell, 1987). It has been applied in some detail to the explanation of social influence more or less contemporaneously with conversion theory. It supposes that one only expects to agree with people categorized as similar to self, and that only disagreement with similar people produces uncertainty (Turner, 1991). To reduce such uncertainty one can recategorize self and others as different in relevant respects, redefine the objective stimulus situation as one that is not shared (as illustrated by participants in an experiment by Sperling, reported in Moscovici, 1976, and Asch, 1952, who failed to take part in the group's emerging consensus when informed that the stimulus movement they were judging was an illusion) or engage in mutual influence to try to produce the expected agreement (i.e., persuade and/or be persuaded).

Where one disagrees with people categorized as outgroup members, their perceived difference from self explains and justifies the disagreement, no uncertainty arises and there is no psychological pressure for mutual influence. No cognitive pressure for uniformity arises with different people, since their very difference explains why they are wrong and why one should not be persuaded: One does not want to agree with people who are, as conversion theory consistently characterizes minorities, *by definition* wrong.

The theory is therefore explicit that persuasion can only be effected by people who are psychological ingroup members on a relevant dimension. Any evidence that psychological outgroup membership can produce influence is contrary to the theory. The social categorization of others as outgroup members is an alternative to being influenced, since if one can dismiss the deviant opinions of deviant others, there is no uncertainty to be resolved. As Festinger concretely put it ". . . it is not necessary for a Ku Klux Klanner that some northern liberal agree with him in his attitude towards Negroes" (Festinger, 1950, p. 273).

The first two studies in our program set out to test our fundamental assumption that people will not be influenced by others who are different from them on a dimension relevant to the influence attempt (David & Turner, 1996). However, as Festinger discovered, "the problems of independently defining which groups are and which groups are not appropriate reference groups for a particular opinion or attitude is a difficult one" (1950, p. 273).

We believe that, in a desire for methodological rigor (i.e., the noncon-founding of categorization with message), some researchers have employed social categorizations which are irrelevant for subjects. Just because, for example, the targets of influence are women and the source men, gender would not be the relevant dimension for categorization unless the topic of the influence message was one on which women could be expected to hold consensual attitudes and beliefs which differed systematically from the con-sensual attitudes and beliefs of men: Women will not necessarily be the appro-priate reference group for women, and gender may well be a "pre-packaged surrogate variable" (Clark & Maass, 1988, p. 348).

To avoid such psychologically empty social categorizations our studies employed ingroup–outgroup categorizations on the dimension directly related to the influence message. A topic of continuing relevance to our Australian participants is the logging of old-growth forests. Numerous rural communities rely economically on the timber industry and are in favour of loosening existing restrictions on old-growth logging ("People are more important than trees!"), while other Australians, primarily city-dwellers, favor the imposition of even tighter restrictions in order to retain remaining wilder-ness areas in their pristine condition ("Saving our wildness for future gener-ations is more important than the temporary needs of a few"). Their position on the logging/conservation issue is central to any Australian political party's platform and most Australians identify strongly with one side or the other. Participants in our studies were self-identified as proconservation or prolog-ging and the influence message was a proconservation policy statement from either a majority or minority of "Friends of the Forest" or a prologging policy statement from a majority or minority of "Friends of the Timber Industry." We employed a full ingroup–outgroup, majority–minority design since it is possible that some findings of outgroup influence may be the result of using only a partial design (Volpato, Maass, Mucchi-Faina, & Vitti, 1990, found a significant outgroup minority effect when employing a reduced design but no significant outgroup minority effects when they employed the full design). Participants indicated their attitudes to logging the rain forest on a ques-tionnaire which was administered before and immediately after the influence message and again at a delay of two weeks.

Examination of Table 5.1 shows that while immediate influence was sig-nificant for all subjects, that is, all subjects evinced a significant pretest to posttest shift, this was in the direction of the source when it was the ingroup for subjects, and away from the source when it was the outgroup for sub-jects. Thus immediate ingroup influence was positive and immediate out-group influence was negative.

Table 5.1 *Study 1: Mean Influence Scores for Two Types of Message by Source of Influence (SD in brackets)*

Source		Message			
Identity	Status	Proconservation		Prologging	
		Immediate influence	Delayed influence	Immediate influence	Delayed influence
Ingroup	Majority	1.94	0.42[a]	1.66	1.28
		(0.60)	(0.71)	(0.56)	(0.74)
	Minority	0.74	2.02	0.90	1.71
		(0.75)	(0.77)	(0.61)	(0.69)
Outgroup	Majority	−1.34	−1.23[b]	−1.69	−1.90[b]
		(0.57)	(0.46)	(0.63)	(0.87)
	Minority	−1.20	−1.25[b]	−1.94	−1.73[b]
		(0.46)	(0.65)	(0.72)	(0.91)

Notes: Comparisons exceeded Bonferroni *t* crit., alpha .05 = 3.15 for 24 comparisons with 140 d.f. except where otherwise indicated.
All immediate influence is significant (posttest significantly different from pretest).
[a] Nonsignificant delayed influence (delayed posttest not significantly different from pretest).
[b] Delayed influence not significantly different from immediate influence.

For subjects in the outgroup source conditions there was no diminution of their immediate negative influence on the delayed measure, while in all ingroup source conditions there was a significant difference between immediate and delayed influence. Table 5.1 shows that for subjects in the ingroup majority conditions, immediate influence was greater than delayed influence, while for subjects in the ingroup minority conditions, delayed influence was greater than immediate influence.

There is one cell that can be seen to disrupt the symmetry of the results: While the long-term diminution of majority influence for proconservation participants returned them to a position which was not significantly different from that of their pretest, diminished long-term majority influence for prologging participants showed their ultimate position to remain significantly closer to that of the source than it had been in the pretest (their "compliance" contained some degree of "conversion"). As part of the pretest, prologging participants had indicated that they were moderately to strongly on the side of the loggers, compared to proconservation participants who indicated that conservationists received their mild to moderate support. A further indication of participant groups' differential involvement with the source and issue at question was provided in the control condition of the study (not shown here). Prologging controls, even though their "influence message" concerned student fees, showed a significant posttest increase in prologging attitudes, while proconservation controls did not polarize. Thus the results in the prologging ingroup majority condition may be an illustration of the point which will be taken up in Studies 5 and 6: People are differentially involved with/committed to/defined by different social identities, and the degree of salience of their self-categorizations will be a crucial determining factor in the nature of their relationship with the source, and hence of the nature of the influence outcome.

Returning to a sequential discussion of our studies, Study 2 employed the same conceptual design as Study 1, with public and private rather than immediate and delayed measures of influence. We employed only proconservationists. Participants indicated their attitudes to rain forest logging, were exposed to the influence message, and again responded to the rain forest logging questionnaire. They were led to believe that there would be a future session where the issue would be discussed among participants and that their responses to the questionnaire would either be read aloud at the beginning of this session (public condition) or would remain anonymous and confidential (private condition)

As can be seen from Table 5.2, results follow the same pattern as those from the first study. Participants in the outgroup majority and minority conditions showed significant pre–post shifts away from the influence source in both public and private conditions. In the ingroup public conditions, participants showed a significant shift towards the source, although for ingroup minority participants, this was significantly less than private influence and for ingroup majority participants it was significantly greater.

We would thus claim Studies 1 and 2 as firm support for our belief that outgroup status confers no "advantage" on a would-be source of influence. In our studies, which maximized the salience of self-and-source categorization on the dimension relevant to the influence attempt, participants in fact showed a significant shift away from the outgroup sources and the sources' numerical status appeared to have no effect at all.

However, the numerical status of ingroup sources did effect influence outcomes: Ingroup majorities exerted greater immediate and public influence, than delayed or private influence, and ingroup minority sources had the opposite effect; thus the pattern of majority compliance and minority conversion was found in our ingroup conditions. Our next two studies concen-

Table 5.2 *Study 2: Mean Public and Private Influence Scores by Source of Influence (SD in brackets)*

Source		Measure	
Identity	Status	Public	Private
Ingroup	Majority	1.88	0.48[a]
		(0.51)	(0.93)
	Minority	0.80	2.09
		(0.65)	(0.78)
Outgroup	Majority	−1.88[b]	−1.48[b]
		(0.54)	(0.61)
	Minority	−1.61[c]	−1.51[c]
		(0.46)	(0.57)

Notes: Comparisons exceeded Bonferroni *t* crit., alpha 0.05 = 2.9 for 12 comparisons with 117 d.f. except where otherwise indicated.
[a] Nonsignificant difference between pretest and posttest.
[b] Nonsignificant difference between public and private majority conditions.
[c] Nonsignificant difference between public and private minority conditions.

trated on a proposal to explain ingroup minority conversion without needing to conceptualize the source as essentially deviant.

Conversion

As already expounded, conversion theorists place great emphasis on the inherently deviant nature of minority sources of influence. Our understanding of their explanation for the frequently found patterns of majority compliance and minority conversion is that it is based on this characterization of minorities. When one finds oneself confronted by a discrepant majority, one does not question the message, since the majority is by definition correct, but enters into the process of social comparison which blocks any subsequent processing of the message content. In contrast a discrepant minority is instantly rejected because the source is by definition incorrect and, Mugny and Papastamou (1982) add, because one does not want to identify with its given negatively valued status. However, free from the need for social comparison, one subsequently enters into the validation process which focuses on the message, trying to understand why the source has presented it.

We find little to disagree with in most of this proposal: It is not inconsistent with self-categorization theory that intense social comparison might result from the discovery that most of "us" (the ingroup majority) are urging something unusual, or that less social comparison would be necessary when only a few of us dissent (a small number can be understood to be idiosyncratic individuals, "most of us" cannot). However, where we take issue with conversion theory is the leap that it makes from rejecting the message from an inherently invalid source, to subsequent validation of it. The rationale the theory provides is that the consistent, confident manner in which the message is presented causes it to be given attention, but we would claim that if a source is deviant by its very nature, the same behavior that could be perceived as *consistent* and *confident* in "normal" people, could as easily be interpreted as *dogmatic* and *arrogant* or *obsessive* and *opinionated* in those who are deviant: There is no reason to validate a mesage perceived as wrong, just because it is presented confidently and consistently.

Our explanation is based on the understanding that no social group has a fixed status (valid/invalid, powerful/powerless, valued/devalued, etc.), but rather that one's evaluation of others' social identity, as of one's own, is fluid and context-dependent. In David and Turner (1996) we present the general argument for this position, supported by an extensive range of current research into social context effects on group polarization, illusory correlation, stereotyping, perceived ingroup/outgroup homogeneity and so forth. The exigencies of space confine us to presenting here a condensed version which suggests simply that one rejects an ingroup minority when comparing it to the ingroup majority and accepts it in a broader field of comparison.

A number of studies support the proposal that, as comparative social context becomes broader, a person who has been perceived as different can come to be perceived as comparatively similar (Gaertner, Mann, Murrell, & Dovidio, 1989; Haslam & Turner, 1992, 1995; Wilder & Thompson, 1988). For example, in Haslam and Turner (1992, Expt. 1) "slightly pragmatic" participants perceived a pragmatic target as most similar to self when presented in a context ranging from "predominantly pragmatic" to "predominantly nonpragmatic," and least similar to self when presented in a restricted range of "predominantly pragmatic" to "slightly pragmatic." Building on these kind of findings, we suggest that immediate, direct, public measures make the discrepancy between ingroup majority and minority highly salient when an ingroup minority attempts to influence the majority. This is to say that measures of immediate influence restrict the frame of reference to the two ingroup factions. On the other hand, because they remove participants from the need to confront the ingroup conflict, delayed, indirect, and private measures are believed to attenuate the salience of the factional conflict. In other words, measures of delayed influence allow the frame of reference to broaden and include the more fundamental ingroup–outgroup conflict.

To test our proposal we employed moderate feminist participants because they had a nomic social identity and a relationship with a nomic ingroup minority, separatist feminists, who were considered by participants to be important members of the "sisterhood," yet a subfaction on the grounds of their total rejection of all things male.

Participants indicated their attitudes to feminism on a questionnaire which was administered before and immediately after an influence message from separatist feminists, and again at a delay of two weeks. We manipulated the context in which the message was presented by informing participants that "a typical group of participants" had produced a statement to be evaluated. The intragroup context was induced in a statement which endorsed moderate feminist values, and the intergroup context was induced in a statement which endorsed antifeminist values. We expected that an intragroup context – making salient comparison of the separatist views with those of the moderate feminist majority – would cause the influence message to be rejected, while an intergroup context – making salient comparison of separatist feminist views with those of antifeminists – would cause the influence message to be accepted.

Since our proposed explanation of conversion is that time attenuates the salience of intragroup conflict, we introduced conditions in which the context was repeated immediately prior to the delayed posttest. We expected that controls who received the influence message without an explicit context would evince an immediate rejection of the message, comparable to participants in the intragroup context conditions. Further, we expected no-context controls to evince delayed acceptance of the message (i.e., to "convert"), as would subjects in the intergroup restated context condition.

As can be seen from Table 5.3, our predictions were supported. Participants for whom no context was explicitly induced (i.e., those in the "normal" minority influence situation) evinced no immediate influence, followed by significant delayed influence. This conversion pattern was also exhibited by intragroup context participants who had the context induced before the immediate measure only. For them, explicit induction of an intragroup context caused an initial move away from the source but it seems that time did ameliorate the conflict of comparison with the ingroup majority, and resulted in acceptance of the ingroup minority's message. That such apparent

Table 5.3   *Study 3: Mean Immediate and Delayed Shift for Control and Experimental Conditions*

Condition	n	Shift	
		Immediate	*Delayed*
Intragroup Context single statement	19	−0.71[a]	0.18
		(0.82)	(1.07)
Intragroup Context repeated statement	18	−0.86[a]	−0.78[a]
		(0.82)	(0.85)
Intergroup Context single statement	18	1.69[a]	1.63[a]
		(0.86)	(0.76)
Intergroup Context repeated statement	19	1.78[a]	1.85[a]
		(0.86)	(0.79)
No-context Control	19	−0.06	0.53[a]
		(0.71)	(0.56)
Irrelevant-message Control	21	0.07	0.08
		(0.32)	(0.29)

Notes: Numbers in brackets are standard deviations.
[a] indicates shift exceeding Bonferroni critical *t* at 0.01 significance level.

delayed acceptance was not merely a product of increased familiarity with the repeated measure was made clear by participants for whom the intragroup context was repeated immediately prior to the delayed measure: They evinced no positive immediate or delayed influence. Comparison of the ingroup minority message with the outgroup (the intergroup context) also led to the effect we predicted, with participants shifting towards the ingroup minority source.

When considering this study we realized that it contained a possible confound: The context inducers were in the form of messages. While they were shorter and less complex than the influence message, they left open interpretation of the results being a product of competing messages. Thus, in Study 4 we replicated Study 3 using a less confounded induction of context. Participants were given a marked feminism scale and told that this represented the position of most women who had taken part in the study so far. Participants in the intragroup context conditions received a scale with a mean which indicated that most participants were moderately feminist, and those in the intergroup condition received a scale which indicated a mean moderately antifeminist position.

Results largely replicated those of Study 3 (for discussion of minor exceptions see David & Turner, 1999). Thus our proposed explanation of conversion received support. We must make it very clear, however, that the support we are claiming is indirect and inferential rather than direct, since we have no measure of subjects' perceptions of the social identity of the source of influence. This was not an oversight but rather the result of difficulty in finding a nonreactive measure of such perceptions: If we are correct in asserting that direct measures induce an intragroup context, it follows that direct questions regarding the source will elicit a perception of the ingroup minority as different from self. For example, a person with moderately liberal political views who is taking part in a demonstration against fascism will probably be thinking of extreme liberals as ingroup members because of the psychological presence of fascists, the relevant outgroup. However, if explicitly asked any of the usual social identification questions regarding extreme liberals (how much do you like these people? how similar to yourself are they? etc) fascists are not in the frame of reference, and the difference the participant is being asked to focus on is between their (moderate) self and (extreme) liberals. In other words the context will have narrowed from intergroup to intragroup and people who were previously thought of as ingroup will now be thought of as essentially different from self.

In spite of the inferential nature of our findings, the fact that we were able to create the "classic" conversion pattern by providing an intragroup context prior to the immediate measure and, more importantly, that we were able to prevent conversion by repeating the intragroup context prior to the delayed measure, and facilitate immediate minority influence by providing an intergroup context prior to the immediate measure, strongly supports a self-categorization analysis of minority conversion. None of the results are consistent with the suggestion we understand conversion theory to make – that perception of a source of influence as similar to self inhibits validation and hence conversion, while perception of the source as different from self facilitates validation and conversion. If this were the case we should have found minority influence in the intragroup but not in the intergroup context, the exact opposite of our actual results.

Having established to some extent that successful minority influence is not predicated by a fixed or enduring evaluation of the source as different from self, we turn to addressing the issue of the processing of influence messages. We will suggest that the nature of processing is determined by complex interactions between participants' social identity, their categorization of the source, and the nature of the influence message, rather than by fixed attributes of the source.

Differential Processing

It stands to reason that the amount of attention one devotes to a communication, and whether the attention focuses in a systematic way on the message content or on a search for social comparative or cognitive cues as to its correctness, will have an impact on whether the communication is rejected out of hand, conditionally rejected, conditionally accepted, or becomes a part of a more enduring belief system. Thus it is not surprising that a large body of research in the field of social influence has been devoted to the processing of influence messages.

Neither is it surprising, given that most researchers espouse a single or dual process model of influence, and that many believe that either majorities or minorities exert "true" influence, that the processing literature contains as many varied and often conflicting findings as the literature that focuses on outcomes. While there is little argument that message elaboration (systematic or central processing) leads to a greater likelihood of attitude change than heuristic or peripheral processing (Chaiken, 1980, 1987; Petty & Cacioppo, 1981, 1986), there is less agreement about who and what stimulates these processes. Conversion theorists argue, for instance, that conflict with the normative majority will elicit a concerned search for social comparative cues to the conflict and that such a search is at the expense of processing the content of the message (Moscovici, 1980; Mugny, 1975). Others have proposed, in a similar vein, that the numerical might and given attractive and normative nature of a majority acts as a consensus or desirability heuristic which allows its message to be accepted without need of further consideration (Axson, Yates, & Chaiken, 1987; Chaiken, 1980; Chaiken & Stangor, 1987; De Vries, De Dreu, Gordijn, & Schuurman, 1996; Kelman, 1961). In contrast, Mackie (1987), following self-categorization theoretical principles, proposes that the same normative nature of majorities which others suggest acts as a heuristic cue may ". . . increase concern with the object truth value of the issue, making *systematic* processing more likely" (Mackie, 1987, p. 42, emphasis added).

Concerning processing of minority communications, conversion theorists claim that minorities elicit a validation process, one which involves systematic evaluation of their message. Stepping beyond the strict confines of conversion theory, Nemeth (1986; Nemeth & Kwan, 1985; Nemeth, Mosier, & Chiles, 1992; Nemeth & Rogers, 1996; Nemeth & Wachtler, 1983) claims that majorities exert both normative and informational pressure, while conflict with a minority raises neither informational nor normative concerns about the *message*, but fosters contemplation of the *issue* from all viewpoints, many of them new and creative.

Baker and Petty (1994, Study 1) supported Mackie's (1987) assertion that majorities stimulate systematic processing in their finding that a counterattitudinal position, supported by strong or weak arguments, was carefully scrutinized only when the source was a majority. A second study reported in the same paper shed an even more interesting light on the issue, demonstrating that a majority or minority message was systematically scrutinized when it ran counter to the attitudes that targets expected of the source.

In our fifth and sixth studies we took up the issue of source–position discrepancy as a determinant of message scrutiny, since it seemed a unique opportunity to test our central tenet that when deviant people present a deviant message it will be dismissed out of hand and the converse that when the same source presents a normative message, the need to explain a flouted expectation may result in increased message elaboration, as it does in the "normal" influence situation of a normative source and counternormative message.

To this end we again employed participants with clear, nomic social identities – moderate feminists in Study 5 and separatist feminists in Study 6. Crano and Hannula-Bral (1994) have shown that the numerical status of the targets of influence may play a part in influence outcomes, and our participant groups demonstrated from the start that they perceived themselves in different ways. In pretest responses to the question "How strong a feminist do you consider yourself to be?", moderate feminists indicated that they were mild to moderate, while separatists indicated that they were strong feminists. Prior to making individual responses, participants were asked to come to consensus as a group about the numerical status of three social categories (subsequently the influence sources) and their decisions can be seen in Table 5.4: Moderate feminists saw themselves as a majority and both separatists and antifeminists as minorities, while separatists attributed majority status to antifeminists and minority status to themselves. The group was not prepared to call moderate feminists either majority or minority and asked if they could qualify the numerical status, which they did by defining moderate feminists as a "mainstream" minority (and themselves, by implication, as marginalized). Clearly moderate feminists live in a more pleasant world, where most people are like them, than separatists, for whom most people are outgroup.

Participants were given two statements attributed either to moderate feminists, separatists, or antifeminists, or no source attribution was made. One of the statements had been determined in pilot testing to be *normative*, and one to be *counternormative*, for feminists. Pilot testing also indicated that feminists would be surprised if the normative statement was made by antifeminists, while they would not be surprised if antifeminists made the counternormative statement. Participants indicated the extent to which they agreed or disagreed with each statement on a 1–9 scale where 1 indicated total disagreement and 9 complete agreement. Each recording of agreement or disagreement was followed by the opportunity to list any additional thoughts they had on the matter.

In the top portion of Table 5.4 it can be seen that moderate feminists endorsed a normative message no matter who the source was (or even, in fact when there was none), while source identity affected the amount of elaboration the message received: They appeared to think little about the normative message when there was no source attribution or when it was attributed to themselves, the ingroup majority, but gave it considerable extra thought when it was attributed to their ingroup minority or outgroup minority. The counternormative message received endorsement only when attributed to the ingroup majority or minority, in which conditions it also received considerable elaboration. This is not surprising since it would not have been expected from the ingroup sources, and controls showed that it was elaborated to some degree even when no source attribution was made. Importantly, attribution of the counternormative message to the counternormative source (antifeminists, the outgroup minority) led to fewer additional thoughts than when it was attributed to no one, suggesting, as we had proposed, that a deviant source explains a deviant message which thus requires no further processing.

In the bottom portion of the table, separatist feminists show an interestingly different response: They indicated agreement with the normative message when it received no source attribution or was attributed to themselves or their ingroup minority, but disagreed with it when it was attributed to their outgroup majority. The amount of elaboration the normative message received followed the same, although exaggerated, pattern as displayed by moderate participants: little elaboration when the message was attributed to themselves or no one, and elaboration when it was attributed to the ingroup minority or the outgroup. Agreement with the counternormative message followed the same patterns as for moderate feminists (although again in a more extreme form): no agreement in the control and outgroup conditions, and endorsement in the ingroup conditions. Processing of the counternormative message was also an exaggerated form of the moderate feminists' response pattern, with the outgroup source condition being the only one where considerable elaboration was not forthcoming.

Table 5.4 Studies 5&6: Agreement and Mean Number of Additional Thoughts as a Function of Participants' Self-categorization, Source and the Normative or Counternormative Nature of a statement

Participants' self-categorization	Source and perceived source status†							
	Modfem		*Sepfem*		*Antifem*		*Control*	
Modfem	*majority*		*minority*		*minority*			
	norm	counter	norm	counter	norm	counter	norm	counter
agreement	7.8	6.3^b	7.2	5.9^b	6.8^a	1.4	7.8	1.2
additional thoughts	1.6	8.6^a	6.4^b	9.7^b	1.2	1.3^b	1.2	4.6
Sepfem	*mainstream minority*		*minority*		*majority*			
	norm	counter	norm	counter	norm	counter	norm	counter
agreement	8.0	5.4^b	7.9	7.1^b	4.0	1.0	8.4	1.0
additional thoughts	5.3^b	8.9	0.7	8.7	8.8^b	0.5^b	0.7	8.9

Notes: † italics indicate the numerical status of the source as consensually defined by participants.

modfem = moderate feminists.

sepfem = separatist feminists.

norm = normative statement.

counter = counternormative statement.

[a] indicates comparison with control exceeding Bonferroni critical *t* at 0.05 significance level.

[b] indicates comparison with control exceeding Bonferroni critical *t* at 0.01 significance level.

In summarizing agreement and number of additional thoughts it is clear that the social identity of respondents was a factor in determining outcomes. Unlike moderate feminists, who endorsed a normative message regardless of source, separatists indicated that they did not agree with the message when they believe it had been delivered by their outgroup. Separatists also reacted more strongly than moderate feminists in elaborating the normative message when it did not issue from themselves. Where the counternormative message was concerned, moderate and separatist feminists differed little in rejecting it when no source attribution was made or when it was attributed to the outgroup, and accepting it in the ingroup source conditions. The pattern of counternormative message processing was similar for both groups of participants but again more extreme for separatists: moderate to intense processing of the message either alone or from ingroup sources, with minimal evidence of processing when it was attributed to the outgroup.

Simple agreement or disagreement with a statement, and number of additional thoughts elicited, however, are relatively gross measures. Table 5.5 shows the results of content analysis of the additional thoughts, breaking them down into those that supported the statements and those that argued against them (note that some additional thoughts fit neither category, thus numbers here may not sum to numbers in Table 5.4).

Maass and Clark (1983, Study 2) found no difference in the absolute number of thoughts elicited in response to a majority or a minority message. They did find, however, that respondents made more arguments in favor of the message and fewer against it in the minority condition. Alvaro and Crano (1996) suggest that participants who agree with a message will not argue against the message, no matter who endorses it. Results in Table 5.5 largely support Alvaro and Crano in suggesting that for our participants the valence of arguments was determined primarily not by identity of the source but by the nature of the message (more for a normative message than against it, and the reverse for a counternormative message), but there was also seen to be an interaction between target identity, source identity, and nature of message: In the separatist feminist source condition for separatist feminist participants responding to a counternormative message, the response pattern of more arguments against than for the counternormative position can be seen to have been disrupted. It will be remembered that these participants indicated that they agreed with the message when believing that they, themselves, originated it so it is not surprising that they might attempt to rationalize their agreement in an attempt to lessen cognitive dissonance. If this is, in fact, what they were doing, why did not moderate feminists, who had also indicated agreement with the counternormative message from an ingroup source,

Table 5.5 Studies 5&6: Mean Number of Additional Thoughts For and Against a Statement as a Function of Participants' Self-categorization, Source and the Normative or Counternormative Nature of a Statement

Participants' self-categorization	Source and perceived source status[†]							
	Modfem		Sepfem		Antifem		Control	
	majority		*minority*		*minority*			
	norm	counter	norm	counter	norm	counter	norm	counter
Modfem								
for	1.3	1.1	3.1[a]	2.0[a]	1.2	0.0	1.1	0.8
against	0.0	1.2[a]	1.8[a]	4.1[a]	0.3	0.8[a]	0.0	3.2
Sepfem	*mainstream minority*		*minority*		*majority*			
for	4.1[a]	0.0	0.5	5.4[b]	5.6[b]	0.0	0.5	0.0
against	0.2	3.4[a]	0.0	0.6[b]	2.7[a]	0.2[b]	0.8	5.7

Notes: [†] italics indicate the numerical status of the source as consensually defined by participants.

modfem = moderate feminists.

sepfem = separatist feminists.

norm = normative statement.

counter = counternormative statement.

indulge in similar cognitive work? We will be suggesting that there are other indications that separatists experienced themselves as a minority and as extremists, which may well have accounted for this, and other anomalies in the data (see Haslam & Turner, 1995, 1998 for discussion of extremists and extreme judgement).

Another apparent anomaly is the fact that, although separatist feminists had indicated that they disagreed with the normative message when it was attributed to antifeminists, Table 5.5 shows that they generated more arguments in favor of it than against it. This suggests a strange kind of negative compliance, in the sense that the direct response reflects salient social categorical norms – "We are very different from them so disagree with everything they say" – while the indirect responses reflect an unchanged opinion about the content of the message. There is a parallel here with the conversion theory explanation of response to a majority message: One acts in accordance with the social categorical norm (in the case of a majority source, this means assumed similarity and agreement) and underlying beliefs are unchanged (in the majority case the underlying belief is usually disagreement, since the message is usually nonnormative). Separatist participants' display of outgroup compliance, albeit negative compliance, lends weight to one of the points we will be making at greater length in our conclusion: An influence outcome is the result of interactions involving source, target, and nature of message, rather than a predictable product of the nature of the source.

In the process of content analyzing the data into pro and con arguments, raters noted a further two frequently occurring content categories – redefining the argument and questioning the source – which might be worth investigating, and these are shown in Table 5.6. While they indicate message-relevant thought (which Mackie, 1987, found to be a better predictor of majority than of minority influence) versus source-relevant thought (perhaps indicative of the social comparison process which has been associated with normative influence and majority compliance, see Alvaro & Crano, 1996), they are more exact descriptors of thought content. Redefining the argument took the form of such responses as "Antifeminists wouldn't understand why women need the right to abortion, they probably look on it as a kind of contraception that allows men to **** around as much as they want to without having to take responsibility," or "I don't think these women understood what they were saying. They meant that men should support women in whatever they decide to do with their own bodies." Questioning the identity of the source took the form of such responses as "These guys think that they're feminists because their girlfriend goes to work" or "No separatist in her right mind would say this."

Table 5.6 *Studies 5&6: Mean Number of Additional Thoughts Devoted to Reinterpreting a Statement and Questioning the Identity of the Source as a Function of Participants' Self-categorization, Source and the Normative or Counternormative Nature of a Statement*

Participants' self-categorization	Source and perceived source status[†]							
	Modfem		*Sepfem*		*Antifem*		*Control*	
Modfem	*majority*		*minority*		*minority*			
	norm	counter	norm	counter	norm	counter	norm	counter
reinterpret statement	0.0	3.3[a]	0.0	7.1[b]	1.8[a]	0.0	0.0	0.0
question source identity	0.0	5.1[b]	0.0	2.1[a]	5.0[b]	0.0	0.0	0.0
Sepfem	*mainstream minority*		*minority*		*majority*			
	norm	counter	norm	counter	norm	counter	norm	counter
reinterpret statement	0.1	0.5	0.0	7.3[b]	7.7[b]	0.0	0.0	0.0
question source identity	0.2	8.1[b]	0.0	0.8[a]	0.4	0.0[b]	0.0	4.1

Notes: [†] italics indicate the numerical status of the source as consensually defined by participants.

modfem = moderate feminists.

sepfem = separatist feminists.

norm = normative statement.

counter = counternormative statement.

Table 5.6 shows that additional thought took these explicit forms when there was a need to explain source–message discrepancy, except for separatist feminists who questioned the identity of the source of a counternormative message, even when one was not provided, writing such things as "The blokes must have got pissed round the bar one night to produce this . . . unless Freddy got all his girls to learn to read and write" (refering to the female congregation of a well-known Australian fundamentalist preacher) and "Who reckons this? The chauvinist pig brigade?".

For moderate feminists, a focus on the message rather than the source, or vice versa, was comparative rather than absolute. They can be seen to have devoted relatively more thought to questioning the source than to reinterpreting the message when antifeminists endorsed the normative message, or when they themselves endorsed the counternormative message, and relatively more thought to reinterpreting the message than to questioning the source when separatist feminist endorsed the counternormative message. Separatists were, as in many other of their responses, more given to extremes. They devoted considerable thought to the message when a counternormative statement was attributed to themselves and when a normative message was attributed to the outgroup, and this was to the virtual exclusion of focus on the putative source. In contrast, they strongly queried the notion that moderate feminists were "real" feminists when they were attributed with the counternormative message, and hardly bothered to question that they really meant what they were saying.

There is a danger here that it will be suggested that separatist responses illustrate the distinction between normative and informational influence, and the idea that normative influence (social comparison) blocks processing of the message (a search for information). This is clearly not the case for two reasons: the first, the obvious fact that moderate feminists showed no such exclusive concern with source versus message; the second that the only times participants reinterpreted the statements were when they had been attributed to an unexpected source, and the discrepancy would not have been apparent if no attention had been paid to the supposed social identity of the source. Conversely, one will only perceive a need to question the identity of the source if the thrust of the message is understood.

Turning to the separatists, their distinctive social identity can be interpreted as having played a major role in the extremity of their responses, as we suggested was true for the prologging participants in Study 1. That separatists were conscious of themselves as a minority received direct confirmation. Interestingly they felt the need to differentiate, not only between themselves and the outgroup which they perceived as a majority, but between themselves and their moderate feminist sisters whom they referred to as "mainstream" which, as we have already observed, makes themselves marginalized. A number of recent studies suggest that social identity is more salient for minorities than for majorities (Mullen, 1991; Simon & Brown, 1987). The self-categorization explanation for this is that "as a group becomes smaller within a given comparative context it will tend to be making more intergroup comparisons than intragroup ones, whilst the reverse is true for majorities" (Haslam, Turner, Oakes, McGarty, & Hayes, 1992, p. 5). Since, in accordance with the meta-contrast principle (see Hogg and Turner, 1987; Hogg, Turner, & Davidson, 1990; Turner,1985, 1991; Turner et al., 1987; Turner & Oakes, 1986, 1989) intergroup comparisons stress the large differences between categories and the small differences within, minorities are more likely than majorities to perceive themselves as a unified group, devote cognitive effort to maximizing their positive distinctiveness, and to act in term of prototypical ingroup norms (for links with the literature on extremists and polarized judgment see Haslam & Turner, 1995, 1998).

Thus separatists argued against the counternormative message even when no source attribution was made, were more disturbed by disruption of normative expectations (at least as indicated by elaborative processing in cases of source–message discrepancy), and were more extreme than moderate feminists in their rejection of a counternormative message when it was attributed to the outgroup and more intense in their acceptance of it when it supposedly came from the ingroup. The latter outcome may at first seem to contradict our proposal, since if ingroup norms are so important for separatists they should never, presumably, endorse a counternormative stance. We argue, however, that more important than normative stance on a particular issue is that the group will always maximize the difference between themselves and the outgroup in a direction that favors themselves. When correctness is at issue this means that "We are right and they are wrong." Thus separatists were even prepared to reject a normative message when it was attributed to antifeminists ("Nothing they say can be correct"). Their need to defend their own correctness was apparently so great that they argued for the counternormative message when they, themselves were identified as the source, yet against it when it was attributed to their "mainstream" factional sisters (moderate feminists never argued for the counternormative message, no matter to whom it was attributed).

Our post-hoc interpretation of the effects of separatists' social identity as minority and extremist is something we will pursue in the future, by which time we hope to have overcome the previously mentioned problem of finding a measure of perceived target–source relationship which will not activate the intergroup comparison, guaranteeing perception of any source other than one's immediate ingroup as different from self. At this time we will simply add our results to the growing body of indirect and inferential support.

The important finding of Studies 5 and 6 which does not rest on inference is that relatively little elaboration of a message is necessary when it matches participants' expectations, which runs counter to the suggestion from conversion theory that a minority influences because it is essentially different from self and the content of its message is processed systematically. Experimental results also argue against a social comparison/validation (read normative/informational) dichotomy, with evidence that participants both attend to the message and the identity of the source in the same influence encounter.

Summary and Conclusion

The aim of the program of studies presented here has been to demonstrate some of the patterns of influence that result from different social relationships between sources and targets. We have shown that when the social identity of both is clear and relevant to the issue under consideration, people are not influenced by outgroup others, regardless of the numerical status of the source, but respond differently to ingroup majorities and minorities (Studies 1 and 2). In Studies 3 and 4 we demonstrated that people reject the messages of a dissenting ingroup minority when the only available comparison is with the ingroup majority, but accept the same message from the same source when the outgroup enters the field of comparison. Manipulating context over time, we were able to demonstrate one ingroup minority source and message stimulating three different patterns of influence: immediate influence which lasted over time, immediate rejection which was not ameliorated by time, and immediate rejection followed by delayed acceptance – the classic pattern of minority conversion. The fifth and sixth studies focused on differential processing of influence messages, demonstrating that additional thought could result from the counternormative nature of a message alone, or from violation of expectancies when the counternormative message was attributed to an ingroup source or a normative message to an outgroup. The studies also demonstrated that informational and social comparative processing are interrelated and, importantly, that although a counternormative message stimulated additional (arguably divergent) thinking when no source attribution was made, it did not do so when attributed to the outgroup. Thus we contend that any suggestion that minority stimulation of divergent thinking is a product of disapprobation of the source must be seriously questioned.

The last point returns us to the central focus of our work: Positive influence is the product of disagreement with people who are perceived as the relevant reference group in the context of the issue at question, the ingroup. We have shown that disagreement with an outgroup results in neither influence nor consideration of the issue, since the fact that an outgroup is expected to hold incorrect attitudes explains their point of view and no more attention need be given to the matter. Thus we challenge the central tenet of conversion theory, that minority conversion is a product of a validation process which is made possible because the deviant, incorrect, negatively valued nature of a minority frees one from the need for social comparison with it and enables one to consider the issue from its point of view. We contend that it is only when the discrepant view is attributed to people who are positively valued, and who we expect to be correct, that we are motivated to consider their position.

How, then, do we explain the different patterns of influence which we agree may sometimes be stimulated by ingroup majorities and minorities? In the majority situation one is confronted with most of "us" saying something we have never said before. It stands to reason that one's assessment of the situation and response to it would be very different from one's assessment and response in a situation where only a few of us say something discrepant. In the latter situation one can decide that the dissenters are idiosyncratic individuals. Initially their ideas may be rejected because, after all, they are saying something that we do not believe. If there is some relevant dimension on which the dissenters can be recategorized as different from us (if one had believed, for example, that people who say that blue is green were normally sighted like us, but subsequently find that they are color-blind), one's initial rejection will firm and result in the dissidents' total failure to influence. However, if there is no reason other than their dissenting opinion on which to reject them, time attenuates the shock and sharpness of the conflict. The dissenters are essentially ingroup members, individuals who are valued and whose opinions are worth considering because one knows them to be based on shared values and beliefs, thus their opinion will need to be included in the "latitude of acceptance" (Hovland, Harvey, & Sherif, 1957). Studies 3 and 4 presented the conversion pattern from a perspective that emphasizes the importance of shifting comparative context: The ingroup minority opinion is rejected when narrowly compared to the ingroup majority opinion as it will be in the first instance, since the ingroup majority are the arbiters of correctness, but the minority's opinions will be perceived as within the latitude of acceptance when considered in a broader context which includes the outgroup, who are wrong by definition.

When we find ourselves in a situation where most of "us" express a discrepant opinion, the dissent cannot be attributed to idiosyncrasy and may well cause one to question one's social identity ("Am I really one of these people who say such strange things?") or the identity of the majority ("Can they really be X when they say such strange things?"). If the identity question can be resolved by concluding that the source is not majority or ingroup, or that one is not an ingroup member oneself, no influence will result. Since, however, a well-planned experiment will control for variables which allow such a resolution, an experimental participant may well decide to endorse the majority view *conditionally*. In making this proposal it can be seen that we do not disagree with Moscovici's suggestion that majority dissent may sometimes stimulate more social comparison and less message scrutiny than minority dissent – moderate feminist subjects in Study 5 devoted a large part of their thinking to questioning the identity of a source which they believed to be majority, at the relative expense of examining the message. However, there are two important qualifications we would make:

The first is that we have emphasised that majority dissent *may* stimulate more social comparison, rather than that it *does* so. We do not believe that the numerical status of a source of influence automatically confers negativity upon it, causing it to have a predictable set of effects on passive, "neutral" targets. The targets of influence bring to the encounter their own identities, which determine the relationship between themselves and the source, and it is this relationship rather than source qualities alone which crucially determines the success or failure of an influence attempt and of the form it will take. In fact we suggest that in using the terms *majority influence* – characterizing it as public, direct, immediate influence, accompanied by convergent thought and heuristic processing – and *minority influence* – characterizing it as private, indirect, delayed influence, accompanied by divergent thought and systematic processing – we risk repeating one of the fundamental mistakes of the functionalists. As Moscovici so clearly pointed out in his revolutionary treatise (1976), the functionalist model of influence presupposes that it can only flow in one direction, from those with access to particular resources to the targets of influence who are in a passive, dependent position. While Moscovici was criticizing an exclusive focus on conformity and majority influence, we believe that the same criticism arises when we focus exclusively on the sources of influence (be they majority or minority) and ignore the fact that any qualities they may have interact with qualities of the target. Influence does not, as Moscovici pointed out, flow in only one direction.

The second qualification we would make to the idea that ingroup majorities may stimulate more social comparison and less message scrutiny than ingroup minorities is our belief that, when such an effect occurs, it is comparative rather than in any way absolute. The idea that, in conflict with a majority one is concerned with social variables to the exclusion of message content, or that, free from the social comparison demanded by a majority, one devotes all one's attention to the content of a minority message, has led to the association of majorities with normative influence and minorities with informational influence (Alvaro & Crano, 1996; cf. Deutsch & Gerard, 1955). We believe that the normative–informational distinction is as false a dichotomy today as it was in 1976 when Moscovici so cogently identified it as such. Moscovici argued that no information is free from social input: Even when referring to a source as inanimate and seemingly objective as a ruler, the meaning we attach to the marks on it is socially mediated. Similarly a desire to belong cannot be separated from the belief that those we want to affiliate with hold a correct view of reality (Turner, 1991; Turner & Oakes, 1997).

Our debt to Moscovici does not end there. In his 1976 book he challenged Festinger's (1950, 1954) contention that uncertainty is a precondition for influence, arguing that it is a " 'result' rather than a 'given'" (Moscovici, 1976, p. 58). In proposing a genetic model of influence, Moscovici expounded upon this observation to make the creation of uncertainty through conflict the necessary first step in a influence attempt. We completely agree with this, but would add that people will only doubt their current beliefs (i.e., experience uncertainty) when they are challenged by others with whom agreement is expected. No amount of consistent, confident repetition of a discrepant point of view by people we perceive as essentially deviant, people whose opinion we do not value, will create conflict for us since we know that deviant people say deviant things. Indeed we may question our view of reality when such people say something with which we *agree* (Baker & Petty, 1994, Study 2; Haslam et al., 1996; Studies 5 & 6 presented here). The participants in Studies 5 and 6 support our assertion that a norm-challenging message from a counternormative source is dismissed out of hand, while a normative message from a normative source is accepted relatively unthinkingly.

Returning to our starting point, we propose that the influence process begins with the uncertainty created by similar others espousing a counternormative position, that one searches for alternatives which allow one to maintain current beliefs, and that when no alternative is possible, one may scrutinize the message content for understanding and move toward including it in one's latitude of acceptance. Throughout, both social–comparative and message-focused processing is occurring and such variables as salience of the relevant self-categorization, its perceived status as majority or minority, moderate or extreme, perception of the source as majority or minority, ingroup or outgroup, nature of the message (normative, nonnormative, irrelevant), social context of the encounter, and so forth, will interact in a panoply of dynamic ways which question the usefulness of such terms as "majority" or "minority" influence.

REFERENCES

Alvaro, E. M., & Crano, W. D. (1996). Cognitive responses to minority- or majority-based communications: Factors that underlie minority influence. *British Journal of Social Psychology, 35* (1), 105–122.

Asch, S. E. (1952). *Social psychology.* Englewood Cliffs, NJ: Prentice-Hall.

Axson, D., Yates, S., & Chaiken, S. (1987). Audience response as a heuristic cue in persuasion. *Journal of Personality and Social Psychology, 53,* 30–40.

Baker, S. M., & Petty, R. E. (1994). Majority and minority influence: Source–position imbalance as a determinant of message scrutiny. *Journal of Personality and Social Psychology, 67,* 5–19.

Chaiken, S. (1980). Heuristic versus systematic processing and the use of source versus message cues to persuasion. *Journal of Personality and Social Psychology, 39,* 752–766.

Chaiken, S. (1987). The heuristic model of persuasion. In M. P. Zanna, J. M. Olson, & C. P. Herman (Eds.), *Social influence: The Ontario symposium* (Vol. 5, pp. 3–39). Hillsdale, NJ: Erlbaum.

Chaiken, S., & Stangor, C. (1987). Attitudes and attitude change. *Annual Review of Psychology, 38,* 575–630.

Clark, R. D. III, & Maass, A. (1988). The role of social categorization and perceived source credibility in minority influence. *European Journal of Social Psychology, 18,* 381–394.

Crano, W. D., & Hannula-Bral, K. A. (1994). Context/categorization model of social influence: Minority and majority influence in the formation of a novel response norm. *Journal of Experimental Social Psychology, 30,* 247–276.

David, B., & Turner, J. C. (1996). Studies in self-categorization and minority conversion: Is being a member of the out-group an advantage? *British Journal of Social Psychology, 35* (1), 179–199.

David, B., & Turner, J. C. (1999). Studies in self-categorization and minority conversion: The ingroup minority in intragroup and intergroup contexts. *British Journal of Social Psychology, 38,* 115–134.

Deutsch, M., & Gerard, H. B. (1955). A study of normative and informational social influence upon individual judgment. *Journal of Abnormal and Social Psychology*, *51*, 629–636.

De Vries, N. K., De Dreu, C. K. W., Gordijn, E., & Schuurman, M. (1996). Majority and minority influence: A dual role interpretation. *European Review of Social Psychology*, *7*, 145–172.

Festinger, L. (1950). Informal social communication. *Psychological Review*, *57*, 271–282

Festinger, L. (1954). A theory of social comparison processes. *Human Relations*, *7*, 117–140

Gaertner, S., Mann, J., Murrell, A., & Dovidio, J. F. (1989). Reducing intergroup bias: The benefits of recategorization. *Journal of Personality and Social Psychology*, *57*, 239–249.

Haslam, S. A., Oakes, P. J., McGarty, C., Turner, J. C., Reynolds, K., & Eggins, R. (1996). Stereotyping and social influence: The mediation of stereotype applicability and sharedness by the views of in-group and out-group members. *British Journal of Social Psychology*, *35*, 369–397.

Haslam, S. A., & Turner, J. C. (1992). Context-dependent variation in social stereotyping 2: The relationship between frame of reference, self-categorization and accentuation. *European Journal of Social Psychology*, *22*, 251–277.

Haslam, S. A., & Turner, J. C. (1995). Context-dependent variation in social stereotyping 3: Extremism as a self-categorical basis for polarized judgement. *European Journal of Social Psychology*, *22*, 341–371.

Haslam, S. A., & Turner, J. C. (1998). Extremism and deviance: Beyond taxonomy and bias. *Social Research*, *65*, 2, 435–448.

Haslam, S. A., Turner, J. C., Oakes, P. J., McGarty, C., & Hayes, B. K. (1992). Context-dependent variation in social stereotyping 1: The effects of intergroup relations as mediated by social change and frame of reference. *European Journal of Social Psychology*, *22*, 3–20.

Hogg, M. A., & Turner, J. C. (1987). Social identity and conformity: A theory of referent informational influence. In W. Doise & S. Moscovici (Eds.), *Current issues in European social psychology* (Vol. 2, pp. 139–182). Cambridge, UK: Cambridge University Press.

Hogg, M. A., Turner, J. C., & Davidson, B. (1990). Polarized norms and social frames of reference: A test of the self-categorization theory of group polarization. *Basic and Applied Social Psychology*, *11*, 77–100.

Hovland, C. I., Harvey, O. J., & Sherif, M. (1957). Assimilation and contrast effects in reactions to communication and attitude change. *Journal of Abnormal and Social Psychology*, *55*, 244–252.

Kelman, H. C. (1961). Processes of opinion change. *Public Opinion Quarterly*, *25*, 57–78.

Maass, A., & Clark, R. D. (1983). Internalization versus compliance: Differential processes underlying minority influence and conformity. *European Journal of Social Psychology*, *13*, 197–215.

Maass, A., & Clark, R. D. III (1986). Conversion theory and simultaneous majority/minority influence: Can reactance offer an alternative explanation? *European Journal of Social Psychology, 16*, 305–309.

Mackie, D. M. (1987). Systematic and non-systematic processing of majority and minority persuasive communications. *Journal of Personality and Social Psychology, 53*, 41–52.

Moscovici, S. (1976). *Social influence and social change*. London: Academic Press.

Moscovici, S. (1980). Towards a theory of conversion behavior. In L. Berkowitz (Ed.), *Advances in experimental social psychology* (Vol. 13, pp. 209–239). New York: Academic Press.

Moscovici, S., & Lage, E. (1976). Studies in social influence III: Majority versus minority influence in a group. *European Journal of Social Psychology, 6*, 148–174.

Moscovici, S., & Lage, E. (1978). Studies in social influence IV: Minority influence in a context of original judgment. *European Journal of Social Psychology, 8*, 349–365.

Moscovici, S., Lage, E., & Neffrechoux, M. (1969). Influence of a consistent minority on the responses of the majority in a colour perception task. *Sociometry, 32*, 365–380.

Moscovici, S., & Mugny, G. (1983). Minority influence. In P. B. Paulus (Ed.), *Basic group processes* (pp. 43–64). New York: Springer.

Moscovici, S., & Neve, P. (1973). Studies in social influence III: Instrumental and symbolic influence. *European Journal of Social Psychology, 3*, 461–471.

Mugny, G. (1975). Negotiations, image of the other and the process of minority influence. *European Journal of Social Psychology, 5*, 209–228.

Mugny, G. (1982). *The power of minorities*. London: Academic Press.

Mugny, G., & Papastamou, S. (1982). Minority influence and psycho-social identity. *European Journal of Social Psychology, 12*, 379–394.

Mugny, G., Pérez, J. A., & Sanchez-Mazas, M. (1993, July). *Changing attitudes: Conflict elaboration and social influence in xenophobia and racism*. Paper presented to the Summer School "Migration Conflicts," Munster University, Germany.

Mullen, B. (1991). Group composition, saliance and cognitive representations: The phenomenology of being in a group. *Journal of Experimental Social Psychology, 27*, 1–27.

Nemeth, C. J. (1986). Differential contributions of majority and minority influence. *Psychological Review, 93*, 1–10.

Nemeth, C. J., & Kwan, J. L. (1985). Originality of word associations as a function of majority versus minority influence. *Social Psychology Quarterly, 48*, 277–282.

Nemeth, C. J., Mosier, J., & Chiles, C. (1992). When convergent thought improves performance: Majority versus minority influence. *Personality and Social Psychology Bulletin, 18*, 139–144.

Nemeth, C. J., & Rodgers, J. (1996). Dissent and the search for information. *British Journal of Social Psychology, 35* (1), 67–76.

Nemeth, C. J., & Wachtler, J. (1983). Creative problem solving as a result of majority versus minority influence. *European Journal of Social Psychology, 13*, 45–55.

Oakes, P., Haslam, S. A., & Turner, J. C. (1998). The role of prototypicality in group influence and cohesion: Contextual variation in the graded structure of social categories. In S. Werchel, J. F. Morabs, D. Paez, & J. C. Deschamps (Eds.), *Social identity perspectives* (pp. 75–92). London: Sage.

Pérez, J. A., & Mugny, G. (1987). Paradoxical effects of categorization in minority influence: When being an outgroup is an advantage. *European Journal of Social Psychology, 17*, 57–169.

Pérez, J., Mugny, G., Butera, F., Kaiser, C., & Roux, P. (1994). Intergrating minority and majority influence: Conversion, consensus, and uniformity. In S. Moscovici, A. Mucchi-Faina, & A. Maass (Eds.) *Social influence* (pp. 74–98). Chicago: Nelson Hall.

Personnaz, B., & Personnaz, M. (1992). Contextes intergroupes et niveaux d'influence. *Bulletin de Psychologie, 405*, 173–182.

Petty, R. E., & Cacioppo, J. T. (1981). *Attitudes and persuasion: Classic and contemporary approaches.* Dubuque, IA: Wm C. Brown.

Petty, R. E., & Cacioppo, J. T. (1986). The elaboration likelihood model in persuasion. In L. Berkowirz (Ed.), *Advances in experimental social psychology* (Vol. 19, pp. 123–205). New York: Academic Press.

Simon, B., & Brown, R. J. (1987). Perceived intragroup homogeneity in minority–majority contexts. *Journal of Personality and Social Psychology, 53*, 703–711.

Sorrentino, R. M., King, G., & Leo, G. (1980). The influence of the minority on perception: A note on a possible alternative explanation. *Journal of Experimental and Social Psychology, 16*, 293–301.

Turner, J. C. (1982). Towards a cognitive redefinition of the social group. In H. Tajfel (Ed.), *Social identity and intergroup relations* (pp. 15–40). Cambridge, UK: Cambridge University Press.

Turner, J. C. (1985). Social categorization and the self-concept: A social cognitive theory of group behavior. In E. J. Lawler (Ed.), *Advances in Group Processes* (Vol. 2, pp. 77–121), Greenwich, CT: JAI Press.

Turner, J. C. (1988). Comments on Doise's "Individual and social identities in intergroup relations." *European Journal of Social Psychology, 18*, 113–116.

Turner, J. C. (1991). *Social influence.* Milton Keynes, UK: Open University Press.

Turner, J. C., Hogg, M. A., Oakes, P. J., Reicher, S. D., & Wetherell, M. S. (1987). *Rediscovering the social group: A self-categorization theory.* Oxford: Blackwell.

Turner, J. C., & Oakes, P. J. (1986). The significance of the social identity concept with reference to individualism, interactionism and social influence. *British Journal of Social Psychology, 25*, 237–252.

Turner, J. C., & Oakes, P. J. (1989). Self-categorization theory and social influence. In P. B. Paulus (Ed.), *The psychology of group influence* (2nd ed., pp. 233–275). Hillsdale, NJ: Erlbaum.

Turner, J. C., & Oakes, P. J. (1997). The socially structured mind. In C. A. McGarty & S. A. Haslam (Eds.), *The message of social psychology* (pp. 355–373). Oxford: Blackwell.

Turner, J. C., & Onorato, R. S. (1999). Social identity, personality, and the self-concept: A self-categorization perspective. In T. Tyler, R. Kramer, & O. John (Eds.), *The psychology of the social self.* Hillsdale, NJ: Erlbaum.

Volpato, C., Maass, A., Mucchi-Faina, A., & Vitti, E. (1990). Minority influence and social categorization. *European Journal of Social Psychology, 20,* 119–132.

Wilder, D. A., & Thompson, J. E. (1988). Assimilation and contrast effects in the-judgements of groups. *Journal of Personality and Social Psychology, 54,* 62–73.

6

Social Influence, Social Identity, and Ingroup Leniency

William D. Crano

Three major theoretical developments have reinvigorated contemporary social psychology: the dual process models of persuasion; social identity theory and its variants; and the study of minority-induced and, by implication, majority-induced social influence. These advances have had their salubrious effect for many reasons, not the least of which is their undeniable relevance to the two central preoccupations of the discipline, social influence and persuasion, and intragroup and intergroup relations. It is my purpose in this chapter to propose a theoretical model, the leniency contract, that provides an explanation of past findings that appear inconsistent with earlier theories of minority influence and suggests new avenues for future research designed to lead to a better understanding of group-attributed social influence. The major predictive parameters of the model derive from the integration of the three central theoretical developments noted here. Given the leniency model's dependence on these disparate building blocks, the proffered approach has the potential to foster an integration of fundamental elements of social psychology that, heretofore, have remained mutually and resolutely incommunicado.

From its inception, social psychology has divided its focus between individualistic and group concerns (Jones, 1998). Arguably, overconcentration on one research strand at the expense of the other may have retarded progress in the underrepresented subfield. Rarely mentioned but equally arguable is the proposition that supposed overconcentration in the favored subfield may have inordinately accelerated progress, thereby offsetting the resultant losses incurred in the other. As such, it is difficult, if not impossible, to calculate the net gain or loss attributable to such swings of interest to the discipline as a whole. Recent commitments (or overcommitments) by the social psychology community to more individualistic, social-cognitive considerations may indeed have suppressed potential progress in research on social groups. While large, the talent pool of excellent researchers in social psychology is, after all, finite. This overcommitment should not be seen as an opportunity lost, however. The knowledge gained by the social-cognitive research community is valuable in its own right, and may also have important ramifications for the study of groups and group processes. As such, imbalances of research commitments in competing subsectors of the field may be adjudged regrettable only in the short run, if at all.

Theoreticians have commented on the ebb and flow of interest in the quintessentially social concerns of social influence and intergroup relations (e.g., McGuire, 1985), but only rarely could their observations be interpreted as being optimistic about their integration or cross-fertilization, largely because there was so little communication between the branches of the social psychological tree. As such, the possibility of a constructive fusion appeared unlikely, perhaps even unfeasible. True to form, the three important developments noted here – dual process models of persuasion, social identity theory, and majority/minority influence theories – have proceeded more or less independently, with some noteworthy exceptions (Turner, 1991). A central premise of this chapter is that their incipient integration may provide the basis for major theoretical advance. My goal in this chapter is to suggest one specific variant of an integrative model of this type. To facilitate developing this theoretical integration, important and relevant features of the three central elements of contemporary social psychology are presented briefly. Given the aims of this chapter, special emphasis is laid on the minority influence literature, as it is the focus of the model to be detailed and discussed. Nonetheless, the relevance of the observations presented for the other critical areas under consideration should be evident as well.

Dual Process Models

One of the leading dual process exemplars, the elaboration likelihood model (ELM) of Petty and Cacioppo (1986a, 1986b) is remarkable in its resemblance to, dependence upon, and expansion of, the pioneering work of Hovland and his associates (e.g., Hovland, Janis, & Kelley, 1953; Sherif & Hovland, 1961; Hovland & Weiss, 1951; Janis & Hovland, 1959). In developing their model, Petty and Cacioppo appended two important considerations to Hovland's basic message-learning framework, and in the process produced a predictive device that has changed the way social psychologists think about the process of persuasion. The additions are a strong focus on a target's motivation to work through or elaborate a message, and the strength of the message being elaborated. Message strength in the ELM refers to the persuasive power of the communication delivered by source to target. There continues to be controversy about the proper way of conceptualizing and operationalizing message strength (e.g., Mongeau & Stiff, 1993), and the necessity of two processes versus a single process of change (Kruglanski, Thompson, & Spiegel, 1999). Even so, it remains the case that adding elaboration motivation and message strength to the predictive equation has had a profound and positive effect on the accuracy of the prediction of acquiescence or resistance to persuasion. The importance of the dual process models has been discussed earlier and so will not be reiterated here. It is sufficient to say that these models, in addition to stimulating mountains of new, interesting, and valuable research, also may be used in retrospect to explain unexpected faults in the topology of prior years' research landscape (e.g., Petty & Wegener, 1998). As will be shown, features of the dual process approach also augment the predictive model under present consideration, the leniency contract.

An important augmentation of Hovland's approach is the ELM's emphasis on motivation to elaborate a message as prerequisite to predicting (and understanding) targets' responses to persuasive communications. Though certainly present in Hovland's model, motivation (and ability) to elaborate was not strongly emphasized. Motivation to understand is a notable feature of the dual process models (see also Chaiken's, 1987, heuristic-systematic approach). Theoretical emphasis on motivation to process (and thus, understand) has important ramifications for a host of issues in contemporary influence research, including the controversy surrounding the effects of self-interest or vested interest on attitude–behavior consistency (Crano, 1995, 1997a, 1997b; Crano & Prislin, 1995; Sivacek & Crano, 1982), and the consequence of attitude strength on the persistence of beliefs, and their resistance to counterattitudinal communication (Petty & Krosnick, 1995). This factor also has an important bearing on social influence in minority and majority influence contexts (Crano & Chen, 1998).

Social Identity and Intragroup Relations

Even a cursory review of social psychology as practiced in Europe and North America reveals the importance the field attaches to issues of social identity. The theory of social identity (e.g., Tajfel, 1979, 1982; Tajfel, Billig, Bundy, & Flament, 1971; Tajfel & Turner, 1986) and its issue, self-categorization theory

(Turner, Hogg, Oakes, Reicher, & Wetherell, 1987), are centered on the fundamentally human concerns of identity and belongingness, and hold that we come to know who we are, at least in part, as a consequence of our memberships in diverse social groups. If our group memberships are so central to identity, it stands to reason that our relationships with our membership and, especially, our reference groups would have critically important implications for behavior (Dobbs & Crano, in press; Kelley, 1952; Turner, 1991). Threats to the group should incite active defense. The more important the group to the self, the more vigorous will be the self in the group's defense. Similarly, if great value is derived from a particular group membership, then the threat of ostracism from the group should cause not only consternation but also energetic attempts to divine ways of avoiding exile or exclusion. These defensive behaviors may involve conversion, that is, attempts to change the group to one's own way of thinking, or subterfuge, that is, a deliberate deceit enacted to afford the appearance of compliance and orthodoxy. Of course, if the group is not highly valued, if it does not play a fundamental role in one's self-definition, it is not in a particularly powerful position to lay on threats. If it does, the response to the group is more likely to be rejection and derogation than compliance. Wise groups, groups that persist across time, pick their fights carefully and avoid skirmishes whose ultimate effect is to cause members to seek identity definition elsewhere.

This is not to suggest that the typical social group that serves as an identity-maker for the individual is necessarily monolithic in its demands for conformity or uniformity. On the basis of considerable observation and research, it seems reasonable to posit that most groups, except the most extreme, do not make strong demands for orthodoxy on all issues, even on issues that are obviously relevant to group interests. Members are not constantly forced to toe the line; indeed, they may hold a variety of positions on a variety of issues, so long as the position does not threaten the continued existence or raison d'être of the group. Degrees of allowable latitude may well vary from group to group, but in general, intragroup research regarding allowable beliefs and behaviors suggests that most enduring groups do not play the role of the stern totalitarian taskmaster in terms of required beliefs and behaviors (Quattrone, 1986; Quattrone & Jones, 1980) unless the group is under considerable external threat (Doosje, Ellemers, & Spears, 1995; Haslam & Oakes, 1995; Simon, Pantaleo, & Mummendey, 1995). To do otherwise would raise to intolerable levels the risk of defection. Views regarding the openness of different groups to discrepancies from absolute orthodoxy probably vary as a consequence of membership status, time in the group, and so on, as suggested by Worchel (1998; Worchel, Grossman, & Coutant, 1994).

Variations of (attitudinal) positions within one's membership or reference group are seen as common and not particularly troublesome except, again, at the extremes. We are familiar with the groups to which we belong, and from which we take our identity. As such, we also are familiar with the range of opinions that exist within the group on all but the most central, group defining, beliefs. We expect ingroup diversity because diversity is consistent with our own past histories of group involvement.

We assume less variation in the belief systems of outgroup members. Outgroups are likely to be seen as more unidimensional in their belief systems, in part because we know less about them (Brewer & Brown, 1998). They are outgroups partly because they are out of our range of experience. As such, we are more likely to impute a more simple structure to them, and to assume that outgroup members are more likely to think alike, even on issues of little moment. Whether their more monolithic views are antithetical to ours is for present purposes irrelevant. Holding this simplistic picture allows ingroup members to categorize the outgroup in black and white, with very little shading. This process facilitates stereotyping, which makes fewer demands on our miserly cognitive systems than a more differentiated and integrated perspective (Fiske, 1998; Gilbert, 1998). As will be shown, the imputations we make about the belief systems of ingroups and outgroups, and the values we place on these groups as a consequence of our membership or non-membership in them, make for very different responses to their calls for belief and behavior change. Before we explore these response divergences and their consequences, it is reasonable to consider in broad outline some of the important regularities arising from the study of minority influence.

Minority Influence

Serge Moscovici's research on minorities signaled an important and generative turn for social psychology. Moscovici focused on the differential impact of minority groups on the beliefs and behaviors of the majority. In an impressive series of studies initiated more than 30 years ago, Moscovici, Lage, and Naffrechoux (1969) discovered that targets' responses to minority influence were decidedly different from those of individuals under majority change pressure. Later research was to replicate and extend his findings (e.g., Moscovici & Lage, 1976, 1978; Moscovici & Personnaz, 1980, 1991), which were summarized in a succession of stimulating, titillating, and, for the times, iconoclastic reviews (e.g., Moscovici, 1974, 1976, 1980, 1985a, 1985b; Moscovici, Mucchi-Faina, & Maass, 1994; Moscovici & Mugny,

1983). Moscovici postulated that majority influence was direct and immediate, but not persistent. The majority could induce change, but its effects did not last, nor did they generalize to related beliefs. Minority influence, on the other hand, was expected to be indirect, delayed, and persistent.

A distinguishing feature of this theoretical position was the insistence on differentiating compliance from conversion. Moscovici was justifiably sensitive to the problems that could arise when these different processes were treated as isomorphic. As has been documented elsewhere (see Crano, in press, 2000), there is a long-standing tradition in social psychology to commingle and confound compliance and conversion when considering social influence. As Festinger (1953) pointed out nearly a half-century ago, this inauspicious coupling can cause considerable confusion. More than merely making a methodological point, Moscovici's insistence on the distinction between compliance and conversion is critical to his theoretical vision. In his scheme, majorities persuade through threats of censure and ostracism. The social pressure they bring to bear to compel members to acquiesce to the will of the group can be formidable, but it is temporary. When majority surveillance is relaxed, the pressure is off, and the old belief or behavior returns because nothing but appearances are changed by the normative social pressure (Deutsch & Gerard, 1955) of the majority.

Minority influence, on the other hand, was seen as persistent, but change in the direction advocated by the minority was expected only after a delay. Moscovici's model assumes that the minority can produce immediate change, but only on beliefs that are associated with, not identical to, the focus of its arguments. Given this set of expectations, it is critical to measure both immediate and long-term conformity to the (majority or minority) influence source, and attitudes on the central, targeted, issue along with attitudes toward objects that may be associated with, but are not identical to, the attitude object under persuasive attack.

Differences in temporal stability of change to minority and majority sources are a function of an assumed difference in the pressures the change agents bring on line in their attempt to influence. Moscovici reasoned that disagreement with the majority could be very threatening, because it called to mind the negative interpersonal ramifications of deviance. These negative features prompt targets to move toward the majority's position. However, this change of position is motivated by a need to avoid censure; it is not the result of message elaboration and acceptance. In Festinger's (1953) terms, public compliance, not private acceptance (conversion), characterizes responses to majority influence pressure.

In theory, the minority prevails in an entirely different way. Almost by definition, the persuasive ingroup minority position is novel and unexpected. Owing to these features of the message itself, (ingroup) targets are motivated to understand how others who are so like themselves can hold deviant views. To achieve this understanding, the targets must process and comprehend the minority's message. In other words, they must elaborate the persuasive communication, "to see what the minority saw" (Moscovici, 1980, p. 215). Such elaboration is the fundamental basis of minority influence. Nemeth (1986) has suggested that minorities stimulate divergent thinking, and DeDreu and DeVries (1996) have supported her hypothesis. This position is consistent with, and extends, the idea that message elaboration is central to minority influence. In Nemeth's view, the minority's message is not only elaborated, it is elaborated openmindedly, in a fashion that is likely to generate links to other ideas.

Clarifications and Extensions

Research over the years has provided substantial, but not unequivocal, support for Moscovici's hypotheses. The "older" research, that is, that which appears in the valuable meta-analysis by Wood and her colleagues (Wood, Lundgren, Ouellette, Busceme, & Blackstone, 1994), generally supports Moscovici's predictions regarding the effects of the majority on the minority. Majority influence often is direct, immediate, and short-lived. However, Wood et al. (1994) found the older research on minority influence somewhat less obliging. In general, and as predicted, Wood's review suggested that direct minority influence is rarely observed. On the other hand, indirect minority influence does occur, but its effect size vis-à-vis that found in response to majority influence is not as large as we might expect on the basis of theory.

Possibly as a result of his long-term association with Tajfel, Moscovici's approach, with its emphasis on the identification of influence sources as being of majority and minority status, explicitly obligates us to consider the social group as an essential feature of the influence process. The relational feature of Moscovici's work creates an important bridge between social influence and group process concerns, the yin and yang of social psychology, and advances us far beyond the classic and undeniably important work of Asch (1951, 1956) and even Sherif (1935, 1936). Furthermore, his insistence on the importance of the group in determining the outcome of social influence processes opens his work to the insights of social identity theory (e.g., Abrams & Hogg, 1990; Hogg & Abrams, 1988; Turner, 1991).

To take advantage of Moscovici's insights, however, it is important that we be clear in our description of ingroup and outgroup, majority and minority. Let us consider opinion minorities, subgroups within the larger collective that hold a position somewhat at odds with that of the bulk of the group's members. The fact that the minority faction of the larger group holds a position at odds with the majority does not make the minority an outgroup. Minority and outgroup are not synonymous, but too often in the literature of minority research the terms are used interchangeably. This distinction, like that of compliance and conversion, is not only important, but all too often blurred. The superordinate group containing both majority and minority factions may be a reference or membership group for both factions; from the perspective of the minority, that is, the majority may be ingroup, just as the minority may be ingroup from the perspective of the majority. The designation *outgroup* should be reserved for organized collectives that perceivers view as not included in, and sometimes antithetical to, the set of persons that comprises their membership and reference groups.

Moscovici's implicit linkage of group membership or social identity to the persuasion process is the pivotal and irreplaceable insight of his theory of minority (and majority) influence. Indeed, predictions of the success or failure of an influence attempt are conditioned largely on group membership considerations. This is a major theoretical advance. However, the approach falls short in its relative neglect of the cognitive processes that individuals may engage when responding to persuasive stress. From the standpoint of the sociology of science, the relative neglect of this fundamentally North American concern is understandable; at the time of the theory's development, Moscovici was not a strong advocate of North American social science. Nonetheless, as the past 30 years of research have demonstrated, the obdurate avoidance of cognitive social psychology did not advance the explanatory power of the model. As will be shown, adding considerations of cognitive process to the equation makes possible the development of a model that more powerfully maps onto the data pattern of the field.

To maximize the predictive power resident in Moscovici's insights requires integrating them with results of the social cognition laboratory. We must delineate carefully the (identity-relevant) features of the influence agent while simultaneously attending to the cognitive processes activated by these features in persuasion. This dual focus on social group and social cognition is not characteristic of much contemporary research in social influence. Rarely are defining aspects of the minority (or majority) specified in other than a gross numeric sense (but see Wood, Pool, Leck, & Purvis, 1996), and this is an important lapse (Crano, 1993, 1994). Without such information the relevance of the minority or majority to the target's self-definition cannot be known, and the contribution of social identity theory in predicting the power of the influence agent is lost. Similarly, measuring the cognitive processes activated in response to a minority-attributed or majority-attributed counterattitudinal communication is not common, though Baker and Petty (1994) and De Dreu and De Vries (1993, 1996), among others, supply good examples of how this can be done. The utility of these additions to the basic model becomes evident when we consider research published after the meta-analytic summary of Wood et al. (1994). These later studies produced results that are clearly contrary to the predictions of Moscovici's standard model. For example, although considerable research has disclosed immediate short-term change in response to the majority, as predicted by the theory, some studies (e.g., Baker & Petty, 1994; Crano & Chen, 1998; Mackie, 1987) have found persistent majority influence effects, or no effects at all, unless the ingroup majority is brought under severe attack (Alvaro & Crano, 1997). Similarly, the standard model holds that minorities will stimulate delayed or indirect changes. Sometimes these expectations are confirmed, but as Wood et al. (1994) have shown, they often are not. Furthermore, the theory does not specify when indirect attitude change, delayed focal change, or both, will occur. It is evident that a more detailed and theoretically elaborated model is necessary if we are to rationalize these inconsistencies, attain greater accuracy of prediction, and develop a better understanding of the ways in which majorities and minorities exert influence.

The Leniency Contract

The literatures of social influence, social identity, and intergroup relations in combination foster development of such a model. The leniency contract is based on a synthesis of these diverse considerations. In many instances, the leniency model produces predictions in accord with those of Moscovici. However, the leniency contract's integration of selected elements of the literatures of social influence, social identity, and intergroup relations supplies a strong social psychological foundation for predicting majority-based and minority-based persuasion effects (see also De Vries, De Dreu, Gordijn, & Schuurman, 1996). The advantage of this more inclusive theoretical approach is that it may produce more accurate predictions while simultaneously promoting a better understanding of the processes at work. Furthermore, its complexity facilitates investigating, understanding, and ultimately eliminating predictive failures, should they occur.

The basic requirement of the model, illustrated in Figure 6.1, is that the persuasive message is attributed to a source of majority or minority status. Theoretically, this attribution provokes a unique set of cognitive reactions that do not ordinarily arise when minority or minority source status is not revealed. These reactions occur because, by virtue of source attribution, the persuasive context has become interpersonal in nature.

Majority influence

The model holds that a target's reactions to the message of an influence agent of majority standing are conditioned on the message's relevance for the target's social identity. Identity relevance is judged in terms of the implications of compliance or resistance for place maintenance in the group from which the message originates. It is for this reason, parenthetically, that the leniency model holds that outgroups will have very little persuasive impact. There is no need to worry about maintaining one's place in the outgroup. The literature is almost overwhelmingly confirmatory of this expectation (see Alvaro & Crano, 1997).

The leniency model assumes that the assessment-of-relevance process occurs as a consequence of the mere specification of source as being of majority or minority status because, as noted, this characterization renders the influence context interpersonal and thus relevant to identity. This context is not like that of earlier research on source characteristics, which identified the source as possessing some special skill, trait, or ability that had little to do with the target's social group and consequent social identity. Hovland et al. (1953) provide many good examples of this earlier form of research, in which a source's expertise or trustworthiness were manipulated. That J. Robert Oppenheimer believed in the feasibility of nuclear submarines (remember, Hovland's research was undertaken in the early 1950s) might prove persuasive, but Oppenheimer's opinion would not necessarily impinge upon his target's sense of social identity. A source designated as representing the majority, however, is generally understood as representing the prevailing opinion on an issue within one's group. If the group is a consequential feature of one's self-definition (if it is self-relevant, in the language of the leniency model), then deviations from it may be threatening. To gauge the extent of threat, the target determines whether or not the majority is a legitimate source of information or influence on the contested issue. Is the issue relevant to group concerns? If the target deems the issue irrelevant to the group, outside the boundaries of its concern or authority, then the majority's

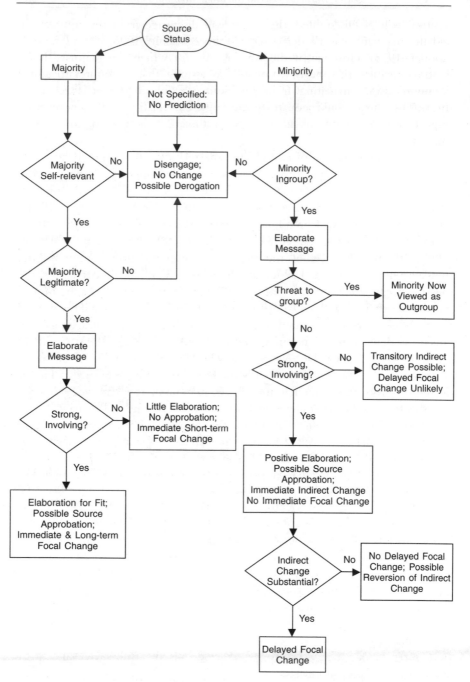

Figure 6.1 *Schematic diagram of the leniency contract.*

position will be discounted, the target will disengage from the interaction, and the majority may be derogated (Alvaro & Crano, 1996, 1997; Crano & Cooper, 1973). However, if the issue is one on which the majority has a legitimate voice, then it is reasonable to assume that a counterattitudinal communication emanating from this source would represent a relational threat. This threat could jeopardize the target's association with a potentially important element of self-identity. Such threats cannot be ignored with impunity.

The specific outcome of considering the relational threat posed by a dis-agreement with the majority will depend upon the judged legitimacy of the source as an agent of social pressure. As noted, if the issue is not one on which the majority is seen as having a legitimate voice, its impact will be attenuated; pressure will be adjudged inappropriate and the group will lose stature in the eyes of the target (Alvaro & Crano, 1996, 1997; Crano & Alvaro, 1998a, 1998b). However, if the issue is relevant to group concerns, the message will be elaborated systematically. If it is weak and unpersuasive, the message might still have an impact, given its (majority) source, but the impact will be short-lived and will not generalize to related attitudes. However, if the message is strongly argued, it may have both immediate and long-term effects, as demonstrated in earlier research (Baker & Petty, 1994; Crano & Chen, 1998; DeDreu & DeVries, 1993, 1996; Mackie, 1987). This result seems inconsistent with the predictions of Moscovici's basic model, but it is a logical derivation from the leniency model. As presented, the leniency contract specifies the conditions under which the majority is expected to have (a) no effect, (b) a short-lived effect, or (c) a lasting impact. These conditions require specification of issue self-relevance, perceived majority legitimacy, and message strength (Crano, 1997a, 1997b; Sivacek & Crano, 1982). This complex predictive pattern is not a feature of any other current theory of majority influence.

Minority influence

The leniency model also provides a theoretical explication of minority influence that accounts for both the delayed focal change and the variable indirect change effects that are a feature of the literature (Wood et al., 1994). When a source is characterized as being in the minority on a given issue, it is by definition deviant with respect to the larger group (Crano & Hannula-Bral, 1994). The importance of this depiction is that it suggests a consequential connection between source and target. Identifying a source as being of minority status describes not only features of the source, but suggests a relationship between source and target that may be of some importance. If this were not so, then describing a source or target as being of minority (or majority) status could not have any persuasive implications. The past 30 years of research on minority influence effects, however, demonstrates conclusively that majority or minority source status has important and variable effects on social influence.

With Moscovici, the leniency contract holds that the majority target will view the ingroup minority's persuasive position as novel or unexpected. The target will be motivated to understand the position, to understand why the deviants believe as they do. Unless the minority's position menaces the existence of the group, there is little apparent threat attached to the minority's position. They are not powerful enough to force their opinions on the majority, and by definition have little apparent power and little ability to administer sanctions for noncompliance. In its initial response to the minority, the majority analyzes any potential threats contained in its position. If the minority position threatens the very existence of the group, it will be ostracized and it will come to be viewed as an outgroup. As an outgroup, it may be derogated or ignored with impunity. By threatening the existence of the group, the minority has removed itself from the ingroup. As an outgroup, its message poses no threat to social identity, and hence can be ignored or denigrated. If the ingroup minority's message does not threaten the continued existence of the group, however, a very different set of accommodative responses are expected. Because it is the ingroup, the deviant minority will receive courteous treatment from the majority. This form of positive response is ultimately defensive, because it is designed to maintain group cohesion and stability, a highly valued goal of all groups. Accordingly, ingroup minorities will not be derogated for propounding their beliefs. Further, the model holds that as part of the lenient accommodation accorded the minority, their message will be elaborated with little counterargument or source derogation. Such an open response would appear to create the ideal venue for persuasion. From Hovland's time, we have known that the likelihood of change is bolstered if a target elaborates a strong message, cannot or does not counterargue, and does not derogate the source (Brewer & Crano, 1994; Crano, 2000). The leniency contract stipulates that this is precisely the majority's response to ingroup deviants – at least when the issue is not essential to the viability of the group. This prediction does not seem to jibe with reality, however. The open-minded and poorly defended elaboration of a counterattitudinal communication should result in continuous change of (the majority's) position, and, accordingly, continual group instability. Yet, it is obvious from considerable research on small groups that the majority's position often is quite persistent, and resistant to change. How can the theoretical claims of the leniency model be sustained?

To answer this question, we must consider one additional feature of the contract. All contracts specify a quid pro quo, and the leniency contract is no exception. In recompense for the lenient elaboration of the minority's message, the model posits a cost. That cost is the implicit understanding that no change will ensue from the persuasive interchange. This implicit agreement is a pivotal feature of the contract. It allows the majority to maintain its core beliefs and at the same time to assuage, or at a minimum, not alienate, the ingroup minority, which may be an important and substantial part of the group. Leniency thus ensures the viability of the group. So long as it is possible to allow a lenient response, the group has a chance to offset the potentially lethal consequences of factional divisiveness. Attitudinal variation on all issues but those that threaten the continued viability of the group may be tolerated. Research on intragroup relations suggests that such apparent beneficence is a common feature of cohesive groups (e.g., Brewer, 1979). The leniency model suggests the mechanism by which the group can tolerate some degree of freedom of expression while simultaneously protecting and maintaining the status quo.

On the surface, such a complex process appears to offer the best of all possible worlds, except for those members who, as minority voices, are truly intent on making an immediate change in the character of the group. This is not likely, but it is not to say that the minority cannot have an appreciable effect on the group's evolution. Although the contractual feature of the leniency model helps foster stability, it also offers a mechanism by which minorities can have an impact. The implicit agreement that majority group members will not change as a result of open-minded elaboration of the minority's position does not counteract the reality that pressures for change are introduced as a result of undefended message elaboration. Such change pressure does not simply dissipate. How is it subdued? To answer this question requires another, easily accepted, assumption. This assumption is simply that one's attitudes do not exist in a cognitive vacuum. That is, our beliefs are, to greater or lesser degrees, interrelated. If this is so, then it is possible that beliefs in close cognitive proximity to the critical issue of minority group contention may be susceptible to change pressure as a result of the majority target's lenient response. Theoretically, the focal belief is contractually unassailable. By the terms of the contract, that is, it will not – perhaps cannot – change. However, related beliefs, which we assume are in close cognitive proximity to the attitude under persuasive attack, will not be defended. The change pressure experienced as a result of the lenient response to the minority may be diffused via spreading activation to these related beliefs (Anderson, 1983). These related attitudes will be easy prey for attitude change because they are not protected via counterargument or other cognitive defenses. After all, why defend a belief that is not under attack? The leniency contract holds that it is in this way that indirect attitude change, a consistent feature of minority influence, comes about. If the minority's message is weak, such indirect change may prove to be transitory and unlikely to persist. However, spreading activation effects may be substantial when strongly argued persuasive messages are employed. Alvaro and Crano (1997) provide evidence consistent with this view. They first established via multidimensional scaling that two attitude objects (gays in the military and gun control) were proximal in multidimensional space. Auxiliary data collected along with this analysis suggested, interestingly, that participants did not believe the attitudes were strongly linked. An ingroup minority strongly arguing against allowing gay soldiers (a counterattitudinal position for the participants) had no apparent impact. However, targets' attitudes on the related object, gun control, moved in a direction consistent with the conservative thrust of the antigay message. This indirect attitude change was evident despite a total lack of change on the focal issue, and despite the fact that gun control was never mentioned in the persuasive communication.

Confidence in this predicted but nonetheless startling result was bolstered in a second study that reversed the direct and indirect attitude objects. In this experiment, Alvaro and Crano (1997) attributed a conservative gun control message to an ingroup minority. The message had no impact on students' gun control attitudes. However, it did have the effect of moving targets' attitudes toward a more conservative position on gays in the military, an attitude object that preliminary research had established as proximal to gun control in multidimensional (cognitive) space. The majority had little impact in either of the studies in this series. According to the leniency model, this null finding came about because participants did not believe that the majority group (fellow students at the targets' university) had a legitimate right to require compliance on either of the controversial issues – these beliefs were not viewed as defining features of student self-identity. As such, the majority was seen as an illegitimate source of influence, and was derogated for attempting to force compliance to its views. It is important to realize that perceptions of legitimacy are not a feature of minority influence. In the minority context, unexpectedness and the need to understand the ingroup's position drives elaboration, not the legitimacy of the source's position.

Persistent and delayed focal change

The leniency model provides a mechanism for delayed focal change, another consistent feature of the literature. If attitudes are interconnected in some way, then when an attitude is changed, those that are contiguous in cognitive space will be put under pressure to change as well. As such, indirect attitude change may cause delayed focal change if the focal attitude is cognitively proximal to the newly changed indirect attitude, and the indirect change is sufficient to destabilize the overall belief structure. Crano and Chen (1998) confirmed this prediction: When a minority source induced substantial indirect attitude change, delayed change on the focal issue was observed, but only among those who had been exposed to a strong message. If the indirect change was not substantial, however, or was not the result of strong message elaboration, then no delayed focal changes were observed. This link between magnitude of indirect change and likelihood of delayed focal change may help explain the variability of delayed focal change (or lack thereof) in the literature. If only modest indirect change occurs, or if it is not the outcome of the elaboration of a strong message, then it seems unlikely that the newly changed indirect attitude would have sufficient strength to pull the focal attitude along.

In Crano and Chen's (1998) research, the majority also had an effect. In this case, the issues were clearly relevant to targets' reference group, fellow students at their university. All the issues involved campus concerns that would have an appreciable effect on students' lives. As such, majority effects were expected, and observed. The majority provoked strong direct attitude change on an issue of high self-interest to the targets. This change persisted when the majority's message was strong; however, it did not generalize to the proximal (indirect) attitude. This result fits with the leniency model's supposition that elaboration of the majority's message is motivated by the need to fit in, not to extract the gist of the message (Crano, in press, 2000). If this is so, then it is unlikely that change in the focal attitude would foster change in the linked belief. What has changed in response to the majority's demand is not the core belief, but the manner in which one presents oneself to the majority. This presentational strategy would not affect the linked attitude, even though it might appear to be a major shift, and even though it might persist indefinitely, even in the absence of majority surveillance.

Summary

Across many studies, the leniency contract has been shown to account for both indirect minority-induced attitude change and delayed focal change. It provides a plausible explanation of the ways minorities and majorities persuade while simultaneously accounting for prior results in the somewhat uneven minority influence literature (Wood et al., 1994). The leniency contract is in accord with a changing emphasis in social influence research, a recognition of the central role of the group, and the social identity derived from the group, in social influence. Over the years, persuasion and social influence research has departed from its interpersonal roots. However, it is apparent that a simultaneous consideration of group identity, intergroup process, and message elaboration – the central building blocks of the leniency contract – fosters creation of a model of considerable depth and predictive power. With continual development, I am hopeful that this approach will provide the means to bring into mutual contact the two central concerns of the discipline, social influence and the social group.

NOTE

Development of this chapter was facilitated by a grant from the National Institute on Drug Abuse (R01 DA 12578-01) for which I am most grateful.

REFERENCES

Abrams, D., & Hogg, M. A. (Eds.) (1990). *Social identity theory: Constructive and critical advances.* New York: Harvester Wheatsheaf.

Alvaro, E. M., & Crano, W. D. (1996). Cognitive responses to minority or majority-based comunications: Factors that underlie minority influence. *British Journal of Social Psychology, 35,* 105–121.

Alvaro, E. M., & Crano, W. D. (1997). Indirect minority influence: Evidence for leniency in source evaluation and counterargumentation. *Journal of Personality and Social Psychology, 72,* 949–964.

Anderson, J. E. (1983). *The architecture of cognition.* Cambridge, MA: Harvard.

Asch, S. E. (1951). Effects of group pressure on the modification and distortion of judgments. In H. Guetzkow (Ed.), *Groups, leadership, and men* (pp. 177–190). Pittsburgh, PA: Carnegie Press.

Asch, S. E. (1956). Studies of independence and conformity: A minority of one against a unanimous majority. *Psychological Monographs, 70* (9), Whole No. 416.

Baker, S. M., & Petty, R. E. (1994). Majority and minority influence: Source-position imbalance as a determinant of message scrutiny. *Journal of Personality and Social Psychology, 67,* 5–19.

Brewer, M. B. (1979). In group bias in the minimal intergroup situation: A cognitive-motivational analysis. *Psychological Bulletin*, *86*, 307–324.

Brewer, M. B., & Brown, R. J. (1998). Intergroup relations. In D. T. Gilbert, S. T. Fiske, & G. Lindzey (Eds.), *The handbook of social psychology* (4th ed., Vol. 2, pp. 554–594). Boston, MA: McGraw-Hill.

Brewer, M. B., & Crano, W. D. (1994). *Social psychology*. Minneapolis/St. Paul, MN: West.

Chaiken, S. (1987). The heuristic model of persuasion. In M. P. Zanna, J. M., Olson, & C. P. Herman (Eds.), *Social influence: The Ontario symposium* (Vol. 5, pp. 3–39). Hillsdale, NJ: Erlbaum.

Crano, W. D. (1993). Context, categorization, and change: Consequences of cultural contrasts on compliance and conversion. In M-F Pichevin, M-C Hurtig, & M. Piolat (Eds.), *Studies on the self and social cognition* (pp. 248–257). Singapore: World Scientific.

Crano, W. D. (1994). Context, comparison, and change: Methodological and theoretical contributions to a theory of minority (and majority) influence. In S. Moscovici, A. Mucchi-Faina, & A. Maass (Eds.), *Minority influence* (pp. 17–46). Chicago: Nelson-Hall.

Crano, W. D. (1995). Attitude strength and vested interest. In R. Petty & J. A. Krosnick (Eds.), *Attitude strength: Antecedents and consequences* (The Ohio State University series in attitudes and persuasion, Vol. 4, pp. 131–157). Hillsdale, NJ: Erlbaum.

Crano, W. D. (1997a). Vested interest, symbolic politics, and attitude–behavior consistency. *Journal of Personality and Social Psychology*, *72*, 485–491.

Crano, W. D. (1997b). Vested interest and symbolic politics – Observations and recommendations: Reply to Sears (1997). *Journal of Personality and Social Psychology*, *72*, 492–500.

Crano, W. D. (2000). Milestones in the psychological analysis of social influence. *Group Dynamics: Theory, Research, and Practice*, *4*, 68–80.

Crano, W. D. (in press). Directed social influence. In J. P. Forgas, K. Williams, & T. Wheeler (Eds.), *The social mind: Cognitive and motivational aspects of interpersonal behavior*. Cambridge, UK: Cambridge University Press.

Crano, W. D., & Alvaro, E. M. (1998a). Indirect minority influence: The leniency contract revisited. *Group Process and Intergroup Relations*, *1*, 99–115.

Crano, W. D., & Alvaro, E. M. (1998b). The context/comparison model of social influence: Mechanisms, structure, and linkages that underlie indirect attitude change. In W. Stroebe & M. Hewstone (Eds.), *European review of social psychology* (Vol. 8, pp. 175–202), Chichester, UK: Wiley.

Crano, W. D., & Chen, X. (1998). The leniency contract and persistence of majority and minority influence. *Journal of Personality and Social Psychology*, *74*, 1437–1450.

Crano, W. D., & Cooper, R. E. (1973). Examination of Newcomb's extension of structural balance theory. *Journal of Personality and Social Psychology*, *27*, 344–353.

Crano, W. D., & Hannula-Bral, K. A. (1994). Context/categorization model of social influence: Minority and majority influence in the formation of a novel response norm. *Journal of Experimental Social Psychology, 30*, 247–276.

Crano, W. D., & Prislin, R. (1995). Components of vested interest and attitude–behavior consisency. *Basic and Applied Social Psychology, 17*, 1–21.

De Dreu, C. K. W., & De Vries, N. K. (1993). Numerical support, information processing, and attitude change. *European Journal of Social Psychology, 23*, 647–662.

De Dreu, C. K. W., & De Vries, N. K. (1996). Differential processing and attitude change following majority and minority arguments. *British Journal of Social Psychology, 35*, 77–90.

Deutsch, M., & Gerard, H. B. (1955). A study of normative and informational social influence upon individual judgment. *Journal of Abnormal and Social Psychology, 51*, 629–636.

De Vries, N. K., de Dreu, C. K. W., Gordijn, E., & Schuurman, M. (1996). Majority and minority influence: A dual role interpretation. In W. Stroebe & M. Hewstone (Eds.). *European review of social psychology* (Vol. 7, pp. 145–172). Chichester, UK: Wiley.

Dobbs, M., & Crano, W. D. (in press). Accountability in the minimal group paradigm: Implications for aversive discrimination and social identity theory. *Personality and Social Psychology Bulletin.*

Doosje, B., Ellemers, N., & Spears, R. (1995). Perceived intragroup variability as a function of group status and identification. *Journal of Experimental Social Psychology, 31*, 410–436.

Festinger, L. (1953). An analysis of compliance behavior. In M. Sherif and M. O. Wilson (Eds.), *Group relations at the crossroads* (pp. 232–256). New York: Harper.

Fiske, S. T. (1998). Stereotyping, prejudice, and discrimination. In D. T. Gilbert, S. T. Fiske, & G. Lindzey (Eds.), *The handbook of social psychology* (4th ed., Vol. 2, pp. 357–411). Boston, MA: McGraw-Hill.

Gilbert, D. T. (1998). Ordinary personology. In D. T. Gilbert, S. T. Fiske, & G. Lindzey (Eds.), *The handbook of social psychology* (4th ed., Vol. 2, pp. 89–150). Boston, MA: McGraw-Hill.

Haslam, S. A., & Oakes, P. J. (1995). How context-independent is the out group homogeneity effect? A response to Bartsch and Judd. *European Journal of Social Psychology, 12*, 469–475.

Hogg, M. A., & Abrams, D. (1988). *Social identifications.* London: Routledge.

Hovland, C. I., Janis, I. L., & Kelley, H. H. (1953). *Communication and persuasion.* New Haven, CT: Yale University Press.

Hovland, C. I., & Weiss, W. W. (1951). The influence of source credibility on communication effectiveness. *Public Opinion Quarterly, 15*, 635–650.

Janis, I. L., & Hovland, C. I. (1959). *Personality and persuasibility.* New Haven, CT: Yale University Press.

Jones, E. E. (1998). Major developments in five decades of social psychology. In

D. T. Gilbert, S. T. Fiske, & G. Lindzey (Eds.), *The handbook of social psychology* (4th ed., Vol. 1, pp. 3–57). Boston, MA: McGraw-Hill.

Kelley, H. H. (1952). The two functions of reference groups. In G. E. Swanson, T. M. Newcomb, & E. L. Hartley (Eds.), *Readings in social psychology* (2nd ed., pp. 410–414). New York: Holt, Rinehart & Winston.

Kruglanski, A. W., Thompson, E. P., & Spiegel, S. (1999). Separate or equal? Bimodal notions of persuasion and a single-process "unimodel." In S. Chaiken & Y. Trope (Eds.), *Dual-process theories in social psychology* (pp. 293–313). New York: Guilford.

Mackie, D. M. (1987). Systematic and nonsystematic processing of majority and minority persuasive communications. *Journal of Personality and Social Psychology, 53*, 41–52

McGuire, W. J. (1985). Attitudes and attitude change. In G. Lindzey & E. Aronson (Eds.), *The handbook of social psychology* (Vol. 2, pp. 233–346). New York: Random House.

Mongeau, P. A., & Stiff, J. B. (1993). Specifying causal relationships in the elaboration likelihood model. *Communication Theory, 3*, 65–72.

Moscovici, S. (1974). Social influence I: Conformity and social control. In C. Nemeth (Ed.), *Social psychology: Classic and contemporary integrations* (pp. 179–216). Chicago: Rand-Nally.

Moscovici, S. (1976). *Social influence and social change.* New York: Academic Press.

Moscovici, S. (1980). Toward a theory of conversion behavior. In L. Berkowitz (Ed.), *Advances in experimental social psychology* (Vol. 13, pp. 209–239). New York: Academic Press.

Moscovici, S. (1985a). Innovation and minority influence. In S. Moscovici, G. Mugny, & E. Van Avermaet (Eds.), *Perspectives on minority influence* (pp. 9–52). Cambridge, UK: Cambridge University Press.

Moscovici, S. (1985b). Social influence and conformity. In G. Lindzey & E. Aronson (Eds.), *The handbook of social psychology* (3rd ed., Vol. 2, pp. 347–412). New York: Random House.

Moscovici, S., & Lage, E. (1976). Studies in social influence III: Majority versus minority influence in a group. *European Journal of Social Psychology, 6*, 349–365.

Moscovici, S., & Lage, E. (1978). Studies in social influence IV: Minority influence in a context of original judgments. *European Journal of Social Psychology, 8*, 349–365.

Moscovici, S., Lage, E., & Naffrechoux, M. (1969). "Sleeper effect" and/or minority effect? Theoretical and experimental study of delayed social influence. *Cahier de Psychologie Cognitive, 1981*, 199–221.

Moscovici, S., Mucchi-Faina, A-M., & Maass, A. (Eds.). (1994). *Minority influence.* Chicago: Nelson-Hall.

Moscovici, S., & Mugny, G. (1983). Minority influence. In P. B. Paulus (Ed.), *Basic group processes* (pp.43–64). New York: Springer

Moscovici, S., & Personnaz, B. (1980). Studies in social influence V: Minority influence and conversion behavior in a perceptual task. *Journal of Experimental Social Psychology, 16,* 270–282.

Moscovici, S., & Personnaz, B. (1991). Studies in social influence: VI. Is Lenin orange or red? Imagery and social influence. *European Journal of Social Psychology, 21,* 101–118.

Nemeth, C. (1986). Differential contributions of majority and minority influence. *Psychological Review, 93,* 1–10

Petty, R. E., & Cacioppo, J. (1986a). *Communication and persuasion: Central and peripheral routes to attitude change.* New York: Springer-Verlag.

Petty, R. E., & Cacioppo, J. (1986b). The elaboration likelihood model of persuasion. In L. Berkowitz (Ed.), *Advances in experimental social psychology* (Vol. 19, pp. 123–205). New York: Academic Press.

Petty, R. E., &. Krosnick, J. A. (Eds.) (1995). *Attitude strength: Antecedents and consequences* (The Ohio State University series in attitudes and persuasion, Vol. 4). Hillsdale, NJ: Erlbaum.

Petty, R. E., & Wegener, D. T. (1998). Attitude change: Multiple roles for persuasion variables. In D. T. Gilbert, S. T. Fiske, & G. Lindzey (Eds.), *The handbook of social psychology* (4th ed., Vol. 1, pp. 323–390). Boston, MA: McGraw-Hill.

Quattrone, G. A. (1986). On the perception of a group's variability. In S. Worchel & W. G. Austin (Eds.), *Psychology of intergroup relations* (2nd ed., pp. 25–48). Chicago: Nelson-Hall.

Quattrone, G. A., & Jones, E. E. (1980). The perception of variability within in groups and out groups: Implications for the law of small numbers. *Journal of Personality and Social Psychology, 38,* 141–152.

Sherif, M. (1935). A study of some social factors in perception. *Archives of Psychology, 27* (187), 1–60.

Sherif, M. (1936). *The psychology of social norms.* New York: Harper & Row.

Sherif, M., & Hovland, C. I. (1961). *Social judgment.* (1961). New Haven, CT: Yale University Press.

Simon, B., Pantaleo, G., & Mummendey, A. (1995). Unique individual or interchangeable group member? The accentuation of intragroup differences versus similarities as an indicator of the individual self versus the collective self. *Journal of Personality and Social Psychology, 69,* 106–119.

Sivacek, J., & Crano, W. D. (1982). Vested interest as a moderator of attitude–behavior consistency. *Journal of Personality and Social Psychology, 43,* 210–221.

Tajfel, H. (1979). Individuals and groups in social psychology. *British Journal of Social and Clinical Psychology, 18,* 183–190.

Tajfel, H. (1982). *Social identity and intergroup relations.* Cambridge, UK: Cambridge University Press.

Tajfel, H., Billig, M., Bundy, R., & Flament, C. (1971). Social categorization and intergroup behavior. *European Journal of Social Psychology, 1,* 149–178.

Tajfel, H., & Turner, J. T. (1986). The social identity theory of intergroup behavior. In S. Worchel & W. Austin (Eds.), *Psychology of intergroup relations* (pp. 7–24). Chicago: Nelson-Hall.

Turner, J. C. (1991). *Social influence*. Milton Keynes, UK: Open University Press.

Turner, J. C., Hogg, M., Oakes, P., Reicher, S., & Wetherell, M. (1987). *Rediscovering the social group: A self-categorization theory*. Oxford: Blackwell.

Wood, W., Lundgren, S., Ouellette, J. A., Busceme, S., & Blackstone, T. (1994). Minority influence: A meta-analytic review of social influence processes. *Psychological Bulletin, 115*, 323–345.

Wood, W., Pool, G. J., Leck, K., & Purvis, D. (1996). Self-definition, defensive processing, and influence: The normative impact of majority and minority groups. *Journal of Personality and Social Psychology, 71*, 1181–1193.

Worchel, S. (1998). A developmental view of the search for group identity. In S. Worchel & J. F. Morales (Eds.). *Social identity: International perspectives* (pp. 53–74). London: Sage.

Worchel, S., Grossman, M., & Coutant, D. (1994). Minority influence in the group context: How group factors affect when the minority will be influential. In S. Moscovici, A. Mucchi-Faina, & A. Maass (Eds.), *Minority influence* (pp. 97–114). Chicago: Nelson-Hall.

7

Self-persuasion: An Alternative Paradigm for Investigating Majority and Minority Influence

Ernestine Gordijn, Nanne K. De Vries, and Tom Postmes

Examples of the effects of majority and minority support can be found in many situations. When discussing certain issues with friends, while watching television, when reading newspapers, or when taking positions in meetings, we are confronted with the fact that some people support our opinions and other people do not. Sometimes we will realize that a majority of people disagrees with us, and sometimes we notice that it is only a minority that does not share our position.

For many years now, researchers have investigated to what extent such knowledge of numerical support for one's own position and for positions of people who disagree with us influence our perceptions, judgments, decisions, attitudes, and behavior (for reviews see, e.g., Latané & Wolf, 1981; Tanford & Penrod, 1984; Wood, Lundgren, Ouellette, Busceme, & Blackstone, 1994; De Vries, De Dreu, Gordijn, & Schuurman, 1996). The influence of majorities and minorities has been studied both in small groups (for a review, see Levine & Russo, 1987; Levine & Kaarbo, chapter 11, this volume; Smith, Tindale & Anderson, chapter 9, this volume), and in situations in which majority or minority support for a certain (counterattitudinal) position is described to participants (e.g., Mackie, 1987; see also Crano, chapter 6, this volume). Furthermore, influence was studied in the case of perception, problem solving, decision making, and attitude change. A meta-analytic review of 97 experiments in which the differential influence of majority and minority support was examined by Wood et al. (1994) showed that recipients of information are motivated to align themselves with the majority point of view, while they want to differentiate from minorities. In general, majorities appear to be more persuasive than minorities, especially on measures of *direct* public and private influence. Minorities, in contrast, have been shown to be more persuasive on privately stated measures that are *indirectly* related to the content of the appeal.

The focus has thus been on the effects of numerical support on the recipient of information, in which both a point of view and underlying arguments are communicated. In some circumstances, however, recipients are actively involved in generating a basis for certain points of view. For instance, when people are preparing for a meeting and thinking about which point of view they will support, they might consider the different positions first by thinking about the pros and cons of each position. People could do this spontaneously, but it may also be more organized. For example, De Dreu and De Vries (1997) discuss the procedure of "devil's advocacy" as a form of institutionalized dissent in organizations. In this case, someone is asked to think of all the arguments against a plan with which everybody agrees. Also, sometimes one might find oneself in a situation in which a position has to be defended that one does not really agree with, on behalf of, for example, a political party that one represents or the company one works for. Other times people have to advocate a position that they do agree with, for example, when they are trying to convince their friends or colleagues. In all these cases, one may realize that the proattitudinal or counterattitudinal position one is defending is supported by a lot of people or only by a few. The question is to what extent such knowledge influences whether people are persuaded by their own arguments.

So, although the influence of majority and minority support has been investigated in many settings, the influence of numerical support on self-persuasion has not received a lot of attention. In the case of self-persuasion one generates arguments for a certain view after which one might be persuaded. In this chapter, recent research will be presented that tested different hypotheses concerning the effect of numerical support in the case of self-persuasion. We will also discuss in what way research on self-persuasion can contribute to our knowledge about minority and majority influence in general.

Self-persuasion

Self-persuasion was initially demonstrated in classic role-playing studies by Janis and King (1954). This research shows that participants who argue a counterattitudinal point of view (devil's advocacy) are more likely to be persuaded (by themselves) than when they are simply exposed to others' arguments that favor this counterattitudinal position (for a review see Eagly & Chaiken, 1993). In general, role playing leads to stronger attitude change towards the position one advocates, than mere reception of similar arguments.

Several explanations have been offered for this self-persuasion effect. Janis (1968), for example, argued that generating counterattitudinal arguments will increase the accessibility of arguments for this position, while arguments opposing this position are suppressed because they are not relevant to the task. Role playing therefore leads to active and biased scanning of a position, resulting in attitude change in the advocated direction, and more so than the reception of a message (which instigates a process of counterargumentation). The most prominent explanation, however, was provided by Festinger (1957) who suggested that self-persuasion is caused by dissonance reduction. He argued that advocating a counterattitudinal opinion leads to cognitive dissonance, which can be reduced by changing one's attitude. Self-persuasion will occur as a function of the strength of the inducement to comply with the experimenters' request to play a certain role. In the case of strong inducement, dissonance will not be experienced, and attitude change is unlikely to occur. However, in the case of weak inducement, there will be insufficient justification for complying with the request. In this case, one will reduce the dissonance experienced under such circumstances by changing one's attitude (Festinger, 1957). Exposure to a discrepant opinion of some other person will, in general, not lead to comparable high states of dissonance.

With these two explanations in mind, several properties of self-persuasion processes seem important. First of all, recent research on the influence of numerical support has tended to focus on the question of *when* people are capable or motivated to elaborate (e.g., Mackie, 1987; Baker & Petty, 1994; Bohner, Moskowitz, & Chaiken, 1995; De Vries et al., 1996; Crano & Alvaro, 1998; Erb, Bohner, Schmälzle, & Rank, 1998; see also several chapters in this book). In general, it can be concluded that (all other things being equal) minorities suffer a disadvantage relative to majorities because disagreement with a majority leads to a higher motivation to scrutinize their message. However, in a self-persuasion task participants are induced to elaborate intensively by the nature of the task. For example, Eagly and Chaiken (1993, p. 504) describe improvisational role playing (i.e., role playing by generating arguments oneself) as follows: "a context that probably encouraged role-players to give thorough consideration to the persuasive arguments generated and delivered. Such scrutiny of information resembles the type of processing that we have labeled systematic." Indeed, Janis's "biased scanning" approach suggests that generating arguments is akin to elaboration of arguments.

Elaboration refers to the extent to which people think about a certain argument or position, but elaboration also contains an element of transformation and refinement in order to improve the argument (cf. Greenwald, 1968). Therefore, a self-persuasion study provides an opportunity to address the question of what happens given that people elaborate, as no differences are expected in the intensity of elaboration (e.g., the number of arguments generated) as a function of numerical support.

Second, a self-persuasion paradigm is interesting with regard to the kind of arguments generated. Using the persuasive message paradigm, it has been demonstrated that numerical support not only affects the likelihood of elaboration, but also the nature of elaboration, that is, the kind of thoughts that people have (Nemeth, 1986, 1995; De Vries et al., 1996; De Dreu, De Vries, Gordijn, & Schuurman, 1999). That is, majority support is likely to produce convergent processing, which is the thought process that explicitly takes the source's position into account. According to De Dreu et al. (1999) such convergent processing leads to direct influence. Minority support, on the other hand, can produce divergent thinking, which is a thought process that focuses on multiple perspectives, including the perspective of the source of influence. De Dreu et al. (1999) showed that such divergent processing is more likely to lead to indirect influence. In a self-persuasion study, it is unlikely that there will be differences in the kind of arguments generated. In such a study, participants are asked to generate arguments in favor of the issue under consideration only. Therefore, they are likely to engage in convergent thinking, independent of numerical support, because they are asked to think about the arguments in favor of the position of the source only.

Thus, in theory, when people have to persuade themselves, both the intensity of elaboration, as well as the kind of arguments generated, are constant across conditions. If so, one can reduce the effects of factors that are known to have influence on elaboration (mainly motivation and capacity-enhancing factors such as numerical support), and examine other routes to persuasion and relevant variables. Therefore, a self-persuasion study allows the assessment of the influence of numerical support on attitude change over and above the traditionally investigated factors.

The Influence of Numerical Support on Self-persuasion

In what way will numerical support influence the extent to which self-persuasion occurs when advocating one's own or a counterattitudinal position? Gordijn, Postmes, and De Vries (in press) examined several hypotheses regarding the influence of numerical support on self-persuasion, including two hypotheses that were derived from dissonance theory. This theory argues that dissonance increases when one experiences more dissonant cognitions, and that dissonance may be reduced by attitude change. Since arguing for a counterattitudinal position (devil's advocacy) is likely to arouse dissonance, it could lead to attitude change. However, the realization that only a minority supports one's point of view may also trigger dissonant cognitions (Festinger, 1957, p. 179). Thus, to argue for a *counterattitudinal majority* position could cause more persuasion than to argue for a *counterattitudinal minority*, because majority support for an issue one disagrees with elicits more dissonance than minority support for the issue. In the proattitudinal case, participants should only experience cognitive dissonance when a minority shares their position. Therefore, arguing for a *proattitudinal minority* position should lead to more persuasion than arguing for a *proattitudinal majority* position.

However, alternative hypotheses can be derived from cognitive dissonance theory. Advocating a counterattitudinal position will cause dissonance when there is insufficient justification for it. It could be argued that advocating a counterattitudinal majority position is justified since the majority provides one with social support and validation of the advocated views (Festinger, 1954; Mackie, 1987). In this view, to argue for a counterattitudinal minority is less justified than to argue for a majority. Therefore, the second prediction is that arguing for a counterattitudinal minority should cause more dissonance, and thereby stronger self-persuasion, than arguing for a counterattitudinal majority. In the case of proattitudinal advocacy, dissonance is not likely to be aroused, because it is justified to argue for one's own position. Thus, numerical support is not expected to lead to differential influence in this case.

Hypotheses regarding the influence of numerical support on self-persuasion can also be based on research that examined the influence of numerical support. For example, the meta-analysis by Wood et al. (1994) has shown that people are motivated to align themselves with majorities and to differentiate themselves from minorities. If it is generally the case that majority viewpoints are more appealing, one has to predict that majority support will lead to more influence than minority support (both in the case of proattitudinal and counterattitudinal advocacy. Therefore, the third hypothesis is that a majority elicits stronger self-persuasion than a minority.

Finally, predictions can be based on the influence of *similarity* on social influence. In line with Festinger (1954), Turner, Hogg, Oakes, Reicher, and Wetherell (1987) argued that people are more likely to be influenced by others who are seen as similar to the self. People with a different attitude than oneself will be seen as more dissimilar to oneself (perhaps belonging to an outgroup) than those holding similar attitudes (perhaps belonging to an ingroup). Thus, if one is asked to advocate the position of a group of people which holds a counterattitudinal position, one will feel less similar to this group and, as a consequence, one will be less influenced in the direction argued for than when advocating a proattitudinal position.

The implicit causal link within the above argument can also be reversed. If the people one argues for are seen as relatively similar to oneself, one is more likely to follow them if they hold a majority position than a minority position, because the majority opinion is normative for the group (Turner, 1991; cf. Wood et al., 1994). Thus, in the case of proattitudinal advocacy, it is predicted that advocating a majority position will lead to more self-persuasion than advocating a minority position. However, when asked to be the devil's advocate for people who are seen as relatively dissimilar, it seems less likely that one is persuaded by the majority than by the minority (cf. Gordijn, De Vries, & De Dreu, 1998). According to Gordijn et al. (1998) the reason for this is that a large dissimilar group is more threatening to one's own group than a small dissimilar group. Therefore, in the case of counter-attitudinal advocacy, it is predicted that advocating a majority position leads to less self-persuasion than advocating a minority position.

Examining the Influence of Numerical Support on Self-persuasion

Gordijn et al. (in press) examined these different hypotheses in four studies. In the first study, participants, all students of the University of Amsterdam, were asked to generate arguments in favor of their own position or for a counterattitudinal position. They were told either that a majority of 80% of students of the University of Amsterdam supported the position they had to defend or only a minority 20% of the students. After generating the arguments they were asked to report their attitude. It was shown that advocating a proattitudinal majority position led to more self-persuasion (i.e., polarization) than advocating a proattitudinal minority position. Conversely, advocating a counterattitudinal majority position led to less self-persuasion than advocating a counterattitudinal minority position. Moreover, no evidence was found for differences in elaboration: The length of the appeals provided did not differ, nor did the time spent on writing them as a function of the manipulations. In addition, the content of the appeals that were rated on persuasiveness and originality by independent judges also did not differ depending on the manipulations. The second study, in which a different attitude topic was used, replicated these results. Thus, it appears that there is an influence of numerical support over and above the impact of elaboration.

What do the results imply for the different hypotheses? The first hypothesis, derived from dissonance theory, suggests that devil's advocacy for a majority causes more dissonant cognitions, and consequently, more self-persuasion, than devil's advocacy for a minority. This hypothesis is not confirmed: Results showed the opposite effect. On the basis of dissonance theory, it was predicted with respect to proattitudinal advocacy that arguing for a minority leads to more dissonant cognitions, and consequently, more self-persuasion (i.e., polarization), than arguing for a majority. This hypothesis is also not confirmed: Again, results were in the opposite direction.

Hypotheses derived from the "insufficient justification" explanation (an alternative explanation based on dissonance) suggested that devil's advocacy for a majority is more justifiable than for a minority. Consequently, advocacy for the counterattitudinal majority should cause less dissonance, and thereby less self-persuasion, than advocacy for a counterattitudinal minority. Results were in line with this hypothesis. With respect to proattitudinal advocacy, no differences in justification were expected, and therefore, numerical support should not affect the degree of self-persuasion. This hypothesis was not confirmed, however, because numerical support did have an influence in the proattitudinal case.

The third set of hypotheses was based on research findings that indicate a motivation to align with the majority and to differentiate oneself from a minority. This motivation should result in more self-persuasion when arguing for a majority than when arguing for a minority. This hypothesis was only supported in the case of proattitudinal advocacy. However, results were opposite to what was expected for devil's advocacy.

Finally, hypotheses derived from the "similarity" explanation with respect to devil's advocacy suggested that one would be less likely to embrace a position shared by a (dissimilar) majority than a (dissimilar) minority. In the case of proattitudinal advocacy it was predicted that one would rather associate oneself with a (similar) majority than a (similar) minority. The findings are in line with these hypotheses.

In sum, hypotheses derived from the view that one is motivated to align with the majority partially accounted for the results, that is, the proattitudinal self-persuasion effects. With respect to devil's advocacy, evidence was found to support the "insufficient justification" explanation. The "similarity" explanation was the only one to predict the complete pattern of results. If similarity moderated the effects of numerical support in the case of proattitudinal and counterattitudinal advocacy, the effects of proattitudinal advocacy (i.e., more influence of a majority than of a minority) should be replicated in the case of counterattitudinal advocacy when the group argued for is very similar (except for its opinion) to the advocate. Moreover, the effects of counterattitudinal advocacy (i.e., more influence of a minority than of a majority), should be replicated in the case of proattitudinal advocacy when the group argued for is very dissimilar (except for its opinion) to the advocate. This was examined in the two remaining studies by Gordijn et al. (in press).

In Study 3, the influence of similarity and numerical support in the case of counterattitudinal advocacy was investigated. Participants, all psychology students, were asked to argue for a counterattitudinal point of view that was supported by either a minority or a majority of other psychology students. In the low similarity conditions, participants were told that proponents and opponents of the issue under consideration not only differed with respect to their opinion on the issue, but also with respect to their political orientation. In the high similarity conditions, participants were told that opponents and proponents only differed with respect to their opinion on the issue under consideration, while there were absolutely no differences on other dimensions such as political orientation. The results of this study showed that when one advocated a counterattitudinal position that was shared by a dissimilar minority, self-persuasion occurred. When a dissimilar majority shared the position, no influence was found. These results are in line with the findings of Study 1 and 2 for counterattitudinal advocacy. On the other hand, when a counterattitudinal minority was said to be similar, arguing for its position did not cause self-persuasion. Rather, a counterattitudinal majority was influential if this group was perceived as similar. These findings are comparable to the findings for proattitudinal advocacy in Study 1 and Study 2. Thus, perceived similarity of the group argued for moderated the influence of numerical support in the case of self-persuasion. Moreover, in this study no differences were found for any of the elaboration variables (the same as used in the first study), indicating that persuasion occurs independent of the level of elaboration.

In the final study, the influence of similarity and numerical support in the case of proattitudinal advocacy was investigated. Moreover, in order to strengthen the manipulation of similarity, real groups, that is, political parties, were used to provide direct evidence for the social situation of the similarity effect as a property of ingroup and outgroup memberships. The participants were asked to advocate a position that they supported, but which was also supported by either a majority or a minority of the political party that they would vote for (i.e., similar group) or that they would never vote for (i.e., dissimilar group). It was shown that proattitudinal advocacy for the majority of a party that one would vote for was more self-persuasive than advocacy for a minority of a party one would vote for. However, the reverse was found in the case of proattitudinal advocacy for a party that one would never vote for: In this case a minority is more persuasive than a majority.

Once more, the differences caused by numerical support and similarity appeared not be the result of differences in elaboration. It seemed that the instruction to generate arguments for a certain position is motivating in itself, causing intensive elaboration independently of numerical support and the direction argued for (cf. Eagly & Chaiken, 1993, p. 504). If so, it could be argued that the self-persuasion paradigm provides the opportunity to keep elaboration more or less constant across conditions, and to look for influential factors other than elaboration, such as similarity between advocate and the people advocated for. In persuasion paradigms, such a variable would probably affect the intensity of elaboration itself.

Why are people persuaded after advocating the position of a similar majority or a dissimilar minority? It was argued that, unlike dissimilar majorities, dissimilar minorities do not impose a threat to one's group, which makes their influence more likely. This idea was examined in Study 4 by Gordijn et al. (in press). Evidence was provided that people feel more threatened when advocating for a large rather than a small dissimilar group of people. Moreover, it was shown that such threat mediated self-persuasion. It was further argued that, unlike similar minorities, similar majorities are perceived as normative (Turner, 1991; Wood, Pool, Leck, & Purvis, 1996) and provide validation ("consensus implies correctness"; see Axsom, Yates, & Chaiken, 1987), which accounts for their influence. However, research by Gordijn et al. (in press) did not provide direct evidence for these underlying processes. Therefore, future research should study such processes. For example, advocates could be directly asked or it could be manipulated to what extent they perceive the group argued for as normative for their own opinion, and to what extent the group argued for provides validation for their opinion.

Implications for Persuasive Messages Research on Minority and Majority Influence

What are the implications of these findings for other research that investigates majority and minority influence? Most research on the influence of numerical support on attitudes has investigated to what extent people process persuasive messages, and to what extent such processing influenced attitudes (e.g., Mackie, 1987; Baker & Petty, 1994; Bohner et al., 1995; De Vries et al., 1996; Crano & Alvaro, 1998; Erb et al., 1998). In this research it is argued that when people process information in a systematic manner, attitude change will occur. It is usually examined under conditions in which systematic processing will be likely. The current research suggests, however, that even under conditions of high elaboration, persuasion does not necessarily occur. That is, even under such conditions, persuasion will only be found when people perceive the majority source as relatively similar or the minority source as dissimilar and nonthreatening. Similarity to the source should therefore also be taken into account when examining the influence of numerical support in the persuasive message paradigm.

Gordijn et al. (1998, Study 2) examined to what extent participants were persuaded by counterattitudinal minority and majority messages as a function of similarity. It was argued that people are only persuaded by a counterattitudinal source that is relatively similar to the recipient. In this research, participants, who were all students of the University of Amsterdam, received strong counterattitudinal arguments that were either supported by a majority of 83% of students of the University of Amsterdam, or by a minority of only 17% of these students. Furthermore, similarity was manipulated in the same way as in Study 3 by Gordijn et al. (in press). When proponents and opponents differed only with respect to their opinion, that is, when similarity is high, positive influence was shown in the case of majority support and no influence in the case of minority influence. Furthermore, in line with the self-persuasion study by Gordijn et al. (in press, Study 3), the majority lost its influence when recipients were told that the source did not only hold different opinions than the recipient, but also was dissimilar to the recipient in other ways. In this case, a majority source is not more influential than a minority source (i.e., the pattern of influence is reversed, suggesting somewhat more influence of the dissimilar minority).

These findings imply that the persuasive message of a counterattitudinal majority source is only more persuasive, as evidenced by attitude change, when the source is perceived to be relatively similar. Yet, one may argue that most research has shown that counterattitudinal persuasive messages supported by a majority are more persuasive than when they are supported by a minority (e.g., Mackie, 1987; Baker & Petty, 1994; Gordijn et al., 1998, Study 1). How does this relate to research on self-persuasion that has shown that a counterattitudinal majority is more persuasive only when its similarity to the advocate is explicitly made salient? We would like to argue that when one is offered a counterattitudinal message that is supported by a certain faction of a group to which one belongs, one is inclined to perceive the source as relatively similar to oneself. In this case, an intragroup context appears to be salient (see also David & Turner, chapter 5, this volume): The counterattitudinal majority position is normative. On the other hand, when one is asked to advocate a counterattitudinal position which is supported by a certain population of a group to which one belongs, one is inclined to perceive the people advocated for as relatively dissimilar to oneself. In this case, an intergroup context appears to be salient. It is this difference in the way that supporters of the counterattitudinal position are perceived that seems to account for the reversal of influence on attitudes between the two types of research.

Some theories predict more processing and, as a result, influence on attitudes in the case of a counterattitudinal majority message than of a minority message, because the counterattitudinal majority position is unexpected (see Baker & Petty, 1994), but normative. We would like to argue that a counterattitudinal majority position is only unexpected, but normative, when recipients perceive themselves to be relatively similar to the source. Thus, theories that explain the role of numerical support on the influence of persuasive messages should take similarity to the source into account.

Implications for Small Group Research on Minority and Majority Influence

Research discussed in this chapter examined the influence of numerical support in anonymous situations in which one does not expect to encounter the people holding other views. Yet, there are many situations in which one is directly confronted with disagreeing people. Small group research has extensively studied how minorities respond to an opposing majority, and how majorities react to deviance (for an overview, see Levine, 1980; and several chapters in this volume). It has been shown that minorities within small groups are very likely to conform to the majority point of view. However, minorities within small groups also exert influence. For example, Van Dyne and Saaverdra (1996) showed how minorities within interacting groups stimulated divergent thinking of majority members. They further showed that groups with deviant minorities developed more original products compared to groups in which nobody deviated from the majority point of view (see also Nemeth & Kwan, 1985, 1987).

In what way would people be influenced when they are asked to defend a proattitudinal or counterattitudinal majority or minority position within such a small group? Will people still be likely to conform to the majority or will processes occur as described in this chapter with respect to self-persuasion? There are a number of differences between the anonymous situation that we described and the public situation within the small group. Most importantly, people will be likely to experience more social pressure, because they publicly have to defend the position, which might encourage conformity to the majority position. However, similarity between the different factions within the group may moderate such conformity. That is, people may only experience social pressures from people within the small group who appear relatively similar to themselves, especially when those similar people form a large faction. For example, it can be predicted that in a small group situation, such as a meeting between four employers and four employees concerning issues at work, people will feel most social pressure from the majority of people within their small subgroup, and will be most likely persuaded in such a case. The opinion of the majority of the subgroup to which they do not belong is less likely to be persuasive. However, current research suggests they could be persuaded by a minority of people of the other subgroup, because their opinion is less threatening. It would be interesting to study such small group processes. Moreover, it would be interesting to examine if similar results are obtained if people are asked to be the devil's advocate, by arguing contrary to their personal beliefs within such a small group.

More recently, research has started to focus on the influence of numerical support when anticipating interaction with the group (Levine & Russo, 1995; Zdaniuk & Levine, 1996). Before going to meetings in which decisions have to be made or opinions have to be formed, people will prepare themselves. They search for information and generate arguments which can be used to persuade others, and think about who might disagree with them. In particular, the number of people from whom they expect support will be considered. In line with this, this anticipation of numerical support has been shown to affect cognitive activity. For example, research by Levine and Russo (1995) showed that those who expected to be confronted with a disagreeing majority spent more time preparing themselves for the meeting compared to those who only expected resistance from a minority. Also, people who expected to be part of a small minority had more negative thoughts about their own point of view, and were more likely to change their attitude in the direction suggested by the majority (Zdaniuk & Levine, 1996).

What is not clear from this research is in what way similarity between the majority and minority would have an impact on cognitive activity and persuasion when anticipating interaction. On the basis of research presented in this chapter it could be expected that people are more likely to prepare themselves for discussions when their opponents are in the majority rather than in the minority in the case of high similarity, but also when their opponents are in the minority rather than in the majority in the case of low similarity. Moreover, in such a case they may be persuaded by the arguments they think of when preparing themselves. In future research the influence of minority and majority support on anticipated interaction should be examined, because it has interesting implications for group decision making and attitude change.

Practical Implications

Often people will find themselves in situations, such as meetings or discussion groups, in which they have to defend their position to others, while being part of a minority or of a majority. The findings of research regarding the influence of numerical support on self-persuasion imply that people are less convinced about their own ideas in such circumstances when realizing that they are defending a minority position. However, this will only be true when the other people are seen as relatively similar to themselves. When their opponents are seen as members of outgroups it is less likely that they will give up their own ideas. This suggests that if a majority wants to influence a small group of people, they should show that they are similar to the people they want to influence. On the other hand, if the minority group wants to be influential, they should emphasize the fact that they are dissimilar to the people they want to influence, and not threatening. In this case, the majority might be persuaded. Thus, supposing that two political parties have to decide about which decision has to be taken, the larger party is more likely to be persuasive when they show the smaller party that the two parties are alike. On the other hand, the smaller party should only be persuasive if it is able to show that the two parties are not alike. It would be interesting to investigate whether these opposing strategies for majority and minority groups work in "real life," for example, by analyzing notes of meetings.

Conclusion

In this chapter, self-persuasion was discussed as an alternative paradigm for investigating majority and minority influence. Recent research was presented that tested some hypotheses concerning the influence of numerical support in the case of self-persuasion. Furthermore, it was discussed in what way research on self-persuasion could contribute to our knowledge about minority and majority influence. The main conclusion is that a self-persuasion study provides an opportunity to examine the influence of numerical support on persuasion in the case of high elaboration. Under such conditions, persuasion is most likely to occur when a majority is perceived to be similar and a minority as dissimilar. Future research could examine other factors, such as the extent to which the source is seen as threatening, valid, or normative, that might be relevant for persuasion to occur.

REFERENCES

Axsom, D., Yates, S., & Chaiken, S. (1987). Audience response as a heuristic cue in persuasion. *Journal of Personality and Social Psychology, 53*, 30–40.

Baker, S. M., & Petty, R. E. (1994). Majority and minority influence: Source–position imbalance as a determinant of message scrutiny. *Journal of Personality and Social Psychology, 67*, 5–19.

Bohner, G., Moskowitz, G., & Chaiken, S. (1995). The interplay of heuristic and systematic processing of social information. In W. Stroebe & M. Hewstone (Eds.), *European review of social psychology* (Vol. 6, pp. 33–68). Chichester, UK: Wiley.

Crano, W. D., & Alvaro, F. M. (1998). The context/comparison model of social influence: Mechanisms, structure, and linkages that underlie indirect attitude change. In M. Hewstone & W. Stroebe (Eds.). *European review of social psychology* (Vol. 8, pp. 175–188). Chichester, UK: Wiley.

De Dreu, C. K. W., & De Vries, N. K. (1997). Minority dissent in organizations. In C. K. W. De Dreu & E. Van de Vliert (Eds.), *Using conflict in organizations* (pp. 72–86). London: Sage.

De Dreu, C. K. W., De Vries, N. K., Gordijn, E. H., & Schuurman, M. S. (1999). Effects of convergent–divergent processing on attitude change towards majority and minority supported arguments. *European Journal of Social Psychology, 29*, 329–348.

De Vries, N. K., De Dreu, C. K. W., Gordijn, E., & Schuurman, M. (1996). Majority and minority influence: A dual role interpretation. In W. Stroebe & M. Hewstone (Eds.), *European review of social psychology* (Vol. 7, pp. 145–172). Chichester, UK: Wiley.

Eagly, A. H., & Chaiken, S. (1993). *The psychology of attitudes*. Fort Worth, TX: Harcourt Brace Jovanovich.

Erb, H., Bohner, G., Schmälzle, K., & Rank, S. (1998). Beyond conflict and discrepancy: Cognitive bias in minority and majority influence. *Personality and Social Psychology Bulletin, 24*, 620–633.

Festinger, L. (1954). A theory of social comparison processes. *Human Relations, 7*, 117–140.

Festinger, L. (1957). *A theory of cognitive dissonance.* Evanston, IL: Row, Peterson.

Gordijn, E. H., De Vries, N. K., & De Dreu, C. K. W. (1998). *The influence of counterattitudinal numerical support on persuasion: The role of information processing and identification with the source.* Unpublished manuscript.

Gordijn, E. H., Postmes, T., & De Vries, N. K. (in press). Advocate of the devil or advocate of oneself: The effects of pro- and counterattitudinal argumentation and numerical support on self persuasion. *Personality and Social Psychology Bulletin.*

Greenwald, A. G. (1968). Cognitive learning, cognitive response to persuasion, and attitude change. In A. G. Greenwald, T. C. Brock, & T. M. Ostrom (Eds.), *Psychological foundations of attitudes* (pp. 147–170). New York: Academic Press.

Janis, I. L. (1968). Attitude change via role playing. In R. P. Abelson, E. Aronson, W. J. McGuire, T. M. Newcomb, M. J. Rosenberg, & P. H. Tannenbaum (Eds.), *Theories of cognitive consistency: A source book* (pp. 810–818). Chicago: Rand McNally.

Janis, I. L., & King, B. T. (1954). The influence of role playing on opinion change. *Journal of Abnormal and Social Psychology, 49,* 211–218.

Latané, B., & Wolf, S. (1981). The social impact of majorities and minorities. *Psychological Review, 88,* 438–453.

Levine, J. M. (1980). Reaction to opinion deviance in small groups. In P. B. Paulus (Ed.), *Psychology of group influence* (pp. 375–430). Hillsdale, NJ: Erlbaum.

Levine, J. M., & Russo, E. M. (1987). Majority and minority influence. In C. Hendrick (Ed.), *Review of personality and social psychology* (Vol. 8, pp. 13–54). Newbury Park, CA: Sage.

Levine, J. M., & Russo, E. M. (1995). Impact of anticipated interaction on information acquisition. *Social Cognition, 13,* 293–317.

Mackie, D. M. (1987). Systematic and non-systematic processing of majority and minority persuasive communications. *Journal of Personality and Social Psychology, 53,* 41–52.

Nemeth, C. J. (1986). Differential contributions of majority and minority influence. *Psychological Review, 93,* 23–32.

Nemeth, C. J. (1995). Dissent as driving cognition, attitudes, and judgments. *Social Cognition, 13,* 273–291.

Nemeth, C. J., & Kwan, J. L. (1985). Originality of word associations as a function of majority vs. minority influence. *Social Psychology Quarterly, 48,* 277–282.

Nemeth, C. J., & Kwan, J. L. (1987). Minority influence, divergent thinking and detection of correct solutions. *Journal of Applied Social Psychology, 17,* 788–799.

Tanford, S., & Penrod, S. (1984). Social influence model: A formal integration of research on majority and minority processes. *Psychological Bulletin, 95,* 189–225.

Turner, J. C. (1991). *Social influence.* Pacific Grove: Brooks/Cole.

Turner, J. C., Hogg, M. A., Oakes, P. J., Reicher, S. D., & Wetherell, M. S. (1987). *Rediscovering the social group: A self-categorization theory.* Oxford: Blackwell.

Van Dyne, L., & Saavedra, R. (1996). A naturalistic minority influence experiment: Effects on divergent thinking, conflict and originality in work-groups. *British Journal of Social Psychology, 35,* 151–167.

Wood, W., Lundgren, S., Ouellette, J. A., Busceme, S., & Blackstone, T. (1994). Minority influence: A meta-analytic review of social influence processes. *Psychological Bulletin, 115*, 323–345.

Wood, W., Pool, G., Leck, K., & Purvis, D. (1996). Self-definition, defensive processing, and influence: The normative impact of majority and minority groups. *Journal of Personality and Social Psychology, 71*, 1181–1193.

Zdaniuk, B., & Levine, J. M. (1996). Anticipated interaction and thought generation: The role of faction size. *British Journal of Social Psychology, 35*, 201–218.

8

Conflicts and Social Influences in Hypothesis Testing

Fabrizio Butera and Gabriel Mugny

Introduction

How many times have we, as researchers, thought: "This other representative of the field has demonstrated the opposite of what my work shows. I must prove that he or she is wrong"? Of course, it is difficult to admit having such unfriendly and antiepistemic thoughts. However, it is not uncommon to think like this when coping with disagreement or conflict. This issue has been very well documented by sociologists of science, and Lemaine (1984) pointed out that in the scientific community social comparison is a very frequent phenomenon, that generally aims at acquiring "visibility."

What do conflict and social comparison – which are relational processes – have to do with science, which is, after all, a matter of reasoning and testing hypotheses? The idea that will be put forward in this chapter is that, in order to understand the mechanisms that underlie reasoning in general and hypothesis testing in particular, it is important to consider that people always reason for a purpose, surrounded as they are by people who sometimes agree but at other times disagree, and that therefore science never happens in an ivory tower but is most of the time a matter of social influence. On this basis, it becomes apparent that many mechanisms in reasoning and hypothesis testing that are generally seen as biases or errors when compared to normative theories (such as formal logic, laws of probability, etc.), can be understood as useful mechanisms when social needs such as the confrontation of viewpoints are taken into account. In this chapter we will show how conflicts that arise during social influence situations affect, and are affected by, reasoning strategies.

Hypothesis Testing and Confirmation "Bias"

Hypothesis testing has been extensively studied by both cognitive and social psychologists. The reason for such an interest is twofold. First, hypothesis testing is a central human activity, from everyday inferences (e.g., Kruglanski, 1980; Kruglanski & Ajzen, 1983) to inductive reasoning in scientific thinking (e.g., Mitroff, 1974; Tweney, Doherty, & Mynatt, 1981). Second, research on hypothesis testing has shown a peculiar systematic tendency toward confirmation: Individuals asked to test their hypotheses appear to do so most of the time through procedures aiming at providing support for these hypotheses, even in tasks where disconfirmation would be more diagnostic. After Wason's pioneer work (1960), this "bias" has been found in work on inductive reasoning (e.g., Mynatt, Doherty, & Tweney, 1977; Gorman & Gorman, 1984), deductive reasoning (e.g., Wason, 1966; Evans, 1982), and information selection (e.g., Snyder, 1981; Snyder & Swann, 1978), to name but a few tasks and situations (for reviews, see e.g., Evans, 1989; Holyoak & Spellman, 1993; Leyens, Dardenne, Yzerbyt, Scaillet, & Snyder, 1999).

The explanations that have been put forward to account for this "bias" (or "error") are as numerous as the researchers that have studied this phenomenon. However, three trends seem to be quite well accepted. One line of research considers the "confirmation bias" as a form of positivity bias in reasoning, because of cognitive difficulties in considering negative information. Evans, for instance, proposes an explanation in terms of "cognitive failures": "Subjects confirm, not because they want to, but because they cannot think of the way to falsify" (1989, p. 42). Another line of research explains that there is a general bias in information processing that leads individuals to focus on the first sufficient hypothesis, without taking into account the alternatives that could lead to the "true hypothesis" (McDonald, 1990; see also Green, 1990; Legrenzi, Girotto, & Johnson-Laird, 1993). The third line of research considers that, since people do not possess a "mental logic" (the capacity to use the rules of logic without having studied it, as proposed by the Piagetian tradition), disconfirmation in hypothesis testing is just too difficult. As Johnson-Laird (1983) proposed, taking alternatives into account needs several "mental models" to be built, which takes a great amount of working memory.

These lines of research nevertheless have a common ground: They seem to agree about the fact that confirmation as a "bias" is due to a lack of activation, analysis, and articulation of alternative solutions to a problem (cf. Gorman & Carlson, 1989; Green, 1990; Johnson-Laird, 1983; Kruglanski &

Mayesless, 1988; McDonald, 1990; Trope & Mackie, 1987). In fact, it has been noted that disconfirmation is indeed possible, but only when the reasoner is able to consider alternative solutions (Gorman & Carlson, 1989).

The question that arises from this work then, is why some people are able to activate cognitive mechanisms that can lead them to be less "biased." Is it a matter of acquired competences? Research on scientific thinking, showing that scientists can be just as biased as lay people, seems to reject this idea (e.g., Mahoney, 1976; Mitroff, 1974). The analysis that led to the research paradigm presented in this chapter considers that hypothesis confirmation and disconfirmation are reasoning processes that are specific to some particular social situations (Butera, Legrenzi, Mugny, & Pérez, 1991–92). Indeed, hypothesis testing most often takes place during situations of social confrontation, that is, in situations where one may be confronted by the alternative hypothesis proposed by someone else; this is particularly evident in the case of scientific reasoning. It thus appears that it is of utmost importance to study the conflicts that arise from these social influence situations in order to understand the differential use of confirmation and disconfirmation in inductive reasoning.

High-status and low-status source influence in inductive reasoning

The social psychology of influence has shown that exposure to a majority's model or proposal induces conformity (Moscovici, 1980) and cognitive functioning of a convergent type, that is, confined to the use of information at hand (Nemeth, 1986; Nemeth, Mosier, & Chiles, 1992). This means that the presence of a majority's proposal would induce individuals to use the source's hypothesis when formulating their own. Convergent thinking should then orientate people's reasoning to take into account only the characteristics of this hypothesis and its elements; thus, it is likely that individuals, when testing a hypothesis, would formulate positive examples, that is, examples that are compatible with the hypothesis under test. In short, individuals would be oriented toward the use of confirmation in social situations characterized by a consensus expectation leading to conformity to the majority.

Furthermore, research in social influence has shown that when a model is given by a minority source, individuals are not motivated to adopt it (Moscovici, 1980), because the source does not guarantee the validity of its proposal (Nemeth, 1986). Thus, in a problem-solving task, where individuals must come to a reliable solution, it is difficult to trust a minority source when assessing a judgment. The notion of divergent thinking (Nemeth, 1986) is useful to account for the cognitive processes occurring during problem solving when faced with a minority source. On the one hand, "minorities stimulate a greater consideration of other alternatives" (Nemeth, 1986, p. 25); in fact, several studies show that confrontation with a minority source actually induces a search for alternatives (Nemeth & Kwan, 1985; De Dreu & De Vries, 1993; De Dreu, De Vries, Gordijn, & Schuurman, 1999; Volpato, Maass, Mucchi-Faina, & Vitti, 1990). Moreover, a study by Huguet, Mugny, and Pérez (1991–92) suggests that minority influence implies an activity of decentration, that is, the induced possibility of taking into account several points of views when formulating a judgment. In the case of the formulation of a hypothesis, it is thus legitimate to think that individuals confronted with a minority's proposal would be less motivated to adopt it and would then be led to choose or formulate alternative hypotheses.

On the other hand, from an information-processing point of view, individuals exposed to minority influence "are stimulated to attend to more aspects of the situation" (Nemeth, 1986, p. 25). Nemeth suggests furthermore (1986, p. 28) that divergent thinking leads to a kind of information processing that can be described as more systematic (cf. Chaiken, 1980). The same idea underlies Moscovici's notion of validation, when he argues that confrontation with a minority source leads to a greater focusing on the issue under consideration in order to check the validity of one's own judgment as well as that of the minority's judgment (Moscovici, 1980, p. 215), and also in order to check the limits of the validity of a judgment (Mugny, Butera, Pérez, & Huguet, 1993).

The above implies that, in hypothesis testing, minority influence induces mechanisms that make it possible to question the limits of the validity of a hypothesis, and therefore the use of negative examples, that is, examples that are not compatible with the hypothesis under test. This in turn should favor the use of disconfirmation. Thus, the possibility of considering the existence of alternative hypotheses gives disconfirmation its necessary condition: the possibility of imagining a replacement solution (it would be absurd to test through disconfirmation the only available hypothesis). In short, individuals would be oriented toward the use of disconfirmation in social situations where the existence of alternative solutions is elicited by the opposition between one's own hypothesis (which it is not necessary to give up for conformity reasons) and the minority alternative hypothesis.

Majority and Minority Studies

In a preliminary study (Legrenzi, Butera, Mugny, & Pérez, 1991), participants had to discover the rule underlying a given number triad (e.g., 2-4-6). This task, devised originally by Wason in 1960, is one of the most widely used tasks for the study of inductive reasoning. It is an interesting task for the current purposes because, although using disconfirmation would be more diagnostic (as it makes it possible to increase the generality of tested hypotheses), confirmation is used by the large majority of participants. In our experimental setting, participants were asked to formulate a hypothesis and to propose a number triad for testing it. Before doing so, participants had been informed of the hypothesis ("Each new number is greater than the previous one") and of the triad proposed by either a majority (82%) or a minority (12%) of people who had already participated in the study. The triad proposed by the majority or minority source was either confirmatory (e.g., 8-10-12), or disconfirmatory (e.g., 12-10-8) with respect to the source's hypothesis. The results showed that, when formulating hypotheses, more participants used the source's hypothesis in the majority conditions (even if it was in order to reformulate it), whereas more participants formulated completely new hypotheses when the minority used a confirmatory strategy. As for the hypothesis–testing strategies, although confirmation was the dominant strategy in all conditions, more participants used disconfirmation when this strategy was proposed by the source (which is in line with the results of Gorman & Gorman, 1984). More importantly, when the source proposed confirmation for testing hypotheses, participants confronted with a majority almost never used disconfirmation, while participants confronted with a minority (those who proposed the highest rate of completely new hypotheses) formulated disconfirmatory triads more often than majority condition participants. The latter result occurred in spite of the fact that disconfirmation was proposed neither by the source, nor by experimental instructions. In a second experiment (Butera & Mugny, 1992), again a majority induced more hypotheses derived from its own hypothesis as well as more confirmatory examples than a minority did; moreover, a minority induced more participants to formulate completely new hypotheses and to use disconfirmatory hypothesis testing.

Taken together, these two experiments showed that individuals consider the majority's hypothesis as informative, since they use it more frequently to elaborate their own hypotheses; in contrast, when confronted with the minority's hypothesis, they elaborate new and original hypotheses. In hypothesis testing, confirmation is the most frequent strategy, but individuals confronted

Table 8.1 *Majority or Minority Source: Mean Number of Yielding (from 0 to 2) and Mean Number of Disconfirmations (from 0 to 4)*

	Majority		Minority	
	Unity	Plurality	Unity	Plurality
Yielding	1.74[a]	0.74[b]	0.78[b]	0.32[c]
Disconfirmation	0.31[a]	1.26[b]	0.98[b]	2.97[c]

Note: For each measure, means sharing the same subscript are not significantly different at $p < 0.05$.

with a minority use disconfirmation more than those confronted with a majority. These results suggest that confirmation would be more typical of confrontation with majority sources, while disconfirmation would occur when confronted with minority sources.

These intitial studies did not explain why this pattern of results was found. A subsequent experiment was designed to test the idea that confirmation would be more typical of confrontation with majority sources because they exert a pressure toward considering one single answer, disconfirmation would be more typical of confrontation with minority sources because they induce subjects to be open to alternative solutions (Brandstätter et al., 1991). This would explain why confirmation is so frequently found, since inductive reasoning is generally at work in very normative settings, whether the experimental setting of a laboratory or the actual functioning of a scientific research team.

An experiment was devised to test the hypothesis that a majority source induces more yielding and more confirmation because it produces a representation of the task in terms of unity, and that a minority source induces the consideration of alternative hypotheses and the use of disconfirmation because it produces a representation of the task in terms of plurality (Butera, Mugny, Legrenzi, & Pérez, 1996). In a 2 × 2 design, the first variable concerned the nature of the source (either a majority or a minority), and the second the representation of the task; with this variable, participants were told that the task allowed either one single correct answer (unity), or several possible answers (plurality).

Results showed (see Table 8.1) that the nature of the source induced differential effects, as found in previous experiments. Importantly, the representation of the task induced differential effects too, as this is supposed to be the mediating variable accounting for the source's effects. As for the correspondence between nature of the source and representation of the task, results show that participants confronted with a majority engaged in more yielding to the source's hypothesis and in more confirmation when the task was represented as unidimensional. Moreover, participants confronted with a minority engaged in a greater use of alternative hypotheses (different from those suggested by the source) and in more disconfirmation when the task was represented as allowing a certain diversity of solutions.

These results suggest that a majority source focuses hypothesis elaboration on its proposed model. Representation of the task in terms of unity induces a similar effect, as participants focus more on the source's model. These processes are more pronounced when the majority nature of the source matches the corresponding representation of the task, in which case informational dependence on the majority source produces imitation. This need for consensus renders the search for alternative hypotheses not only useless (Kruglanski, 1990) but also dangerous, as the focus on a single hypothesis necessitates its validity and therefore calls for a testing strategy that does not contradict it – confirmation. The effects attributed to majority influence in problem solving would then be mediated by a representation of the task in terms of unity, and would be less pronounced when plurality is allowed.

When the proposal of a problem-solving model comes from a minority, very few participants adopt its proposal and, when possible, they formulate more new hypotheses. The same happens when a representation of the task in terms of plurality is induced. This specifies that divergent thinking implies avoiding focusing on a single judgment. This idea is supported by the fact that the minority's effects are more pronounced in case of a correspondence with the representation of the task in terms of plurality. It is in this case that the highest rate of disconfirmation is found, which shows that the possibility of considering alternatives is a fundamental factor for a problem-solving procedure leading to validation, in the sense of a search for the validity and the limits of validity of the source's proposal as well as that of other possible alternatives. In this context disconfirmation is likely to be used, as it is no longer aimed at invalidation, but at integrating the alternatives.

These findings have interesting implications for group decision making; they actually show the finer mechanisms underlying the "groupthink" phenomenon (Janis, 1972). In fact, Janis showed that during group decision making, the presence of a single dominant position reduces the likelihood of appearance of alternative hypotheses, thereby reducing the likelihood of challenging a potentially bad decision. The above results demonstrated that when people are confronted with a majority in a context that allows one single answer, not only is the dominant (majority) position adopted, but the very process of reasoning is adapted (through confirmation) to produce a mindset that avoids taking alternatives into account. Groupthink produces confirmatory reasoning, which in turn reduces the likelihood of diagnostic decision making.

Competence and Uncertainty

Induction is a form of reasoning that is used in specific sets of problems, those that need a general law to be inferred from the observation of a regularity. The *conflict elaboration theory* (Mugny, Butera, Sanchez-Mazas, & Pérez, 1995; Pérez & Mugny, 1993, 1996) contends that when people are confronted with an influence source during problem solving, what is really at stake is aptitude. In fact, solving a problem shows mastery of intellectual or technical tools that assigns people to a certain hierarchical position on some competence scale.

When aptitude is at stake in a task, individuals are particularly motivated to give a correct answer, or at least the best possible answer (cf. Festinger, 1954). Therefore, when solving problems in a social influence situation, targets are motivated to estimate the probability that the source can be informative about the correct or the most adequate solution. According to conflict elaboration theory, two different mechanisms are at work depending on the source's attributed competence. If the source is an expert, a competent source, its solution will be regarded as an *informational support*: Expertise guarantees validity (cf. Chaiken, 1980). This would induce imitation, with little task processing, since the expert source's answer is adopted on the basis of the guarantee given by the expert's (high) status. If the source is a novice, a low-competence source, the target cannot adopt its answer since the probability that it is the correct answer is low. However, the target cannot discard the source's answer, since in problem solving individuals are typically uncertain and they are not sure they have the correct or the best possible solution. Therefore, confronting a low-status source in an aptitude task leads to a *conflict of incompetences* (Butera & Mugny, 1995; Maggi, Butera, & Mugny, 1996), that of the source (who has no status to be considered competent) and that of the target (who is judging under uncertainty). This would lead to a close examination of the task and to a decentration from the two existing points of view, in search of an answer that would guarantee validity; latent, constructivistic influence should then appear.

If one applies this theoretical framework to the third study presented in the previous section (Butera et al., 1996), the observed results appear to be consistent. A high-status source (a majority) induced imitation and a low-status source (a minority) induced constructivism. However, this experiment manipulated the majority or minority nature of the source, and not directly its competence. It is true that according to Nemeth (1986) there is a relation between the source's numerical support and the inferences that people make about the probability that the source holds a correct answer: People are motivated to consider that majorities are generally right and minorities are generally wrong. However, both Nemeth and Butera et al. (1996) only manipulated the numerical support of the source and there was no proof that manipulating the source's competence would produce the same results (imitation of the high-status source and constructivism when confronting the low-status source).

In a fourth experiment (Butera, Mugny, & Tomei, 2000, Study 1), the source's status was manipulated directly on the basis of its declared competence. Participants were again asked to solve two inductive reasoning problems (choosing a hypothesis and testing it), being confronted with a source that was either an expert or a novice (plus a control condition without influence). Following conflict elaboration theory, individuals consider the high-status source's model as an informational support or they find themselves in a conflict of incompetence when confronting a low-status source because they are uncertain, the typical condition of someone attempting to solve a problem. Therefore, half of the subjects were led to believe that the solution was either highly unpredictable (uncertainty) or easily predictable (certainty): The hypothesized influence effects should appear under uncertainty and not under certainty (cf. also Festinger, 1950).

A significant interaction between the two variables showed that the predicted influence effects appeared only under uncertainty, and this for both yielding and disconfirmation (see Table 8.2). With yielding, the high-status source is the one that participants imitated the most and the low-status source the one that participants imitated the least. However, this was true only under uncertainty: When participants were certain, the imitation rate was the same whatever the source. With disconfirmation, the reverse was observed: The highest rate of disconfirmatory testing was used by participants confronted with a low-status source, whereas the lowest rate appeared when participants were confronted with a high-status source, again only under uncertainty.

Table 8.2 *Competence of Source: Mean Number of Yielding (from 0 to 2) and Mean Number of Disconfirmations (from 0 to 4)*

	Uncertainty			Certainty		
	Expert	Novice	Control	Expert	Novice	Control
Yielding	1.42[a]	0.40[b]	0.96[c]	0.88[c]	0.90[c]	0.88[c]
Disconfirmation	0.50[a]	2.60[b]	1.04[c]	1.16[c]	1.21[c]	1.24[c]

Note: For each measure, means sharing the same subscript are not significantly different at $p < 0.05$.

This study showed how, in a task involving aptitude (namely logic), individuals who are uncertain (which is generally the case in problem solving) are highly sensitive to the competence of a source that proposes a model of solution. If the source has a high status – a competent source – individuals rely highly upon the source's model and imitate it. It thus appears that confirmation then has a *protection function*. Since individuals prefer autonomy when competence is at stake (cf. Lemaine, 1974), those who imitate the source then have to be sure that this costly yielding leads to a correct solution, and therefore use a testing strategy that brings support to the borrowed hypothesis and does not imply the risk of invalidating it — confirmation. In fact, participants with the highest yielding rate also had the lowest disconfirmation rate (i.e., the highest confirmation rate).

The highest disconfirmation rate appeared when participants were uncertain and were confronted with a low–status source: These are the conditions that, according to conflict elaboration theory, produce a conflict of incompetences. In fact, not only do individuals not know if they will be able to solve the problem, but the source's status does not seem to guarantee the validity of its answer. In this respect, disconfirmation has a *research function*: It makes it possible to test the limits of validity of a hypothesis. Again it appears that confirmation and disconfirmation are typical of specific social situations, and they seem to serve specific social functions. This idea was tested in sudies summarized in the next section.

Conflicts in Hypothesis Testing

The results observed in the above studies suggest that imitation of a high–status source in aptitude tasks is not a mere form of compliance (Moscovici,

1980), but serves to reduce uncertainty (which is uncomfortable when apti-tude is at stake), to produce more confidence in the validity of one's own judgment, and to establish confidence in one's own competence. Yet, what happens when individuals cannot yield to the high-status source? This is an important question: Not only are people motivated to keep their autonomy when aptitude is at stake (as pointed out before), but there are numerous situations in which people cannot yield. This is the case when individuals have already committed themselves to a particular judgment, when they have a particular status to protect, or when they feel threatened by the source.

So, what happens when individuals are led to oppose a high-status source, an expert? The source's high competence implies that its answer is the good one: People use heuristics such as "Experts hold correct judgments" (Chaiken, 1980). If individuals consider a highly competent source as being right, and they do not yield, this implies that they are incompetent, since their answer is different and therefore wrong. In this situation, the source's competence directly threatens the target's competence, leading to what can be called a *conflict of competences* (Butera, Gardair, Maggi, & Mugny, 1998; Mugny, Butera, & Falomir, in press). This is a conflict produced by the fact that targets cannot recognize the source's competence without implying their own incompe-tence. The consequence would be that individuals whose competence is threatened by a high-status source in a problem-solving task are more con-cerned with relational matters than with the actual features of the task. This should lead to a relational solution of the task (trying to be better that the source), instead of an epistemic solution (aiming at discovering a valid answer). These considerations stemmed from the following study.

The conflict of competences and the conflict of incompetences

This study (Butera et al., 1998, Study 1) was designed to investigate the effect of an inevitable conflict (not to be solved through imitation) in an aptitude task. Again the task involved solving a series of inductive reasoning tasks when confronted with the solution of an influence source. However, in this task the cover story attributed a hypothesis to the participants that they had to defend and justify. When participants had thoroughly appropriated the hypothesis, they were informed of the source's hypothesis, which was different from theirs. The source was either an expert or a novice. The task then continued with hypothesis testing, without providing an opportunity to reformulate the hypothesis: The conflict was apparent and could not be reduced.

In previous studies, participants always tested their own hypothesis. If disconfirmation appeared, it was clearly used for an epistemic purpose (cf. Popper, 1955), that is, testing the limits of validity of their hypothesis. However, Gorman and Carlson (1989) pointed out that, within the scientific community, disconfirmation – although quite rarely used in scientific induction – appears very frequently when testing competing theories or hypotheses: "Disconfirmation of other's ideas can be a successful investment heuristic as well" (p. 101). In this case, disconfirmation does not have an epistemic purpose but a relational one: to discredit the validity of competing hypotheses. We therefore asked half of the sample to test their own hypothesis, and the other half to test the source's hypothesis.

Results showed that when participants confronted a low-status source (a novice), the disconfirmation rate was equally high for the test of their own hypothesis as for the test of the source's hypothesis. This supports the idea that a conflict of incompetence stemming from confrontation with a low-status source orients the individual's activity toward the epistemic purpose of testing the validity of the hypothesis. Therefore no differences appear, whatever the target of testing, a sign that elaboration is directed toward the task and not toward the relationship.

When people confronted a high-status source, disconfirmation rate changed according to the target of testing. If they tested the source's hypothesis, disconfirmation rate was high, as high as that found for the low-status conditions. If they tested their own hypothesis, disconfirmation rate was very low, significantly lower than all the other conditions. So it seems that confrontation with a high-status source is relation-dependent. The almost exclusive use of confirmation in testing one's own hypothesis when confronted with the high-status source can be interpreted as a way of adding support (confirmation brings evidence) in a competitive relationship. If this is true, the use of disconfirmation found in participants testing the high-status source's hypothesis can be interpreted as a way of discrediting, through invalidation, the source's answer. Disconfirmation would then be used in an epistemic way when confronted with a low-status source, and in a relational, competitive way when confronted with a threatening high-status source.

Some observations are in line with the above interpretation. First of all, in the high-status source conditions, participants were more likely to declare that their purpose in testing was to prove that their idea was good and that the other's idea was wrong. Conversely, in the low-status source conditions, participants were more likely to declare that their purpose in testing was to discover which idea, among a set of alternatives, was correct. Second, when participants were asked to rate the source's and their own perceived competence at the task on two independent scales, a significant positive correlation appeared when participants were confronted with the low-status source, while a significant negative correlation appeared when participants were confronted with the high-status source. Therefore, it appears that participants perceive a competitive relationship with the high-status source, and prepare to "fight"; conversely, they perceive a more cooperative relationship with the low-status source and seem to be more task-oriented. However, although these elements provide a hint for interpretation, they do not prove that the disconfirmation that appeared in the high-status source condition is different in origin (namely relational) from that appearing in the low-status source condition (namely epistemic).

Research on the social development of the intellect has shown that constructs developing from a relational conflict disappear as soon as the relationship is over, since they do not correspond to real learning. Conversely, sociocognitive conflict (based on epistemic motives) can lead to a generalization of the effects, leading to true constructivism (Doise & Mugny, 1984). Therefore, the present study – that was also designed to investigate the dynamics of relational versus epistemic disconfirmation – concluded with a generalization problem. This problem was a Wason's 2-4-6 classic task, that had to be completed individually, with no comparison with a source. All participants were requested to test their own hypothesis. Results showed that no more differences appeared in the disconfirmation rate of participants previously confronted with a high-status source: Participants who previously tested their own hypothesis and those who tested the source's hypothesis both displayed the same very low rate of disconfirmation (they mainly used confirmation). However, participants who were previously confronted with a low-status source displayed a significantly higher disconfirmation rate, whatever the target (own or other's hypothesis) previously tested. This presents a more robust argument that in the high-status condition disconfirmation had a relational, invalidating function: It appeared mostly when participants had to test the source's idea (cf. Gorman & Carlson, 1989), and disappeared when the confrontation was over, showing that nothing was learnt from its use. The opposite seems to be true for confrontation with a low-status source: Disconfirmation is used whatever the target of testing, and its use persists after the influence relationship, showing some kind of constructivism.

To sum up, two important conclusions can be drawn from these results. First of all, we can confidently conclude that confirmation is not merely a bias and disconfirmation is not always an ideal diagnostic test, but that they are reasoning strategies adapted to specific social situations. In fact, it was demonstrated that disconfirmation, far from being the idealized tool of scientific falsification, can serve competitive purposes when used to test hypotheses coming from a threatening source. Second, more elements appeared that contribute to characterizing the conflict of competences and the conflict of incompetences. In the conflict of competences, it appears that when one cannot imitate a competent source, one's own competence is threatened: Since disagreement cannot be reduced, because one answer is correct and the other one is not, the implication is that one person is competent and the other one is not. This leads to the perception of a negative interdependence between target and source (as shown by the negative correlation mentioned above). Individuals focus on the conflict with the source (they attempt to invalidate it), rather than on the characteristics of the task, which gives a self-serving, rather than diagnostic, processing of the problem.

The conflict of incompetences was already well documented in previous studies, but the present one presents two additional ideas. First, the positive correlation that participants established between their competence and the source's competence shows that they do not perceive the low-status source as an opponent, but rather as someone "in the same boat." This allows them to concentrate on the characteristics of the tasks, which explains the higher level of constructivism. Second, the lack of a relational problem is clearly shown by the fact that participants used disconfirmation in an epistemic way even when they were testing the source's hypothesis. In the following two sections we will present two experiments that directly manipulate these characteristics.

The conflict of incompetences and independence

The hypothesis tested by the following experiment was that the constructivist impact of a low-status source supposes that individuals do not perceive themselves as much more competent than the source. The condition for a real conflict of incompetences to occur would indeed be for individuals to doubt their own competence as much as that of the source. Our prediction was that the constructivist effect of the low-status source in such an aptitude task will be stronger if the participants regard their degree of incompetence as close to that of the source than if they emphasize their own competence relative to the source's incompetence.

The procedure was exactly the same as in the previous experiment, except that participants were confronted only with a low-status source (a novice). After having appropriated the criterion they were to stand by, and having

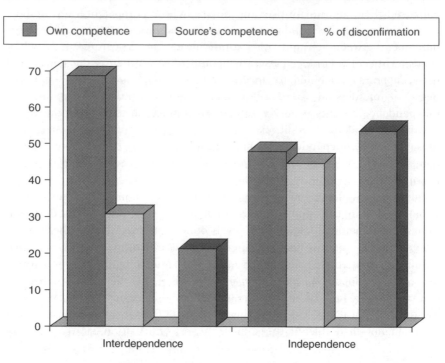

Figure 8.1 Mean points attributed to own and to source's competence, and mean percentage of disconfirmation.

read the one proposed by the novice, participants were asked to compare themselves to the novice on four characteristics: competence, qualification, skill, and expertise. This comparison aimed at operationalizing two modes of relations between participants' competence and that of the source. In the negative interdependence mode, for each characteristic, participants were asked to share a total of 100 points between the source and themselves: The novice's incompetence thus serves as the condition for the participant's competence (what is given to one is denied to the other). In the independent mode, participants had 100 points to attribute to themselves and another 100 points for the novice; this condition was intended to elicit a conflict of incompetences. This experimental manipulation has proved to induce a fairer distribution of points (Mummendey & Schreiber, 1983); in a task dominated by uncertainty, this distribution should reflect the participants' doubts concerning their own competence as well as that of the source.

Results (see Figure 8.1) showed that, although participants generally gave themselves more points, in the negative interdependence condition they enhanced their superiority over the novice, whose competence was denied. In the independence condition participants did not establish such a large difference between self and other. Both means are close to 50%, which is characteristic of a conflict between incompetences. Whereas the correlation between points attributed to oneself and the novice is logically −1 in the negative interdependence condition, it is significantly positive in the independence condition. As for hypothesis testing, participants in the negative interdependence condition used disconfirmation significantly less than those in the independence condition, reaching an overall rate that is comparable to what is called *confirmation bias* in the cognitive psychology literature.

The role of independence within the conflict of incompetence was clearly demonstrated in this study. This is theoretically very important because it shows that individuals display high levels of constructivism when the source's competence is not threatening. When the source's competence is evaluated within a competitive relationship (negative interdependence) individuals are led to produce a *downward comparison* (Wills, 1981), that is, a comparison that aims more at self-enhancement than at self-improvement (Wood & Taylor, 1991). In fact, although they evaluated their competence as being much higher than that of the source, the disconfirmation rate stayed very low.

The conflict of competences, independence, and decentration

Independence proved to be an important factor in the constructivistic effects induced by the conflict of incompetences. In the characteristics that were mentioned above for the conflict of competences, it was noted that one of the problems in the relationship with a high-status source is that individuals spontaneously perceive a negative interdependence between their competence and that of the source. The following study (Butera et al., 2000, Study 3) tested the idea that evaluating independently the source's and the target's competence can decentrate the target from the relational conflict and induce more constructivism. Decentration also seems to be a problem in the conflict of competences. In fact, in this conflict individuals seem to be tied to relational matters without a real motivation to decentrate from this focusing effect (Legrenzi et al., 1993) in order to consider the content of the source's proposal and/or other features of the task. Therefore, the following study investigated the possibility of enhancing constructivism by leading individuals in a conflict of competences to decentrate and to consider the possible complementarity between their hypothesis and that of the source.

The procedure and materials for the present study were the same as for the two previous studies. The source was always a high-status source, and again participants were led to disagree with the source without having the opportunity to reduce this opposition. They then evaluated (as in the previous experiment) their competence and that of the source, either in an independent mode, or in a negatively interdependent mode. Half of the sample was exposed to a decentration procedure (Huguet et al., 1991–92), whereas the other half was not. Participants in the decentration condition were invited to look in a black box, half of them through a hole on the top, the other half through another hole on the side. They then had to write down what they had seen and exchange their sheets of paper: To their great surprise, they discovered that half of them had seen a triangle and the other half a square. They then had to guess what was in the box. Since nobody found the correct answer, the experimenter opened the box and took out a square-based pyramid, and explained that very often in everyday life we have the impression that we face incompatible points of views, but when we make the effort to integrate them, we can find that seemingly incompatible judgments can be different but complementary sides of a more complex reality.

Results showed two main effects: Independence in judgments of competence induced more disconfirmation than negative interdependence, and the decentration condition induced more disconfirmation than did the condition without this procedure (see Figure 8.2). Therefore, the basic conflict of competences condition – negative interdependence and no decentration – induced the lowest rate of disconfirmation. When the two postulated problems that create a conflict of competences are counterbalanced, the disconfirmation rate improves, and in the condition with both independence and decentration, the highest disconfirmation rate appears. In this condition, target and source are no longer opposed by a conflict of competences, but the high-status source can be beneficial as it is related to the target in a sort of *informational interdependence* (Mugny et al., in press; Quiamzade, Mugny, Falomir & Butera, 1999). This is an important result for the present line of research and has practical implications for the use of expertise, for instance in work settings. In fact, previous studies showed that confrontation with a high-status source in problem solving leads either to yielding (if the source can be imitated), or to a relational conflict (if the opposing positions are seen as incompatible). Only confrontation with a low-status source produced an appreciable level of constructivism. However, solving problems efficiently with an expert is possible, as shown every day by work groups. This last experiment shows

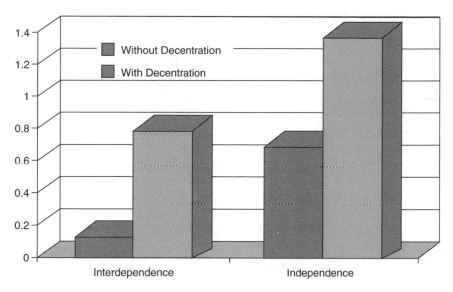

Figure 8.2   Mean number of disconfirmations (from never to twice).

the conditions in which it is possible to find constructivistic effects when confronted with an expert, even if a divergence opposes the two points of view. First, competences must be evaluated in an independent way: One of the problems with the relation with a high-status source is that its competence can be perceived as a threat to the target's competence. Second, targets must be able to defocus, to decentrate, and to consider that an opposing view can bring a complementary contribution toward a correct judgment. When these two conditions are met, target and source are in informational interdependence: They can use both judgments to construct a more complex reality.

Conclusions

The work presented in this chapter leads us to draw two kinds of conclusions, one concerning hypothesis-testing mechanisms, and another concerning social influence when aptitude is at stake. With hypothesis testing, the work done in individuating the social factors that influence the use of confirmation showed that "confirmation bias" is not a bias: Its use is neither wrong nor uncoercible. It was shown that confirmation is used in particular social influence situations and that it seems to have a specific function of protecting individuals' competence. When individuals give up their autonomy in order to imitate a high-status source, confirmation warrants that this costly yielding does not prove to be wrong. When individuals are in blatant disagreement with a threatening high-status source, confirmation makes it possible to bring support to their own position. It was also demonstrated that disconfirmation — which can indeed be diagnostic when the motivation is epistemic — is not always used as a strategy for testing validity and the limits of validity. It was shown how disconfirmation can serve competitive motives in the attempt to denigrate the opposing source. To sum up, confirmation appears as a bias — that is, a systematic behavior — only because reasoning over difficult problems leads to uncertainty, and if competence is at stake this can be threatening; confirmation can then bring the necessary support.

In the case of social influence, inductive reasoning seems to be determined by the specific type of conflict between targets and the source. Since competence is at stake in reasoning tasks, the regulation of competence organizes the dynamics of influence in these tasks. When the source is low in status, acquiring competence needs an effort, since the source does not guarantee the validity of its answer, but targets' uncertainty does not allow them to discard it; they must therefore decentrate and take into account the characteristics of the task, instead of using relational heuristics. This is the conflict of incompetences, which is an epistemic one, based on the fact that a low-status source does not threaten the targets' competence, which gives them freedom to work on the task. In fact it was shown that when targets are forced into competition by a negative interdependence with the source, they are led to produce a downward comparison that relieves their perceived competence, but that dissolves all the constructivistic effects typical of confrontation with a low-status source.

When the source is high in status, it is possible to reach a correct answer by imitating the competent source. Although keeping one's own autonomy is very important, in particularly constraining situations (e.g., representation of unity) targets use the source's answer as an informational support to their own judgment. But there are times when the high-status source cannot be imitated and the disagreement cannot be reduced. Targets are then in a conflict of competences: They cannot conceive that two different answers can be two facets of the same reality, since they focus more on the comparison of competences than on the task; however, they are threatened by the high competence of the source, since it is considered as a negation of their own competence. The result of this conflict is that targets concentrate on protecting their point of view and on denigrating the source's, instead of working on the properties of the task. However, if targets can overcome this threatening conception of the relation to a high-status source, they can process the characteristics of the task, and social influence can result in constructivistic effects, because targets can consider the source as being in an informational interdependence: A sort of nonthreatening cooperation between competent people. Learning and developing are a matter of social influence.

NOTE

We wish to thank Paolo Legrenzi and Juan Antonio Pérez who participated in developing this research paradigm. This work was supported by the Swiss National Foundation for Scientific Research and by the "Avenir" fund of the French Rhône-Alpes Regional Council.

REFERENCES

Brandstätter, V., Ellemers, N., Gaviria, E., Giosue, F., Huguet, P., Kron, M., Morchain, P., Pujal, M., Rubini, M., Mugny, G., & Pérez, J. A. (1991). Indirect majority and minority influence: An exploratory study. *European Journal of Social Psychology*, *21*, 199–211.

Butera, F., Gardair, E., Maggi, J., & Mugny, G. (1998). Les paradoxes de l'expertise: Influence sociale et (in)compétence de soi et d'autrui. In J. Py, A. Somat, & J. Baillé (Eds.), *Psychologie sociale et formation professionnelle: Propositions et regards critiques* (pp. 109–123). Rennes, France: Presses Universitaires de Rennes.

Butera, F., Legrenzi, P., Mugny, G., & Pérez, J. A. (1991–92). Influence sociale et raisonnement. *Bulletin de Psychologie*, *45*, 144–154.

Butera, F., & Mugny, G. (1992). Influence minoritaire et falsification. *Revue Internationale de Psychologie Sociale*, *5* (2), 115–132.

Butera, F., & Mugny, G. (1995). Conflict between incompetences and influence of a low-expertise source in hypothesis testing. *European Journal of Social Psychology*, *25*, 457–462.

Butera, F., Mugny, G., Legrenzi, P., & Pérez, J. A. (1996). Majority and minority influence, task representation and inductive reasoning. *British Journal of Social Psychology*, *35*, 123–136.

Butera, F., Mugny, G., & Tomei, A. (2000). Incertitude et enjeux identitaires dans l'influence sociale. In J. L. Beauvois, R. V. Joule, & J. M. Monteil (Eds.), *Perspectives cognitives et conduites sociales* (Vol. 7, pp. 205–229). Neuchâtel, Switzerland: Delachaux et Niestlé.

Chaiken, S. (1980). Heuristic versus systematic information processing and the use of source versus message cues in persuasion. *Journal of Personality and Social Psychology*, *39*, 752–766.

De Dreu, C. K. W., & De Vries, N. K. (1993). Numerical support, information processing and attitude change. *European Journal of Social Psychology, 23,* 647–662.

De Dreu, C. K. W., De Vries, N. K., Gordijn, E. H., & Schuurman, M. S. (1999). Convergent and divergent processing of majority and minority arguments: Effects on focal and related attitudes. *European Journal of Social Psychology, 29,* 329–348.

Doise, W., & Mugny, G. (1984). *The social development of the intellect.* Oxford: Pergamon Press.

Evans, J. St. B. T. (1989). *Bias in human reasoning: Causes and consequences.* Hove, UK: Erlbaum.

Evans, J. St. B. T. (1982). *The psychology of deductive reasoning.* London: Routledge & Kegan Paul.

Festinger, L. (1950). Informal social communication. *Psychological Review, 57,* 271–282.

Festinger, L. (1954). A theory of social comparison processes. *Human Relations, 7,* 117–140.

Gorman, M., & Carlson, B. (1989). Can experiments be used to study science? *Social Epistemology, 3,* 89–106.

Gorman, M., & Gorman, M. E. (1984). A comparison of confirmatory, disconfirmatory and control strategy on Wason's 2-4-6, task. *Quarterly Journal of Experimental Psychology, 36 A,* 629–648.

Green, D. W. (1990). Confirmation bias, problem solving and cognitive models. In J. P. Caverni, J. M. Fabre, & M. Gonzales (Eds.), *Cognitive biases* (pp. 553–562). Amsterdam: Elsevier (North Holland).

Holyoak, K. J., & Spellman, B. A. (1993). Thinking. *Annual Review of Psychology, 44,* 265–315.

Huguet, P., Mugny, G., & Pérez, J. A. (1991–92). Influence sociale et processus de décentration. *Bulletin de Psychologie, 45,* 155–163.

Janis, I. L. (1972). *Victims of groupthink.* Boston: Houghton-Mifflin.

Johnson-Laird, P. N. (1983). Mental models. Cambridge, UK: Cambridge University Press.

Kruglanski, A. (1980). Lay epistemo-logic process and contents: Another look at attribution theory. *Psychological Review, 87,* 70–87.

Kruglanski, A. W. (1990). Motivations for judging and knowing: Implications for causal attribution. In E. T. Higgins & R. M. Sorrentino (Eds.), *The handbook of motivation and cognition: Foundation of social behavior* (Vol. 2, pp. 333–368). New York: Guilford Press.

Kruglanski, A., & Ajzen, I. (1983). Bias and error in human judgement. *European Journal of Social Psychology, 13,* 1–44.

Kruglanski, A. W., & Mayseless, O. (1988). Contextual effects in hypothesis testing: The role of competing alternatives and epistemic motivations. *Social Cognition, 6,* 1–20.

Legrenzi, P., Butera, F., Mugny, G., & Pérez, J. A. (1991). Majority and minority influence in inductive reasoning: A preliminary study. *European Journal of Social Psychology, 21,* 359–363.

Legrenzi, P., Girotto, V., & Johnson-Laird, P. N. (1993). Focusing in reasoning and decision making. *Cognition, 49,* 37–66.

Lemaine, G. (1974). Social differentiation and social originality. *European Journal of Social Psychology, 4,* 17–52.

Lemaine, G. (1984). Social differentiation in the scientific community. In H. Tajfel (Ed.), *The social dimension* (pp. 338–359). Cambridge, UK: Cambridge University Press.

Leyens, J.-Ph, Dardenne, B., Yzerbyt, V., Scaillet, N., & Snyder, M. (1999). Confirmation and disconfirmation: Their social advantages. In W. Stroebe & M. Hewstone (Eds.), *European Review of Social Psychology* (Vol. 10, pp. 199–230). Chichester, UK: Wiley.

Maggi, J., Butera, F., & Mugny, G. (1996). Conflict of incompetences: Direct and indirect influences on representation of the centimetre. *International Review of Social Psychology, 9,* 91–105.

Mahoney, M. J. (1976). *Scientist as subject: The psychological imperative.* Cambridge, MA: Ballinger.

McDonald, J. (1990). Some situational determinants of hypothesis-testing strategies. *Journal of Experimental Social Psychology, 26,* 255–274.

Mitroff, I. (1974). Norms and counter-norms in a selected group of Apollo moon scientists: A case study of the ambivalence of scientists. *American Sociological Review, 39,* 579–595.

Moscovici, S. (1980). Toward a theory of conversion behaviour. In L. Berkowitz (Ed.), *Advances in experimental social psychology* (Vol. 13, pp. 209–239). New York: Academic Press.

Mugny, G., Butera, F., & Falomir, J. M. (in press). Social influence and threat in social comparison between self and source's competence: Relational factors affecting the transmission of knowledge. In F. Butera & G. Mugny (Eds.), *Social influence in social reality.* Bern, Switzerland: Hogrefe & Huber.

Mugny, G., Butera, F., Sanchez-Mazas, M., & Pérez, J. A. (1995). Judgements in conflict: The conflict elaboration theory of social influence. In B. Boothe, R. Hirsig, A. Helminger, B. Meier, & R. Volkart (Eds.), *Perception – evaluation – interpretation. Swiss monographs in psychology* (Vol. 3, pp. 160–168). Bern, Switzerland: Huber.

Mugny, G., Butera, F., Pérez, J. A., & Huguet, P. (1993). Les routes de la conversion: Influences majoritaires et minoritaires. In J. L. Beauvois, R. V. Joule, & J. M. Monteil (Eds.), *Perspectives cognitives et conduites sociales* (Vol. 4). Cousset, Switzerland: Delval.

Mummendey, A., & Schreiber, H. J. (1983). Better or just different? Positive social identity by discrimination against, or by differentiation from outgroups. *European Journal of Social Psychology, 13,* 389–397.

Mynatt, C. R., Doherty, M. E. & Tweney, R. D. (1977). Confirmation bias in a simulated research environment: An experimental study of scientific inference. *Quarterly Journal of Experimental Psychology, 29,* 85–95.

Nemeth, C. (1986). Differential contributions of majority and minority influence. *Psychological Review, 93,* 23–32.

Nemeth, C., & Kwan, J. (1985). Originality of word associations as a function of majority vs. minority influence. *Social Psychology Quarterly*, *48*, 277–282.

Nemeth, C., Mosier, K., & Chiles, C. (1992). When convergent thought improves performance: Majority versus minority influence. *Personality and Social Psychology Bulletin*, *18*, 139–144.

Pérez, J. A., & Mugny, G. (1993). *Influences sociales. La théorie de l'élaboration du conflit.* Neuchâtel, Switzerland: Delachaux et Niestlé.

Pérez, J. A., & Mugny, G. (1996). The conflict elaboration theory of social influence. In E. H. Witte & J. Davis (Eds.), *Understanding group behavior: Consensual action by small groups* (Vol. 2, pp. 191–210). Mahwah, NJ: Erlbaum.

Popper, K. R. (1955). *The logic of scientific discovery.* New York: Harper & Row.

Quiamzade, A., Mugny, G., Falomir, J. M., Butera, F. (1999). Gestion identitaire vs. épistémique des compétences. In H. Hansen, B. Sigrist, H. Goorhuis, & H. Landolt (Eds.), *Bildung und Arbeit: Das Ende einer Differenz?* (pp. 267–276). Aarau, Switzerland: Sauerländer.

Snyder, M. (1981). Seek and ye shall find: Testing hypotheses about other people. In E. T. Higgins, D. C. Herman, & M. P. Zanna (Eds.), *Social cognition: The Ontario symposium on personality and social psychology* (Vol. 1, pp. 277–303). Hillsdale, NJ: Erlbaum.

Snyder, M., & Swann, W. B. (1978). Hypothesis-testing processes in social interaction. *Journal of Personality and Social Psychology*, *36*, 1202–1212.

Trope, Y., & Mackie, D. M. (1987). Sensitivity to alternatives in social hypothesis-testing. *Journal of Experimental Social Psychology*, *23*, 445–459.

Tweney, R. D., Doherty, M. E., & Mynatt, C. R. (Eds.) (1981). *On scientific thinking.* New York: Columbia University Press.

Volpato, C., Maass, A., Mucchi-Faina, A., & Vitti, E. (1990). Minority influence and social categorisation. *European Journal of Social Psychology*, *20*, 119–132.

Wason, P. C. (1960). On the failure to eliminate hypotheses in a conceptual task. *The Quarterly Journal of Experimental Psychology*, *12*, 255–274.

Wason, P. C. (1966). Reasoning. In B. M. Foss (Ed.), *New horizons in psychology.* Harmondsworth, UK: Penguin.

Wills, T. A. (1981). Downward comparison principles in social comparison. *Psychological Bulletin*, *90*, 245–271.

Wood, J. V., & Taylor, K. L. (1991). Serving self-relevant goals through social comparison. In J. M. Suls & T. A. Wills (Eds.), *Social comparison: Contemporary theory and research.* Hillsdale, NJ: Erlbaum.

9

The Impact of Shared Representations on Minority Influence in Freely Interacting Groups

Christine M. Smith, R. Scott Tindale, and Elizabeth M. Anderson

Until the early 1970s, social influence researchers tended to assume that social influence was asymmetrical or, in other words, that majorities were the sources of social influence and minorities were the targets (e.g., Asch, 1951; Festinger, 1950, 1954). Following the publication of *Social Influence and Social Change* (1976), in which Moscovici adroitly pointed out the weaknesses in construing the phenomenon of social influence so narrowly, much more attention was directed toward minority influence. Since the mid-1970s, minority influence research has flourished and generated a number of interesting theories and empirical findings (see Wood, Lundgren, Ouellette, Busceme, & Blackstone, 1994, for review). This literature has supported the notion that minorities have their greatest impact when measures of influence are delayed, indirect, and taken in private (e.g., Maass & Clark, 1984; Maass, West, & Cialdini, 1987; Wood et al., 1994). Minorities also appear to be more powerful sources of influence when they argue in favor of the position that is prevalent in the general population (i.e., the *Zeitgeist*) than when they argue against the Zeitgeist (Clark & Maass, 1988a, 1988b, 1990; Paicheler, 1976, 1977). In addition, minority impact is determined, in part, by how consistently (Moscovici, 1980; Maass and Clark, 1984; Mugny, 1982; Nemeth, 1986) and flexibly (Mugny, 1975) the minority position is argued. Finally, relative to majority influence, minority influence tends to be weak when subjective opinion judgments are studied (Wood et al., 1994).

It is interesting to note that social psychological evidence of minority influence predated Moscovici's seminal work by several decades (Shaw, 1932) but this work was carried out and interpreted within a "group performance" rather than a "social influence" context. Even today, the small group decision-making and problem-solving literature is rarely construed as being relevant to minority influence research. This lack of cross-referencing is unfortunate because there are empirically demonstrated predictive parameters common to each area (e.g., faction size). The goal of the present chapter is to demonstrate the relevance of both classic and contemporary work on group processes and performance to minority and majority influence research. In particular, we hope to show that a construct that has helped to explain variation across tasks in group, as compared to individual, performance – *shared task representations* (Tindale, Smith, Thomas, Filkins, & Sheffey, 1996) – is quite useful for understanding how and when minorities and majorities will be influential.

Small Group Performance: Problem Solving and Decision Making

Much of the research we discuss below was based on a theoretical framework called *social decision scheme (SDS) theory* (Davis, 1973). Within this framework it is assumed that groups reach consensus by combining individual preferences into a single collective group choice. Assuming a set of discrete response alternatives, the model defines the consensus process in terms of a social decision scheme (SDS) matrix, which is an m (number of potential preference distributions) by n (number of response alternatives) matrix. For example, a five-person group choosing between two response alternatives (Plan A vs. Plan B) can have six distinguishable preference distributions (i.e., 5-0, 4-1, 3-2, . . . , 0-5). The entries in the SDS matrix represent the conditional probabilities of the group choosing a particular response alternative (Plan A) given a particular preference distribution (three members prefer Plan A and two prefer Plan B). This approach allows both for testing a priori models of the group consensus process against empirical data (where the matrix entries are set by theory or logical intuition), and describing the consensus process by empirically estimating the matrix entries. (See Davis, 1973, 1982, or Kameda, Tindale, & Davis, in press for a more thorough description of the theory.)

The SDS approach has generated a large body of research findings regarding the correspondence between differing task demands and the related group consensus processes (see Davis, 1982; Stasser, Kerr, & Davis, 1989 for reviews). Although a number of factors have been found to influence group decision processes (Davis, 1982; Laughlin, 1980), one of the more consistent and robust findings from this research has been that "majorities/pluralities win" most of the time. In other words, the largest faction in the group tends to have the most influence. Majority/plurality type processes have been found for groups working on a variety of decision tasks and situations, including mock juries (Kameda, 1991; Tindale & Davis, 1983), risk taking (Davis, Kameda, & Stasson, 1992), duplex bets (Davis, Kerr, Sussman, & Rissman, 1974), choosing political candidates (Stasser & Titus, 1985), reward allocation decisions (Tindale & Davis, 1985), investment decisions (Smith, Tindale, & Steiner, 1998), and promotion decisions (Tindale, 1989).

Although majority processes in group performance research are quite prevalent, one of the earliest studies comparing group to individual performance found that groups were quite good at solving problems that very few individuals could solve on their own (Shaw, 1932). Shaw argued that groups outperformed individuals because groups could engage in error checking, but later work by Lorge and Solomon (1955) showed that this assumption was not necessary to account for the difference between individual and group performance. Lorge and Solomon's *Model A* – an early group performance model – states that the probability of a group solving a particular problem correctly is equal to the probability that the group contains at least one member who is capable of solving the problem correctly. In other words, the group will accept and adopt a single member's proposed solution to a problem if that solution is correct. Within the SDS framework, this model has been referred to as *truth wins* (Steiner, 1972; Laughlin, 1980).

Laughlin's intellective–judgmental task dimension can be used to predict when majority and minority factions will prevail in group decision-making contexts (Laughlin 1980; Laughlin & Ellis, 1986). Intellective tasks are those for which there is a "demonstrably correct" solution, whereas judgmental tasks do not have demonstrably correct solutions. According to Laughlin and Ellis (1986), a problem has a demonstrably correct solution when it meets the following four criteria: (1) The group members share a symbolic system that may be utilized in solving the problem, (2) the group members collectively possess enough information to solve the problem within the system, (3) every group member possesses enough knowledge about the system to recognize the correct response when proposed, and (4) individuals who correctly solve the problem must be able and motivated to explain and demonstrate why the response is correct. Conversely, none of the response alternatives for a judgmental task can be demonstrated as correct. In such cases, the "correctness" of a particular alternative depends, in part, on the degree to which most people feel it is the best alternative.

According to Laughlin and Ellis, group consensus processes will vary as a function of the position of the task along the intellective–judgmental continuum. *Eureka* tasks are extremely high in demonstrability (thus well to the intellective end of the continuum), and once a single individual within the group generates the correct response, she or he has little problem convincing the group of the solution's correctness. For example, when a group is presented with the words *cookie, sixteen,* and *heart,* and asked for a fourth word that is related to all three, as is done in the Remote Associates Test (Mednick & Mednick, 1967), the individual who suggests *sweet* will have little difficulty convincing her or his fellow group members that the solution is correct (Laughlin, 1980). A *truth wins* SDS (which is identical to Lorge and Solomon's (1955) Model A) appears to be the best fitting model for most problems with extremely high demonstrability, although in some instances it overpredicts group performance. Laughlin found truth wins to be the best fitting SDS for five-person groups working on a highly demonstrable mathematics problem (Laughlin & Ellis, 1986) and for the remote associates task (Laughlin, Kerr, Munch, & Haggarty, 1976).

Groups working on tasks that are lower in demonstrability (relative to Eureka tasks) typically operate under a *truth supported wins* SDS. That is, there must be at least two group members who can agree regarding what the truth is before the group will adopt their solution as the correct one. Examples of intellective tasks lower in demonstrability include basic vocabulary problems (Laughlin, Kerr, Davis, Halff, & Marciniak, 1975) and verbal analogies (Laughlin et al., 1976). Although it is difficult to construe Laughlin's early work on intellective tasks, showing the best fitting SDS to be truth supported wins (Laughlin et al., 1975, 1976), as evidence of minority influence, because the faction arguing for "truth" was never a numerical minority, his later work (e.g., Laughlin & Adamopoulos, 1980) replicated the truth supported wins findings within the context of six-person groups working on verbal analogies. In this context the two group members arguing for the truth were in fact a minority faction. Finally, his work showing truth wins as the best fitting SDS should also stand as strong evidence of minority influence within decision-making groups (e.g., Laughlin, et al., 1976).

When there is no demonstrably correct solution, groups tend to operate under a majority/plurality type process (Davis, 1982; Stasser et al., 1989). Majority/plurality processes are based on the power of large factions. When no other mechanism exists for deciding which alternative is best, optimal, correct, and so forth, the amount of social support for a given alternative tends to guide the decision process. Thus, the decision regarding which of two products to market first, or whether to convict or acquit a defendant, will most often be determined by the size of the factions favoring each alternative. Minority factions are not predicted to prevail when the group's task is judgmental in nature.

The relatively weak direct minority influence found on subjective opinion judgments in the minority influence literature, coupled with the strong direct minority influence found on tasks high in demonstrability in the small group decision-making literature, suggests that position verifiability is an important predictor of social influence. For issues where an objectively correct position cannot be determined, social support is often used to gauge the validity of a given position. In contexts where the consensus heuristic of truth is likely to be used, minority sources of influence will necessarily be at a disadvantage (Chaiken & Stangor, 1987). This point is further supported by the Zeitgeist literature, where minority sources of influence are more influential when they argue in favor of the position that is most prevalent within the general population than when they argue against this position. Clark (1990) argues that minority arguments in line with the Zeitgeist may be perceived as more valid than arguments that run against the spirit of the times because of the implied social support for the position being argued. With respect to the findings regarding consistency, minority arguments presented consistently may be perceived as more valid because of the attributions made regarding the minority member's confidence in her or his position (Moscovici & Nemeth, 1974). Finally, noting the importance of position verifiability, Mugny and Pérez (1991) argue that minorities can validate their counternormative position by appealing to some common normative principle that is shared by members of both the majority and the minority. In doing so, they increase dramatically their chances of being influential. This, in essence, is how minorities in the group decision-making literature become powerful. When they appeal to a shared symbolic system and can demonstrate the validity of a given response within that system, both single and supported minorities often prevail in group decision-making contexts.

Shared Preferences Versus Shared Cognitions: Alternate Ways of Defining Truth?

The prevalence of evidence supporting majority influence in group decision making indicates that shared preferences are quite powerful for defining truth in a group context. When most of the group members favor a particular response alternative, the alternative is quite likely to become the group's collective choice. However, we have seen that for intellective tasks, even when most of the members have chosen an incorrect alternative, minority factions favoring the correct alternative tend to win. One of the key aspects of Laughlin and Ellis's (1986) definition of a demonstrably correct solution is that the members share a symbolic system that can be used to solve the particular problem. Another way of thinking about this is that shared preferences/choices become powerful when there is no shared system of thought that group members can use to define truth/correctness. Thus, we can conceptualize the two different situations as representing two different types of "sharedness" – one at the preference or choice level and one at the cognitive or representation level (Kameda, Tindale, & Davis, in press; Tindale & Kameda, in press).

Recently, Tindale et al. (1996) have used such a distinction to predict minority–majority faction impact in several different decision-making situations. Their arguments are based on the concept of *shared task representations*. Tindale et al. define such shared representation as "any task/situation relevant concept, norm, perspective, or cognitive process that is shared by most or all of the group members" (p. 84). Whenever such a shared task representation exists, factions that prefer alternatives consistent with the representation, regardless of their minority or majority status, will be at a distinct advantage with respect to social influence. The shared representation provides the context within which arguments favoring a particular alternative are seen as valid or plausible. Thus, they allow "truth" to be defined in a way other than social consensus.

Laughlin and Ellis's (1986) idea of a *shared symbolic system* is probably the best and strongest example of a shared task representation. However, Tindale et al. argue that there is evidence that other types of cognitive sharing can affect the group consensus processes. Specific examples of shared representations include cultural or societal norms, learned rules or axioms, processing goals or objectives, perspectives on or ways of framing a particular problem, and cognitive heuristics. Tindale et al. (1996) have argued that when there is no salient task-relevant shared representation that can readily be applied to the decision or judgment at hand (which is often, but not always, the case with subjective opinion judgments), influence or the group consensus process is best described by some type of majority model. These are also the contexts where the consensus heuristic of truth is most salient and most likely to be used. When a shared task representation does exist, asymmetries in the social influence patterns are expected, with factions favoring the alternative consistent with the shared representation being more influential than those arguing against it. However, these asymmetries will not necessarily follow "truth" in some absolute sense, but only truth in relation to the shared representation. Thus, tasks typically defined as judgmental on the intellective–judgmental continuum can also show evidence of minority influence. A number of examples of such instances are described below.

Shared processing objectives

An area of group decision making that has received a large amount of attention (particularly in the USA) is jury decision making. One of the more interesting early findings in this research was that, even though juries are typically mandated to reach a unanimous decision, a two-thirds majority model tends to provide an adequate description of the group decision process (Davis, 1980; Tindale & Davis, 1983). However, most of the recent research has found that when a two-thirds majority does not exist, juries are very unlikely to reach a guilty verdict (Davis, Kerr, Stasser, Meek, & Holt, 1977; Kerr & MacCoun, 1985; Nemeth, 1977; Tindale, Davis, Vollrath, Nagao, & Hinsz, 1990). Thus, even if 7 members of a 12-person jury favor guilty at the beginning of the deliberation, the final verdict is more likely to be defined by the 5-person minority favoring not guilty. This "bias" or asymmetry has been referred to as the *defendant protection norm* (Tindale & Davis, 1983) or the *leniency bias* (Stasser, Kerr, & Bray, 1982).

Tindale et al. (1996) have argued that the processing goal given to juries in the USA (i.e., the reasonable doubt criterion) operates as a shared representation. Jurors are informed that they should vote for guilty if and only if they cannot find any reasonable doubts concerning the defendant's guilt. Since all jurors receive the same instructions, this "processing goal" is shared by all of the group members. Thus, it is quite likely that arguments concerning potential reasonable doubts as to guilt will be rather persuasive in the group discussion. In a group with a slight majority favoring guilt, such arguments would come from the minority. This shared processing goal makes arguing in favor of acquittal much easier than arguing in favor of conviction because only one reasonable doubt needs to be generated in order to lend credence to the acquittal position. Evidence consistent with this idea was found by Kerr and MacCoun (1985), who demonstrated that the leniency bias basically disappears when the reasonable doubt criterion is replaced by a "preponderance of the evidence" criterion.

A similar asymmetry in the group consensus process was observed in a study originally designed to explore the impact of feedback on group decision making. Tindale (1989) asked five-person groups to make decisions regarding the promotion of 48 candidates for middle-level management positions. Half of the candidates, presented in blocks of eight, were "promotable" and the other half were not. At the outset of the study, participants were given instructions to avoid promoting candidates who would not succeed in the upper level positions. In addition, they were given several practice candidates with feedback that successfully reinforced these instructions – leading to a "do not promote" bias in the participants. During the experimental session Tindale (1989) manipulated the amount of feedback that groups received regarding their decision-making accuracy. One third of the groups received total feedback (given after every decision), one third received partial feedback (given after each decision to promote), and one third of the groups received no feedback at all.

Across the six trial blocks, the "do not promote" bias disappeared almost immediately in the total feedback condition. The group consensus process in the total feedback condition was best described by a four-fifths majority wins-proportionality otherwise model. That is, when four or five members of the group favor either alternative (promote or do not promote), the group was predicted to collectively endorse that alternative 100% of the time. Additionally, groups with three-person majorities are predicted to win proportionately to their relative size (approximately 60% of the time the group will endorse the three-person majority's alternative as its own). In the partial and no feedback conditions the "do not promote" bias also diminished over the trial blocks but the social decision scheme matrices revealed strong asymmetries, where those who favored "do not promote" were more influential than those who were in favor of promotion. In two trial blocks for each feedback type, two-person minorities who favored the "do not promote" alternative were just as influential (and in two instances considerably more influential) than their three fellow group members who favored promotion. However, minorities favoring "promote" decisions were never more influential than majorities favoring "do not promote."

Shared beliefs and values

There is some evidence in the literature that minorities holding positions that match specific beliefs or values can also be persuasive in groups. Typically, it is assumed that peoples' preferences in groups are in part defined by their beliefs and values. However, many different beliefs and/or values may be relevant to a particular issue. Thus, the degree to which people's preferences correspond with specific beliefs or values can vary and will rarely be perfect. In addition, Nemeth (1986) has argued that minorities often lead people to think more divergently about a given problem or issue. Thus, minorities may set the stage for majority members to view a wider range of values and beliefs relevant to the issue at hand. If the minority can then link their preferred position to a value or belief that is shared by most or all of the group members, they should be able to be influential in terms of the group's final position.

Risk as a value was used as an explanation for the "risky shift" in group decision making until cautious shifts were also observed (see Myers & Lamm, 1976). A number of studies have shown that decisions involving risk can produce minority influence. A study by Tindale, Sheffey, and Scott (1993) showed fairly strong asymmetries in observed SDS matrices favoring the risky alternative when problems were framed in terms of losses. Consistent with Kahneman and Tverskys' (1979) prospect theory, minorities favoring the risky alternative were more powerful when most of the members were presented with the loss version of the "Asian Disease" problem. Laughlin and Early (1982) found minority influence for choice dilemma items that showed the greatest amount of group polarization. Using two problems that showed very strong shifts (one in the direction of risk, and the other in the direction of caution), Laughlin and Early found that *risk supported wins* and *caution supported wins* SDS models did a good job of describing the group consensus processes for the items that typically shifted in those directions. For items that showed less polarization, majority models tended to produce the best fits to the data. Thus, for items where the respective values of risk or caution are strong, minorities favoring the value-consistent positions are more influential. Similarly, Clark's (1988) group polarization study found strong minority influence on risky choice dilemmas when the minority argued in favor of risk.

The issue-specific Zeitgeist may not be the only shared value system that can be used by a minority to gain influence. Smith, Dykema-Engblade, Walker, Niven, and McGough (2000) used five-person freely interacting groups discussing the death penalty to compare numerical minorities arguing in favor of and against the same attitudinal issue. Half of the groups were asked to render a group judgment regarding the issue (i.e., we are in favor of/against capital punishment) and the other half of the groups were simply asked to discuss the issue for a predetermined amount of time. As we mentioned earlier, the literature on Zeitgeist effects has consistently shown that minorities arguing in favor of the spirit of the times are at a distinct advantage relative to minorities arguing against the Zeitgeist. However, Smith et al. found the exact opposite pattern of results in their attitude change data for the participants who had rendered a group judgment regarding the death penalty. That is, minorities who argued against the death penalty (the minority opinion in the USA) were significantly more influential than those who argued in favor of capital punishment (the Zeitgeist).

Smith et al. argued that the strongly shared religious values of their participants may have affected the ease with which the anticapital punishment position was argued, because antideath penalty minorities could present arguments that appealed to their fellow group members' Christian identities and values. Indeed, Smith et al. found that majority members' attitude change could be predicted according to whether or not the minority member presented arguments grounded in religious principles (e.g., thou shalt not kill, God can deliver far more severe punishment than can humans, only God can be just). Further support for this argument was found in the content-analyzed thought listing data, where religion was mentioned more frequently by members exposed to minorities arguing against the death penalty than for a group of control subjects.

Shared beliefs affected group performance in another study reported by Smith et al. (1998). In this study the authors also demonstrated that multiple competing representations can limit the degree to which minorities can be influential. Smith et al. compared individual to group performance on an investment problem involving sunk costs. A sunk cost situation is one where individuals are likely to continue supporting a particular course of action (or to forego a more lucrative change in plans) because of the amount of time, effort, and/or resources already committed to that action. Thus, people often remain committed to a project or decision because of sunk costs even when it would be economically more viable to change direction and refrain from putting more resources into the current project (see Arkes & Blumer, 1985, or Staw, 1976 for review). Smith et al. used a revised problem reported by Arkes and Blumer (1985) involving a printing company that had either recently purchased a new and expensive printing press or a fleet of delivery trucks. Subsequently, the company is given the opportunity to obtain a better printing press at a bargain basement price. Arkes and Blumer found that participants were less likely to purchase the better printing press when they had just spent a significant amount of money on a press because of the perceived wastefulness of the initial printing press purchase. That is, the belief that being wasteful is bad prevents people from making the "economically rational" choice.

Smith et al. predicted that minorities favoring the sunk cost position might be particularly influential in this situation, and thus groups might actually perform worse (from a normative perspective) than individuals on this task. However, in the sunk cost condition, groups and individuals performed equally poorly (only made the rational choice about 50% of the time). In addition, a majority model did an adequate job of accounting for the group decision. There was some evidence of minority influence but that influence was not a function of the position being argued for. That is, although minority influence was rare, it was equally as likely when the minority was arguing against buying the press as it was when the minority argued in favor of buying the press. Each group member was asked to justify in writing her or his decision regarding the purchase of the press. Two reasons were stated with equal frequency and these two reasons were almost perfectly negatively correlated within the written justifications. Just under 40% of the group members (prior to group discussion) mentioned that they did not buy the press because they had just purchased one. An approximately equal number of the members mentioned that they had bought the press because it was the economically rational thing to do (e.g., it was a better press at a very good price). Thus, there were two prominent beliefs relevant to the choice alternatives and these beliefs were shared by approximately 40% of the population of group members.

Analyses involving the number of group members who stated a particular belief showed that both representations (i.e., sunk cost logic versus economically rational choice) had a powerful impact upon final group decisions. For example, when only two members used sunk cost logic to justify their preference, the minority faction prevailed in their decision not to buy the press in over half of the groups. A similar trend was found for minority factions using the economically rational logic. In instances where there were two competing representations the representation with the most advocates tended to prevail. Consequently, minority influence was reduced and groups were neither better nor worse (in most cases) than individuals working alone.

Shared cognitive processes

Tindale et al. (1996) reported the preliminary results of a series of probability estimate studies where members of minority factions who put forth preferences consistent with heuristic strategies were often much more influential than their numbers would predict. In each study, individuals and four-person groups were asked to estimate a series of probabilities, some of which involved conjunctive events. As demonstrated by Tversky and Kahneman

(1983), people often estimate the probabilities of conjunctions much higher than their estimate for at least one of the component events, thus violating the laws of probability. The initial probability estimate studies were oriented toward ascertaining whether group error rates would exceed those of individuals working alone.

Three different types of conjunctive events were used in these studies. Some of the conjunctions included two highly likely events (i.e., two events with high initial probability estimates). Others were defined by either one likely and one unlikely event, or by two unlikely events. Work by Yates and Carlson (1986) has shown that a typical way in which people estimate probabilities for conjunctions is by *signed summation*. When both events are highly likely, people rate the conjunctive event as even more likely than either single event. When both events are highly unlikely, they estimate the probability for the conjunction as even less likely than either single event. However, when one event is likely and the other unlikely, they tend to split the difference and average the estimates from the two component events. Thus, people are likely to violate the laws of probability when estimating conjunctive probabilities when the two component events are likely, or when one is likely and one is unlikely, but are less likely to make such errors when both component events are unlikely.

In the studies reported by Tindale et al. (1996), individual estimates conformed well to the predictions of the signed summation model. For likely–likely and likely–unlikely conjunctions, individuals were more likely than not to make errors. However, they were considerably less likely to make errors for the unlikely–unlikely conjunctions. Groups tended to exacerbate these patterns, such that groups were more likely than individuals to make errors on the likely–likely and likely–unlikely conjunctions, but less likely than individuals to make errors on the unlikely–unlikely conjunctions. Perhaps more interesting, the patterns of majority and minority influence also shifted as a function of conjunction type. For likely–likely and likely–unlikely conjunctions, groups containing only one member whose prediscussion estimates violated the laws of probability made the conjunction error more than 50% of the time. On the other hand, when estimating the unlikely–unlikely conjunctions, single-person minorities were more powerful when their estimates did not violate the laws of probability than when they made the conjunction error. Thus, factions whose preference matched the implications of the signed summation strategy were more powerful than those whose preference did not. Although the size of the faction was not irrelevant, even single-member minorities facing three-person majorities defined the groups response more often than not when their position was consistent with the shared strategy.

A recent follow-up to these studies (Tindale, Anderson, Smith, Steiner, & Filkins, 1998) attempted to explore further the group processes underlying the pattern of results presented above. In addition, we also varied the degree of familiarity participants would have with the components making up the conjunctions (hypothetical people described in the abstract versus people described as fellow university students). The group discussions were videotaped and coded with respect to how the group members reached consensus on a final judgment. Two rather interesting findings have emerged thus far (the data are still being analyzed). First, when making judgments about the category memberships of students at their own university (e.g., likelihood of student X being a math major and holding down a part-time job), participants were relatively unlikely to make conjunction errors, particularly for the unlikely–unlikely and the likely–unlikely conjunctions. In addition, for the familiar items, minorities making conjunction errors tended not to overpower majorities that did not make the error. We believe this is because the students were more likely to use their knowledge of the population of students to make their estimates than the signed summation or some other heuristic strategy. For the unfamiliar items, results were similar to those found in the earlier studies. It is interesting to note that the videotaped group discussions revealed that groups rarely discussed strategies for making the judgments – they simply mentioned their estimates and then negotiated about which estimate to use for the group. In over 60% of the cases, the groups simply went with one of their members' preferences. However, in all but the unlikely–unlikely condition, the group preference was more likely than chance to reflect the conjunction error. For example, more than 50% of the groups made the conjunction error when they comprised two individuals who made the error and two members who did not. It seems that preferences normatively defined as errors were more acceptable or seemed more plausible to group members than preferences that did not violate the laws of probability. That is, group members did not discuss whether specific estimates were more or less likely to be valid; they simply went along with suggested estimates that fit with the shared heuristic strategy.

Summary and Implications

Much of the work discussed in this chapter used a different paradigm than is typically used for minority influence research. On the other hand, any situation that involves reaching consensus also involves social influence. Therefore, we believe that thinking about small group decision making in terms of majority and minority influence can simultaneously inform the group performance and minority influence literatures. For example, Wood et al.'s (1994) meta-analytic summary of the minority influence literature concluded that evidence of minority influence is most readily found in contexts where measurements of influence are delayed, indirect, and taken in private. It is interesting to note that much of the work discussed here revealed minority influence that was immediate, direct, and public. Although it is not our aim to invalidate these earlier findings, we would like to suggest that the notion that minority influence is private, indirect, and more likely found after a delay is most likely a paradigm-specific conclusion. In situations where consensus must be reached, the task has a correct or optimal solution, and the members share an appropriate task representation for solving the problem, minorities favoring the correct solution are quite influential, in a direct, immediate, and public way. An increased focus on tasks that are intellective, as opposed to judgmental in nature, will certainly allow for a richer understanding of minority influence processes. (cf. Kerr, this volume; Pérez & Mugny, 1996; Maass, Volpato, & Mucchi-Faina, A., 1996).

Our discussion of judgmental tasks where shared task representations were present also serves to broaden the context in which minority influence is predicted. This work is consistent with the vast majority of the Zeitgeist research (Clark & Maass, 1988a; 1988b; 1990; Paicheler, 1976, 1977). Arguing a local minority position for which there is majority support in the general population allows one to tie one's arguments to generally accepted norms, value, beliefs, and so forth that are shared by fellow group members. When the minority faction is able to make these shared perspectives salient, one would expect significant minority influence. The work by Smith et al. (2000) also demonstrates that the Zeitgeist specific to the influence topic is only one type of shared representation, and that other related representations might enhance minority influence.

Finally, recent work on social influence processes in decision-making groups has emphasized that preferences are not the only things that can be viewed as shared in a group (Hinsz, Tindale, & Vollrath, 1997; Kameda, Tindale, & Davis, in press; Tindale & Kameda, in press). Although majorities and minorities are often defined at the preference level, this is only one of many levels that can be addressed. Thus, a member of a preference minority may be able to take advantage of cognitions shared with majority members in an attempt to enhance the influence she or he exerts. Although shared preferences are a powerful component of social influence in groups, shared ideas, beliefs, values, goals, identities, and so forth can also be used to provide a context for increased minority influence. In other words, sharedness on many different levels has the potential to define truth for the group.

NOTE

Preparation of this chapter was supported by NSF Grant #SBR-9730822 to the first and second author.

REFERENCES

Arkes, H. R., & Blumer, C. (1985). The psychology of sunk cost. *Organizational Behavior and Human Decision Processes*, *35*, 124–140.

Asch, S. E. (1951). Effects of group pressure upon the modification and distortion of judgments. In H. Guetzkow (Ed.), *Groups, leadership and men* (pp. 177–190). Pittsburgh, PA: Carnegie Press.

Chaiken, S., & Stangor, C. (1987). Attitudes and attitude change. *Annual Review of Psychology*, *38*, 575–630.

Clark, R. D., III. (1990). Minority influence: The role of argument refutation of the majority position and social support for the minority position. *European Journal of Social Psychology*, *20*, 489–497.

Clark, R. D., III. (1988). On predicting minority influence. *European Journal of Social Psychology*, *18*, 515–526.

Clark, R. D., III., & Maass, A. (1988a). Social categorization in minority influence: The case of homosexuality. *European Journal of Social Psychology*, *18*, 347–364.

Clark, R. D., III., & Maass, A. (1988b). The role of social categorization and perceived source credibility in minority influence. *European Journal of Social Psychology*, *18*, 381–394.

Clark, R. D., III., & Maass, A. (1990). The effects of majority size on minority influence. *European Journal of Social Psychology*, *20*, 119–132.

Davis, J. H. (1973). Group decision and social interaction: A theory of social decision schemes. *Psychological Review*, *80*, 97–125.

Davis, J. H. (1980). Group decision and procedural justice. In M. Fishbein (Ed.), *Progress in social psychology* (Vol. 1, pp. 157–229). Hillsdale, NJ: Erlbaum.

Davis, J. H. (1982). Social interaction as a combinatorial process in group decision. In H. Brandstatter, J. H. Davis, & G. Stocker-Kreichgauer (Eds.), *Group decision making* (pp. 27–58). London: Academic Press.

Davis, J. H., Kameda, T., & Stasson, M. (1992). Group risk taking: Selected topics. In F. Yates (Ed.), *Risk taking behavior* (pp. 163–199). Chichester, UK: Wiley.

Davis, J. H., Kerr, N. L., Stasser, G., Meek, D., & Holt, R. (1977). Victim consequences, sentence severity, and decision processes in mock juries. *Organizational Behavior and Human Performance*, *18*, 346–365.

Davis, J. H., Kerr, N. L., Sussman, M., & Rissman, A. (1974). Social decision schemes under risk. *Journal of Personality and Social Psychology*, *30*, 248–271.

Festinger, L. (1950). Informal social communication. *Psychological Review*, *57*, 217–282.

Festinger, L. (1954). A theory of social comparison processes. *Human Relations, 7,* 117–140.

Hinsz, V. B., Tindale, R. S., & Vollrath, D. A. (1997). The emerging conceptualization of groups as information processors. *Psychological Bulletin, 121,* 43–64.

Kahneman, D., & Tversky, A. (1979). Prospect theory: An analysis of decisions under risk. *Econometrica, 47,* 263–291.

Kameda, T. (1991). Procedural influence in small-group decision making: Deliberation style and assigned decision rule. *Journal of Personality and Social Psychology, 61,* 245–256.

Kameda, T., Tindale, R. S., & Davis, J. H. (in press). Cognitions, preferences, and social sharedness: Past, present and future directions in group decision making. In S. L. Schneider & J. Shanteau (Eds.), *Emerging perspectives on judgment and decision research.* Cambridge, UK: Cambridge University Press.

Kerr, N. L., & MacCoun, R. J. (1985). The effects of jury size and polling method on the process and product of jury deliberation. *Journal of Personality and Social Psychology, 48,* 349–363.

Laughlin, R. R. (1980). Social combination processes of cooperative, problem-solving groups on verbal intellective tasks. In M. Fishbein (Ed.), *Progress in social psychology* (Vol. 1, pp. 127–155). Hillsdale, NJ: Lawrence Erlbaum.

Laughlin, P. R., & Adamopoulos, J. (1980). Social combination processes and individual learning for six-person cooperative groups on an intellective task. *Journal of Personality and Social Psychology, 38,* 941–947.

Laughlin, P. R., & Early, P. C. (1982). Social combination processes, persuasive arguments theory, social comparison theory, and choice shifts. *Journal of Personality and Social Psychology, 42,* 273–280.

Laughlin, P. R., & Ellis, A. L. (1986). Demonstrability and social combination processes on mathematical intellective tasks. *Journal of Experimental Social Psychology, 22,* 177–189.

Laughlin, P. R., Kerr, N. L., Davis, J. H., Halff, H. M., & Marciniak, K. A. (1975). Group size, member ability, and social decision schemes on an intellective task. *Journal of Personality and Social Psychology, 31,* 522–535.

Laughlin, P. R., Kerr, N. L., Munch, M. M., & Haggarty, C. A. (1976). Social decision schemes of the same four-person groups on two different intellective tasks. *Journal of Personality and Social Psychology, 33,* 80–88.

Lorge, I., & Solomon, H. (1955). Two models of group behavior in the solution of Eureka-type problems. *Psychometrika, 20,* 139–148.

Maass, A., & Clark, R. D., III. (1984). The hidden impact of minorities: Fifteen years of minority influence research. *Psychological Bulletin, 95,* 428–450.

Maass, A., Volpato, C., & Mucchi-Faina, A. (1996). Social influence and the verifiability of the issue under discussion: Attitudinal versus objective items. *British Journal of Social Psychology, 35,* 15–26.

Maass, A., West, S. G., & Cialdini, R. (1987). Minority influence and conversion. In C. Hendrick (Ed.), *Review of personality and social psychology* (Vol. 8, pp. 55–79). Beverly Hills, CA: Sage.

Mednick, S. A., & Mednick, M. T. (1967). *Examiner's manual: Remote associates test.* Boston: Houghton-Miffin.

Moscovici, S. (1980). Toward a theory of conversion behavior. In L. Berkowitz (Ed.), *Advances in experimental social psychology* (Vol. 13, pp. 209–239). New York: Academic Press.

Moscovici, S., & Nemeth, C. J. (1974). Social influence II: Minority influence. In C. J. Nemeth (Ed.), *Social psychology: classic and contemporary integrations* (pp. 217–249). Chicago: Rand McNally.

Mugny, G. (1975). Negotiations, image of the other and the process of minority influence. *European Journal of Social Psychology, 5,* 209–229.

Mugny, G. (1982). *The power of minorities.* London: Academic Press.

Mugny, G., & Pérez, J. A. (1991). *The social psychology of minority influence.* Cambridge, UK. Cambridge University Press.

Myers, D. G., & Lamm, H. (1976). The group polarization phenomenon. *Psychological Bulletin, 83,* 602–627.

Nemeth, C. (1977). Interactions between jurors as a function of majority vs. unanimity decision rules. *Journal of Applied Social Psychology, 7,* 38–56.

Nemeth, C. (1986). Differential contributions of majority and minority influence. *Psychological Review, 93,* 23–32.

Paicheler, G. (1976). Norms and attitude change: I. Polarization and styles of behavior. *European Journal of Social Psychology, 6,* 405–427.

Paicheler, G. (1977). Polarization of attitudes in homogeneous and heterogeneous groups. *European Journal of Social Psychology, 9,* 85–96.

Pérez, J. A., & Mugny, G. (1996). The conflict elaboration theory of social influence. In E. Witte & J. Davis (Eds.), *Understanding group behavior: Consensual action by small groups* (Vol. 2, pp. 191–210). Hillsdale, NJ: Erlbaum.

Shaw, M. E. (1932). Comparison of individuals and small groups in the rational solution of complex problems. *American Journal of Psychology, 44,* 491–504.

Smith, C. M., Dykema-Engblade, A., Walker, A., Niven, T., & McGough, T. (2000) Asymmetrical social influence in freely interacting groups discussing the death penalty: A shared representations interpretation. *Group Processes and Intergroup Relations, 3* (4), 387–401.

Smith, C. M., Tindale, R. S., & Steiner, L. (1998). Investment decisions by individuals and groups in "sunk cost" situations: The potential impact of shared representations. *Group Processes and Intergroup Relations, 1,* 175–189.

Stasser, G., Kerr, N. L., & Bray, R. (1982). The social psychology of jury deliberations: Structure, process and product. In N. Kerr & R. Bray (Eds.), *The psychology of the courtroom* (pp. 186–219). New York: Academic Press.

Stasser, G., Kerr, N. L., & Davis, J. H. (1989). Influence processes and consensus models in decision-making groups. In P. Paulus (Ed.), *Psychology of group influence* (2nd ed., pp. 279–326). Hillsdale, NJ: Erlbaum.

Stasser, G., & Titus, W. (1985). Pooling of unshared information in group decision making: Biased information sampling during discussion. *Journal of Personality and Social Psychology, 48,* 1467–1478.

Staw, B. M. (1976). Knee deep in the big muddy: A study of escalating commitment to a chosen course of action. *Organizational Behavior and Human Performance, 16,* 27–44.

Steiner, I. (1972). *Group process and productivity.* New York: Academic Press.

Tindale, R. S. (1989). Group vs. individual information processing: The effects of outcome feedback on decision making. *Organizational Behavior and Human Decision Processes, 44,* 454–473.

Tindale, R. S., Anderson, E. M., Smith, C. M., Steiner, L., & Filkins, J. (1998, September). *Further explorations of conjunction errors by individuals and groups.* Paper presented at the British Psychological Society Social Psychology Section Conference, Canterbury, UK.

Tindale, R. S., & Davis, J. H. (1983). Group decision making and jury verdicts. In H. H. Blumberg, A. P. Hare, V. Kent, & M. F. Davies (Eds.), *Small groups and social interaction* (Vol. 2, pp. 9–38). Chichester, UK: Wiley.

Tindale, R. S., & Davis, J. H. (1985). Individual and group reward allocation decisions in two situational contexts: The effects of relative need and performance. *Journal of Personality and Social Psychology, 48,* 1148–1161.

Tindale, R. S., Davis, J. H., Vollrath, D. A., Nagao, D. H., & Hinsz, V. B. (1990). Asymmetrical social influence in freely interacting groups: A test of three models. *Journal of Personality and Social Psychology, 58,* 438–449.

Tindale, R. S., & Kameda, T. (in press). "Social sharedness" as a unifying theme for information processing in groups. *Group Processes and Intergroup Relations.*

Tindale, R. S., Sheffey, S., & Scott, L. A. (1993). Framing and group decision making: Do cognitive changes parallel preference changes? *Organizational Behavior and Human Decision Processes, 55,* 470–485.

Tindale, R. S., Smith, C. M., Thomas, L. S., Filkins, J., & Sheffey, S. (1996). Shared representations and asymmetric social influence processes in small groups. In E. Witte & J. Davis (Eds.), *Understanding group behavior: Consensual action by small groups* (Vol. 1, pp. 81–103). Hillsdale, NJ: Erlbaum.

Tversky, A., & Kahneman, D. (1983). Extensional vs. intuitive reasoning: The conjunction fallacy in probability judgments. *Psychological Review, 90,* 293–315.

Wood, W., Lundgren, S., Ouellette, A., Busceme, S., & Blackstone, T. (1994). Minority influence: A meta-analytic review of social influence processes. *Psychological Bulletin, 115,* 323–345.

Yates, J. F., & Carlson, B. W. (1986). Conjunction errors: Evidence for multiple judgment procedures including signed summation. *Organizational Behavior and Human Decision Processes, 37,* 230–253.

10

Is It What One Says or How One Says It?: Style vs. Substance from an SDS Perspective

Norbert L. Kerr

In a recent chapter, Moscovici (1994) draws on Gibbon's (e.g., see Trevor-Roper, 1966) historical analysis to examine the growth of the early Christian church (which, of course, began as a very small minority at the beginning of the last millennium). Moscovici writes:

> Gibbon firmly suggests that the reason for the influence of a small group cannot be sought in the cognitive value of its doctrine and even less in a supernatural intervention. Consequently, the problem of the ascension of the Christian doctrine on the world stage has to be approached from another side. If firstly the minority is in a disadvantageous situation, and secondly the cognitive value of its ideas and message does not make up for it, then there needs to be a third factor explaining the influence it manifestly exerts on the majority. We have surmised (Moscovici and Faucheaux, 1972; Moscovici and Nemeth, 1974) that this factor is what has been termed behavioral style ... one has to observe how [an individual or group] express themselves rather than listen to what they say. (Moscovici, 1994, p. 246)

Moscovici suggested that there was nothing distinctive or compelling about the message of the early Christian minority (a position which goes well beyond Gibbon's, as I will later argue). He argued that one could not plausibly attribute the ascendancy of this religion to "... the cognitive value of its doctrine." Rather, Moscovici suggested, it was the conviction, courage, and certainty – elements of behavioral style – with which those early advocates (and martyrs) expressed their faith that won converts. It was not what they said that explained their influence, it was how they said it (e.g., how consistently, how firmly, how inflexibly). Or, as this chapter's title would put it, when it comes to minority influence, style is much more important than substance.

There is by now a substantial body of empirical work on minority influence that has convincingly documented that aspects of a minority source's behavioral style – such as the degree of flexibility (Mugny & Pérez, 1991) and the degree of consistency (e.g., Moscovici et al., 1969) – can indeed moderate its social influence (for reviews, see Levine & Russo, 1987; Maass & Clark, 1984; Wood, Lundgren, Ouellette, Busceme, & Blackstone, 1994). In the present chapter, however, I would like to consider the rather stronger position advanced by Moscovici in his analysis of the rise of Christianity (and in other theoretical writings)[1] – not that a minority's behavioral style can sometimes matter, but that style is essentially all that matters (particularly when compared with the substance of the minority's message).

I shall approach this issue from a theoretical and empirical perspective that is very different from Moscovici's, or for that matter, from most other contemporary minority influence theorists' (e.g., Crano, 1994; Trost & Kenrick, 1994; Pérez, Mugny, Butera, Kaiser, & Roux, 1994; Nemeth, 1986; De Vries, De Dreu, Gordijn, & Schuurman, 1996). My general perspective is the study of small group decision making; my specific perspective is that of social combination models of group decision making, such as Davis's (1973, 1996) social decision scheme (SDS) model (see the chapter by Smith, Tindale, and Anderson in this volume for another application of this perspective to minority influence). Since relatively few readers are likely to be familiar with – much less share – this perspective, a good place to begin might be to provide a brief introduction to it (for a fuller discussion of the assumptions and application of the SDS model, see Baron, Kerr, & Miller, 1992; Davis, 1973; Kerr, Stasser, & Davis, 1979; and Stasser, 1999).

The Social Combination/SDS Approach to the Study of Group Decision Making and Problem Solving

About the same time that interest in minority influence first arose (around 1970; e.g., Moscovici, Lage, & Naffrechoux, 1969), another research program was also just beginning – the program of research developing and applying the social decision scheme (SDS) model (Davis, 1973, 1996; Stasser, Kerr, & Davis, 1989). The minority influence research program grew out of (and in many ways, challenged) the early social influence literature in general and the conformity literature in particular (Nemeth, 1994). The SDS program's roots are rather different; they lie in the early group performance literature (e.g., Davis, 1969; Steiner, 1972) in general and in formal, mathematical modeling of group processes (e.g., Lorge & Solomon, 1955; Smoke & Zajonc, 1962) in particular. The SDS model is the prototype of the "social combination approach" (Davis, 1982; Laughlin, 1980). That approach tries to predict a product of group interaction (such as a group decision, a group performance, or a group solution to a problem) as a combination of the resources (e.g., group member preferences, levels of performance, or solutions) that members bring to the group. The function relating group member inputs and group outputs takes the form of a stochastic matrix in the SDS model, the *social decision scheme* matrix (usually denoted D). D specifies the probability that the group will eventually arrive at each possible group outcome for each possible distribution of member inputs.

There are a few noteworthy differences between the minority influence and SDS research traditions. First, minority influence work has tended to focus on the *processes* of social influence, whereas SDS models are, first and foremost, designed to account for group *products*. The immediate goal for most SDS analyses has been to identify the applicable decision scheme for a particular group task, that is, the D that will most accurately predict the group product. Explication of the processes of mutual social influence that must occur in the group between the two principal points of assessment for SDS – the assessment of prediscussion opinion/dissensus and the assessment of postdiscussion group consensus – has generally been of less immediate concern. That is not to say that understanding group processes is of little concern in SDS work. Construction of a priori, candidate D matrices does not take place in a process vacuum. Because the D matrix is a summary of the net effect of all social influence processes that occur during group interaction (Kerr, MacCoun, & Kramer, 1996), one cannot construct a D matrix without making process assumptions (at least implicitly). And, when a best-fitting D matrix is estimated from one's data (rather than being tested as an a priori model), its content will usually carry useful process implications. So, although there are clear differences in emphasis, the minority influence and the SDS research programs continually confront the same basic social psychological questions: How do majorities influence minorities and how do minorities influence majorities.

The second noteworthy difference is in the types of social influence upon which these two programs focus most closely. Minority influence theorists have conceded that it is difficult and uncommon for minorities to produce overt, public conversion of the majority to their positions. However, it has been argued that minorities can and do have more indirect or delayed impact

– on private opinion and on related issues (cf. Mugny & Pérez, 1991; Crano & Chen, 1998), or producing more original, divergent thinking about the focal issue (Nemeth, 1986). By contrast, most SDS work has concentrated on mutual social influence in face-to-face groups striving to reach a mutually acceptable decision or solution. SDS's research context has several potentially important implications. Specifically in the SDS social-influence crucible:

1. When there are majority and minority factions, both are simultaneously trying to influence one another. (Contrast this situation with most other social influence work – conformity, attitude change, and, of course, minority influence research – where a single source – majority/minority person or faction – attempts unilaterally to influence a single target – a majority/minority person or faction that is typically passive and not attempting counterinfluence). Thus, one side's substance is likely to be challenged by the other side. One person's style can provide a model for other sources of social influence (who do and don't share his or her position). Social influence is likely to be much more dynamic; for example, early position changes may affect subsequent opinion changes (Kerr, 1981, 1992a; Kerr, MacCoun, Hanseu, & Hymes, 1987).

2. There is nearly always an explicit or implicit requirement for some level of ultimate agreement. This criterion is referred to by proponents of SDS as a *decision rule*. Examples are a simple majority requirement or (in most US juries) a requirement of unanimity. Until the group reaches that criterion, it cannot complete its work and in most instances (including most laboratory groups) cannot end its deliberation. A number of minority influence scholars (e.g., Trost & Kenrick, 1994) have suggested that the unexpectedness or novelty of a minority advocacy can attract attention and (perhaps) more thorough processing of the minority's message (see Trost, Maass, & Kenrick, 1992). In decision-making groups, minorities that block satisfaction of the decision rule compel the majority to consider and try to refute its views. When the decision rule is extreme – near unanimity – even very small minorities can force such attention.

3. There is a considerable level of interdependence between group members. The need to satisfy a decision rule before quitting, discussed above, is one such source of interdependence. The process of group decision making or problem solving is one in which one's own position must often be defended, and there are salient consequences of taking a popular versus an unpopular position, well documented in social influence research (e.g., Levine, 1989; Schachter, 1951). (Contrast this with the

usual minority influence setting, where there is usually little interdependence between source and target, and targets often face no external social consequences for their agreement or disagreement with a source of influence.)

Besides these distinctive features, the social influence of most interest in an SDS analysis is immediate, public, and on the focal issue (although occasionally some attention is given to private and/or postdeliberation opinion; e.g., Kerr, Davis, Meek, & Rissman, 1975). Moscovici and others have argued that the social influence processes that explain public compliance to majorities are qualitatively and fundamentally different than those that explain opinion change that is private, delayed, or indirect – ostensibly the province of minorities. This has become a point of theoretical contention that will not be rehashed or settled here. But it is best to be clear about my own position: I tend to agree with those (e.g., Kruglanski & Mackie, 1990; Latané & Wolf, 1981) who argue that the existence and importance of these differences are exaggerated. Hence, I assume that the insights that SDS researchers have had largely through the study of public opinion change can be of interest and value to minority influence scholars, even those who have been relatively uninterested in such forms of direct social influence.

As is sadly so often the case, these two programs – minority influence and SDS – have progressed with little apparent mutual awareness, and much less active cross-fertilization. The primary objective of the rest of this presentation will be to argue that SDS work has something interesting to say to scholars of minority influence, specifically on the "style versus substance" question.

Minority Influence from an SDS Perspective

Within the admittedly distinctive context which is the focus of SDS research, when do minorities prevail? The work of Laughlin and his colleagues (e.g., Laughlin, 1980; Laughlin & Ellis, 1986) is particularly informative. In work begun in the 1970s (e.g., Laughlin, Kerr, Davis, Halff, & Marciniak, 1975; Laughlin, Kerr, Munch, & Haggerty, 1976), Laughlin and his colleagues attempted to apply the SDS model to predicting the performance of groups working on simple intellectual tasks with correct answers, such as tests of word meanings or associations. Laughlin found that for certain tasks (e.g., the Remote Associates Test; Mednick & Mednick, 1967), a single correct group member was sufficient to insure (or nearly insure) that the group also solved the problem. For other tasks (e.g., verbal analogies or vocabulary tests), the D that best fit the data indicated that a single advocate of the correct answer was not sufficient, but that two such advocates were – hence, the D was termed "truth-supported wins." These results stood in sharp contrast to other SDS work going on about the same time, which was examining other group tasks, such as jury decision making (e.g., Davis, Kerr, Atkin, Holt, & Meek, 1975; Kerr et al., 1976), attitude polarization (e.g., Kerr et al., 1975), and selection among bets (Davis, Kerr, Sussman, & Rissman, 1974). Minority factions, even fairly large ones, rarely prevailed in the latter groups.

Laughlin (e.g., Laughlin, 1980; Laughlin & Ellis, 1986) suggested that these differences in the power of minorities could be traced to a crucial task feature.[2] He suggested that tasks could be ordered on a dimension anchored at one end by purely *intellective* tasks, and at the other end by purely *judgmental* tasks. Intellective tasks are ones which have an "objective," "correct" answer. This is not as transparent a criterion as it might seem. Laughlin argues that what makes one particular answer "objectively correct" is a widely shared conceptual system. For example, agreement on the meaning of numbers and simple arithmetic operations (e.g., adding, subtracting) makes the solutions to simple arithmetic problems "objectively correct." Ideally, this conceptual system is not only universally shared, but clear and complete enough to permit one to deduce from available information whether any particular possible solution is, within this system, correct or not. Of course, this ideal is only rarely met. The conceptual systems with which we must evaluate most of the problems or decisions we face are shared incompletely, have missing or ambiguous links, or rely upon nondeterministic reasoning. When the conceptual systems become too idiosyncratic and/or fragmentary, our choices become largely or completely matters of personal preference – the realm of judgmental tasks. For example, Laughlin suggests that many ethical, aesthetic, or attitudinal issues are judgmental because they have no demonstrably "correct" answer within a shared conceptual system.

Laughlin goes on to suggest (as have others, e.g., Festinger, 1954) that when there is no "objective" basis for evaluation, we rely upon social consensus to validate alternative positions. Hence, the more judgmental the task, the more majorities are likely to prevail. The more intellective the task, the lower the level of social support required to prevail for a demonstrably correct alternative. Thus, Laughlin does not argue that any minority gains power as the task becomes more intellective. Rather, he argues that minorities (or, for that matter, majorities) can prevail at such tasks as long as they are advocating a correct alternative. This analysis suggests that the minority position must have substance to prevail.

"Substance" from an SDS perspective

Although minority influence scholars have had much that is useful to say about what constitutes an effective style of advocacy (e.g., see Moscovici, 1976), they have devoted much less attention to what constitutes impactful substance for advocates. Perhaps this is not surprising, given the relative importance many such scholars have attached to style over substance. Laughlin's analysis does, however, offer a useful conception of what gives a social influence attempt "substance." It roots such substance in a shared conceptual system (e.g., beliefs, values, assumptions, logic). The more widely shared a particular system is, the larger the potential pool of targets of influence who will recognize and accept the substance of a persuasive message. Hence, "substance" is not a disembodied property of the message itself, but depends directly on the beliefs of the targets of influence – what they see as relevant and probative for the issue at hand. In this sense, "correctness" is a social construction. This admits the possibility that certain arguments could have great "substance" for certain target audiences, while having little "substance" for others. For example, Gibbon suggests that mere claims of miracles and prophecies were highly probative of the power and validity of the claimant's religion in the minds of many in the first century AD. There apparently was a widely (although not universally) accepted conceptual system that (a) granted the reality of miracles, and (b) required little systematic, observable evidence to credit specific claims of miracles. It seems likely that the shared conceptual system of 21st century targets would attach less substance to such unsubstantiated claims.

Between the two extremes of purely intellective and purely judgmental tasks lie decision tasks with more or less widely shared and coherent conceptual systems. So, for example, among fluent English speakers, there is fairly wide agreement on the meaning of English words, but for many words there is disagreement and/or no knowledge. Laughlin finds (e.g., Laughlin et al., 1975; Laughlin et al., 1976) that a truth-supported wins D best accounts for the performance of groups at verbal analogies or vocabulary tests – correct minorities must be somewhat larger than for purely intellective tasks (cf. Laughlin et al., 1976; Laughlin & Ellis, 1986). Other tasks are closer to the judgmental extreme (e.g., juries deciding guilt or innocence; groups providing advice to actors facing risky choices), but still can tap into a shared conceptual system which gives advocates of certain "correct" positions greater influence than one would expect simply from their numbers. For example, the shared and accepted belief (traditional in common law) that an accused person deserves the benefit of any doubts as to his or her guilt should give advocates of acquittal (who voice such doubts) greater influence in jury deliberation than advocates of conviction, all other things – including the size of their factions – being equal. And, indeed, such an asymmetry of influence in juries has been documented (MacCoun & Kerr, 1988). Another example is group polarization. Laughlin and Earley (1982) have shown that an asymmetric decision scheme, one that gives greater influence to an advocate of risk-taking (relative to an advocate of caution), best predicts group decision for classic choice dilemma items that routinely produce risky shifts. Such items tap partially shared conceptual systems which give certain arguments greater substance than others.

This line of reasoning helps explain a regularity noted by several minority influence scholars – that minorities which advocate positions that are consistent with the inclinations of the (majority of the) target population (Clark, 1994), or that gain legitimacy with the dominant social norm (Moscovici, 1976) or with the current Zeitgeist (e.g., Clark & Maass, 1988) are, all else being equal, more likely to be influential. The SDS analysis would suggest that such opinion trends reflect a shared conceptual system which lends the arguments of minority (or, for that matter, majority) sources weight and substance.

"Style" from an SDS perspective

Laughlin also argues that even when there exits a "correct" answer within a widely shared conceptual system, it is not sufficient for a source simply to favor that answer personally. First, the targets of influence must be sufficiently able and willing to listen – to recognize the fit of the source's substance into their shared conceptual system. The latter requirement has been recognized and documented of late by theorists who have applied dual-process models of attitude change to minority influence (e.g., Baker & Petty, 1994; Trost & Kenrick, 1994; de Vries et al., 1996). So, for example, there is evidence that the relevant arguments of a minority source may be discounted when the target is highly motivated to reject the source's message (Trost et al., 1992). Secondly, and more important for our present discussion, Laughlin suggests that the advocate of a "correct" alternative must be sufficiently motivated to share the substance of his or her position with the group. In most cases, the "truth" of the correct solution will not be immediately evident – it will be necessary for the advocate of such "truth" actively to demonstrate the truth of his or her position by appeal to the shared conceptual system. Thus, for example, advocates of acquittal may have to do more than simply assert and defend their personal beliefs in a defendant's innocence. To have more substance than the views of an advocate of conviction, they must do more (e.g., remind the jury that the prescribed burdens of proof require them to give the defendant the benefit of every doubt). This might well be viewed as a requirement that the "correct" minority advocate must be assertive, dogged, consistent, persistent – that is, exhibit a certain behavioral style.

There is some suggestive evidence for this viewpoint in the group problem-solving literature. A number of studies have shown that groups containing a single member who can correctly solve a relatively intellective task (the horse trader problem, Maier & Solem, 1952) do not invariably solve the problem. It matters who the solver is and how that person behaves. For example, a low-status solver is less likely to prevail than a high-status solver (Torrence, 1954), an unconfident solver is less likely to prevail than a confident one (Johnson & Torcivia, 1967), and a reticent, untalkative solver is less likely to prevail than a more talkative solver (Thomas & Fink, 1961). It is quite possible that such low-status, unconfident, and reticent minority advocates fail fully to exploit the substance of their position due to their ineffectual behavioral style.

It is interesting to consider the reasons that minority influence theorists have given for why certain behavioral styles increase the effectiveness of a minority source (see Levine & Russo, 1987, for a review). For example, it has been argued that a consistent minority advocate (a) establishes the existence of a clear alternative to the dominant majority viewpoint, (b) suggests that one would have a steadfast ally if one were to defect from the majority to the minority, (c) wins the respect and attention of the target for the source's courage in taking an unpopular position, and (d) suggests to the target that there is a simple and correct solution to the problem at hand. The latter are implied by Laughlin's analysis. When one knows – within some coherent and presumably widely shared conceptual system – that one's position is "correct" and can be so demonstrated, it is reflected in one's style of advocacy. One is more likely to be adamant, persistent, unyielding, stubborn – in a word, consistent. We come to expect those who take consensually agreed upon "correct" positions to act with a certain behavioral style, and may eventually come to infer substance from style (perhaps even heuristically). Thus, the power of a consistent behavioral style may well, at least in part, derive from a consistent relationship between substance and style. Style implies substance (cf. Crano, 1994).

SDS Concepts from the Perspective of Minority Influence Research

Before I try to extend Laughlin's ideas to addressing the more general question, "When does a minority's (or majority's) style matter and when does its substance," I will note how minority influence theorists have addressed two of the issues raised by Laughlin's analysis: (a) the insufficiency of style and (b) the intellective/judgmental task distinction.

The insufficiency of style

Laughlin's SDS analysis suggests that as group decision tasks become more intellective, substance becomes more important. At the limit, for a purely intellective task, style may be largely irrelevant. As long as one presents one's position explicitly so that its substance can be recognized within the relevant shared conceptual system, it really should not matter with what style one advocates that position. Conversely, this suggests that for more intellective tasks, one may require at least some substance to be effective and that no level of type of behavioral style could compensate for the absence of sufficient substance.

It is fairly simple to substantiate this basic argument. It is not difficult to find delusional mental patients who, for example, assert that they are Napoleon, that their brains are being controlled by Martians, and so forth. And, in many cases, they make these assertions with exemplary behavioral style. They show conviction and consistency. They are willing to stick to their position even when others tell them they're crazy and otherwise stigmatize them. They may even show a willingness to be flexible and grant certain points to the skeptical observer. But no matter what style they adopt, if their position is wholly inconsistent with widely and deeply shared conceptual systems (e.g., that Napoleon is dead; that Martians do not exist), I maintain that they will have no influence at all (direct or indirect).

I will readily confess to being a casual scholar of the minority influence literature. My casual scholarship suggests, though, that the necessity of at least a minimum of substance (for at least some decision tasks) is addressed only implicitly or indirectly by minority influence scholars. For example, Cialdini and Trost (1998) say that the majority will examine the validity of the minority source's position if "... the minority presents a *realistic* consistent alternative viewpoint" (p. 165, emphasis added). Thus, unless the minority position passes some minimal substantive threshold, the majority will not even consider it. This theme also runs through Moscovici's writings. He suggests, for example, that "On the whole, it is not enough for [a minority] to display a consistent behavioral style. It helps if its position also appears objective . . ." (Moscovici, 1985, p. 390). (The SDS work of Laughlin and others would ground such objectivity in a shared conceptual system that gives a position "substance.") Elsewhere, Moscovici suggests that substance (". . . he cognitive value of its ideas and messages," Moscovici, 1976, p. 246) can compensate for the disadvantages of advocating a minority position, and that the "effectiveness of arguments depends *not only* on their content, but also on their form or style" (Moscovici, 1985, p. 401, emphasis added). Thus, a minority's power can apparently stem from its substance as well as from its style. But it remains unclear just how much substance is required, and whether and when there is a minimum substance threshold required for effective minority influence.

Intellective vs. judgmental tasks

The distinction between intellective and judgmental tasks – or something much like it – has been incorporated into theorizing on at least four recent minority influence models. A brief review of those models will provide a useful preface to a presentation of a model based explicitly upon the SDS model and its use of the distinction.

Pérez, Mugny, et al.'s model. In their model of minority influence, Pérez, Mugny, and their colleagues (Pérez, et al., 1994; Pérez & Mugny, 1996) utilize a distinction between issues which they term *objective* (which have a correct answer, like intellective tasks) and *opinion* issues (which do not, like judgmental tasks). The distinction is, they suggest, of special relevance for situations in which the credibility of a source of influence has been questioned (what they call *denial*). They argue that for objective tasks a *norm of objectivity* is engaged; targets of influence believe that there is a single correct answer. For such a task, denial of the source of influence would be more harmful to the credibility of a minority source than a majority source, at least in terms of latent influence (i.e., indirect or delayed influence). On opinion issues, on the other hand, a *preference norm* is engaged; there is no unique correct answer and ". . . the situation of influence allows for a certain pluralism" (Pérez et al., 1994, p. 190). Denial of the source on such an issue is, they argue, more harmful to the credibility of a majority than a minority source, and a minor-

Table 10.1 Summary of Predictions of Minority Influence Models Incorporating Intellective/Judgmental Distinction

Author of Model	Type of Influence	Influence Task Type	
		Intellective	Judgmental
		Model Prediction on Social Influence	
Pérez, Mugny, et al.	Direct	–	–
	Indirect	Denial of Source: Maj > Min	Denial of Source: Min > Maj
Maass, Vopato, & Mucci-Faina	Direct & Indirect?	Maj > Min	Min = Maj
Crano	Direct	Maj > Min	Maj > Min
	Indirect	Min > Maj	Maj > Min
De Vries & De Dreu	Direct	If Substance High: Min = Maj	Maj > Min
	Indirect	If Substance High: Maj = Min	Min > Maj

Notes: Cells with dashes signify that the model makes no explicit prediction for this set of conditions. Question marks signify that the prediction of the model is ambiguous. Direct influence refers to public opinion/position change on the focal issue; indirect change here refers broadly to change that is private, delayed, or on related issues.

ity should therefore exert greater latent influence. The predictions of this model, along with the other three models discussed below, are summarized in Table 10.1.

Maass, Vopato, and Mucci-Faina's model.   In an interesting paper, Maass, Vopato, and Mucci-Faina (1996) lay out a model of social influence in which they distinguish between objective (intellective) and attitudinal (judgmental) tasks. Using logic similar to that of Pérez et al., they suggest that people expect a single answer to be correct for the former but allow for many valid, acceptable answers to the latter kind of task. They make two other suggestions about objective tasks: (1) that there is a greater concern with holding the right, correct position (than for an attitudinal/judgmental issue), and (2) there is a presumption that there will be greater consensus on that correct position (relative to attitudinal/judgmental issues). Thus, they argue, a majority should be more influential than a minority on objective/intellective issues (see Table 10.1). (Although they include a manipulation of public vs. private change in their first study, their model does not make different predictions for direct/public vs. indirect/private change.) However, on an attitudinal/judgmental issue, being in the minority does not automatically imply being wrong, and thus minorities should be more influential (relative to objective/intellective tasks). Although the authors suggest that for certain attitudinal/judgmental issues (e.g., fashion, taste in literature), it may even be an advantage to be in the minority, the model is unclear about just how influential a minority can become at attitudinal issues (see Table 10.1). At the limit (i.e., purely judgmental tasks), their logic suggests (to me anyway) that minorities should be no less (or more) influential than majorities.

Crano's model.   Crano's context/comparison model of social influence (e.g., Crano, 1994) gives a central role to the choice of referent or comparison other. Crano suggests that whether or not the targets will see the minority as a legitimate or useful source of information will depend upon the nature of the influence task. He distinguishes between objective (intellective) and subjective (judgmental) tasks, and argues that for the latter, subjective task, one is particularly reliant upon the opinions of similar others (e.g., ingroup members). Although he considers many cases, for us the most interesting one is the prototypical minority influence situation in which the targets of influence comprise a majority (or, lacking any information about the popularity of their own views, presume they are in the majority). In this case, the target (in the majority) should view a minority source as a particularly poor source of valid information if the task is subjective, and thus, a majority source would be more likely to produce indirect social influence (which, for Crano, includes both private change on the focal issue and change on related, non-focal issues; see Table 10.1). When the task is objective, on the other hand, Crano suggests that a minority source will be even more influential than a majority source, at least for indirect change (see Table 10.1). As with many other minority influence models, Crano predicts that majorities will generally produce greater overt, public change than minorities (see Table 10.1).

De Vries, De Dreu, and colleagues' model.   Finally, De Vries, De Dreu and their colleagues (e.g., De Vries et al., 1996) speculate about the affect of Laughlin's intellective/judgmental task distinction within their dual role model of social influence. For judgmental tasks (the primary focus of their model), they predict that majority sources will be more influential than minority sources for direct, focal change, but that minorities have an advantage for indirect change (see Table 10.1; also see De Vries et al. for a fuller discussion of the dual role theory and the rationale for these predictions). On the other hand, they speculate that intellective tasks engender (a) a strong desire to be accurate, and (b) careful, systematic processing of source information (without certain biases in that processing that can arise for judgmental tasks). Thus, if a source is endorsing the correct response on an intellective task, it should make no difference – either for direct or indirect change – whether or not the source is a minority or a majority (see Table 10.1).

Implications of these models.   Several common themes emerge from our review of the preceding models. First, with only one exception (De Vries et al., 1996), the models do not consider the substance of the source's message. Both theoretically (and, in most cases, operationally), these scholars tend to focus on social influence without substance – for example, an influence source's simple assertion of preference with minimal explanation and justification for that preference. This is, of course, an interesting and common social influence context. But it almost never arises in SDS research; it is rare for a group member or faction in a face-to-face, consensus-seeking group simply to assert a preference without explanation or justification. In a sense, the models are most interested in the effects of source minority/majority status (first and foremost) and task type (as a moderating variable) on a target's thinking about several matters prior to receiving, or regardless of the substance of, the source's message. Thus, in these models, the important thing is the targets' perception of issue objectivity, not whether or not a position actually can be demonstrated as correct within a conceptual system that is widely shared among targets.

Second, these models identify some of the ways a source's thinking may be thus affected. Most suggest that targets are more likely to (1) presume that there is a correct answer, and (2) be concerned with choosing that correct answer when the issue is intellective than when it is judgmental. Where they consider this point, they do not always agree on which type of source is relied more upon for each task type. For example, Maass et al. suggest that, all else being equal, a majority source is seen as more credible for an intellective task (because of the consensus heuristic, which holds that the larger a faction, the more likely it is to be correct; Chaiken & Stangor, 1987), whereas Crano suggests that, all else being equal, a majority source is particularly credible for a judgmental task (because one seeks majority support on issues without objectively correct answers).

In the next section, I will present a social influence model which (1) is explicitly built upon SDS theory and research, (2) explicitly incorporates the role of the substance of a source's message, and (3) might illuminate both some of the points of agreement and of conflict in the preceding models.

An SDS Model of Minority Influence

To begin with, let us add another general type of influence to the distinction between "direct" (i.e., public change on the focal issue) and "indirect" (i.e., private change, immediate or delayed, on the focal or on other issues) which runs through the minority influence literature. It is the kind of influence which occurs in the group contexts usually studied by investigators within the SDS tradition – changes of position that are made publicly on the focal issue in a context where consensus is being sought.[3] We will call this kind of social influence *consensus-seeking* change (see Table 10.2). Such change may (but need not be) only in the service of reaching an agreement. So, for example, even in groups which reach consensus on attitudinal or choice dilemma tasks, there is typically some regression in publicly endorsed opinion to the predeliberation position of individual members (e.g., Davis et al., 1974; Kerr et al., 1975). Surprisingly, even members of juries will agree to a verdict (with potentially serious consequences for a defendant) with which they will subsequently, publicly disagree (e.g., Davis et al., 1974). Because the SDS model has been developed and applied primarily to consensus-seeking change, the model I am proposing here is most (but not exclusively) relevant and least speculative for this form of social influence.

With this trichotomy of social influence (consensus-seeking vs. direct, no-consensus seeking vs. indirect) in hand, let us consider the roles that

Table **10.2** *An SDS Model of Minority Influence*

Level of Substance in Source Message	Type of Influence	Type of Social Influence Issue/Task		
		Purely Intellective	*Partially Intellective*	*Purely Judgmental*
High Substance	Consensus-seeking	Minority = Majority	Majority > Minority	Not Defined
	Direct, no consensus	Minority = Majority	Majority > Minority	
	Indirect	Minority = Majority / Majority > Minority	–	
Low Substance	Consensus-seeking	Majority > Minority	Majority >> Minority	Target committed: Majority > Minority / Target uncommitted: Maj = Min
	Direct, no consensus	Majority > Minority	Majority > Minority	Minority = Majority
	Indirect	–	–	–
Importance of Style		Substance trumps Style and/or Popularity	Substance and/or Style can compensate for Unpopularity	Style trumps "Substance" (or Popularity?)

Note: Cells with dashes signify that the model makes no explicit prediction for this set of conditions.

substance, style, and the popularity of a source of influence's position have in its likely social influence for different points along the intellective–judgmental dimension.

Purely intellective tasks

Let us begin with tasks near the intellective end of the dimension. For these tasks there should be a widely shared and coherent conceptual system within which a particular alternative is, in Laughlin's words, demonstrably correct. For such a task, when I speak of a source position having "high substance," I mean that the source of social influence advocates this correct position and is able and willing to defend that position relying upon the shared conceptual system. As Table 10.2 indicates, for such a source and such a task, it should make no difference whether the source espouses a popular, majority position or an unpopular, minority position; either source should be highly and equally influential. This prediction has been confirmed for consensus-seeking change (e.g., Laughlin et al., 1976; Laughlin & Ellis, 1986). If, as the previous models argue, a target is particularly concerned with adopting the correct position for what he or she perceives to be an intellective task,[4] and because a position that has been demonstrated correct in the target's own mind is equally correct whether or not one is required to reach consensus, like de Vries et al. (1996), I suspect that this pattern will not be restricted to consensus-seeking contexts, but will characterize direct and indirect change as well (see Table 10.2).

When in Table 10.2 I refer to a source whose message has "low substance" at a purely intellective task, I mean a source that either (a) is advocating a position that is (in principle) demonstrably incorrect, or (b) if he or she does favor the correct position, is unwilling or unable to demonstrate its correctness within the shared conceptual system that defines it as correct, or (c) offers no defense for his or her preferred position (much like Asch's confederates). Under such conditions, most SDS work suggests that, without a compelling (high substance) argument, there is considerable "strength in numbers" (see Stasser et al., 1989, for a review), so we would expect majority advocates to be more influential than minority advocates in consensus-seeking contexts. Furthermore, much SDS work suggests that the power of majorities persists, for the most part, to postdeliberation personal opinion. And so I suggest in Table 10.2 that majorities are also more influential for direct opinion change. An SDS analysis does not seem to suggest a clear prediction for indirect influence (so no prediction is offered in Table 10.2). However, the consensus of the minority influence models which have considered this case (see Table 10.1) is also that, all else being equal, majority sources should be more influential than minority sources.

Two additional points deserve mention here. First, for a genuinely intellective task, substance should be paramount. When one is right and everyone can see that one is right, a source of influence does not need to be (or particularly profit from being) in the majority. Or, as I put it in Table 10.2, using a card–game analogy, substance should "trump" style. A corollary of this position is that a minority that is demonstrably right should prevail over a majority that is demonstrably wrong (cf. Latané & Wolf, 1981). Second, compared to less intellective tasks, style should have its weakest effect for purely intellective tasks – that is, substance should also trump style. A source with substance should prevail even if his or her style is weak (e.g., not highly consistent, forceful), and a great style will not help a source without substance who is contending with a source with substance. Only in a contest of advocates where none of the positions have much or any substance should the benefits of style suggested by minority influence theorists emerge.

Purely judgmental tasks

Let us now move to the other, opposite extreme on the intellective dimension, to purely judgmental tasks (see rightmost column of Table 10.2). For these tasks there is no widely shared and coherent conceptual system within which any particular alternative is, in Laughlin's words, "demonstrably correct." For such a task, it is not meaningful to characterize a source of influence having "high substance" (except, perhaps within his or her own conceptual system, which few, if any, share). Good examples might be trying to decide in a group what the most pleasing color is or which of several lights will next light up in a probability matching experiment (Davis, Hornick, & Hornseth., 1970). For such tasks, no source of influence can defend his or her preference with much substance (see Table 10.2).

Prior SDS work suggests that the nature of social influence in a consensus-seeking context may well depend upon just how committed the group members are to their positions. By that I mean just how strong their own preference is and how "correct" it seems to them within their own personal conceptual system. Davis (e.g., 1982) has suggested that when there is very high uncertainty in such a task context, there will be little commitment to member preferences nor much strength in numbers; thus, minority factions will be just as likely to prevail as majority factions. In support of this conjecture, Davis et al. (1970) have found that group performance on a probability matching task (guess which of several lights will next light up – an extremely uncertain, judgmental task context) is best accounted for by an equiprobability social decision scheme, which gives every faction an equal probability of prevailing regardless of its size. Elsewhere (Kerr, 1992b), I have suggested that minorities gain in influence as task importance (and hence, member commitment) declines. At the limit, tasks which are of no importance to group members are also likely to be tasks for which no good arguments can be marshaled (i.e., highly judgmental). I suggest that in such contexts, when consensus is sought, majority factions are unlikely to press their numerical advantage. If no one really cares about the issue, a majority is more willing to yield to a minority, if only to help maintain group harmony. In support of this logic, I found some evidence of an inverse relationship between issue importance and minority influence in decision-making groups.

If, on the other hand, group members are highly committed to their positions on a purely judgmental task, and there are no widely shared beliefs which give one position a greater claim to correctness than any other, groups which must reach consensus are most likely to settle on the most popular positions, and majority factions are more likely to prevail than minority factions (Laughlin & Ellis, 1986). This argument suggests that majority influence in this context is compliance without conversion. Therefore, if the requirement for consensus is removed (i.e., we consider direct influence with no need for consensus), majorities and minorities should be equally and only weakly influential. (This, I suspect, corresponds to Maass et al.'s attitudinal task condition.)

Again, an SDS analysis does not seem to suggest a clear prediction for indirect influence (so no prediction is offered in Table 10.2). This is the case, however, for which most of the minority influence theories predict that minority influence can equal or even exceed that of the majority (see Table 10.1).

What is the likely role of behavioral style for purely judgmental tasks? Since there is little if any "substance" that one can use to persuade, a source's style gains in importance (i.e., style trumps apparent "substance"), relative to more intellectual tasks. The suggestion that certain behavioral styles (e.g., consistent, confident, flexible) imply that one's position is "substantial" should bolster the influence of a source for such tasks. Should style also trump popularity (e.g., will a consistent minority tend to prevail over an inconsistent, vacillating majority)? The preceding analysis suggests that this will depend upon at least two factors: how strongly the group seeks consensus on the issue and how committed group members are to their positions. The less the press for consensus and the lower members commitment, the more important source style is likely to be.

Partially intellective tasks

The vast majority of issues do not lie at either extreme of the intellective–judgmental dimension, but somewhere in between. For such issues, there are some shared beliefs, values, assumptions, and so forth which, if appealed to, give certain arguments substance. But these conceptual systems lack (a) uniform acceptance and (b) coherence. If one were to use Venn diagrams to represent group members' issue-relevant conceptual systems, they would completely overlap for purely intellective tasks, and be completely disjoint, nonoverlapping for purely judgmental tasks. But for the type of issue we consider now, they would, to varying degrees, be partially overlapping. And the areas of nonoverlap can thwart consensual agreement on a "correct" alternative. Consider, for example, the contentious issue of whether pregnant women should be permitted to have abortions. There is wide agreement on a number of points (e.g., that human life must be treated with respect and dignity; that women should not be forced to rely on dangerous means of ending pregnancies), but far less agreement on many other points (e.g., exactly how shall we define a human life?; is abortion murder?).

Disagreements over values is a particularly common area of nonoverlap. For example, which is more important, the health of a mother or the life of a fetus; how does one weigh the quality of an unwanted child's life against preserving a fetus' life; how much are such decisions private versus public ones? By coherence I mean how complete and interconnected the elements of a conceptual system are. For example, the basic rules of arithmetic constitute a highly coherent system. It is possible to deduce and thereby defend a particular answer as correct. The conceptual system relevant for evaluating one's stance on abortion, on the other hand, is likely to be far less coherent. There will be conflicting values, unexamined assumptions, preferences based on mood and emotion, unsubstantiated facts, and so forth. There may be no clear logic within one's system that makes one position on this issue indisputably more defensible than another.

It is, nevertheless, meaningful to distinguish between influence attempts with more versus less substance for such issues. By a "high substance" appeal, I mean an appeal which concentrates on shared elements of group members' conceptual systems and/or which effectively employs shared logical or rhetorical values (e.g., making one's position clearly and as simply as possible, avoiding non sequiturs, avoiding internal inconsistency in one's arguments). Such substance lends impact to an appeal, but the less intellective the task, the less likely that such a high substance argument can be decisive. As considerable SDS research has shown, majorities are much more likely to prevail than minorities in consensus-seeking groups facing such partially intellective tasks (e.g., group attitudinal judgments; jury decision making; see Stasser et al., 1989, for a review). And even when consensus is not required, the uncertainty about the correctness of one's own position gives majority sources an advantage for direct opinion change (see Table 10.2).

A low substance appeal fails to exploit shared conceptual elements and/or is poorly structured (e.g., internally inconsistent, ambiguous). When one fails to exploit what substance is possible, social consensus becomes a potent means to define "correctness" (Festinger, 1954; Laughlin & Ellis, 1986), particularly when the group must reach some consensus. Thus, majorities sources are more influential than minority sources (see Table 10.2).

For this broad set of tasks, both substance and style can counteract and compensate for the unpopularity of one's position. A minority with sufficiently high substance and/or style can prevail over a majority with neither. For all the good reasons offered by minority influence scholars, style of advocacy can have impact, and especially for partially intellective tasks, where there is enough agreement on essentials to conclude that some alternatives are better than others, but not enough agreement to make any one alternative demonstrably correct.[5] The ability of substance to compensate for low numbers is illustrated in jury decision making, a good example of a partially intellectual task. All jurors in US courts are instructed that they must give the defendant the benefit of any reasonable doubt of guilt. This becomes a shared element of the jury's conceptual system. And, reasonably large minorities advocating acquittal (i.e., raising doubts) are consequently more likely to prevail in jury deliberation than equally large majorities favoring conviction (MacCoun & Kerr, 1988).

Style vs. Substance: The Early Christian Church Revisited

I would like to conclude by returning to the interesting historical example of minority influence used by Moscovici (1994) – the rise of the Christian religion. You'll recall that he identified this as an instance of behavioral style triumphing for a minority with no unique substantive advantage. However, other scholars (e.g., Stark, 1996, Chapters 9 & 10) have developed a different argument – that the rise of Christianity can be attributed in large part to the substance of the message. This is not simply a reiteration of Christian religious conviction or doctrine (e.g., ours is the one true faith, and its validity had to be evident to the nonbelieving majority of the Roman empire). Rather, in the language we have been using in this chapter, it is an argument that Christian theology was more demonstrably correct than its contemporary competitors within a widely shared conceptual system. No doubt the conceptual system used to evaluate religions is not purely intel-lective, but neither is it purely judgmental. What then are the widely shared beliefs and values that might have given the early Christian minority's message greater substance than the messages of competing religions (e.g., Judaism, paganism)?

Here are a few possibilities (cf. Stark, 1996; Trevor-Roper, 1966). Chris-tianity (a) was relatively more simple and parsimonious, with one deity and behavioral requirements that were easy to understand – if not to practice (e.g., love thy neighbor as thyself); (b) was open to all (even those of low status, like slaves); (c) offered hope for an afterlife (contrary to both pagan-ism and Judaism); (d) promised a terrifying afterlife to nonbelievers; (e) pre-scribed and modeled widely admired human virtues (e.g., mercy, love, charity); and (f) offered proof of its validity with evidence that was credible to many at this period of history (e.g., reports of miraculous healings, resur-rections, accurate prophecies, the gift of tongues). Moscovici was correct in suggesting that Gibbon emphasizes the importance of early Christians' behav-ioral style. But Gibbon also acknowledges a number of substantive advantages of the Christian religion. For example (all quotes from Gibbon, excerpted in Trevor-Roper, 1966):

> we may perceive several defects inherent to the popular religions of Greece and Rome . . . 1. The general system of their mythology was unsupported by any solid proofs; . . . 2. The description of the infernal regions had been abandoned . . .; 3. The doctrine of a future state [of immortality] was hardly considered . . . (pp. 101–2)

> The careless Polytheist, assailed by new and unexpected terrors, against which neither his priests nor his philosophers could afford him any certain protec-tion, was very frequently terrified and subdued by the menace of eternal tor-tures. His fears might assist the progress of his faith and reason; and if he could once persuade himself that the Christian religion might possibly be true, it became an easy task to convince him that it was the safest and most prudent party that he could possibly embrace. (p. 108)

> The primitive Christians perpetually trod on mystic ground, and their minds were exercised by the habits of believing the most extraordinary events. (p. 112)

Christians allured into their party the most atrocious criminals, who . . . were easily persuaded to wash away, in the water of baptism, the guilt of their past conduct, for which the temples of the gods refused to grant them any expiation. (p. 113)

the *New Jerusalem*, the seat of this blissful kingdom [of a Christian afterlife] was quickly adorned with all the gayest colours of the imagination. . . . A city was therefore erected of gold and precious stones, and a supernatural plenty of corn and wine . . . The assurance of such a Millennium was carefully inculcated by a succession of fathers . . . it seems so well adapted to the desires and apprehensions of mankind, that it must have contributed in a very considerable degree to the progress of the Christian faith. (pp. 104–5)

Thus, even Gibbon acknowledges that it was not just how the early Christians expressed their religious views, it was, in some large part, what they had to say. If, as I have argued, an adult's choice among alternative religions is a partially intellective task, and if there are a common set of human concerns ("the desires and apprehensions of mankind") that gave the message of the early Christians substance, then we might more accurately understand the rise of Christianity (and other striking historical examples of minority influence) as an instance of both style and substance combining to compensate for lack of popularity.

NOTES

The author wishes to express his appreciation to John Levine for some early suggestions, and to the editors of this volume for their extraordinary patience.

1 For example, Moscovici (1976), in discussing minority influence, asserts that behavioral style is ". . . the only variable with explanatory power" (p. 110), and that the primary source of a minority's power lies in its behavioral style (e.g., p. 109). In fairness, it should be noted that Moscovici also suggests elsewhere that a consistent behavioral style may be necessary but not sufficient to produce minority influence (e.g., see review by Levine, 1980).

2 McGrath (1984) suggested that there have been three important "schools" of research on small groups: the Harvard school (exemplified by the work of Bales and his colleagues), the Michigan school (exemplified by the work of Lewin, Festinger, and other early group dynamicists), and the Illinois school (exemplified by the work of Steiner, McGrath, Hackman, Komorita, Davis, Laughlin, and others). A central theme in the Illinois school, of which the SDS program is a prominent part, is the crucial importance of task features as moderators of group processes. Laughlin's argument linking minority influence to task features is clearly consistent with this tradition.

3   Festinger (1954), in his social comparison theory, suggests that we strive for consensus in opinions and abilities even when there is not explicit requirement for
consensus, such as those imposed in decision-making or problem-solving groups
with an implicit or explicit decision rule. However, my primary concern here is
with the latter type of consensus requirement.

4   It should be noted that the perception of a task's objectivity and the "intellec-
tualness" of the task (in Laughlin's sense) are not perfectly related. Targets can
believe, within their own conceptual system, that their preference is "correct,"
even though that system is not shared widely enough to make their position
demonstrably correct to others. The opposite (highly intellective task perceived
to be highly subjective) is also possible. However, it seems likely that perception
tends to mirror reality for most tasks, particularly those that are most intellective.

5   Maass et al. suggest that for certain issues (e.g., fashion, taste in reading), it may
actually be an advantage to be in the minority. I suspect, though, that such tasks
are not really purely judgmental, but partially intellective ones for which there is
some agreement on the value of novelty or innovation – a shared conceptual
system that actually favors the minority.

REFERENCES

Baker, S., & Petty, R. E. (1994). Majority and minority influence: Source advocacy
as a determinant of message scrutiny. *Journal of Personality and Social Psychology, 67,*
4–19.

Baron, R. S., Kerr, N. L., & Miller, N. (1992). *Group process, group decision, group action.*
Pacific Grove, CA: Brooks/Cole.

Chaiken, S., & Stangor, C. (1987). Attitudes and attitude change. *Annual Review of
Psychology, 38,* 575–630.

Cialdini, R., & Trost, M. (1998). Social influence: Social norms, conformity, and compliance. In D. Gilbert et al. (Eds.), *The Handbook of Social Psychology* (4th ed., Vol.
2, pp. 151–192). Boston: McGraw-Hill.

Clark, R. D. (1994). A few parallels between group polarization and minority influence. In S. Moscovici et al. (Eds.), *Minority influence* (pp. 47–66). Chicago: Nelson-
Hall.

Clark, R. D. III, & Maass, A. (1988). Social categorization in minority influence: The
case of homosexuality. *European Journal of Social Psychology, 18,* 347–364.

Crano, W. D. (1994). Context, comparison, and change: Methodological and
theoretical contributions to a theory of minority (and majority) influence. In
S. Moscovici et al. (Eds.), *Minority influence* (pp. 17–46). Chicago: Nelson-Hall.

Crano, W. D., & Chen, X. (1998). The leniency contract and persistence of majority
and minority influence. *Journal of Personality and Social Psychology, 74,* 1437–
1450.

Davis, J. H. (1969). *Group performance.* Reading, MA: Addison-Wesely.

Davis, J. H. (1973). Group decision and social interaction: A theory of social decision schemes. *Psychological Review, 80,* 97–125.

Davis, J. H. (1982). Social interaction as a combinational process in group decision. In H. Brandstatter et al. (Eds.), *Group decision making* (pp. 27–58). London: Academic Press.

Davis, J. H. (1996). Group decision making and quantitative judgments: A consensus model. In E. Witte & J. Davis (Eds.), *Understanding group behavior: Consensual action by small groups* (Vol. 1, pp. 35–59). Mahwah, NJ: Erlbaum.

Davis, J. H., Hornik, J., & Hornseth, J. P. (1970). Group decision schemes and strategy preferences in a sequential response task. *Journal of Personality and Social Psychology, 15,* 397–408.

Davis, J. H., Kerr, N. L., Atkin, R., Holt, R., & Meek, D. (1975). The decision processes of 6- and 12-person mock juries assigned unanimous and 2/3 majority rules. *Journal of Personality and Social Psychology, 32,* 1–14.

Davis, J. H., Kerr, N. L., Sussman, M., & Rissman, A. (1974). Social decision schemes under risk. *Journal of Personality and Social Psychology, 30,* 248–271.

De Vries, N. K., De Dreu, C. K. W., Gordijn, E., & Schuurman, M. (1996). Majority and minority influence: A dual role interpretation. In W. Stroebe & M. Hewstone (Eds.), *European Review of Social Psychology* (Vol. 7, pp. 145–172). Chichester: J. Wiley.

Festinger, L. (1954). A theory of social comparison processes. *Human Relations, 7,* 117–140.

Johnson, H. H., & Torcivia, J. (1967). Group and individual performance on a single-stage task as a function of distribution of individual performance. *Journal of Experimental Social Psychology, 3,* 266–273.

Kerr, N. L. (1981). Social transition schemes: Charting the group's road to agreement. *Journal of Personality and Social Psychology, 41,* 684–702.

Kerr, N. L. (1992a). Group decision making at a multialternative task: Extremity, interfaction distance, pluralities, and issue importance. *Organizational Behavior and Human Decision Processes, 52,* 64–95.

Kerr, N. L. (1992b). Issue importance and group decision making. In S. Worchel, W. Wood, & J. Simpson (Eds.), *Group process and productivity* (pp. 68–90). Newberry Park, CA: Sage.

Kerr, N. L., Atkin, R., Stasser, G., Meek, D., Holt, R., & Davis, J. H. (1976). Guilt beyond a reasonable doubt: Effects of concept definition and assigned decision rule on the judgments of mock jurors. *Journal of Personality and Social Psychology, 34,* 282–294.

Kerr, N. L., Davis, J. H., Meek, D., & Rissman, A. (1975). Group position as a function of member attitudes: Choice shift effects from the perspective of social decision scheme theory. *Journal of Personality and Social Psychology, 35,* 574–593.

Kerr, N. L., MacCoun, R. J., Hansen, C. H., & Hymes, J. A. (1987). Gaining and losing social support: Momentum in decision-making groups. *Journal of Experimental Social Psychology, 23,* 119–145.

Kerr, N. L., MacCoun, R., & Kramer, G. P. (1996). Bias in judgment: Comparing individuals and groups. *Psychological Review, 103,* 687–719.

Kerr, N. L., Stasser, G., & Davis, J. H. (1979). Model-testing, model-fitting, and social decision schemes. *Organizational Behavior and Human Performance, 23,* 339–410.

Kruglanski, A. W., & Mackie, D. M. (1990). Majority and minority influence: A judgmental process analysis. In W. Stroebe & M. Hewstone (Eds.), *European review of social psychology* (Vol. 1, pp. 229–261). Chichester, UK: Wiley.

Latané, B., & Wolf, S. (1981). The social impact of majorities and minorities. *Psychological Review, 88,* 438–453.

Laughlin, P. R. (1980). Social combination processes of cooperative problem-solving groups on verbal intellective tasks. In M. L. Fishbein (Ed.), *Progress in social psychology* (Vol. 1, 127–155). Hillsdale, NJ: Erlbaum.

Laughlin, P. R., & Earley, P. C. (1982). Social combination models, persuasive arguments theory, social comparison theory, and choice shift. *Journal of Personality and Social Psychology, 42,* 273–280.

Laughlin, P. R., & Ellis, A. L. (1986). Demonstrability and social combination processes on mathematical intellective tasks. *Journal of Experimental Social Psychology, 22,* 17–189.

Laughlin, P. R., Kerr, N. L., Davis, J. H., Halff, H. M., & Marciniak, K. A. (1975). Group size, member ability, and social decision schemes on an intellective task. *Journal of Personality and Social Psychology, 31,* 522–535.

Laughlin, P. R., Kerr, N. L., Munch, M., & Haggerty, C. A. (1976) Social decision schemes of the same four-person groups on two different intellective tasks. *Journal of Personality and Social Psychology, 33,* 80–88.

Levine, J. M. (1980). Reaction to opinion deviace in small groups. In P. Paulus (Ed.), *Psychology of group influence* (pp. 375–429). Hillsdale, NJ: Erlbaum.

Levine, J. M. (1989). Reaction to opinion deviance in small groups. In P. Paulus (Ed.), *Psychology of group influence* (2nd ed., pp. 187–231). Hillsdale, NJ: Erlbaum.

Levine, J. M., & Russo, E. M. (1987). Majority and minority influence. In C. Hendrick (Ed.), *Review of personality and social psychology* (Vol. 8, pp. 13–54). Newbury Park, CA: Sage.

Lorge, I., & Solomon, H. (1955). Two models of group behavior in the solution of eureka-type problems. *Psychometrika, 20,* 139–148.

Maass, A., & Clark, R. D. III (1984). Hidden impact of minorities: Fifteen years of minority influence research. *Psychological Bulletin, 95,* 428–450.

Maass, A., Vol.pato, C., & Mucchi-Faina, A. (1996). Social influence and the verifiability of the issue under discussion: Attitudinal versus objective items. *British Journal of Social Psychology, 35,* 15–26.

MacCoun, R. J., & Kerr, N. L. (1988). Asymmetric influence in mock jury deliberation: Jurors' bias for leniency. *Journal of Personality and Social Psychology, 54,* 21–33.

Maier, N., & Solem, A. (1952). The contribution of a discussion leader to the quality of group thinking: The effective use of minority opinions. *Human Relations, 5,* 277–288.

McGrath, J. E. (1984). *Groups, interaction, and performance.* Englewood Cliffs, NJ: Prentice-Hall.

Mednick, S., & Mednick, M. (1967). *Examiner's manual: Remote Associates Test.* Boston: Houghton-Mifflin.

Moscovici, S. (1976). *Social influence and social change.* New York: Academic Press.

Moscovici, S. (1985). Social influence and conformity. In G. Lindzey & E. Aronson (Eds.), *The handbook of social psychology* (3rd ed., Vol. 2, pp. 347–412). New York: Random House.

Moscovici, S. (1994). Three concepts: Minority, conflict, and behavioral style. In S. Moscovici, A. Mucchi-Faina, & A. Maass (Eds.), *Minority influence* (pp. 233–251). Chicago: Nelson-Hall.

Moscovici, S., & Faucheaux, C. (1972). Social influence, conformity bias and the study of active minorities. In L. Berkowitz (Ed.), *Advances in experimental social psychology* (Vol. 6, pp. 149–202). New York: Academic Press.

Moscovici, S., Lage, E., & Naffrechoux, M. (1969). Influence of a consistent minority on the responses of a majority in a color perception task. *Sociometry, 32,* 365–380.

Moscovici, S., & Nemeth, C. (1974). Social influence II: Minority influence. In C. Nemeth (Ed.), *Social psychology: Classic and contemporary integrations* (pp. 217–249). Chicago: Rand-McNally.

Mugny, G., & Pérez, J. A. (1991). *The social psychology of minority influence.* Cambridge, UK: Cambridge University Press.

Nemeth, C. (1986) Differential contributions of majority and minority influence. *Psychological Review, 93,* 23–32.

Nemeth, C. J. (1994). The value of minority dissent. In S. Moscovici, A. Mucchi-Faina, & A. Maass (Eds.), *Minority influence* (pp. 3–15). Chicago: Nelson-Hall.

Pérez, J. A., & Mugny, G. (1996). The conflict elaboration theory of social influence. In E. Witte & J. Davis (Eds.), *Understanding group behavior: Consensual action by small groups* (Vol. 2, pp 185–208). Mahwah, NJ: L. Erlbaum.

Pérez, J. A., Mugny, G., Butera, F., Kaiser, C., & Roux, P. (1994). Integrating minority and majority influence: Conversion, consensus, and uniformity In S. Moscovici, A. Mucchi-Faina, & A. Maass (Eds.), *Minority influence* (pp. 191–210). Chicago: Nelson-Hall.

Schachter, S. (1951). Deviation, rejection, and communication. *Journal of Abnormal and Social Psychology, 46,* 190–207.

Smoke, W. H., & Zajonc, R. B. (1962). On the reliability of group judgments and decisions. In J Criswell, H. Solomon, & P. Suppes (Eds.), *Mathematical methods in small group processes* (pp. 233–333). Stanford, CA: Stanford University Press.

Stark, R. (1996). *The rise of Christianity: A sociologist reconsiders history.* Princeton, NJ: Princeton University Press.

Stasser, G. (1999). A primer of social decision scheme theory: Models of group influence, competitive model-testing, and prospective modelling. *Organizational Behavior and Human Decision Processes, 80,* 3–20.

Stasser, G., Kerr, N. L., & Davis, J. H. (1989). Influence processes and consensus models in decision-making groups. In P. Paulus (Ed.), *Psychology of group influence* (2nd ed., pp. 279–326). Hillsdale, NJ: Erlbaum.

Steiner, I. (1972). *Group process and productivity*. New York: Academic Press.

Thomas, E., & Fink, C. (1961). Models of group problem solving. *Journal of Abnormal and Social Psychology, 63*, 53–63.

Torrence, E. (1954). Some consequences of power differences on decision making in permanent and temporary three-man groups. *Research Studies, State College of Washington, 22*, 130–140.

Trevor-Roper, H. (1966). *Gibbon: "The Decline and Fall of the Roman Empire" and other selections from the writings of Edward Gibbon*. London: New English Library.

Trost, M., & Kenrick, D. T. (1994). Ego inVol.vement in the minority influence paradigm: The double-edged sword of minority advocacy. In S. Moscovici, A. Mucchi-Faina, & A. Maass (Eds.), *Minority influence* (pp. 149–161). Chicago: Nelson-Hall.

Trost, M., Maass, A., & Kenrick, D. T. (1992). Minority influence: Personal relevance biases cognitive processes and reverses private acceptance. *Journal of Experimental Social Psychology, 28*, 234–254.

Wood, W., Lundgren, S., Ouellette, J. A., Busceme, S., & Blackstone, T. (1994). Minority influence: A meta-analytic review of social influence processes. *Psychological Bulletin, 115*, 323–345.

11

Minority Influence in Political Decision-making Groups

John M. Levine and Juliet Kaarbo

Social psychological research on minority influence has yielded many important insights, but it has been remarkably silent about the role that social interaction plays in innovation. This neglect of social processes is surprising when we recall that Moscovici's ground-breaking work on minority influence was stimulated, not by an interest in individual cognitive dynamics, but rather by an interest in group dynamics. In particular, he wanted to understand historical cases in which small, obscure minorities with little prestige and few resources were able to triumph over entrenched majorities and produce revolutionary changes in religion, politics, science, and the arts.

Rejecting the idea that influence springs from dependence, Moscovici argued that disagreement produces conflict and that the essence of influence is conflict negotiation. This approach puts strong emphasis on the role of social, or interpersonal, conflict, as indicated by the assertion that "in social influence, relations with others take precedence over relations with objects, and inter-individual dynamics take precedence over intra-individual dynamics" (Moscovici, 1976, p. 106). Thus, an emphasis on the social basis of conflict is at the heart of Moscovici's analysis, and it has been adopted, either explicitly or implicitly, by most other researchers who study minority influence. It is therefore curious that research on minority influence has paid little attention to the social interactions that occur within and between majority and minority factions and has focused instead on how majorities resolve the cognitive conflict that minorities presumably elicit (Levine, 1989; Levine & Thompson, 1996).

How might we explain the fact that minority influence research has emphasized the individual, rather than the group, level of analysis and intrapersonal, rather than interpersonal, processes? There are three probable reasons.

First, in spite of the important role that Moscovici accorded to social conflict, his theoretical explanation of minority influence, or conversion, emphasized perceptual and cognitive processes rather than social processes. His focus on majority members' attention to and processing of the minority's message, as opposed to their behavioral interaction with the minority, no doubt set the stage for later work by others on the cognitive mediators of minority influence. A second, and related, reason involved the popularity of cognitive analyses in social psychology. Markus and Zajonc's characterization of the field rings as true today as it did in 1985, when they asserted that "The cognitive approach is now clearly the dominant approach among social psychologists, having virtually no competitors" (p. 137). So, in emphasizing cognitive processes in minority influence, Moscovici was clearly in step with the Zeitgeist. Finally, a third reason for researchers' apparent lack of interest in social processes is methodological, namely the difficulty of conducting group research. It takes a lot of work to assemble groups in the laboratory, to record the complex interactions that occur between group members, and to analyze and interpret these interactions in theoretically meaningful ways. And, of course, studying group processes outside the laboratory is even harder. To get around these problems, some minority influence researchers bring subjects together in groups and inform them of one another's ostensible positions, but do not allow any conversation or interaction between group members. Other researchers simply inform individual subjects that a majority or minority of prior respondents, whom they will never meet, expressed a particular opinion on a topic.

It is not the case, of course, that researchers have totally ignored the social context in which minority influence occurs. Work has been done, for example, on the impact of ingroup versus outgroup minorities (e.g., Alvaro & Crano, 1997; David & Turner, 1996; Mugny & Pérez, 1991) and minorities espousing evolutionary versus regressive positions vis-à-vis societal norms (e.g., Maass, Clark, & Haberkorn, 1982; Paicheler, 1976). In addition, attention has been given to how temporal changes in groups affect minority motivation and ability to exert influence (e.g., Levine & Moreland, 1985; Worchel, Grossman, & Coutant, 1994) and how social support within majority and minority factions affects minority influence (e.g., Doms & Van Avermaet, 1985; Gerard, 1985). Finally, efforts have been made to analyze minority influence in various real-world groups, particularly organizations (e.g., De Dreu & De Vries, 1997; Gruenfeld, 1995; Nemeth & Staw, 1989). While helpful in clarifying minority influence, most of this work has not dealt explicitly with the social dynamics of groups containing majorities and minorities. Of greater relevance is recent work examining reciprocal majority and minority influence in interacting groups (e.g., Smith, Tindale, & Dugoni, 1996; Tindale, Davis, Vollrath, Nagao, & Hinsz, 1990). But even these studies are primarily designed to study opinion change, rather than interactive behavior (for an exception, see McLeod, Baron, Marti, & Yoon, 1997).

Political Decision-making Groups as a Context for Minority Influence

The relevance of group level analysis and interpersonal processes becomes apparent when we consider how minority influence operates in decision-making groups outside the laboratory. In this chapter, we will focus on politi cal decision-making groups, which include school boards, city councils, legislative and bureaucratic committees, cabinets, and leaders' advisory circles. These groups, which are widely distributed throughout society, share several important characteristics that are frequently absent in laboratory groups. Members know one another and interact face to face. The group has role and status differentiation, such that members have different rights and obligations vis-à-vis one another. The group exists over time, and hence members have knowledge about its past and expectations about its future. The group is embedded in a larger organizational and societal context, and members are typically accountable to constituencies outside the group. Group members are charged with making decisions that affect the welfare of people who do not belong to the group. And influence efforts within the group are often directed toward changing members' overt behaviors (e.g., votes on a particular issue) rather then their underlying beliefs.

Political scientists recognize the importance of small groups in political decision making (e.g., Anderson, 1987; Gaenslen, 1992; Stewart, Hermann, & Hermann, 1989), and they have investigated a variety of group phenomena, including norms, leadership, and risk taking. Interestingly, however, although factional conflict would seem to lie at the heart of politics, this feature of intragroup relations has not been emphasized in political science. One reason for this neglect may be the popularity of Janis's (1982) *groupthink* model (e.g., Tetlock, 1979; t' Hart, 1994; Walker & Watson, 1989). This formulation stresses cohesion, concurrence, and conflict avoidance, rather than active management of conflict between different factions. A second reason may be the dominance of information-processing models for explaining behavior in groups. These models focus on how groups acquire, exchange, and interpret information about political events, with special emphasis on group biases and errors (Purkitt, 1992). Scholars using these models tend to minimize noncognitive aspects of decision making and concentrate on either the group or individual level of analysis, ignoring the factional level. In contrast to the groupthink and information-processing perspectives, the "bureaucratic politics" perspective on small group decision making does acknowledge the role of factional conflict, but it typically assumes that the factions are equal in strength (Hermann, 1993; Huntington, 1960). This assumption is the basis for the prediction that intragroup conflict produces either a failure to reach any decision (deadlock) or a decision that no faction intially desired (resultant). Thus, the three dominant perspectives on small group decision making in political science have either ignored factional conflict or assumed that it always occurs between equally strong factions.

Although equal strength factions occur in some political groups, in many groups factions differ substantially in strength. Often groups contain two factions – a larger majority faction and a smaller minority faction. There are many examples of minorities in political groups, including a dissenter in a presidential advisory group, a small faction in a single party cabinet or a junior partner in a coalition, a small ideological subgroup on a legislative committee, and representatives of a small bureaucratic unit in an interdepartmental meeting. Because numerically smaller factions are often weaker than numerically larger factions, conventional wisdom suggests that when there is an opinion or policy conflict between a minority and a majority, the majority will prevail. However, like many truisms, this one may be valid only under certain circumstances. In fact, minorities can sometimes be quite influential. For example, the British cabinet decision to pursue an alliance with the Soviet Union just prior to the Molotov–Ribbentrop Pact in 1939 was the result of a minority gradually influencing the majority through discussion (Hill, 1991). In addition, the National Religious Party in Israel and the Free Democratic Party in Germany are almost always members of ruling coalition governments and, despite their numerical disadvantage, frequently have significant impact on government policy (Kaarbo, 1996). A final example of minority influence was provided by President Abraham Lincoln, who is reported to have concluded an advisory meeting by saying, "Gentlemen, the vote is eleven to one, and the one has it."

In the remainder of this chapter, we will suggest several ways in which social psychological research on minority influence might be enriched by attention to factional conflict in political groups. In so doing, we will pay particular attention to the social dynamics of groups, as opposed to the cognitive dynamics of individuals. Because minority influence in political groups has received little theoretical or empirical attention, our presentation will necessarily be speculative. First, we will discuss dimensions of minority influence

Table 11.1 *Minority Impact on Change by Type of Change*

		Type of Change	
		---	---
		Forward	Backward
Minority Impact on Change	Promotion	Progressive	Reactionary
	Blockage	Conservative	Modernist

that are of special relevance to political groups. Second, we will analyze how structural features of political groups can affect a minority's ability to exert influence. Third, we will talk about strategies that a minority faction can use to gain acceptance for its position. Finally, we will conclude with some general observations regarding minority influence in political decision-making groups.

Dimensions of Minority Influence

Social psychologists have assumed that effective minorities invariably promote change, producing innovation in otherwise conservative groups (e.g., Moscovici, 1976, 1985). This often translates into a heroic conception of the minority and a villainous conception of the majority. Yet minorities can also block change advocated by majorities, and it may often be easier for minorities to exert this kind of influence than to promote change. In conceptualizing change promotion versus blockage on the part of minorities, it is also important to consider whether the change is forward-oriented (i.e., reflects a new group decision or policy) or backward-oriented (i.e., reflects a prior group decision or policy). Four cases can be identified by crossing the minority's impact on group change (promotion versus blockage) and the type of change it produces (forward-oriented versus backward-oriented). We label these four cases *progressive influence*, *reactionary influence*, *conservative influence*, and *modernist influence* (see Table 11.1).

Progressive influence occurs when the minority successfully promotes change to a decision or policy that is new for the group (e.g., if the head of the Environmental Protection Agency convinces the president and the cabinet to adopt path-breaking environmental laws). *Reactionary influence* occurs when the minority successfully promotes change to a decision or policy that the group previously held (e.g., if hardliners in the Israeli cabinet push through a proposal to scrap the current peace plan and return to a nonrecognition policy toward the PLO). *Conservative influence* occurs when the minority successfully blocks the majority's attempt to produce change to a decision or policy that is new for the group (e.g., if legislators on a congressional committee prevent adoption of a proposal to extend welfare benefits to cover child care). Finally, *modernist influence* occurs when the minority successfully blocks the majority's attempt to produce change to a decision or policy that the group previously held (e.g., if a minority faction on a Southern school board prevents the majority from creating "separate and equal" schools for African American students). Interesting questions arise about the relative difficulty of producing these four kinds of change and the particular behaviors that are likely to be successful in each case (e.g., persuasive communications may be most effective in promotion cases, whereas delaying tactics may work best in blockage cases). In addition, minorities may sometimes produce one kind of change in the short run with the goal of producing a different kind of change in the long run (e.g., modernist influence at time 1 and progressive influence at time 2).

So far, our discussion of minority influence has focused on the majority's external, or overt, change toward the minority's position. However, minority influence can also involve internal, or covert, change on the part of the majority. The distinction between external change (compliance) and internal change (conversion) toward the minority's position has elicited a great deal of theoretical and empirical attention from social psychologists (see Moscovici, 1976, 1980; Pérez & Mugny, 1996; Personnaz & Personnaz, 1994; Wood, Lundgren, Ouellette, Busceme, & Blackstone,1994). Several criteria have been used to distinguish compliance from conversion, including temporal lag of influence (immediate versus delayed), duration of influence (short-term versus long-term), response context (public versus private), and specificity of influence (directly versus indirectly related to the minority's message) (Maass, West, & Cialdini, 1987). Thus, compliance has been assumed if the majority exhibits immediate, short-term, public, and/or direct influence, whereas conversion has been assumed if the majority exhibits delayed, long-term, private, and/or indirect influence.

The possible forms of minority influence are more complex than this typology suggests, however. For one thing, the various indices assumed to reflect compliance and conversion may not always pattern as suggested above. For example, there may be cases in which public agreement is delayed rather than immediate and long-term rather than short-term (cf. Allen, 1965). In addition, rather than moving toward the minority's position (positive influence), the majority could move further away from that position (negative influence), and this movement could occur at either the public or private level (cf. Mucchi-Faina, 1994; Nail, 1986; Paicheler, 1976). Finally, minority influence could involve response consistency rather than movement (Levine & Russo, 1987; Sorrels & Kelley, 1984). This might occur, for example, when the majority is tempted to shift further away from the minority's position, but resists this impulse because of persuasive arguments from the minority.

To illustrate some of these complexities, let us consider possible causes of delayed public influence. A minority might produce this kind of influence by highlighting a new of piece of information that supports its position. Awareness of this information might cause the majority to attend to additional information consistent with the minority's position and thereby produce eventual public (as well as private) agreement with the minority. In addition, delayed public influence might occur because of the majority's accountability to its constituency. Consider the case in which a majority, after hearing persuasive minority arguments, fails to agree publicly with the minority because of fear of retaliation from its constituency. If the majority subsequently learns that its constituency is unlikely to punish it for publicly agreeing with the minority, the majority may finally do so. This is not to say, of course, that majority accountability to a constituency always produces delayed public influence toward the minority position. Consider the case in which the minority is able to convince the majority to publicly adopt its position when the group is isolated from external pressures. If the majority subsequently learns that its constituency is angry about its agreement with the minority, the majority may revert to its original position and demand that the group reconsider the issue.

In general, it seems likely that minorities in political decision-making groups are more interested in traditional indices of compliance than conversion. That is, they are probably more motivated to elicit immediate, short-term, public, and direct influence than delayed, long-term, private, and indirect influence. However, if we are to extrapolate from social psychological research on minority influence in laboratory groups, the goal of producing public influence may be hard to achieve. In a recent meta-analysis of this work, Wood et al. (1994) found that minorities generally produce more private indirect influence than either public influence or private direct influence.[1] Given the problem minorities have inducing public change in laboratory settings, it would not be surprising if they encountered even greater difficulty in political groups. This is because majorities are reluctant to agree publicly with minorities when, as is often the case, they are accountable to constituencies outside the group, they believe these constituencies can monitor their behavior inside the group, and they assume that agreement with the minority will be punished. To the extent a majority fears reprisal for adopting a minority position, it is unlikely to do so even if convinced of the validity of the minority's arguments. Conversely, a majority has more flexibility if its constituency does not have knowledge of its behavior during group deliberations.[2]

Although minorities in political decision-making groups often want to elicit compliance from majorities, they also may be interested in producing certain aspects of conversion. This is because factions in political decision-making groups rarely have conflict over isolated issues and typically anticipate future interactions. For example, a minority that cannot produce direct influence by changing the majority's position on a given policy might nevertheless seek to produce indirect influence by inducing the majority to justify that position in a way that advances the minority's long-term agenda. Consider a minority faction in a cabinet that is opposed to sending troops on a United Nations peacekeeping mission, but is generally supportive of the UN. If, in capitulating to the majority's wish to send troops, the minority convinces the majority to justify troop commitment in pro-UN terms, the minority would indirectly influence the majority to move closer to its position at a general policy level. A classic form of indirect minority influence in political settings, which will be discussed in more detail later, involves inducing the majority to make concessions on an entirely separate issue in exchange for compliance on the issue in conflict (logrolling).

A subtle but important form of indirect influence is the minority's ability to affect the quality of the group's decision making. Nemeth (1986, 1995) argues that minority dissent, even when it does not produce movement toward the minority's position, can stimulate the majority to engage in certain forms of cognitive activity (e.g., divergent thinking) that often lead to better problem solving (see also Maass & Volpato, 1994; Mucchi-Faina, 1994; Butera, Mugny, Legrenzi, & Pérez, 1996). This kind of indirect influence may also occur in political groups. For example, a minority's objection to the majority's position on a controversial issue might lead the majority to search for more information and consider more alternatives. The presence of a minority might also cause the majority to engage in more contingency planning, if only to avoid a politically embarrassing situation in which the minority could later say "we told you so." These indirect effects of minority dissent are considered indices of good decision making by most policy analysts (e.g., George, 1980), even if the final decision was the one originally favored by the majority.

Although divergent thinking by the majority is often an unintended consequence of minority dissent, in certain cases minorities may seek to foster such thinking. This might occur, for example, if the minority were more interested in helping the group make high quality decisions than in winning converts to its own position. It is interesting that social psychologists have not considered the possibility that minorities may rise above narrow factional concerns and work toward larger group goals, even though many political minorities view their behavior in precisely this light.

Finally, there may be cases in which the minority seeks to produce direct influence that is superficially harmful to its cause, because of the hidden benefits that accompany the influence. For example, in certain cases a minority might secretly try to provoke a counterreaction (negative influence) in the majority. This might happen because the minority believes that the majority will be driven to an extreme position that will cause it to lose support from its constituency. In addition, a change toward greater extremity on the part of the majority might also alter the group's structure or process in ways that help the minority (e.g., new majority leaders may arise who are sympathetic to the minority, the majority may lose members).

Structural Features of Groups

Several structural features of political decision-making groups may affect how majority and minority factions behave toward one another and thereby the minority's ability to influence the majority. Although these features would probably strike political scientists as obvious candidates for study, social psychologists have tended to ignore them. One reason for this lack of interest is methodological, namely the constraints of laboratory paradigms for studying groups. Some important structural characteristics of political groups, such as a long history of interaction between factions, are difficult to create in laboratory settings. A second reason is theoretical, namely the absence of models of minority influence that emphasize social, as opposed to cognitive, factors.

Relative size of the minority faction

One structural feature of groups that has received attention from social psychologists is the size of the minority (e.g., Latané & Wolf, 1981; Moscovici & Lage, 1976; Tanford & Penrod, 1984). It has often been argued that larger minorities are more effective than smaller ones, although one can think of many cases in which small minorities, such as political elites, have high status and power (cf. Crano, 1994; Latané, 1996; Levine & Russo, 1987). In fact, plausible arguments can be made for a variety of relationships between minority size and influence in political groups.

There are several reasons why larger minorities might be more influential than smaller minorities. First, larger minorities may be seen as more correct than smaller minorities (Nemeth, Wachtler, & Endicott, 1977). This presumably occurs because the more people who espouse a position, the less likely their response will be attributed to some idiosyncratic personal characteristic and the more likely it will be seen as reflecting objective reality. Second, in political groups, larger minorities may be viewed as posing a more credible threat of retaliation if they are rejected than do smaller minorities. This is because larger minorities have more resources to punish the majority in the future (e.g., by refusing to compromise on subsequent votes), and thus the majority is more likely to acquiesce to larger minorities. Both of these arguments are based on majority perceptions of the minority. In addition, larger minorities may exert more influence than smaller minorities because they are more motivated to prevail, which in turn leads to more assertive behaviors. Larger minorities may be highly motivated because they do not fear retribution or because they feel optimistic about taking over the group (they can "taste victory").

Conversely, there are also reasons why smaller minorities might be more influential than larger minorities. First, smaller minorities (which confront relatively large majorities) may be seen as more confident and courageous than larger minorities (which confront relatively small majorities) (Nemeth et al., 1977). This is because internal attributions are more likely to be made for targets that resist strong external pressure than for targets that resist weak pressure. Second, smaller minorities may be more influential than larger minorities because they are more distinct and salient, which in turn increases majority attention to their message (Maass et al., 1987). Third, in many political groups, smaller minorities may be more influential than larger minorities because they are less likely to be viewed as viable competitors for power. Whereas agreeing with a small minority typically does not threaten a majority's dominance in the group, agreeing with a large minority does. Fourth, smaller minorities may be more influential than larger minorities because they have greater internal stability (i.e., less tendency to form subfactions). Because of this reduced factionalism, smaller minorities may spend less time fighting intrafactional battles and more time creating persuasive arguments for their position. Finally, in contrast to the argument presented earlier, smaller minorities may be more motivated to prevail than larger minorities, which in turn leads to more assertive behaviors. This could occur because smaller minorities feel they have nothing to lose by pushing their point of view or because their members are highly committed to the minority position. Regarding the latter point, there is reason to believe that smaller minorities may be more highly identified with their faction and more biased toward it than are larger minorities (Mullen, Brown, & Smith, 1992).

Both of the above hypotheses predict a linear relationship between a minority's size and its ability to influence a majority. However, the impact of minority size may not be so simple. For one thing, the benefits and costs of minority size may cancel out in some situations, producing a curvilinear relationship between minority size and influence. That is, both very small and very large minorities may be less influential than medium-sized minorities, because small minorities are dismissed as cranks and large minorities are perceived as threatening (cf. Nemeth et al., 1977). For another thing, even if minority influence increases as a function of minority size, the relationship may not be linear. Both Latané and Wolf (1981) and Tanford and Penrod (1984) postulate a positive, but nonlinear, relationship between minority size and influence. Finally, the impact of minority size may vary as a function of the type of influence the minority is exerting. In a recent meta-analysis of laboratory studies, Wood et al. (1994) found that minority size was positively related to public influence and private direct influence, but was negatively related to private indirect influence. Wood and her colleagues suggested that the former relationship may reflect normative influence, whereas the latter relationship may reflect informational influence. Assuming, as we did earlier, that minorities in political groups are usually motivated to produce public influence, larger minorities will be more effective than smaller ones.

Faction history

Given that political groups often exist over time, the relationship that the majority and minority had in the past may affect the minority's ability to exert influence in the present. Consider the case in which the minority has a history of negative interactions with the majority. Here, we would expect the minority to have a difficult time convincing the majority to adopt its position, even on an issue they had never dealt with before. This could occur for several reasons. The majority might attribute the minority's position to a biased perception of reality and therefore discount the validity of this position (Maass et al., 1982). In addition, the majority might view the minority as an outgroup rather than as part of the ingroup and therefore feel less normative as well as informational pressure to agree with it (Abrams & Hogg, 1990; David & Turner, 1996; but see Mugny & Pérez, 1991). Finally, the majority's antipathy and distrust toward the minority might elicit reactance, which in turn would cause rejection of the minority's position (cf. Maass & Clark, 1986).

In contrast, consider the case in which the minority has a history of positive interactions with the majority. Compared to the minority described above, this minority should have a relatively easy time convincing the majority to accept its position. In addition, this minority should also be more effective than a "new" minority composed of either people who just entered the group or people who defected from the majority. The former minority would be at a disadvantage because the majority does not understand its position or know its members, whereas the latter minority would be at a disadvantage because the majority resents its "treasonous" behavior.

In addition to the positivity of the relationship between the majority and minority, other dimensions of faction history may also be important. One such dimension is faction stability, specifically whether the majority and minority have always occupied the same relative positions or whether the majority was once the minority and vice versa. Compared to stable factions, reversed factions may be more knowledgeable about one another's influence strategies and therefore more resistant to them. In addition, compared to stable factions of the same size, those that recently underwent "downward mobility" (from majority to minority) may be particularly motivated to regain their old status, whereas those that recently underwent "upward mobility" (from minority to majority) may be particularly motivated to maintain their new status. A second potentially important dimension of faction history is faction permeability, specifically whether there is a tradition of majority members switching to the minority and continuing to have positive rela tions with their former colleagues. To the extent that this is the case, and ex-majority members are given the task of presenting the minority position, faction permeability may enhance minority influence.

Finally, it is important to note that factions with different histories may have learned different ways of exerting influence. For example, minority factions that have a history of positive relations with majorities may have learned accommodative strategies involving persuasive arguments and willingness to compromise. In contrast, minority factions that have a history of negative relations with majorities may have learned confrontational strategies involving threats and intransigence. Though not without pitfalls, both kinds of strategies can be useful in certain situations (cf. Levine, Sroka, & Snyder, 1977; Mugny, 1982; Nemeth & Brilmayer, 1987).

Number of minority factions

Social psychologists interested in majority–minority conflict have restricted their attention to groups that contain a single minority. Moreover, they have focused on three types of influence between majority and minority factions – majority influence, in which the minority moves toward the majority position; minority influence, in which the majority moves toward the minority position; and reciprocal influence, in which both factions move toward a compromise position. These three types of influence have been labeled conformity, innovation, and normalization, respectively (Moscovici, 1976).

The situation in many political groups is not so simple, however. Not only do such groups often contain two or more minority factions, but the patterns of influence between these factions can become quite complex. Sometimes, by allying with one another, minority factions can create a new faction that is large enough to extract concessions from the majority or, in extreme cases, to unseat the majority. To the extent this is possible, each minority faction will be motivated (a) to join a winning alliance (a cooperative goal vis-à-vis other minorities and a competitive goal vis-à-vis the majority) and (b) to maximize its influence within that alliance (a competitive goal vis-à-vis other minorities). Theoretical and empirical work on coalition formation sheds light on this process (e.g., Cook & Gillmore, 1984; Kahan & Rapoport, 1984; Komorita, 1984; Polzer, Mannix, & Neale, 1995). For example, minority factions may be especially drawn to "minimal winning coalitions," which are just large enough to win and thereby maximize the outcomes of each coalition member.

It is important to note, however, that minority factions do not always form coalitions with other minority factions. In some cases, they may join forces with the majority faction instead. This might occur for several reasons. First, it may be easier for a minority to negotiate the formation of a coalition with a single large faction than with several smaller factions. Second, the majority may provide disproportionately large rewards to the minority (i.e., rewards greater than its relative size would warrant) because of the minority's pivotal power in forming the coalition. And third, the minority may have closer ideological ties to the majority than to other minorities (Miller & Komorita, 1986). To the extent the issue under consideration has strong ideological underpinnings, ideological similarities between factions may be a critical determinant of coalition formation and maintenance.

Of course, majorities are not simply passive observers of minorities' efforts to form coalitions. If they are not large enough to prevail against any pos-

sible minority coalition, majorities will be motivated to join a winning coalition with one or more minorities and to maximize their influence within
that coalition. Moreover, they will be motivated to thwart any possible
winning coalition that excludes them. This in turn may cause them to adopt
a "divide and conquer" strategy, which pits minority factions against one
another and thereby reduces their ability to work together.

So far, we have assumed that majorities and minorities are homogeneous,
in the sense that all faction members are equally committed to the "official"
faction position. This is not always the case, however. In political groups, factions are often divided into subfactions, and the relationships between these
subfactions can affect coalition formation. For example, consider the case in
which the minority faction is unified, but the majority faction is composed
of majority and minority subfactions. Here, the majority wing of the majority faction and the minority faction might find it strategically useful to form
an alliance against the minority wing of the majority faction. This tactic was
used by Chancellor Kohl of Germany in the 1980s and 1990s. As leader of
the majority wing of the majority party, Kohl often allowed the minority
party in his coalition to have influence, not because he agreed with them,
but rather because they posed less threat to his leadership than did the minority wing of his own party (Berry, 1989; Clemens, 1988; Kaarbo, 1996).

Minority Influence Strategies

The structural factors described above set limits on the amount and type of
influence that a minority can produce, but they do not, in and of themselves,
account for this influence. In order to do this, we must consider the strategies that minority members use in trying to persuade majority members to
agree with their position. These fall into three categories – informational
strategies, punishment/reward strategies, and compositional and procedural
strategies.

Informational strategies

In explaining minority influence, social psychologists have emphasized informational influence, or a minority's provision of information about reality
(Deutsch & Gerard, 1955). This is because, following Moscovici's lead, social
psychologists have restricted their attention to minorities with low power and
status. It is assumed that such minorities have no means of coercing majori-

ties into accepting their position and therefore must convince majorities of the validity of this position.

The dominant informational strategy studied by social psychologists is behavioral consistency. According to Moscovici (1985), a minority that consistently maintains its position demonstrates confidence in and commitment to that position, indicates its willingness to endure conflict, and signals its refusal to compromise. In so doing, the minority makes clear that the majority is solely responsible for resolving the conflict and must change its position to do so. Although there is evidence that both objective consistency (e.g., Moscovici, Lage, & Naffrechoux, 1969) and perceived consistency (Wood et al., 1994) can enhance minority influence, this is not always the case. For example, at least one kind of inconsistent minority (i.e., a majority member who moves to a minority position) is more effective than a consistent minority on attitudinal issues (Levine, Saxe, & Harris, 1976; Levine, Sroka, & Snyder, 1977). Moreover, consistency need not involve mere repetition in order to be effective (Nemeth, Swedlund, & Kanki,1974), and too much consistency can backfire – an extreme, rigid minority is less effective than a moderate, flexible minority in producing public change (Mugny, 1982). All of this suggests that minorities wishing to exert influence in political groups must do more than follow the simple admonition to respond consistently.

Several additional informational strategies may prove useful to minorities in political groups. All of these involve impression management directed toward convincing the majority that the minority is a valid source of information. For example, the minority can attempt to convey the impression that it is behaving autonomously, that is, arriving at its position through independent thought and objective analysis (Moscovici, 1985). If the minority can convince the majority that its position is based on careful analysis of the facts rather than preconceived notions or self interest, it is likely to be more effective in exerting influence. A powerful demonstration of autonomy is evidence that the minority is taking a stand against its own constituency (cf. Koeske & Crano, 1968).

Similarly, if the minority can convince the majority that it has special expertise on the issue under consideration, it is more likely to be influential (cf. Hovland, Janis, & Kelley, 1953). In most political decision-making groups, different members are responsible for different policy areas (e.g., the foreign minister, the defense minister, the finance minister). If the issue under consideration lies within the jurisdiction of a member of the minority faction, that faction can legitimate its arguments by asserting its expertise on the matter (Halperin, 1974). And even if it cannot claim jurisdiction, the minority faction can attempt to frame the issue in a way that emphasizes its expertise (e.g., the foreign minister might argue that although balance of trade looks like a domestic fiscal problem, it is really a foreign relations problem). Finally, when the minority faction is responsible for gathering and presenting information to the group, it can manipulate the information in order to emphasize its expertise (e.g, by using selective information sources, by presenting only part of the information, by outright lying) (Halperin, 1974).

In order to increase its credibility, a minority might also seek to manipulate the perceived popularity of its position outside the group. In implementing this strategy, the minority does not have to convince the majority that it has support from an overwhelming number of outsiders. Instead, the minority may simply need to make a case that its position is attractive to important elements of the majority's constituency or to a small number of high-status people who are not affiliated with either the majority or the minority. In fact, the outside support for the minority's position does not have to involve specific people at all, but instead may involve such abstractions as the "spirit of the times" (or _Zeitgeist_). Laboratory studies demonstrate that minorities taking "progressive" positions in line with emerging social values are more effective than those taking "reactionary" positions that oppose these values (e.g., Clark & Maass, 1988; Maass et al., 1982). Social psychologists who have studied the impact of the Zeitgeist on minority influence have tended to view minorities and majorities as passive respondents to wider societal trends (but see Mugny & Pérez, 1991). However, minorities in political groups may seek to alter the Zeitgeist, for example by campaigning to change laws or by leaking confidential information to the public. Whether a minority merely refers to the exisiting Zeitgeist or alters the Zeitgeist to suit its purposes, claiming support outside the group is likely to be an effective informational strategy.

Finally, a minority faction can seek to enhance its credibility by characterizing its motives in positive terms (Levine & Ruback, 1980). For example, the minority might assert that its intransigence is designed to further group-level (rather than faction-level) goals, for example stimulating open discussion or reaching the best possible group decision (cf. Allison & Halperin, 1972; Ridgeway, 1982). Alternatively, the minority might seek to justify its position in terms of overarching moral principles that the majority endorses (Halperin, 1974). Thus, weak actors often use an _issue escalation strategy_, in which they convert a practical question into a matter of principle and then appeal to this principle in justifying their position (Lindell & Persson, 1986). Similarly, appeals to such principles as justice and fairness may prove useful to minority factions in political decision-making groups.

Clearly, minorities have several potential avenues for increasing their credibility and hence their capacity to produce informational influence. They are often handicapped, however, by pre-existing negative attributions about their behaviors and motives (Islam & Hewstone, 1993; Levine, 1989), which in turn reduce their ability to exert influence (cf. Bohner, Erb, Reinhard, & Frank, 1996; Moskowitz, 1996).

Punishment/reward strategies

As noted above, social psychologists have assumed that minorities rely exclusively on information-based strategies, because minorities lack the status and power to employ intimidation-based strategies. Yet in many political decision-making groups, the majority needs the minority's support (or at least acquiescence) in order to achieve its goals, and in these groups the minority wields considerable power. This power has been ignored, at least in part, because social psychologists interested in minority influence have not studied situations in which group members are interdependent in terms of outcomes. In such situations, minorities can often get their way by using threats of punishment and promises of reward. It is often assumed that threats and promises produce only public change (Raven & Kruglanski, 1970), but this is not necessarily a problem. As noted earlier, minorities in political groups are often more concerned with public than private change – their main goal is to win votes, not hearts and minds.

In an effort to exert influence, minorities in political groups can threaten majorities in several ways. For example, a minority can threaten to frustrate the majority's desire to reach a quick decision on an issue by disrupting the decision-making process. This could involve filibustering or otherwise stalling the process (e.g., by parliamentary procedures, by absence from meetings) so that the decision is delayed beyond the majority's deadline for resolution or, in extreme cases, is never made at all. In addition, a minority can threaten to form a coalition with another minority in the group and thereby obtain sufficient power to thwart the majority's will on the issue in question and perhaps on future issues that the majority cares about. "Uncommitted thinkers" or "cue-takers" play a pivotal role in foreign policy decision-making groups (Stewart et al., 1989), and hence minorities often seek to recruit these members to their cause. A minority can also threaten to withdraw from the group altogether, either by simply leaving or by forming a competing group. Junior partners in coalition cabinets, for example, often use threats to withdraw from the coalition and form an alliance with opposition parties in parliament to pressure senior partners for concessions (Kaarbo, 1996). Finally, the minority can threaten (a) to increase outside pressure on the majority to adopt its position (e.g., by mobilizing external constituencies); (b) to discredit the majority (e.g., by revealing improprieties of its members); or (c) even to undermine the survival of the entire group (e.g., by engaging in whistle-blowing about group crimes, by discouraging new members from joining the group).

These threats that a minority faction can issue are reminiscent of well-known bargaining and negotiation strategies based on costs and punishments (e.g., Deutsch, 1973; Rubin & Brown, 1975; Snyder & Diesing, 1977). Although much of what we know about such strategies is derived from studies of symmetrical negotiation between actors of equal power, researchers interested in asymmetrical negotiation have discovered threat-based strategies that weak actors successfully employ against strong actors (see Lindell & Persson, 1986). It has been found, for example, that threatening to deadlock negotiations through veto and to build coalitions outside the group are useful strategies for weak actors (Habeeb, 1988). Moreover, weak actors can some-times exploit their weakness by arguing that if strong actors do not accept their position, the weak actors will face a dangerous external threat and may even disintegrate. Lindell and Persson (1986) label this the *blackmail out of weakness* strategy. A minority faction in a small group could similarly turn a negative attribute (disunity) into an influence strategy by arguing that if the majority faction does not concede, the minority will fall apart and thus endanger the structure and possibly existence of the group. Another strategy that weak actors use is *actor linkage*, in which they claim they cannot make concessions because they are committed to third parties that share their position (Lindell & Persson, 1986). This, of course, is what a minority faction in a group does when it uses its constituency as an excuse for not compromising.

Whether unique to weak actors in asymmetrical negotiation or relevant to all actors in symmetrical negotiation, threat-based strategies are more likely to be used and to prove effective under some circumstances than others. Thus, in addition to "objective" criteria such as cost, benefit, and magnitude, "per-ceived" criteria such as legitimacy, credibility, and precision of contingencies will determine how actors use and respond to threat (Deutsch & Shichman, 1986). Moreover, we might expect these latter threat criteria to be more criti-cal to successful influence for minority factions than for majority factions. Consistent with this argument, Habeeb (1988) concluded that a small power's demonstrated commitment to a preferred outcome is the most important determinant of its influence.

In addition to strategies based on threats, a minority can use strategies based on promises. An example is "whitemail." A minority employing this strategy offers not to do something beneficial to itself in exchange for concessions from the majority. For example, a minority might promise that, if the majority agrees with its position, it will not recruit new members or adopt a potentially effective influence tactic. A minority may also promise a side-payment on a separate issue if the majority goes along with its position on the current issue (logrolling). This promise can involve either an immediate payback or a future payback. The probability of logrolling is influenced by the importance that the majority and minority attach to various issues. Thus, logrolling is possible if the two factions have different priorities (e.g., the minority cares about foreign policy, whereas the majority cares about domestic policy), but not if they have the same priority (e.g., they both care about foreign policy). Only the former situation is conducive to integrative bargaining (Bazerman & Neale, 1983).

Compositional and procedural strategies

The informational and punishment/reward strategies discussed above involve particular behaviors that minority members can use to induce majority members to agree (privately and/or publicly) with their position. Another category of minority strategies eschews active influence and instead relies on the minority's ability to alter the group in ways that increase the likelihood that its position will eventually prevail.

Compositional strategies are based on the assumption that group decisions are often determined by the "strength in numbers" effect, that is, the tendency for larger factions to prevail over smaller factions (Stasser, Kerr, & Davis, 1989). Thus, compositional strategies involve controlling who is present in the group with the aim of insuring that the minority faction is as large as possible (Hoyt, 1997; Levine, Moreland, & Ryan, 1998).[3] Kaarbo and Beasley (1998) have identified four compositional strategies that minorities can use to increase the likelihood that their position will triumph (see Kaarbo, 1998, for a discussion of these strategies in a bureaucratic context).

The first strategy involves enlarging the group to include allies (Halperin, 1974). This can be done, for example, by convincing the majority that the group needs people with special expertise and then nominating people who, besides having this expertise, are likely to endorse the minority's position. The second strategy involves shrinking the group to exclude opponents (cf. Levine, 1989; Levine & Thompson, 1996). For example, the minority might try to convince the majority that certain members (who disagree with the minority's position) should be excluded for security reasons (Destler, 1972). If this fails, the minority might define the topic of discussion in ways that make opponents' expertise irrelevant, fail to inform them of critical meetings, or schedule such meetings when they cannot attend.

The third strategy involves changing the decision forum, that is, moving the locus of authority to another group that is dominated by members of the minority (Halperin, 1974; Kaarbo, 1996). This might be done, for example, by substituting a departmental committee for an interdepartmental committee or persuading the group leader to appoint an ad hoc committee. Finally, the fourth strategy involves quitting the group.[4] Although quitting eliminates the minority's chance to directly influence the group's decision, it can nonetheless advance the minority's agenda. For example, by quitting, the minority may highlight the value of its position to remaining group members, who may then champion this position in the minority's absence. In addition, quitting may stimulate the minority's constituency to exert pressure on the group and may change the roles and responsibilities of remaining group members in ways that are helpful to the minority's cause.

Procedural strategies are based on the assumption that group decisions are often determined by the group's procedures for processing information and reaching consensus (Hoyt, 1997; Kaarbo & Beasley, 1998). Sometimes, a group's procedural rules (e.g., majority voting) are so strongly rooted in tradition that any effort to alter them will be met with rebuff and even outright hostility. Often, however, group members can and do manipulate procedural rules to benefit their faction. As Maoz (1990) argued, "a decision maker who can determine the procedure by which the group decides is in a position to affect the choice outcome without having to induce individual preference change" (p. 83). We would add that such a person is also able to exert influence without having to make threats or promises. Similar arguments for procedural control were advanced by Riker (1986), in his discussion of "heresthetics."

One obvious way to influence the group decision is to exert control over the decision rule that is used to aggregate members' individual preferences. If the majority rule is used, a faction maintaining a minority position at the end of the discussion will surely lose. But if the minority can convince the group to adopt the unanimity rule instead, the minority is more likely to influence the final decision (Miller, 1989). Furthermore, adoption of the unanimity rule will also affect majority members' private preferences following the discussion. As Miller (1989) noted:

Whereas under majority rule the majority members can remain intransigent and ignore minority members, under unanimity they must move their positions toward those of the more extreme members, if they wish to attain a group decision. This appears to lead to greater changes, not just in majority members' publicly expressed opinions . . . but also . . . in their privately held preferences. (p. 338)

In addition to changing the decision rule, a minority faction might attempt to change other procedural factors. One such factor is the manner in which alternatives are compared during the decision process. Social choice theory predicts that different outcomes will occur depending on whether decisions are structured as simultaneous choices between multiple alternatives or as sequential pairwise choices (Maoz, 1990). If the minority faction can adroitly manipulate this choice structure, it may increase its chances of prevailing. A minority faction might also try to induce the group to make decisions incrementally rather than all at once. Maoz (1990) discussed the "salami tactic" of making big decisions through small steps, with each successive change only marginally different from the one that preceeded it. By using the salami tactic, a minority might be able to convince a majority to accept a radical change that it otherwise would have rejected out of hand. Such a strategy, Maoz pointed out, was successfully used by Israeli Defense Minister Sharon to convince a reluctant Israeli cabinet to invade Lebanon in 1982. Finally, the minority might seek to influence other aspects of the timing of the decision, for example, whether it comes early or late in a series of decisions and whether it is preceded by a small or a large amount of discussion (cf. Davis, Hulbert, & Au, 1996).

Conclusions

In this chapter, we argued that social psychological research on minority influence would benefit from more attention to the social dynamics of groups, as opposed to the cognitive dynamics of individuals. Moreover, we argued that the social dynamics of political decision-making groups suggest a number of interesting hypotheses about minority influence. We first discussed some dimensions of minority influence that are of special relevance to political groups. In so doing, we presented a new typology of minority influence (encompassing progressive, reactionary, conservative, and modernist influence) and indicated limitations of the traditional compliance–conversion model favored by social psychologists. Next we discussed several structural features of political decision-making groups that may affect majority–minority interactions and thereby minority influence. These features include the relative size of the minority faction, the past relations between minority and majority factions, and the number of minority factions. Finally, we discussed various strategies that minorities can use to influence majorities. These include informational strategies, punishment/reward strategies, and compositional and procedural strategies.

A number of additional issues might be raised about minority influence in political decision- making groups. For example, although we emphasized influence between factions, in particular how minorities influence majorities, it is also important to consider influence within factions (Levine & Thompson, 1996). One interesting question is how minorities retain allies (i.e., members of their own faction) when they are simultaneously trying to convert opponents (i.e., members of the majority faction). This task is difficult because of the "dual audience" problem, which occurs when arguments presented to one faction are also known to the other faction (cf. Fleming, 1994). The difficulty stems from the fact that arguments used to retain allies may drive away opponents, whereas arguments used to convert opponents may alienate allies.

In order to avoid these problems, minorities may try to segregate their audiences, so that they can deliver different arguments to people in their own and the majority faction. In addition, minorities may use different influence strategies when trying to retain allies versus convert opponents. As mentioned earlier, social psychologists have assumed that minorities rely on informational influence when attempting to win over majorities. Although, as we suggested, this is not always the case, informational influence may in fact be the dominant strategy used against majorities. In contrast, when trying to retain allies, minorities may rely heavily on punishment and reward. Threats of punishment and promises of reward should be particularly effective within minority factions, because such factions often have strong norms against "treason" and surveillance of faction members is relatively easy when faction size is small.

Space constraints prevent us from discussing other issues, such as the social dynamics that produce escalation and de-escalation of conflict between majority and minority factions (Levine & Thompson, 1996). Nevertheless, we hope our comments are sufficient to indicate the importance of studying how interpersonal processes affect minority influence and the utility of considering how majority–minority relations operate in natural groups, particularly political decision-making groups.

NOTES

1 See Wood (1999) for a thoughtful analysis of motivational and cognitive mechanisms underlying minority influence.
2 Research on representative bargaining, in which negotiators feel responsible to external constituents, is consistent with this hypothesis (Pruitt & Carnevale, 1993).
3 As discussed earlier, the assumption that large minorities are more effective than small minorities may not always be valid.
4 Note that in this case we are talking about actually leaving the group, rather than simply threatening to leave, as was discussed above.

REFERENCES

Abrams, D., & Hogg, M. A. (1990). Social identification, self-categorization and social influence. In W. Stroebe & M. Hewstone (Eds.), *European review of social psychology* (Vol. 1, pp. 195–228). Chichester, UK: Wiley.

Allen, V. L. (1965). Situational factors in conformity. In L. Berkowitz (Ed.), *Advances in experimental social psychology* (Vol. 2, pp. 133–175). New York: Academic Press.

Allison, G., & Halperin, M. (1972). Bureaucratic politics: A paradigm and some policy implications. *World Politics, 24*, 40–79.

Alvaro, E. M., & Crano, W. D. (1997). Indirect minority influence. Evidence for leniency in source evaluation and counterargumentation. *Journal of Personality and Social Psychology, 72*, 949–964.

Anderson, P. (1987). What do decision makers do when they make a foreign policy decision? The implications for the comparative study of foreign policy. In C. F. Hermann, C. W. Kegley, & J. N. Rosenau (Eds.), *New directions in the study of foreign policy*. Boston: Allen & Unwin.

Bazerman, M. H., & Neale, M. A. (1983). Heuristics in negotiation: Limitations to effective dispute resolution. In M. H. Bazerman & R. J. Lewicki (Eds.), *Negotiating in organizations* (pp. 51–67). Beverly Hills, CA: Sage.

Berry, P. A. (1989). *The West German Federal Chancellory and its role in chancellor leadership*. Ph.D. Dissertation, Georgetown University, Washington, DC.

Bohner, G., Erb, H.-P., Reinhard, M.-A., & Frank, E. (1996). Distinctiveness across topics in minority and majority influence: An attributional analysis and preliminary data. *British Journal of Social Psychology, 35*, 27–46.

Butera, F., Mugny, G., Legrenzi, P., & Pérez, J. A. (1996). Majority and minority influence, task representation and inductive reasoning. *British Journal of Social Psychology, 35*, 123–136.

Clark, R. D., & Maass, A. (1988). Social categorization in minority influence: The case of homosexuality. *European Journal of Social Psychology, 18*, 347–364.

Clemens, C. (1988). The CDU/CSU and arms control. In B. M. Blechman & C. S.

Fisher (Eds.), *The silent partner* (pp. 61–127). Cambridge, MA: Ballinger Publishing.

Cook, K. S., & Gillmore, M. R. (1984). Power, dependence, and coalitions. In E. J. Lawler (Ed.), *Advances in group processes* (Vol. 1, pp. 27–58). Greenwich, CT: JAI Press.

Crano, W. D. (1994). Context, comparison, and change: Methodological and theoretical contributions to a theory of minority (and majority) influence. In S. Moscovici, A. Mucchi-Faina, & A. Maass, (Eds.), *Minority influence* (pp. 17–46). Chicago: Nelson-Hall.

David, B., & Turner, J. C. (1996). Studies in self-categorization and minority conversion: Is being a member of the out-group an advantage? *British Journal of Social Psychology, 35*, 179–199.

Davis, J. H., Hulbert, L., & Au, W.-T. (1996). Procedural influence on group decision making: The case of straw polls – observation and simulation. In R. Y. Hirokawa & M. S. Poole (Eds.), *Communication and group decision making* (2nd ed., pp. 384–425). Thousand Oaks, CA: Sage.

De Dreu, C. K. W., & De Vries, N. K. (1997). Minority dissent in organizations. In C. K. W. De Dreu & E. Van De Vliert (Eds.), *Using conflict in organizations* (pp. 72–86). London: Sage.

Destler, I. M. (1972). *Presidents, bureaucrats and foreign policy: The politics of organizational reform.* Princeton, NJ: Princeton University Press.

Deutsch, M. (1973). *The resolution of conflict.* New Haven, CT: Yale University Press.

Deutsch, M., & Gerard, H. B. (1955). A study of normative and information social influences upon individual judgment. *Journal of Abnormal and Social Psychology, 51*, 629–636.

Deutsch, M., & Shichman, S. (1986). Conflict: A social psychological perspective. In M. G. Hermann (Ed.), *Political psychology* (pp. 219–250). San Francisco: Jossey-Bass.

Doms, M., & Van Avermaet, E. (1985). Social support and minority influence: The innovation effect reconsidered. In S. Moscovici, G. Mugny, & E. Van Avermaet (Eds.), *Perspectives on minority influence* (pp. 53–74). Cambridge, UK: Cambridge University Press.

Fleming, J. H. (1994). Multiple-audience problems, tactical communication, and social interaction: A relational-regulation perspective. In M. P. Zanna (Ed.), *Advances in experimental social psychology* (Vol. 26, pp. 215–292). San Diego, CA: Academic Press.

Gaenslen, F. (1992). Decision-making groups. In E. Singer & V. Hudson (Eds.), *Political psychology and foreign policy.* Boulder, CO: Westview.

Gerard, H. B. (1985). When and how the minority prevails. In S. Moscovici, G. Mugny, & E. Van Avermaet (Eds.), *Perspectives on minority influence* (pp. 171–186). Cambridge, UK: Cambridge University Press.

George, A. (1980). *Presidential decision making in foreign policy: The effective use of information and advice.* Boulder, CO: Westview.

Gruenfeld, D. H. (1995). Status, ideology, and integrative complexity on the U.S. Supreme Court: Rethinking the politics of political decision making. *Journal of Personality and Social Psychology, 68*, 5–20.

Habeeb, W. M. (1988). *Power and tactics in international negotiation.* Baltimore, MD: Johns Hopkins University Press.

Halperin, M. (1974). *Bureaucratic politics and foreign policy.* Washington, DC: Brookings.

Hart, P. t' (1994). *Groupthink in government.* Baltimore, MD: Johns Hopkins University Press.

Hermann, C. F. (1993). Avoiding pathologies in foreign policy decision groups. In D. Caldwell & T. J. McKeown (Eds.), *Diplomacy, force and leadership* (pp. 179–207). Boulder, CO: Westview.

Hill, C. (1991). *Cabinet decisions on foreign policy.* Cambridge, UK: Cambridge University Press.

Hovland, C. I., Janis, I. L., & Kelley, H. H. (1953). *Communication and persuasion: Psychological studies of opinion change.* New Haven, CT: Yale University Press.

Hoyt, P. D. (1997). The political manipulation of group composition: Engineering the decision context. *Political Psychology, 18,* 771–790.

Huntington, S. P. (1960). Strategic planning and the political process. *Foreign Affairs, 38,* 285–299.

Islam, M. R., & Hewstone, M. (1993). Intergroup attributions and affective consequences in majority and minority groups. *Journal of Personality and Social Psychology, 64,* 936–950.

Janis, I. L. (1982). *Groupthink* (2nd ed.). Boston, MA: Houghton Mifflin.

Kaarbo, J. (1996). Power and influence in foreign policy decision making: The role of junior coalition partners in German and Israeli foreign policy. *International Studies Quarterly, 40,* 501–530.

Kaarbo, J. (1998). Influencing peace: Junior partners in Israeli coalition cabinets. *Cooperation and Conflict, 31,* 243–284.

Kaarbo, J., & Beasley, R. K. (1998). A political perspective on minority influence and strategic group composition. In M. A. Neale, E. Mannix, & D. H. Gruenfeld (Eds.), *Research on managing groups and teams* (Vol. 1, pp. 125–147). Greenwich, CT: JAI Press.

Kahan, J. P., & Rapoport, A. (1984). *Theories of coalition formation.* Hillsdale, NJ: Erlbaum.

Koeske, G. F., & Crano, W. D. (1968). The effect of congruous and incongruous source-statement combinations upon the judged credibility of a communication. *Journal of Experimental Social Psychology, 4,* 384–399.

Komorita, S. S. (1984). Coalition bargaining. In L. Berkowitz (Ed.), *Advances in experimental social psychology* (Vol. 18, pp. 183–245). Orlando, FL: Academic Press.

Latané, B. (1996). Strength from weakness: The fate of opinion minorities in spatially distributed groups. In E. Witte & J. Davis (Eds.), *Understanding group behavior: Consensual action by small groups* (Vol. 1, pp. 193–219). Mahwah, NJ: Erlbaum.

Latané, B., & Wolf, S. (1981). The social impact of majorities and minorities. *Psychological Review, 88,* 438–453.

Levine, J. M. (1989). Reaction to opinion deviance in small groups. In P. Paulus (Ed.), *Psychology of group influence* (2nd ed., pp. 187–231). Hillsdale, NJ: Erlbaum.

Levine, J. M., & Moreland, R. L. (1985). Innovation and socialization in small groups. In S. Moscovici, G. Mugny, & E. Van Avermaet (Eds.), *Perspectives on minority influence* (pp. 143–169). Cambridge, UK: Cambridge University Press.

Levine, J. M., Moreland, R. L., & Ryan, C. S. (1998). Group socialization and intergroup relations. In C. Sedikides, J. Schopler, & C. A. Insko (Eds.), *Intergroup cognition and intergroup behavior* (pp. 283–308). Mahwah, NJ: Erlbaum.

Levine, J. M., & Ruback, R. B. (1980). Reaction to opinion deviance: Impact of a fence straddler's rationale on majority evaluation. *Social Psychology Quarterly, 43,* 73–81.

Levine, J. M., & Russo, E. M. (1987). Majority and minority influence. In C. Hendrick (Ed.), *Review of personality and social psychology: Group processes* (Vol. 8, pp. 13–54). Newbury Park, CA: Sage.

Levine, J. M., Saxe, L., & Harris, H. J. (1976). Reaction to attitudinal deviance: Impact of deviate's direction and distance of movement. *Sociometry, 39,* 97–107.

Levine, J. M., Sroka, K. R., & Snyder, H. N. (1977). Group support and reaction to stable and shifting agreement/disagreement. *Sociometry, 40,* 214–224.

Levine, J. M., & Thompson, L. (1996). Conflict in groups. In E. T. Higgins & A. W. Kruglanski (Eds.), *Social psychology: Handbook of basic principles* (pp. 745–776). New York: Guilford.

Lindell, U., & Persson, S. (1986). The paradox of weak state power: A research and literature overview. *Cooperation and Conflict, 21,* 79–97.

Maass, A., & Clark, R. D. III (1986). Conversion theory and simultaneous majority/minority influence: Can reactance offer an alternative explanation? *European Journal of Social Psychology, 16,* 305–309.

Maass, A., Clark, R. D., III, & Haberkorn, G. (1982). The effects of differential ascribed category membership and norms on minority influence. *European Journal of Social Psychology, 12,* 89–104.

Maass, A., & Volpato, C. (1994). Theoretical perspectives on minority influence: Conversion versus divergence? In S. Moscovici, A. Mucchi-Faina, & Maass, A. (Eds.), *Minority influence* (pp. 135–147). Chicago: Nelson-Hall.

Maass, A., West, S. G., & Cialdini, R. B. (1987). Minority influence and conversion. In C. Hendrick (Ed.), *Review of Personality and social psychology* (Vol. 8, pp. 55–79). Newbury Park, CA: Sage.

Maoz, Z. (1990). Framing the national interest. *World Politics, 43,* 77–110.

Markus, H., & Zajonc, R. B. (1985). The cognitive perspective in social psychology. In G. Lindzey & E. Aronson (Eds.), *The handbook of social psychology* (3rd ed., Vol. 1, pp. 137–230). New York: Random House.

McLeod, P. L., Baron, R. S., Marti, M. W., & Yoon, K. (1997). The eyes have it: Minority influence in fact-to-face and computer-mediated group discussion. *Journal of Applied Psychology, 82,* 706–718.

Miller, C. E. (1989). The social psychological effects of group decision rules. In P. B. Paulus (Ed.), *Psychology of group influence* (2nd ed., pp. 327–355). Hillsdale, NJ: Erlbaum.

Miller, C. E., & Komorita, S. S. (1986). Coalition formation in organizations: What laboratory studies do and do not tell us. In R. J. Lewicki, B. H. Sheppard, & M. H. Bazerman (Eds.), *Research on negotiation in organizations* (Vol. 1, pp. 117–137). Greenwich, CT: JAI Press.

Moscovici, S. (1976). *Social influence and social change.* London: Academic Press.

Moscovici, S. (1980). Toward a theory of conversion behavior. In L. Berkowitz (Ed.), *Advances in experimental social psychology* (Vol. 13, pp. 209–239). New York: Academic Press.

Moscovici, S. (1985). Social influence and conformity. In G. Lindzey & E. Aronson (Eds.), *Handbook of social psychology* (3rd ed., pp. 347–412). Reading, MA: Addison-Wesley.

Moscovici, S., & Lage, E. (1976). Studies in social influence III: Majority versus minority influence in a group. *European Journal of Social Psychology, 6,* 149–174.

Moscovici, S., Lage, E., & Naffrechoux, M. (1969). Influence of a consistent minority on the responses of a majority in a color perception task. *Sociometry, 32,* 365–380.

Moskowitz, G. B. (1996). The mediational effects of attributions and information processing in minority social influence. *British Journal of Social Psychology, 35,* 47–66.

Mucchi-Faina, A. (1994). Minority influence effects: Assimilation and differentiation. In S. Moscovici, A. Mucchi-Faina, & A. Maass (Eds.), *Minority influence* (pp. 115–133). Chicago: Nelson-Hall.

Mugny, G. (1982). *The power of minorities.* New York: Academic Press.

Mugny, G., & Pérez, J. A. (1991). *The social psychology of minority influence.* Cambridge, UK: Cambridge University Press.

Mullen, B., Brown, R., & Smith, C. (1992). Ingroup bias as a function of salience, relevance, and status: An integration. *European Journal of Social Psychology, 22,* 103–122.

Nail, P. R. (1986). Toward an integration of some models and theories of social response. *Psychological Bulletin, 100,* 190–206.

Nemeth, C. J. (1986). Differential contributions of majority and minority influence. *Psychological Review, 93,* 23–32.

Nemeth, C. J. (1995). Dissent as driving cognition, attitudes, and judgments. *Social Cognition, 13,* 273–291.

Nemeth, C. J., & Brilmayer, A. G. (1987). Negotiation versus influence. *European Journal of Social Psychology, 17,* 45–56.

Nemeth, C. J., & Staw, B. M. (1989). The tradeoffs of social control and innovation in groups and organizations. In L. Berkowitz (Ed.), *Advances in experimental social psychology* (Vol. 22, pp. 175–210). San Diego, CA: Academic Press.

Nemeth, C. J., Swedlund, M., & Kanki, B. (1974). Patterning of the minority's responses and their influence on the majority. *European Journal of Social Psychology, 4,* 53–64.

Nemeth, C. J., Wachtler, J., & Endicott, J. (1977). Increasing the size of the minority: Some gains and some losses. *Eurpoean Journal of Social Psychology, 7,* 15–27.

Paicheler, G. (1976). Norms and attitude change I: Polarization and styles of behaviour. *European Journal of Social Psychology*, 6, 405–427.

Pérez, J. A., & Mugny, G. (1996). The conflict elaboration theory of social influence. In E. Witte & J. Davis (Eds.), *Understanding group behavior: Small group processes and interpersonal relations* (Vol. 2, pp. 191–210). Mahwah, NJ: Erlbaum.

Personnaz, M., & Personnaz, B. (1994). Perception and conversion. In S. Moscovici, A. Mucchi-Faina, & A. Maass, (Eds.), *Minority influence* (pp. 165–183). Chicago: Nelson-Hall.

Polzer, J. T., Mannix, E. A., & Neale, M. A. (1995). Multiparty negotiation in its social context. In R. M. Kramer & D. M. Messick (Eds.), *Negotiation as a social process* (pp. 123–142). Thousand Oaks, CA: Sage.

Pruitt, D. G., & Carnevale, P. J. (1993). *Negotiation in social conflict*. Pacific Grove, CA: Brooks/Cole.

Purkitt, H. E. (1992). Political decision making in small groups: The Cuban missile crisis revisited – one more time. In E. Singer and V. Hudson (Eds.), *Political psychology and foreign policy*. Boulder, CO: Westview.

Raven, B. H., & Kruglanski, A. (1970). Conflict and power. In P. Swingle (Ed.), *The structure of conflict* (pp. 69–109). New York: Academic Press.

Ridgeway, C. L. (1982). Status in groups: The importance of motivation. *American Sociological Review*, 47, 76–88.

Riker, W. H. (1986). *The art of political manipulation*. New Haven, CT: Yale University Press.

Rubin, J. Z., & Brown, B. (1975). *The social psychology of bargaining and negotiation*. New York: Academic Press.

Smith, C. M., Tindale, R. S., & Dugoni, B. L. (1996). Minority and majority influence in freely interacting groups: Qualitative versus quantitative differences. *British Journal of Social Psychology*, 35, 137–149.

Snyder, G. H., & Diesing, P. (1977). *Conflict among nations*. Princeton, NJ: Princeton University Press.

Sorrels, J. P., & Kelley, J. (1984). Conformity by omission. *Personality and Social Psychology Bulletin*, 10, 302–305.

Stasser, G., Kerr, N. L., & Davis, J. H. (1989). Influence processes and consensus models in decision-making groups. In P. B. Paulus (Ed.), *Psychology of group influence* (2nd ed., pp. 279–326). Hillsdale, NJ: Erlbaum.

Stewart, P. D., Hermann, M. G., & Hermann, C. F. (1989). Modeling the 1973 Soviet decision to support Egypt. *American Political Science Review*, 83, 35–59.

Tanford, S., & Penrod, S. (1984). Social influence model: A formal integration of research on majority and minority influence processes. *Psychological Bulletin*, 95, 189–225.

Tetlock, P. E. (1979). Identifying victims of groupthink from public statements of decision makers. *Journal of Personality and Social Psychology*, 37, 1314–1324.

Tindale, R. S., Davis, J. H., Vollrath, D. A., Nagao, D. H., & Hinsz V. B. (1990). Asymmetrical social influence in freely interacting groups: A test of three models. *Journal of Personality and Social Psychology*, 58, 438–449.

Walker, S. G., & Watson, G. L. (1989). Groupthink and integrative complexity in British foreign policy-making: The Munich case. *Cooperation and Conflict, 24,* 199–212.

Wood, W. (1999). Motives and modes of processing in the social influence of groups. In S. Chaiken & Y. Trope (Eds.), *Dual-process theories in social psychology*. New York: Guilford.

Wood, W., Lundgren, S., Ouellette, J. A., Busceme, S., & Blackstone, T. (1994). Processes of minority influence: Influence effectiveness and source perceptions. *Psychological Bulletin, 115,* 323–345.

Worchel, S., Grossman, M., & Coutant, D. (1994). Minority influence in the group context: How group factors affect when the minority will be influential. In S. Moscovici, A. Mucchi-Faina, & A. Maass (Eds.), *Minority influence* (pp. 97–114). Chicago: Nelson-Hall.

12

Minority Influence in Organizations: Its Origins and Implications for Learning and Group Performance

Carsten K. W. De Dreu and Bianca Beersma

Introduction

Social influence is key to managerial effectiveness and an integral part of working in teams and organizations. Members of organizations rely on one another to validate their views of the world, they seek and maintain norms and values about what they deem appropriate or not, and they influence one another to serve their personal or group interests. Some scholars even go as far as defining organizations in terms of social influence processes. For example, Vickers (1967) defines organizations as structures of mutual expectation, attached to roles that define what each of its members shall expect from others and from themselves. Weick (1979, p. 3) argues that "organizing is first of all grounded in agreements concerning what is real and illusory, a grounding that is called consensual validation."

Consensual validation is an ongoing and dynamic activity and the process of gaining consensus constitutes a very basic source of disagreement and social conflict (Taylor, 1992). That is, members of organizations disagree with one another about their views of the world, about their interpretation of facts and figures, about proper norms and values, and about whose interests should prevail. How people deal with opposition has been a core topic in psychology and management science for more than 40 years, starting with now classical studies on bargaining (Deutsch, 1949), norm formation (Sherif, 1936), and conformity (Asch, 1956). A common finding in each of these lines of research is that people tend to yield to the powerful, and align themselves with the majority point of view (Cialdini & Trost, 1998). Studies on bargaining and negotiation show that the more powerful party usually gets the bigger share of the pie, thus reflecting greater and more effective influence (e.g., Rubin & Brown, 1975). Likewise, newcomers in groups quickly adapt to the group norms and values; they side with the majority perspective within their group (e.g., Levine & Moreland, 1998). Evidence suggests that people tend to follow the majority view about reality, even when the majority point of view is obviously wrong (Baron, Kerr, & Miller, 1993). And in organization theory and research, many studies have emphasized compliance and conformity. For example, Yukl and Falbe (1990) examined the effectiveness of certain influence tactics and found that managers produce conformity to a greater extent when they use rational persuasion rather than coercion.

Conformity, however, is but one side of the coin. Because consensual validation is an ongoing and dynamic activity there is, by definition, deviance and dissent. That is, within organizations there always are members who do not conform to the majority perspective, do not comply with organizational policies, rules, and regulations, or do not accept the organization's mission and objectives. Moreover, the mere fact that organizations change suggests that these minority factions are able to influence the majorities' interpretation of the world, the majorities' ideas about proper norms and values, and majorities' position in how resources should be allocated. In other words, in groups and organizations we are likely to encounter minority factions who resist the majority and, to some extent, are able to influence the majority perspective on a number of issues.

In this chapter, our aim is to provide a framework for understanding when and why minority dissent in organizational groups influences attitudes and opinions, group functioning, and group performance. Because minority influence can be seen as the flip side of conformity processes, a better understanding of minority influence brings us one step closer to a comprehensive model of social influence in organizations. Second, modern organizations face an increasing diversity in their workforce. Organization members differ in terms of their demographic, informational, and normative background (Williams & O'Reilly, 1998) and this increases the likelihood of minority factions opposing the dominant majority perspective within organizations. Understanding minority influence helps research and theorizing about the effects of diversity in organizations. Accordingly, we seek answers to three questions. First, what are the origins of minority dissent in groups and organizations – where does it come from? Second, when and why are minority factions able to influence majority attitudes and opinions? And third, when and how do minority factions influence group and organizational performance?

In the first part of the chapter we review recent empirical studies dealing with the nature and origins of minority dissent. Subsequently, we discuss the influence of minority dissent using judgment and decision making research concerned with the "status quo bias," and social psychological research and theory concerned with opinion change as a function of persuasive arguments attributed to majority and minority factions. In the third part of the chapter we review research on the effects of minority dissent on group creativity, innovation and task performance. We conclude with some avenues for future research.

The Definition and Origins of Minority Dissent in Organizational Groups

Minority dissent can be defined as publicly advocating and pursuing beliefs, attitudes, ideas, procedures, and policies that go against the "spirit of the times" and challenge the position or perspective assumed by the majority (De Dreu & De Vries, 1997). Levine and Kaarbo (this volume) argued that in political decision-making groups four types of minorities may be distinguished. *Progressive* minorities advance a new perspective and seek to convince the majority of its value. *Conservative* minorities attempt to block the majorities' tendency to adopt a new, progressive perspective. *Modernist* minorities try to block the majorities' tendency to return to previously held attitudes and policies, while *reactionary* minorities try to persuade the majority to return to previously help opinions and perspectives. As with political decision-making groups, we may also find examples of each of these four types of minorities in organizational settings. An example of a progressive minority is the newly hired medical assistant who consistently advocates implementation of a novel treatment she was taught about at school. An example of a conservative minority is the small faction of employees who resist the introduction of a computer system thought to enhance internal communication between management and employees. An example of a modernist minority is the minority trying to persuade the majority that with time the recently implemented organizational change program should become beneficial and therefore should not be reversed prematurely. Finally, an example of a reactionary minority is the small group of colleagues insisting on dropping affirmative action policies.

Before turning to a discussion of the consequences of minority dissent in organizations we need to address the origins of minority dissent. De Dreu, De Vries, Franssen, and Altink (in press) focused on the antecedents of *willingness to dissent*. They examined personality differences including extraversion, which was expected to be positively related to the individual's willingness to dissent, and group antecedents including past treatment of dissent, clarity of group objectives, and quality of group communication. Respondents were highly educated, with 74% having a university degree or comparable level of education. About one-third of the respondents worked as consultants, another third worked as engineers, and the remaining respondents were general managers, or worked as financial staff members. Their average age was 35, and 59% were male. Willingness to dissent was reliably measured with four items: "I give my opinions when they disagree with the other members of my team," "I adjust to the group, even when I'm not fully convinced" (reverse scored), "I'm inclined to publicly attack the majority point of view," "I dare to take a minority position within the team" (responses could be given on five-point scales, with 1 = never, to 5 = very often). Results showed that more extraverted individuals displayed greater willingness to voice dissent, and that willingness to dissent was greater when the group had reacted positively to dissent in the past. Moreover, willingness to dissent decreased when the group had higher clarity of objectives, especially among extraverted individuals. Finally, results showed that willingness to dissent increased when the group provided for more communication opportunities. However, extraverted individuals benefited from communication opportunities and introverted individuals did not (see Figure 12.1).

Similar findings were obtained by LePine and Van Dyne (1998) when they examined the antecedents to voice in work groups. *Voice* is related to minority dissent and refers to expressing views and searching for alternative methods and strategies to perform the task (Van Dyne & LePine, 1998; see also Rusbult, Farrell, Rogers, & Mainous, 1988). Contrary to voice, minority dissent is explicitly seen as challenging the majority perspective and it is not necessarily constructive and intended to improve. Nevertheless, research and theory on voice may be useful in understanding minority dissent and vice versa. LePine and Van Dyne (1998) discuss two broad classes of antecedents to voice in work groups – person-centered antecedents and situation antecedents. *Person-centered antecedents* are those variables that are rooted in personality and individual differences. An example is satisfaction with one's work. Using Hirschman's (1970) framework, LePine and Van Dyne argued that satisfaction should be positively related to voice in work groups. In addi-

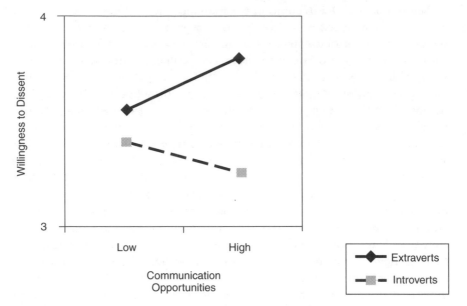

Figure 12.1 *Willingness to dissent as a function of opportunities for communication and individual differences in extraversion (based on De Dreu et al., in press).*

tion, they proposed that global self-esteem – the degree of positive self-worth that individuals ascribe to themselves – is positively related to voice in work groups. *Situation antecedents* are those variables that are independent of the individual but rooted in the situation, including the group to which one belongs. Because larger groups increase anonymity and make individual contributions to group work less identifiable, LePine and Van Dyne expected group size to be negatively related to voice. In a field study involving 95 work groups from 21 firms, they obtained support for their predictions. Satisfaction with the work group predicted voice especially in smaller groups, and global self-esteem predicted voice especially in larger groups.

The research by LePine and Van Dyne (1998) and De Dreu et al. (in press) provides some first insights into the origins of minority dissent in organizations. Person-centered antecedents include extraversion, satisfaction with the work group, and global self-esteem. Situation antecedents include group size, clarity of group objectives, and opportunities for communication. Interestingly, both studies provide good evidence that person-centered and situation antecedents interact to produce willingness to dissent and to voice one's deviant opinions and viewpoints. It is important to realize, however, that these studies were conducted in organizational settings using cross-sectional designs. We need to be cautious with conclusions about causality, although this seems less of a problem with regard to the person-centered antecedents discussed above.

One may speculate about the different origins of different types of dissent. For instance, certain personality characteristics such as high levels of authoritarianism may make it more likely that someone aligns with a reactionary rather than progressive minority. Likewise, individuals with high levels of uncertainty avoidance (Sorrentino & Short, 1986) may be more likely to join modernist and conservative minorities than progressive minorities, while those people with high levels of openness to experience (Barrick & Mount, 1991) may be likely to form a progressive minority. Again, we expect interactions with the situation, and research is needed to examine these issues in more detail. We believe such research is important because it may provide those seeking to enhance or reduce the occurrence of minority dissent in work groups with the tools to do so.

Minority Dissent and Social Influence

Moscovici (1980, 1985) argued that people depend on each other to validate their views of the world, and majority and minority influence should be understood in terms of dependency and social power, the majority being the dominant and the minority being the dominated party. When it comes to the validation of information, consensus provides a solid cue as to whether a particular position, attitude, or preference is correct, appropriate, or justifiable (Chaiken & Stangor, 1987). Seen as such, majority factions have a power advantage over minority factions because of the larger number of people endorsing a majority rather than minority position.

Power affects social attention in ways that predispose powerful individuals to be more biased judges and less powerful individuals to be less accurately judged (Fiske, 1993; Fiske & Depret, 1996). Powerful individuals tend to rely on judgmental heuristics to a greater extent and base their judgments about powerless individuals on social stereotypes. Keltner and Robinson (1997) indeed showed that factions defending the status quo were more prone to polarize the opposing faction's attitudes and underestimate the preferences they shared with their opponents.

The cognitive and motivational processes outlined above translate into behavioral strategies that are likely to be preferred by minority and majority factions in organizations. Research on marital relations reveals that defendants have a strong tendency to withdraw from the debate and remain inactive, while complainants engage in increasingly strong forms of demanding behavior. From a strategic perspective, this demand–withdrawal pattern makes sense, in that complainants often have the best chance of "winning" the dispute by demanding, while defendants often "win" by remaining inactive, that is, by not changing (Kluwer, Heesink, & Van de Vliert, 1997). Rubin, Pruitt, and Kim (1994), in discussing the attack–defend model of escalation, argue that in this kind of conflicts the attacker is assigned blame for the negative consequences of the conflict, and is more easily perceived in negative, derogative terms.

Fighting or defending the status quo

The relative disadvantage due to faction size may be increased or reduced by the type of position the minority faction is advocating. Disagreement between minority and majority factions is often asymmetrical in that one faction (the minority) wants change while the other faction (the majority) wants to maintain the status quo. This is the case for reactionary and progressive minorities alike but not for modernist and conservative minorities that defend the status quo against a majority faction seeking to change it.

Situations in which one party defends and another party seeks to change the status quo are similar to complainant–defendant disputes (Pruitt, 1998). Research on judgment and decision making provides evidence for the status quo bias: the individual's tendency to attach greater subjective weight to the current rather than prospective situation (Samuelson & Zeckhauser, 1988). This status quo bias exists for several reasons. One is that change involves transaction costs including broker's fees, search costs for identifying alternatives, learning costs associated with familiarizing oneself with alternatives, and activity costs involved in motivating a change (Schweitzer, 1994). Second, change involves risk and ambiguity – "the proof of the pudding is in the eating" – and this makes it more difficult to justify the costs of change. Third, change involves gains as well as losses, but losses loom larger and receive greater weight in judgment (Kahneman & Tversky, 1979). Finally, individuals have more knowledge about, and access to, information concerning the current state of affairs than about the prospective situation (Ritov & Baron, 1995). This means that those defending the status quo have an information advantage compared to those seeking to change the status quo. Taken together, change is likely to be evaluated in negative terms while the status quo is likely to be evaluated in positive terms. Defending rather than trying to change the status quo provides one with a relative power advantage and one has an easier task justifying one's position.

The status quo bias is pervasive in organizations. As Weick argues:

> The thick layering of routines in most organizations, coupled with the fact that departures from routine increase vulnerability, mean that discrediting is rare . . . organizations are said to be accountable and . . . must continually give the impression that . . . the organization *knows* what it is doing. Doubts, hesitance, or reevaluation of past enactments are treated . . . as evidence that an organization is unsure of itself rather than as evidence that it is reflecting, preserving adaptability, or preparing for an even more diverse set of circumstances. The moral would seem to be that if you're going to discredit, keep quiet about it. (1979, pp. 225–6)

Weick's observation is supported by research showing that organizations and their employees tend to go to great length to eliminate minority dissent. Minority dissent disrupts harmony and social relations in the group (Schweiger, Sandberg, & Rechner, 1989) and this may lead majority factions to put (informal) pressures on minority dissenters to remain silent and to cooperate. Group members direct a substantial amount of their communica tion toward the dissenting party, press the dissenter to change his or her point of view, or expel the minority from further participation (e.g., Levine, 1980; see also Festinger, Gerard, Hymovitch, Kelley, & Raven, 1952). Frost and Egri (1991) discuss cases in which organizations cover up evidence in support of the dissenter, sabotage the minority's functioning, or manage external committees in ways that automatically silence the dissenter.

Although a minority faction may have a power disadvantage because of its small faction size, this power disadvantage may be bolstered or leveraged depending on whether the minority faction defends the status quo or desires change. We suggest that progressive and reactionary minorities have a double disadvantage (the status quo bias, and a small number) while modernist and conservative minorities blend a power advantage (the status quo) with a power disadvantage (their small number). When minority factions have a (double) power disadvantage, as in the case of progressive and reactionary minorities, their main strategy for getting their way is through increasing use of a demanding, forceful strategy. This reduces their positive image and minority factions are likely to be stereotyped as negative, annoying, and rebellious people. Because change involves costs, and costs tend to loom larger than the potential benefits from change, the arguments advanced by minority factions are easily derogated and ignored. But when the minority faction defends the status quo it mixes a small faction size with an information advantage and has a position that is relatively easy to defend. We expect conservative and modernist minorities to have a relatively positive image and, consequently, to be relatively influential (see also below).

Taken together, minority factions have a power disadvantage due to their small number and consequently majority members may be inclined to develop and maintain stereotypical views of the minority. The specific type of position advocated by the minority faction depends strongly on whether it defends the status quo. Because seeking to change the status quo is diffi-cult to justify and requires a forceful, aggressive strategy, progressive and reac-tionary minorities are expected to be seen as more annoying, rebellious, and negative, and to be less influential, than conservative and modernist minori-ties who seek to defend the status quo.

The Influence of "Powerless" (Progressive) Minorities

Up to this point, our review suggests that minorities have less of a "fighting chance" when it comes to influencing the majority faction, especially when the minority faction seeks to change the status quo. Progressive minorities in particular may be responded to with rather strong reactions by the majority, including tendencies to cover up evidence in support of the dissenter, to sabotage the minority's functioning, and strategies that automatically silence the dissenter (cf. Frost & Egri, 1991). This may be true only, however, when the minority point of view poses an existential threat to the group or orga-nization, as in the case of a whistleblower (Near & Micelli, 1995). When such an existential threat is absent, or when the majority faction needs the minor-ity to cooperate to ensure effective group functioning, the majority reaction is more likely to be ambivalent. Consistent with Crano and Chen (1998; Alvaro & Crano, 1997; Crano, this volume) we suggest that in most cases a minority faction is treated on the basis of a *leniency contract*: Majority members are reluctant to be identified with the minority faction, but at the same time, they want to keep the group together. They listen to the minority, do not derogate its position, but remain inactive as it comes to adopting the minor-ity point of view.

Three categories of variables appear to stimulate the majorities' attention to a minority faction's position and, hence, minority influence (De Vries, De Dreu, Gordijn, & Schuurman, 1996). The first class of variables deals with the behavioral style the minority uses. Social psychological experiments show that minorities are more influential when they are consistent over time as well as in their argumentation (Moscovici, 1985). Consistency makes it difficult for the majority to condone the minority without really considering the content of the minority message, and more thorough, detailed processing of the minority message is the result. Likewise, when the minority uses solid, good arguments for its position, majority members have greater difficulty ignoring the message compared to situations in which the minority only presents its position, or provides weak arguments that are easy to refute (De Vries et al., 1996).

The second class of variables deals with the issue under debate. Majority members are more likely to consider the minority point of view when the issue is of great importance, is involving, and has clear personal (or organizational) consequences (De Dreu & De Vries, 1996; Trost, Maass, & Kenrick, 1992). However, when the minority position can be attributed to self-interest, majority members are more likely to derogate the message and ignore it, compared to when the minority position cannot be "explained away" in terms of self-interest (Moskowitz, 1996; Moskowitz & Chaiken, this volume). Likewise, when the minority position on a particular issue is highly surprising and unexpected it is more likely to attract majority attention (Baker & Petty, 1994).

The third class of variables deals with the defining characteristics of the minority faction. When the minority is categorized as an ingroup rather than outgroup (e.g., does not belong to "our work unit") it is likely to be more influential (Alvaro & Crano, 1997). In this regard, it is important to distinguish between so-called single and double minorities. Single minorities only differ from the majority faction in terms of their attitude position, while double minorities also differ on some other, social dimensions. Consider, for example, a software design team who are used to following a particular strategy to acquire outside contracts. The team has three female and five male members. A minority of two arguing for an alternative, novel acquisition strategy is more likely to be influential when it consists of a man and a women (i.e., is a single minority) rather than when it consists of two women. In the latter case, the deviating position is quickly attributed to a "female bias," thus rendering the minority faction less influential (Maass & Clark, 1984). Finally, expectation states theory (De Gilder & Wilke, 1995) suggests that high status minorities are more likely to be influential than low status minorities. In the example of the software design team, a minority consisting of two males is likely to be more influential than an all-female minority because men tend to be assigned greater expertise and knowledge.

Minority dissent and levels of influence

Minority influence, when it occurs, may result in either one of two types of change in the majority. The first type of change is overt and public – majority members publicly accept the minority position. The second type of change is covert and private – majority members privately accept the minority position but fail to acknowledge it in public. This type of change is much more likely than the first. Public acceptance increases the likelihood that other members of the organization identify the changing majority member as part of the deviating minority faction. Because deviant minority factions have low power, are vulnerable, and in danger of persecution people tend to avoid identification with a minority faction. Therefore, they are reluctant to openly adopt the minority position even when they privately agree (Crano & Chen, 1998; De Dreu, De Vries, Gordijn, & Schuurman, 1999; Mugny, Kaiser, Papastamou, & Pérez, 1984; Wood, Pool, Leck, & Pervis, 1996). A meta-analysis of social psychological research on minority influence supports this reasoning by showing that minority influence is much stronger on private rather than public measures of attitude change (Wood, Lundgren, Ouellette, Busceme, & Blackstone, 1994).

An interesting and robust observation is that private attitude change following minority influence not only occurs on the issue that is under consideration, but spreads to related issues as well. Pérez and Mugny (1987) conducted an experiment in which Spanish schoolgirls were exposed to a minority influence agent advocating in favor of abortion. The authors measured attitude changes on two topics – abortion and birth control. Results revealed that while the minority message had some influence on the girls' attitudes towards abortion, substantial change occurred on attitudes concerning birth control (for replications and extensions, see Crano & Chen, 1998; De Dreu & De Vries, 1993). The meta-analysis cited above found that this pattern – substantial change on related issues – was robust and independent of attitude topics and measurement issues (Wood et al., 1994). Thus, it appears that minority influence provokes deep and thorough processing of information, focused not only on the topic under consideration but also on underlying organizing principles.

Minority Dissent and Group Performance

Earlier we quoted Weick (1979), whose observations pointed to the fact that minority dissent in organizations has to counter an immense pressure to conform and to maintain the status quo, but also reflects the inherent value accorded to dissent – increased reflection and adaptation. Indeed, mounting evidence suggests that organizational groups open to minority dissent perform better. In this section we argue that minority dissent contributes to organizational learning, stimulates creativity and divergent thought, and increases the quality of group decision making.

Minority dissent and learning in organizations

In the section on minority dissent and social influence we reviewed research showing that minority dissent may promote deep and systematic rather than shallow and heuristic processing of information. Deep versus shallow thinking relates to the distinction between single-loop and double-loop learning (Argyris, 1991; Weick, 1979). In *single-loop learning*, individuals focus on identifying and correcting errors in the external environment. In *double-loop learning*, however, managers and employees look inward and reflect critically on their own behavior, identify the ways they often inadvertently contribute to the organization's problems, and then change how they act. In double-loop learning, managers and employees "learn how the very way they go about defining and solving problems can be a source of problems in its own right" (Argyris, 1991, p. 100).

Double-loop learning requires independent thinking, and several studies indicate that the occurrence of minority dissent may stimulate independent thinking in majority members. Nemeth and Chiles (1988) showed that exposure to minority dissent increases individual courage to resist pressures to conformity and the tendency to polarize attitudes toward extreme viewpoints that are undesirable in their consequences. Smith, Tindale, and Dugoni (1996) found that in decision-making groups in which a minority advocated a deviating position, less extreme and less polarized strategy decisions were made than in groups in which such a resisting minority was absent. Another indication comes from a study by Van Dyne and Saavedra (1996) who used a longitudinal design with natural groups who had to analyze two ambiguous cases that emphasized divergent thinking and idea generation. Some group members were given private instructions to adopt a deviant position, that is, to act as a minority dissenter. Results showed that designated minority agents reported their roles to be stressful, yet they received relatively positive evaluations from their peers and received substantial admiration and respect. Also minority agents promoted and facilitated role differentiation and concomitant specialization. Thus, minority dissent may provide an example of courage, may stimulate role differentiation and may counter the polarization of attitudes. Each of these processes stimulates, in turn, independent thinking, and double-loop rather than single-loop learning in organizations (cf., Argyris, 1991; Weick, 1979).

Minority dissent, divergent thought, and team innovation

Research by Nemeth (1986) suggests that being confronted with minority dissent elicits "divergent" thinking. When recipients focus on the dissenter's message they attempt to understand why the minority thinks this way as well as to falsify and counterargue its position. As a result, recipients take into account multiple perspectives and consider various aspects of the issue under debate (Butera & Mugny, 1996, this volume; De Dreu & De Vries, 1993; Gordijn, De Vries, & De Dreu, 2000; Martin & Hewstone, 1999; Nemeth & Kwan, 1985, 1987; Nemeth, Mayseless, Sherman, & Brown, 1990; Nemeth, 1995; Van Dyne & Saavedra, 1996). For example, the study by Van Dyne and Saavedra (1996) discussed earlier showed that work groups with a minority influence agent produced more creative ideas and had more divergent perspectives on the task than groups lacking a minority influence agent.

Related to the divergent thinking research by Nemeth and others is research concerned with integrative complexity. Gruenfeld, Thomas-Hunt, and Kim (1998) studied integrative complexity in majority and minority factions within freely interacting groups. Integrative complexity refers to the individual's tendencies to exhibit (a) conceptual differentiation such as the recognition of multiple alternatives, and (b) conceptual integration such as the recognition of possible tradeoffs among alternatives. Research revealed that majority members tend to have greater integrative complexity than members of minority factions (Gruenfeld, 1995) but this evidence was based on archival materials. Gruenfeld et al. (1998) conducted an experiment to see whether the greater integrative complexity of members of a majority faction was due to their being confronted with minority dissent, or whether it was the result of a communication strategy aimed at converting the minority faction. Results were consistent with the first explanation and showed that members of majority factions scored higher on integrative complexity regardless of whether this integrative complexity was strategically useful or not (i.e., whether their communications would reach the minority faction or not).

That minority dissent in teams increases originality suggests that minority dissent may contribute to *innovation*, defined as the introduction or application within a team of ideas, processes, products, or procedures which are new to that team and which are designed to be useful (cf., Amabile, Conti, Coon, Lazenby, & Herron, 1996; West & Farr, 1990). Examples of team innovations include the development of a computer program to keep track of holidays and sick leave within the team, a protocol for handling complaints, a new strategy to (re)introduce a product in the market, and a new and complementary service for valued customers. De Dreu and West (2000) argued, however, that creativity is a necessary but not sufficient condition for team innovation. In addition to being creative, groups need to process creative ideas critically so as to drop those that appear useless and implement those that have promise, thereby helping the group to adapt to its environment. Thus, group members need to share information and insights, and work together to transform creative ideas into workable methods, products, and services.

De Dreu and West (2000) hypothesized that participation facilitates integration of information and commitment to team decisions (Bowers & Seashore, 1966; Coch & French, 1948; Lawler & Hackman, 1969). To the extent that information and influence over decision making are shared within teams, and there is a high level of interaction amongst team members, cross-fertilization of perspectives is more likely to occur. Through participation, creative ideas and solutions may be critically examined and adopted or rejected on the basis of arguments and evidence. Participation also provides the social support needed for newly adopted ideas to be pursued and implemented. In other words, participation may be key to turning (minority dissent-induced) originality into innovative methods, products, and services. Thus, De Dreu and West (2000) predicted more innovations in teams under high rather than low levels of minority dissent, but especially when these teams had high rather than low levels of participation in decision making. They tested this prediction in two studies. Minority dissent and participation in decision making was assessed through questionnaires filled out by team members. In Study 1 innovations were traced by interviewing team coaches about the innovations in their teams, and in Study 2 team innovation was assessed through questionnaires filled out by the team supervisors. Study 1 involved 21 self-managed teams from a parcel service in The Netherlands. Study 2 involved 28 teams from various organizations involved in a diverse set of tasks, including controlling, consulting, health care, and manufacturing. Results of both studies provided good support for the hypothesis. Innovation was higher when teams had high rather than low levels of minority dissent, but especially when they also had high levels of participation in decision making. Figure 12.2 represents, as an illustration, the results of Study 1.

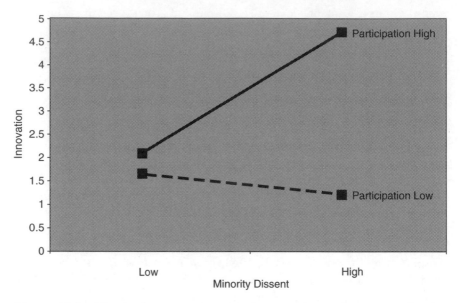

Figure 12.2 *Minority dissent, participation in decision making, and innovations (based on De Dreu & West, 2000).*

Minority dissent and group decision making

As we argued at the outset of this chapter, group leaders often seek compliance and punish deviates (Festinger et al., 1952; Frost & Egri, 1991) and individuals within groups have a strong tendency toward conformity and to align with the majority perspective in their group (Baron et al., 1993; Moscovici, 1980). Although compliance and conformity pressures are functional in that they define the group boundaries and facilitate coordination and task performance, Janis (1972) showed that conformity pressures and (extreme) concurrence seeking may lead to defective decision making with sometimes disastrous consequences (for evidence and reviews, see Aldag & Fuller, 1993; Park, 1990; Tetlock, Peterson, McGuire, Chang, & Feld, 1992; Turner & Pratkanis, 1997). Likewise, Hackman and Morris (1975) noted that an important reason why groups fail to outperform individuals is their premature movement to consensus, with dissenting opinions either being suppressed or dismissed.

The notion that conformity and compliance may be dysfunctional to group decision making has produced three more or less related lines of research. Based on the assumption that compliance and conformity is more likely in homogeneous rather than heterogeneous groups (Hoffman, 1959; Hoffman & Maier, 1961), research considered the relationship between team diversity in terms of personality, training, background, attitudes, and the quality of group decision making (Bantell & Jackson, 1989; O'Reilly, Caldwell, & Barnett, 1989). Team diversity is likely to have its positive effects on the quality of team decision making when it gives rise to debate and disagreement (Simons, Pelled, & Smith, 1999; Williams & O'Reilly, 1998). For example, job-related types of diversity (i.e., functional background and tenure diversity) in top management teams interacts with the amount of debate within teams to predict the extent to which the team attempted to be exhaustive and inclusive in making and integrating strategic decisions (decision comprehensiveness) (Simons et al., 1999).

That diversity fosters high quality decisions is consistent with a rather large set of studies examining the functionality of appointing a devil's advocate – a team member whose role is to consistently criticize the assumptions and directions suggested by the rest of the team (e.g., Janis, 1972). For example, research by Schweiger, Sandberg, and Ragan (1986) compared decision-making groups that used an expert-based approach to groups with a devil's advocate. Their results showed that appointing a devil's advocate improved the quality of the decision-making process, the quality of the decisions, and the group members' commitment to the decision. Schwenk (1990) conducted a meta-analytic review of the research on devil's advocacy and concluded that through exposure to a devil's advocate, group members question their assumptions and come to realize these to be less than optimal. As a result, the quality of group decision making is improved.

That voicing dissenting views is important for the quality of group decision making is consistent as well with research probing the functions and effects of more spontaneous forms of minority dissent. Authentic minority dissent has been shown to increase the quality of team decision making. For example, Dooley and Fryxell (1999) observed that, provided there was loyalty and competence within teams, dissent was associated with higher decision quality and decision commitment in strategic decision-making teams in US hospitals. Peterson (1997) showed that the quality of team processes and outcomes depends on whether the leader was open to dissent. Peterson, Owens, Tetlock, Fan, and Martorana (1998) studied top management teams and found that successful teams encouraged more dissent in private meetings. Other research indicates that exposure to minority dissent increases individual courage to resist group pressures to conformity (Nemeth & Chiles, 1988), and prevents teams from polarizing their attitudes toward extreme viewpoints that are undesirable in their consequences (Smith, Tindale, & Dugoni, 1996). Frey, Schulz-Hardt, and Stahlberg (1992) showed that minority dissent reduces the tendency in teams to search for confirmation rather than dis-confirmation of preferred strategies and solutions. Research by Gruenfeld, Thomas-Hunt, and Kim (1998) showed that in groups composed of majori-ties and minorities members of the majority showed higher levels of cogni-tive complexity. Butera and Mugny (1996; see also Martin & Hewstone, 1999), finally, observed that group members were more likely to find the correct solution for a problem when they were shown a minority rather than majority perspective on the subject matter. Thus, like an appointed devil's advocate, authentic minority dissent appears to prevent teams from biased and defective decision making.

Conclusions and Avenues for Future Research

This chapter sought an answer to three interrelated questions. The first ques-tion was what are the origins of minority dissent in teams and organizations. We reviewed research suggesting that minority dissent is the product of person-centered antecedents including extraversion and global self-esteem, and situation antecedents including group size, opportunities for communi-cation, and the clarity of team and organizational objectives. More research on the antecedents of minority dissent is needed, at the least because the evi-dence to date derives from cross-sectional research designs that do not settle issues of causality. In addition, the theory of minority dissent and minority influence gains practical relevance when we know the conditions that foster or inhibit the occurrence of minority dissent in groups and organizations. One particularly interesting avenue for research is, in our view, the interac-tion between person-centered and situation variables on the one hand, and the type of minority (progressive, modernist, conservative, or reactionary) they trigger on the other.

The second question we asked was when and why minority dissent influ-ences majority factions in organizational settings. We argued that when minority dissent has to overcome a status quo bias, as in the case of pro-gressive and reactionary minorities, the minority is placed in a relatively pow-erless position predisposing the minority to use rather forceful strategies to influence the majority. But because the majority often needs the minority to make the organization function effectively, majority factions tend to condone rather than oppress minority factions. Given solid arguments and a consistent behavioral style, minority dissent may be influential although, as ample research has shown, minority influence will be indirect and latent rather than direct and manifest.

The final question we asked was what consequences minority dissent has for group performance. We reviewed research suggesting that minority dissent in organizations may contribute to double-loop learning because it stimulates independent thinking and strengthens majority members' courage to resist conformity pressures. In addition, much research has shown that minority dissent stimulates creativity and divergent thought. We discussed recent research suggesting that minority dissent induces divergent thought which is associated with team innovation, provided there are high levels of participation in team decision making. Finally, research on group diversity, devil's advocacy, and authentic forms of dissent all indicated that minority dissent is likely to prevent premature moving to consensus, to reduce confirmation bias in information processing, to promote cognitive complexity and, therefore, to prevent defective group decision making.

It should be noted that the emerging literature on minority dissent in (organizational) teams tends to focus on just one side of group and organizational performance. In addition to originality and innovation, group performance depends on member satisfaction and mental as well as physical well-being. Social harmony, interpersonal trust, and psychological safety are key to group functioning and performance (Edmondson, 1999; West, Borrill, & Unsworth, 1998) yet minority dissent may negatively influence these factors. Put differently, to fully understand the influence of minority dissent in groups and organizations, researchers need to expand the repertoire of dependent variables. We need to go beyond originality and innovation and consider "soft" performance parameters including the affective consequences of minority dissent to both the dissenters and the members of the majority faction (cf., Hackman, 1983; Van Dyne & Saavreda, 1996).

Another avenue for future research is closer scrutiny of the issue under debate. Minority influence research has predominantly focused on issues of interpretation, with a minority faction disagreeing with the majority about how to view the world. In many instances, however, a minority faction may disagree with the majority about the distribution and allocation of resources, and adopts a particular position to defend its self-interests. The dynamics involved in conflicts of interpretation and conflicts of interests are different at the cognitive, motivational, and behavioral level (De Dreu, Harinck, & Van Vianen, 1999; Druckman, 1994; Harinck, De Dreu, & Van Vianen, 2000; Levine & Thompson, 1996). Research is needed to examine the influence of minority dissent when divergent interests rather than divergent interpretations of reality are at stake.

A final avenue for future research is to examine the moderating influence of the group task. To date, research has considered group tasks in which creativity and independent thinking is useful and helps the group to perform better. We need to study the effects of minority dissent on attitude change and group performance when the group task requires convergence and consensus decision making (Peterson & Nemeth, 1995; see also Smith, Tindale, & Anderson, this volume). Also, we need to study minority dissent at different phases of group work, such as the generation of ideas and information, the exchange of information and arguments supporting or countering particular decision alternatives, and the choice among decision alternatives including its implementation. The general proposition we would like to end with, but which requires empirical testing, is that in simple, routine tasks requiring convergence in thinking and consensus decision making, minority dissent distracts and hurts group performance. In more complex, nonroutine tasks that require a certain degree of independent thinking, thorough information processing, and the full exchange of information, minority dissent may help groups to perform effectively.

In the field of organizational psychology and management science, scholars have argued that any organizational culture that values the process of continuous learning fosters dissent as a necessary and desirable part of organizational life (Argyris, 1982; Schilit & Locke, 1982; Turner & Pratkanis, 1997; West & Anderson, 1996; see also Janis, 1972). The research discussed in this chapter underlines this advice in that we showed that minority dissent stimulates (double-loop) learning, increases creativity and innovation, and prevents defective group decision making. Future research is needed to examine the influence of different types of minority dissent on these performance parameters, to examine the functionality of minority dissent in different group tasks, and to study the influence of minority dissent on "soft" performance parameters including individual well-being and health. Although the evidence for the benefits of minority dissent is increasing, it is necessary to answer these questions to truly assess the value of minority dissent in teams and organizations.

NOTE

Financial support was provided by a grant of the Netherlands Organization for Scientific Research (NWO-575-31-006). We thank Nanne de Vries for his comments on an earlier version of this chapter.

REFERENCES

Aldag, R. J., & Fuller, S. R. (1993). Beyond fiasco: A reappraisal of the groupthink phenomenon and a new model of group decision processes. *Psychological Bulletin, 113*, 533–552.

Alvaro, E. M., & Crano, W. D. (1997). Indirect minority influence: Evidence for leniency in source evaluation and counterargumentation. *Journal of Personality and Social Psychology, 72*, 949–964.

Amabile, T. M., Conti, R., Coon, H., Lazenby, J., & Herron, M. (1996). Assessing the work environment for creativity. *Academy of Management Journal, 39*, 1154–1184.

Argyris, C. (1982). *Reasoning, learning, and action: Individual and organizational.* San Francisco: Jossey-Bass.

Argyris, C. (1991). *Reasoning, learning, and action: Individual and organizational.* San Francisco: Jossey-Bass.

Asch, S. E. (1956). Studies of independence and conformity: A minority of one against a unanimous majority. *Psychological Monographs: General and Applied, 70*, 1–70.

Baker, S. M., & Petty, R. E. (1994). Majority and minority influence: Source–position imbalance as a determinant of message scrutiny. *Journal of Personality and Social Psychology, 67*, 5–19.

Bantell, K. A., & Jackson, S. E. (1989). Top management and innovations in banking: Does the demography of the top team make a difference? *Strategic Management Journal, 10*, 107–124.

Baron, R. S., Kerr, N., & Miller, N. (1993). *Group process, group decision, group action.* London: Open University Press.

Barrick, M. R., & Mount, M. K. (1991). The Big Five personality dimensions and job performance: A meta-analysis. *Personnel Psychology, 44*, 1–26.

Bowers, D. G., & Seashore, S. E. (1966). Predicting organizational effectiveness with a four-factor theory of leadership. *Administrative Science Quarterly, 11*, 238–263.

Butera, F., & Mugny, G. (1996). Conflict between incompetencies and influence of a low-expertise source in hypothesis testing. *European Journal of Social Psychology, 25*, 457–462.

Chaiken, S., & Stangor, C. (1987). Attitudes and attitude change. *Annual Review of Psychology, 38*, 575–630.

Cialdini, R. B., & Trost, M. R. (1998). Social influence: Social norms, conformity and compliance. In D. T. Gilbert, S. T. Fiske, & G. Lindzey (Eds.), *The handbook of social psychology* (4th ed., Vol. 2, pp. 151–192). Boston, MA: McGraw-Hill.

Coch, L., & French, J. R. (1948). Overcoming resistance to change. *Human Relations, 1*, 512–532.

Crano, W. D., & Chen, X. (1998). The leniency contract and persistence of majority and minority influence. *Journal of Personality and Social Psychology, 74*, 1437–1450.

De Dreu, C. K. W., & De Vries, N. K. (1993). Numerical support, information processing and attitude change. *European Journal of Social Psychology, 23*, 647–662.

De Dreu, C. K. W., & De Vries, N. K. (1996). Differential processing and attitude change following majority & minority arguments. *British Journal of Social Psychology, 35*, 77–90.

De Dreu, C. K.W., & De Vries, N. K. (1997). Minority dissent in organizations. In C. K.W. De Dreu & E.Van de Vliert (Eds.), *Using conflict in organizations* (pp. 72–86). London: Sage.

De Dreu, C. K. W., De Vries, N. K., Franssen, H., & Altink, W. (in press). Minority dissent in organizations: Factors influencing willingness to dissent. *Journal of Applied Social Psychology.*

De Dreu, C. K. W., De Vries, N. K., Gordijn, E., & Schuurman, M. K. (1999). Majority and minority influence under convergent or divergent thinking. *European Journal of Social Psychology, 29*, 329–348.

De Dreu, C. K. W., Harinck, F., & Van Vianen, A. E. M. (1999). Conflict and performance in groups and organizations. In C. L. Cooper & I. T. Robertson (Eds.), *International review of industrial and organizational psychology* (Vol. 11, pp. 367–405). Chichester, UK: Wiley.

De Dreu, C. K. W., & West, M. A. (2000). Minority dissent and team innovation: The importance of participation in decision making. Manuscript submitted for publication.

DeGilder, D., & Wilke, H. A. M. (1995). Expectation states theory and the motivational determinants of social influence. *European Review of Social Psychology, 5*, 243–270.

Deutsch, M. (1949). A theory of cooperation and competition. *Human Relations, 2*, 199–231.

De Vries, N. K., De Dreu, C. K. W., Gordijn, E., & Schuurman, M. (1996). Majority vs. minority influence: A dual-role interpretation. In W. Stroebe & M. Hewstone (Eds.), *European review of social psychology* (Vol. 7, pp. 145–172), Chichester, UK: Wiley.

Dooley, R. S., & Fryxell, G. E. (1999). Attaining decision quality and commitment from dissent: The moderating effects of loyalty and competence in strategic decision-making teams. *Academy of Management Journal, 42*, 389–402.

Druckman, D. (1994). Determinants of compromising behavior in negotiation. *Journal of Conflict Resolution, 38*, 507–556.

Edmondson, A. (1999). Psychological safety and learning behavior in work teams. *Administrative Science Quarterly, 44*, 350–383.

Festinger, L., Gerard, H. B., Hymovitch, B., Kelley, H. H., & Raven, B. H. (1952). The influence process in the presence of extreme deviates. *Human Relations, 5*, 327–346.

Fiske, S. T. (1993). Controlling other people. *American Psychologist, 48*, 621–628.

Fiske, S. T., & Depret, E. (1996). Control, interdependence and power: Understanding social cognition in its social context. In W. Stroebe & M. Hewstone (Eds.), *European review of social psychology* (Vol. 7, pp. 31–62): Chichester, UK: Wiley.

Frey, D., Schulz-Hardt, S., & Stahlberg, D. (1992). Information seeking among individuals and groups and possible consequences for decision making in business and politics. In E. Witte & J. H. Davis (Eds.), *Understanding group behavior* (Vol. 2, pp. 211–226). Mahwah, NJ: Erlbaum.

Frost, P. J., & Egri, C. P. (1991). The political process of innovation. In B. M. Staw & L. L. Cummings (Eds.), *Research on organizational behavior* (Vol. 13, pp. 229–295). Greenwich, CT: JAI Press.

Gordijn, E. H., De Vries, N. K., & De Dreu, C. K. W. (2000). *Minority influence: The impact of expanding and shrinking minorities and argument quality on attitudes and information processing.* Unpublished manuscript, University of Amsterdam.

Gruenfeld, D. H. (1995). Status, ideology, and integrative complexity on the U.S. Supreme Court: Rethinking the politics of political decision making. *Journal of Personality and Social Psychology, 68,* 5–20.

Gruenfeld, D. H., Thomas-Hunt, M. C., & Kim, P. H. (1998). Cognitive flexibility, communication strategy, and integrative complexity in groups: Public versus private reactions to majority and minority status. *Journal of Experimental Social Psychology, 34,* 202–226.

Hackman, R. (1983). The design of effective work groups. In J. W. Lorsch (Ed.), *Handbook of organizational behavior* (pp. 315–342), Englewood Cliffs, NJ: Prentice-Hall.

Hackman, J. R., & Morris, C. G. (1975). Group task, group interaction process and group performance effectiveness: A review and proposed integration. *Advances in Experimental Social Psychology, 8,* 45–99.

Harinck, F., De Dreu, C. K. W., & Van Vianen, A. E. M. (2000) The impact of conflict issue on fixed-pie perceptions, problem solving, and integrative outcomes in negotiation. *Organizational Behavior and Human Decision Processes, 81,* 329–358.

Hirschman, A. O. (1970). *Exit, voice, and loyalty: Responses to decline in firms, organizations, and states.* Cambridge, MA: Harvard University Press.

Hoffman, L. (1959). Homogeneity and member personality and its effects on group problem solving. *Journal of Abnormal and Social Psychology, 58,* 27–32.

Hoffman, L., & Maier, N. (1961). Quality and acceptance of problem solutions by members of homogeneous and heterogeneous groups. *Journal of Abnormal and Social Psychology, 62,* 401–407.

Janis, I. L. (1972). *Victims of groupthink: A psychological study of foreign-policy decisions and fiascos.* Boston: Houghton Mifflin.

Kahneman, D., & Tversky, A. (1979). Prospect theory: An analysis of decision under risk. *Econometrica, 47,* 263–291.

Keltner, D., & Robinson, R. (1997). Defending the status quo: Power and bias in social conflict. *Personality and Social Psychology Bulletin, 23,* 1066–1077.

Kluwer, E. S., Heesink, J. A. M., & Van de Vliert, E. (1997). The marital dynamics of conflict over the division of labor. *Journal of Marriage and the Family, 59,* 635–653.

Lawler, E. E., & Hackman, J. R. (1969). Impact of employee participation in the development of pay incentive plans: A field experiment. *Journal of Applied Psychology, 53,* 467–471.

LePine, J., & Van Dyne, L. (1998). Predicting voice behavior in work groups. *Journal of Applied Psychology, 83,* 853–868.

Levine, J. M. (1980). Reaction to opinion deviance in small groups. In P. Paulus (Ed.), *Psychology of group influence* (pp. 375–430). Hillsdale, NJ: Erlbaum.

Levine, J. M., & Moreland, R. (1998). Small groups. In D. Gilbert, S. Fiske, & G. Lindzey (Eds.), *Handbook of social psychology* (4th ed., Vol. 2, pp. 415–468). Boston, MA: McGraw-Hill.

Levine, J. M., & Thompson, L. L. (1996). Conflict in groups. In E. T. Higgins & A. W. Kruglanski (Eds.), *Social psychology: Handbook of basic principles* (pp. 745–776). New York: Guilford.

Maass, A., & Clark, R. D. III. (1984). Internalization versus compliance: Differential processes underlying minority influence and conformity. *European Journal of Social Psychology, 13,* 197–215.

Martin, R., & Hewstone, M. (1999). Minority influence and optimal problem solving. *European Journal of Social Psychology, 29,* 825–832.

Moscovici, S. (1980). Toward a theory of conversion behavior. In L. Berkowitz (Ed.), *Advances in experimental social psychology* (Vol. 13, pp. 209–239). New York: Academic Press.

Moscovici, S. (1985). Social influence and conformity. In G. Lindzey & E. Aronson (Eds.), *The handbook of social psychology* (3rd ed., pp. 347–412). New York: Random House.

Moskowitz, G. B. (1996). The mediational effects of attributions and information processing in minority social influence. *British Journal of Social Psychology, 35,* 47–66.

Mugny, G., Kaiser, C., Papastamou, S., & Pérez, J. A. (1984). Intergroup relations, identification and social influence. *British Journal of Social Psychology, 23,* 317–322.

Near, J. P., & Micelli, M. P. (1995). Effective whistle-blowing. *Academy of Management Review, 20,* 679–708.

Nemeth, C. (1986). Differential contributions of majority and minority influence processes. *Psychological Review, 93,* 10–20.

Nemeth, C. (1995). Dissent as driving cognition, attitudes, and judgments. *Social Cognition, 13,* 273–291.

Nemeth, C., & Chiles, C. (1988). Modelling courage: The role of dissent in fostering independence. *European Journal of Social Psychology, 18,* 275–280.

Nemeth, C., & Kwan, J. (1985). Originality of word associations as a function of majority versus minority influence. *Social Psychology Quarterly, 48,* 277–282.

Nemeth, C., & Kwan, J. (1987). Minority influence, divergent thinking and detection of correct solutions. *Journal of Applied Social Psychology, 17,* 786–797.

Nemeth, C., Mayseless, O., Sherman, J., & Brown, Y. (1990). Exposure to dissent and recall information. *Journal of Personality and Social Psychology, 58,* 429–437.

O'Reilly, C. A. III., Caldwell, D. F., & Barnett, W. (1989). Work group demography, social integration, and turnover. *Administrative Science Quarterly, 34,* 21–37.

O'Reilly, C. A. III., Williams, K. Y., & Barsade, S. (1998). Group demography and innovation: Does diversity help? *Research on Managing Groups and Teams, 1,* 183–207.

Park, W. (1990). A review of the research on groupthink. *Journal of Behavioral Decision Making, 3*, 229–245.

Pérez, J. A., & Mugny, G. (1987). Paradoxical effects of categorization in minority influence: When being an outgroup is an advantage. *European Journal of Social Psychology, 17*, 157–169.

Peterson, R., & Nemeth, C. (1995). Focus versus flexibility: Majority and minority influence can both improve performance. *Personality and Social Psychology Bulletin, 22*, pp. 14–23.

Peterson, R. S. (1997). A directive leadership style in group decision making can be both virtue and vice: Evidence from elite and experimental groups. *Journal of Personality and Social Psychology, 72*, 1107–1121.

Peterson, R. S., Owens, P. D., Tetlock, P. E., Fan, E. T., & Martorana, P. (1998). Group dynamics in top management teams: Groupthink, vigilance, and alternative models of organizational failure and success. *Organizational Behavior and Human Decision Processes, 73*, 272–305.

Pruitt, D. G. (1998). Social conflict. In D. Gilbert, S. T. Fiske, & G. Lindzey (Eds.), *Handbook of social psychology* (4th ed., Vol. 2, pp. 89–150). New York: McGraw Hill.

Ritov, I., & Baron, J. (1995). Outcome knowledge, regret, and omission bias. *Organizational Behavior and Human Decision Processes, 64*, 119–127.

Rubin, J. Z., & Brown, B. R. (1975). *The social psychology of bargaining and negotiation.* New York: Academic Press.

Rubin, J. Z., Pruitt, D. G., & Kim, S. H. (1994). *Social conflict: Escalation, stalemate, and settlement.* New York: McGraw-Hill.

Rusbult, C. E., Farrell, D., Rogers, G., & Mainous, A. G. III. (1988). Impact of exchange variables on exit, voice, loyalty, and neglect: An integrative model of responses to declining job satisfaction. *Academy of Management Journal, 31*, 599–627.

Samuelson, W., & Zeckhauser, R. (1988). Status quo bias in decision making. *Journal of Risk and Uncertainty, 1*, 7–59.

Schilit, W. K., & Locke, E. A. (1982). A study of upward influence in organizations. *Administrative Science Quarterly, 27*, 304–316.

Schweiger, D., Sandberg, W., & Rechner, P. (1989). Experimental effects of dialectical inquiry, devil's advocacy, and other consensus approaches to strategic decision making. *Academy of Management Journal, 32*, 745–772.

Schweiger, D. M., Sandberg, W. R., & Ragan, J. W. (1986). Group approaches for improving strategic decision making: A comparative analysis of dialectical inquiry, devil's advocacy, and consensus. *Academy of Management Journal, 29*, 51–71.

Schweitzer, M. (1994). Multiple reference points, framing, and the status quo bias in health care financing decisions. *Organizational Behavior and Human Decision Processes, 63*, 69–72.

Schwenk, C. R. (1990). Effects of devil's advocacy and dialectical inquiry on decision making: A meta-analysis. *Organizational Behavior and Human Decision Processes, 47*, 161–176.

Sherif, M. (1936). *The psychology of social norms.* New York: Harper & Row.

Simons, T., Pelled, L. H., & Smith, K. A. (1999). Making use of difference: Diversity, debate, and decision comprehensiveness in top management teams. *Academy of Management Journal, 42,* 662–673.

Smith, C. M., Tindale, R., & Dugoni, B. L. (1996). Minority and majority influence in freely interacting groups: Qualitative versus quantitative differences. *British Journal of Social Psychology, 35,* 137–150.

Smith, C. M., Tindale, S. R., & Dugoni, B. L. (1996). Minority and majority influence in freely interacting groups: Qualitative versus quantitative differences. *British Journal of Social Psychology, 35,* 137–150.

Sorrentino, R. M., & Short, J. C. (1986). Uncertainty orientation, motivation, and cognition. In R. M. Sorrentino & E. T. Higgins (Eds.), *Handbook of motivation and cognition: Foundations of social behavior* (pp. 379–403). New York: Guilford Press.

Taylor, R. N. (1992). Strategic decision making. In M. D. Dunnette & L. M. Hough (Eds.), *Handbook of industrial and organizational psychology* (2nd ed., pp. 651–717). Palo Alto, CA: Consulting Psychologists Press.

Tetlock, P. E., Peterson, R. S., McGuire, C., Chang, S., Feld, P. (1992). Assessing political group dynamics: A test of the groupthink model. *Journal of Personality and Social Psychology, 63,* 403–425.

Trost, M. R., Maass, A., & Kenrick, D. T. (1992). Minority influence: Personal relevance biases cognitive processes and reverses private acceptance. *Journal of Experimental Social Psychology, 28,* 234–254.

Turner, M. E., & Pratkanis, A. (1997). Mitigating groupthink by stimulating constructive conflict. In C. K. W. De Dreu & E. Van de Vliert (Eds.), *Using conflict in organizations* (pp. 53–71). London: Sage.

Van Dyne, L., & LePine, J. (1998). Helping and voice extra-role behaviors: Evidence of construct and predictive validity. *Academy of Management Journal, 41,* 108–119.

Van Dyne, L., & Saavedra, R. (1996). A naturalistic minority influence experiment: Effects on divergent thinking, conflict, and originality in work-groups. *British Journal of Social Psychology, 35,* 151–168.

Vickers, G. (1967). *Towards a sociology of management.* New York: BasicBooks.

Weick, K. E. (1979). *The social psychology of organizing.* New York: Random House.

West, M. A., & Farr, J. L. (1990). Innovation at work. In M. A. West & J. L. Farr (Eds.), *Innovation and creativity at work: Psychological and organizational strategies* (pp. 3–13) Chichester, UK: Wiley.

West, M. A. (1997). *Developing creativity in organizations.* Leicester, UK: British Psychological Society.

West, M. A., & Anderson, N. R. (1996). Innovation in top management teams. *Journal of Applied Psychology, 81,* 680–693.

West, M. A., Borrill, C. S., & Unsworth, K. (1998). Team effectiveness in organizations. In C. L. Cooper & I. T. Robertson (Eds.), *International review of industrial and organizational psychology* (Vol. 13, pp. 1–48). Chichester, UK: Wiley.

Williams, K. Y., & O'Reilly, C. A. III. (1998). Demography and diversity in organizations: A review of 40 years of research. *Research in Organizational Behavior, 20,* 77–140.

Wood, W., Lundgren, S., Ouellette, J. A., Busceme, S., & Blackstone, T. (1994). Minority influence: A meta-analytical review of social influence processes. *Psychology Bulletin, 115,* 323–345.

Wood, W., Pool, G. J., Leck, K., & Purvis, D. (1996). Self-definition, defensive processing, and influence: The normative impact of majority and minority groups. *Journal of Personality and Social Psychology, 71,* 1181–1193.

Yukl, G., & Falbe, C. M. (1990). Influence tactics and objectives in upward, downward, and lateral influence attempts. *Journal of Applied Psychology, 75,* 132–140.

13

Culture and Minority Influence: Effects on Persuasion and Originality

K. Yee Ng and Linn Van Dyne

Introduction

In this chapter, we discuss the role of culture in the minority influence process and develop a theoretical model which proposes contrasting effects for four dimensions of culture (Hofstede, 1984) on two key minority influence outcomes: persuasion and originality (Moscovici, 1976; Nemeth, 1986). Fundamentally, we propose that an individual's cultural values play an important, and underresearched, role in the minority influence process. We suggest that expression of dissent and responses to the expression of dissent are significantly influenced by culture.

Addressing the issue of culture and minority influence is important for various practical and theoretical reasons. From a practical standpoint, two increasingly pervasive phenomena drive the need for a greater understanding of the role of culture in the minority influence process. First, the workforce is becoming more culturally diverse due to a multitude of factors, such as globalization, domestic diversity, advancement in communication technology, and restructuring of businesses (Granrose & Oskamp, 1997). Second, there is growing evidence that conflict may be beneficial to individual, group, and organizational outcomes (Amason, 1996; De Dreu & Van De Vliert, 1997; Jehn, 1995, 1997; Nemeth, 1986; Schweiger, Sandberg, & Rechner, 1989; Schwenk, 1990). However, we contend that although diversity can lead to divergent perspectives, cultural values may be an important boundary condition in determining an individual's response to minority influence. Thus, exploring how the influence process varies for people with different cultural orientations can aid organizations in effectively reaping the potential benefits of productive conflict.

From a theoretical standpoint, incorporating cultural factors explicitly in models of minority influence can serve as a guide for future research. Even though minority influence studies have been conducted in a variety of countries (e.g., Bohner, Erb, Reinhard, & Frank, 1996, in Germany; David & Turner, 1996, in Australia; De Dreu & De Vries, 1996, in The Netherlands; Maass, Volpato, & Mucchi-Faina, 1996, in Italy; Sanchez-Mazas, 1996, in Switzerland; Nemeth & Kwan, 1987 and Van Dyne & Saavedra, 1996, in the USA.), no research has focused explicitly on cultural differences in the minority influence process. Building on the work of Bond and Smith (1996b), who attributed the lack of consistent findings in the conformity literature to the potential effects of culture in the influence process, we focus our theory building specifically on the role of culture. A growing amount of theory and empirical research describes differences in psychological processes based on cultural differences (Bond & Smith, 1996a; Fiske, Kitayama, Markus, & Nisbett, 1998). Hence, assessing the role of culture will enable researchers to examine the ecological validity of current knowledge regarding minority influence, and to develop more refined models for predicting the effects of minority influence in different cultural settings.

Consideration of the effects of culture on minority influence necessitates the inclusion of two perspectives: the minority influence agent (i.e., the person expressing dissent), and the target of influence (i.e., the person exposed to the dissent). The former perspective deals with how culture affects a person's expression of dissenting views, while the latter focuses on how culture influences a person's reactions when exposed to dissenting views. Although both perspectives are important, in this chapter, we focus on the reactions of minority influence targets – in other words, the degree to which targets of influence change their position (persuasion) and/or express divergent ideas (originality). We emphasize these two potential responses based on their practical relevance to work organizations.

In summary, this chapter examines the role of culture in the minority influence process. We begin our exposition with a brief review of the separate literatures on minority influence and culture, followed by a brief discussion on the influence of culture on the expression of dissent. Next, we propose a theoretical model that explicates the effects of Hofstede's (1984) four dimensions of culture (individualism–collectivism, power distance, uncertainty avoidance, and masculinity–femininity) on reactions to dissent (persuasion and originality).

Minority Influence

In the early research on minority influence, scholars modeled the conception of minority influence after the majority influence process where conformity took center stage (e.g., see Latané & Wolf, 1981). Central to the phenomenology of conformity is the distinction between external, or behavioral, consent, and internal consent, which implies personal acceptance of values and beliefs (Moscovici, 1976). For example, Moscovici theorized that external conformity demonstrates compliance, while internal consent indicates conversion. Similarly, Nemeth described this distinction as change at the public (or manifest) level versus change at the private (or latent) level (e.g., Nemeth, 1986).

Thus, most of the research and theory on minority influence differentiates two general responses to influence attempts. An influence target can openly demonstrate agreement with the influence source without necessarily privately accepting the argument (public conformance). Alternatively an influence target can publicly resist the influence but inwardly accept the validity of the argument (private conversion). This distinction is important because past research often demonstrates movement to the minority view at the latent level even though there is no evidence of manifest movement (Moscovici, 1976, 1980; Moscovici, Lage, & Naffrechoux, 1969; Mugny, 1980; Nemeth & Wachtler, 1974).

Another important milestone in the minority influence literature was Nemeth's novel focus on the cognitive processes associated with minority influence. Unlike the classical view of minority influence as conformity, Nemeth contended that the conception of influence should be "broadened from 'prevailing' (whether this be public or private) to issues of attention, thought, and 'novel' judgments or decisions" (1986, p. 23). Based on this perspective, the question is not whether individuals move toward (or away from) the position proposed by the minority influence agent, or whether they do this publicly or privately. Instead, the focus is on how they think about the issues and the consequences of their thought processes for the quality of their solutions and decisions. Empirical studies following Nemeth's conceptualization have demonstrated that minority influence agents stimulate divergent and original thinking, which results in more novel solutions (Nemeth & Kwan, 1985, 1987; Nemeth & Wachtler, 1983; Van Dyne & Saavedra, 1996).

Minority Influence and Culture

Culture

Hofstede defined culture as "the collective programming of the mind which distinguishes the members of one human group from another" (1984, p. 21). A major rationale for examining the effect of culture on minority influence is the notion that culture is a powerful mechanism that shapes social norms (Fiske et al., 1998; Triandis, 1988) and creates "patterned ways of thinking" (Kluckhohn, 1954). These "societal expectations" regarding appropriate and inappropriate behavior are acquired by individuals over time through social learning processes (Bandura, 1986) which, in turn, influence attitude formation and, ultimately, have consequential effects on individual behavior. Eagly and Chaiken defined attitude as "a psychological tendency that is expressed by evaluating a particular entity with some degree of favor or disfavor" (1998, p. 269). One determinant of attitude formation that is particularly relevant to our discussion is subjective norms. A subjective norm is "the person's perception that most people who are important to him think he should or should not perform the behavior in question" (Fishbein & Ajzen, 1975, p. 302). Since individuals with different cultural values possess different "patterned ways of thinking," their subjective norms are likely to vary and influence their attitudes about appropriate behavior and their evaluations of others (for a review of attitude–behavior models, see Eagly & Chaiken, 1998). In other words, culture can influence expression of dissent, reactions to the person who voices the dissent, and responses to the dissent process (persuasion and originality).

Expression of dissent

The notion that cultural conditions affect the level of conformity (or dissent) in a society has long been held by scholars in the field (Bond & Smith, 1996b). Markus and Kitayama noted a popular adage with relevance to cultural differences in the expression of dissent – in individualistic America, "the squeaky wheel gets the grease," while in collectivistic Japan, "the nail that stands out gets pounded down" (1991, p. 224). Popular stereotypes also portray some nations as more conforming and submissive, and others as more independent and self-assertive (e.g., Milgram, 1961; Peabody, 1985). For instance, Milgram (1961) found that Norwegian subjects expressed fewer dissenting opinions than French subjects even when the response elicited was not made public, or when the issue of discussion had critical consequences. Commenting on these findings, Milgram suggested that diversity of opinions was characteristic of the French, who place high value on critical judgment. In contrast, he suggested that emphasis on social cohesiveness predisposed the Norwegians to be more attuned to the needs and interests of those around them.

From a theoretical perspective, the concept of tightness–looseness (Pelto, 1968) suggests differences in the expression of dissent across cultures. In loose cultures, norms are expressed within a wide range of alternative channels. The lack of regimentation and discipline in these cultures allows more tolerance of deviant behavior. In tight cultures, norms are expressed clearly and unambiguously, and the society is highly disciplined and orderly. Deviation from normative behavior is not tolerated, and severe sanctions are imposed on deviants. We submit that individuals' propensity to express dissenting views is conditioned by their societal norms concerning deviant behavior. Since individuals in loose cultures endorse values such as change, tolerance, risk taking, and stimulation (Chan, Gelfand, Triandis, & Tzeng, 1996), they are likely to possess a positive attitude toward voicing a different opinion. On the contrary, individuals in tight cultures emphasize values such as conformity, past tradition, stability, and security (Chan et al., 1996), which predispose them to possess a negative attitude toward dissent. As a result, individuals are more likely to express dissent when they are brought up in a loose culture, than in a tight culture.

We suggest that in addition to influencing the frequency of dissent, culture also affects the manner in which dissent is expressed. Although early work in minority influence has demonstrated the benefits of a consistent and persistent style of persuasion (e.g., Moscovici & Lage, 1976; Nemeth, Swedlund, & Kanki, 1974; Nemeth & Wachtler, 1974), these findings did not consider cultural differences. For instance, negotiation research has shown that although similar negotiation outcomes were obtained in different countries, the process was significantly different. In an experiment, Graham (1983) found that the determinants of business negotiation outcomes were different for American, Brazilian, and Japanese negotiators. Results indicated that for the Americans, the outcomes of the negotiation were primarily determined by information exchange during the negotiation; for the Japanese and Brazilians, the key factor influencing outcomes was the establishment of mutually trusting relationships before the negotiation. Hence, one possible inference from this research is that individualistic and collectivistic individuals differ in the manner in which they attempt to persuade the other party to adopt their viewpoint.

Reactions to dissent

Cultural values can also affect an individual's response to influence attempts. Earlier, we described a causal chain of relationships where cultural values affect subjective norms, subjective norms affect attitudes regarding the appropriateness of a behavior, and attitudes influence behavior in response to others. Here, we propose that the culture–subjective norms–attitudes–behavior process influences the degree to which individuals publicly change their opinions (persuasion) and the degree to which they are stimulated to engage in divergent thinking (originality) when subjected to minority influence. We elaborate our rationale for the effect of culture on persuasion and originality outcomes below.

Persuasion. In defining persuasion, we focus on public movement toward the minority stance. When individuals change their opinion and publicly adopt the minority viewpoint, they resist conformity pressure associated with the majority position. We contend that this process of deciding and publicly adopting the minority versus majority position is influenced by cultural values and subjective norms regarding appropriate behavior (Cialdini & Trost, 1998). When cultural values reinforce normative beliefs regarding conformity to the majority, individuals will be less likely to exhibit public persuasion by the minority influence agent. In contrast, when subjective norms place less emphasis on conforming and more emphasis on independent thinking, individuals experience less pressure to adhere to the majority and have greater latitude to agree with the minority view. Consistent with causal models of attitude–behavior relations, attitudes, in turn, influence the persuasion outcome of minority influence.

Originality. We define originality as enhanced quality and creativity of ideas. Nemeth (1986) theorized that minority influence stimulates divergent thinking (i.e., consideration of multiple perspectives) in contrast to majority influence, which reinforces convergent thinking (Nemeth, Mosier, & Chiles, 1992). Results of empirical studies have demonstrated that those subjected to minority influence develop a wider range of arguments and more original arguments (e.g., Butera, Mugny, Legrenzi, & Pérez, 1996; Martin, 1996; Volpato, Maass, Mucchi-Faina, & Vitti, 1990) as well as more divergent thinking and more creative solutions to problems (see, e.g., Nemeth & Kwan, 1987; Van Dyne & Saavedra, 1996).

Applying this to our focus on cultural influence, we propose that one determinant of the amount of divergent thinking is an individual's attitude toward the minority influence agent's role and behavior. Specifically, we contend that when a minority influence agent (in voicing a dissenting view) violates the influence target's normative beliefs about appropriate behavior, this triggers negative cognitive responses (Petty & Wegener, 1998). Negative evaluation shifts attention away from issue-relevant thoughts to assessment of the minority influence agent and the agent's behavior. We propose that cultural values influence the assessment of appropriateness of the minority influence the agent's behavior. When the influence behavior is evaluated as being inconsistent with role schemas and subjective norms, cognitions about the content of the message decrease and cognitions about the source and the source's motivation increase (Fiske & Talyor, 1991). We propose that this assessment of source credibility and validity distracts attention from message content which reduces divergent thinking and originality.

In the sections that follow, we develop specific propositions for the effect of culture on the minority influence outcomes of persuasion and originality. We argue that cultural orientations of individualism–collectivism, power distance, uncertainty avoidance, and masculinity–femininity influence subjective norms concerning groups, power, ambiguity, and sex roles. Subjective norms influence attitudes toward minority influence and judgments of the appropriateness of the minority influence agent's behavior. These evaluative assessments, in turn, have implications for persuasion and originality. In general, we posit that culture (operating through subjective norms) will have a stronger effect on the public outcome of persuasion than on the private outcome of originality. Figure 13.1 illustrates our overall model and Figure 13.2 summarizes our basic propositions.

Our model is conceptualized as having potential application at both the group and the individual levels of analysis. Although initial research based on Hofstede's framework focused on cross-cultural differences at the national or cultural level (e.g., Bochner & Hesketh, 1994; Chan et al., 1996; Hofstede, 1984), more recent studies have also examined the differences in the cultural values of individuals. Within this group of studies conducted at the individual level of analysis, some emphasized comparisons across cultures (Earley, 1993; Triandis, Bontempo, Villareal, Asai, & Lucca, 1988), while other research focused on within-culture differences (i.e., Chatman & Barsade, 1995; Farh, Earley, & Lin, 1997; Wagner, 1995). We believe that there is value in both approaches and the choice of framing should be a function of the particular research question being addressed in the study. In this chapter, we present our propositions at the individual level of analysis for ease and consistency, and suggest that they could easily be adapted and applied to the group level.

Minority Influence and Individualism–Collectivism

Individualism–collectivism is the most frequently researched dimension of culture. Definitions for individualism–collectivism include "the relationship

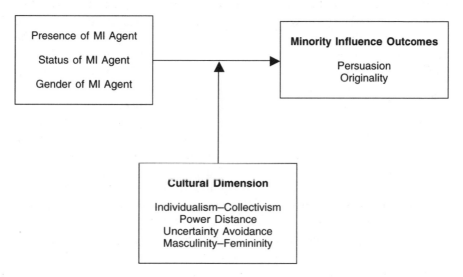

Figure 13.1 *Culture and minority influence.*

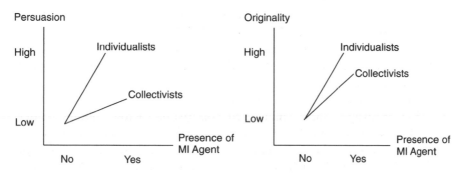

Figure 13.2A *Individualism–collectivism and minority influence.*

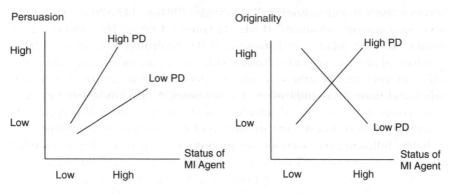

Figure 13.2B *Power distance and minority influence.*

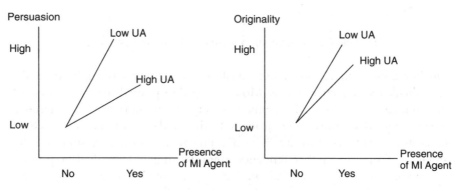

Figure 13.2C *Uncertainty avoidance and minority influence.*

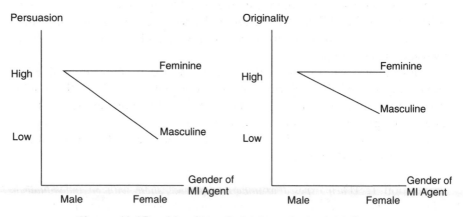

Figure 13.2D *Masculinity–femininity and minority influence.*

between the self and collectivity" (Hofstede, 1984, p. 148), "the social connectedness among individuals" (Earley & Gibson, 1998, p. 266), and the construal of the self (Markus & Kitayama, 1991). According to Triandis's (1995) summary of attributes of individualism–collectivism, an individualist views the self as independent of others, focuses on personal goals, acts upon personal beliefs and values, and emphasizes task outcomes. A collectivist, on the other hand, construes the self as an interdependent entity, adopts group goals, acts according to social norms, and stresses good interpersonal relationships.

In the following two sections, we propose that a person's degree of individualism–collectivism will moderate the effect of minority influence on the outcomes of persuasion and originality. The key difference that we propose is the magnitude of the effect on the two outcomes, as illustrated in Figure 13.2A.

Individualism–collectivism, conformity norms, and persuasion

Our foregoing explication of individualism–collectivism has implications for an individual's subjective norms. Moscovici (1976) posited that the course of the influence process is determined by objectivity norms and preference norms. Objectivity norms give priority to the validation of consensus, which inevitably entails conformity pressure; preference norms presuppose the absence of pressure and a tendency towards unique individual responses. Extending Moscovici's points about social norms to the cultural context, we contend that those with individualistic cultural values stress preference norms as their subjective norms (e.g., independence, self-reliance, pursuit of personal goals) and experience less conformity pressure. On the other hand, those with collectivistic cultural values (e.g., group harmony, group goals) emphasize objectivity norms which reinforce conformity and adherence to the majority view of the group.

Consequently, we anticipate that when exposed to minority influence, conformity toward the majority will be more prevalent among those with collectivistic cultural values than among those with individualistic cultural values. In summary, the minority influence agent has less persuasion power with collectivists (compared to individualists), due to collectivists' cultural values and subjective norms.

Proposition 1: *When exposed to minority influence, those with an individualistic cultural orientation will experience greater persuasion than those with a collectivistic cultural orientation.*

Individualism–collectivism, divergent thinking, and originality

In contrast to persuasion, which is public, divergent thinking is private (Moscovici, 1976, 1980; Nemeth, 1986). We contend that individualists and collectivists will both experience enhanced thought processes and will produce more original outcomes when exposed to minority influence, compared to situations where no minority influence is present. However, we propose that the amount of divergent thinking differs for individualists and collectivists as a result of their culturally influenced attitudes toward the behavior of the minority influence agent.

Since individualists view creativity as a cardinal value to be championed (see Triandis, 1990), they are more likely to regard voicing nonconventional, dissenting opinions as "positive," "creative," or "brave." Another reason to expect individualists to have favorable attitudes toward the minority influence agent is based on Chen, Chen, and Meindl's (1998) argument that the expressive motives of individualistic people center around actualizing the true self. This is reflected by the terms that individualists often associate with those who speak up, such as "individuality," "independence," "self-direction," and "self-reliance." Indeed, studies conducted in Western cultures have found that others described the minority agent as "confident," "independent," "active," "organized" (Nemeth & Chiles, 1988; Nemeth & Wachtler, 1974; Nemeth, Wachtler & Endicott, 1977), and even "respected" (Wolf, 1979). We suggest that these positive evaluations of the minority influence agent made by influence targets with individualistic cultural values will facilitate divergent thinking in response to minority influence attempts.

On the other hand, a collectivistic influence target is likely to view the minority influence agent as "defiant," "disloyal," or as a hindrance to progress toward the group's goal. We predict that those with collectivistic cultural values will view the minority agent negatively and will consider the agent's behavior to be an inappropriate violation of their subjective norms. This negative assessment will distract attention from the issue as those with collectivistic values attempt to understand the motive behind the influence behavior. This results in less issue-related divergent thinking, and hence less originality.

In sum, although we argue that minority influence will increase originality of both collectivists and individualists, we expect that relative to the collectivists, individualists will exhibit greater originality because they will be less distracted by the minority influence agent's behavior and will experience greater issue-related divergent thinking.

Proposition 2: *When exposed to minority influence, those with an individualistic cultural orientation will exhibit greater originality than those with a collectivistic cultural orientation.*

Minority Influence and Power Distance

Hofstede defined power distance as "the extent to which the less powerful members of institutions and organizations within a country expect and accept that power is distributed unequally" (1991, pp. 28–29). In postulating the role of power distance regarding persuasion and originality, we focus on the status of the minority agent, instead of the mere presence of minority influence (as was the case in Propositions 1 and 2). This is consistent with definitions of power distance which are conceptualized in terms of legitimacy accorded to hierarchical relationships (Hofstede, 1991). Because the relation of power distance and influence is meaningful to the extent that the minority influence agent has a hierarchical relationship with the influence target, we conceptualize the status of the minority influence agent on a continuum, ranging from low to high status. We premise the following discussion on the assumption that agents with higher organizational status possess greater power over influence targets.

In the following two sections, we examine the interaction between the status of the minority influence agent and the cultural beliefs of target individuals regarding power distance. Here, we propose a different form of interaction for the two different outcomes of persuasion and originality. Figure 13.2B illustrates our contrasting predictions for persuasion and originality.

Power distance, conformity norms, and persuasion

In our model, we posit that the positive relationship between power (status of the minority influence agent) and influence is moderated by the observer's beliefs regarding power distance. An essential feature of high power distance is the belief that inequality exists between more powerful (e.g., superiors) and less powerful (e.g., subordinates) persons (Hofstede, 1984). In other words, individuals with high power distance hold subjective norms that people with less authority should respect and obey people with authority. For example, studies have found that individuals with high power distance tend to adhere more rigidly to organizational hierarchy and to prefer centralized decision making (Hofstede, 1984; Shane, Venkataraman, & MacMillan, 1995). Accord-

ingly, we suggest that since those with high power distance values hold subjective norms that one should not challenge superiors, they will move publicly toward the minority position (persuasion) when the minority influence
agent has high status.

On the contrary, we predict that those with low power distance values
will be more resistant to influence even when the influence agent has substantial power (high status). For example, people with low power distance
favor participative approaches to management and are less submissive to
authority (Bochner & Hesketh, 1994). Compared to those with high power
distance, they experience less pressure to conform to the views of the powerful. In fact, succumbing to the views of a higher authority is sometimes
interpreted as an indicator of fear or cowardice. Hence, we expect individuals with low power distance cultural values to exhibit less public persuasion
than those with high power distance, when subjected to minority influence
by agents who have high status.

Proposition 3: *When exposed to minority influence agents with high organizational
status, those with a high power distance cultural orientation will experience greater persuasion than those with a low power distance cultural orientation.*

Power distance, divergent thinking, and originality

We propose a different type of influence for power distance cultural
values relative to originality. For persuasion, we proposed an overall positive
effect for the status of the minority influence agent. Here, we suggest
that the effect of subjective norms regarding status will differ for those with
low versus high power distance cultural values. To be more specific, we
argue that influence targets with low power distance beliefs tend to perceive
powerful minority influence agents as domineering and imposing. These
perceptions of negative behavior violate the targets' subjective norms
about equality of power, and as a result they will focus on evaluating the
negative social behavior and trying to uncover potential vested interests.
Consequently, these target individuals will engage in less issue-related divergent thinking.

Conversely, the legitimacy of differential power for those with high power
distance beliefs leads to a genuine respect for power. For example, Shane et
al. (1995) found that those with high power distance prefer innovation cham-
pions to gather support from those in authority before pursuing innovation
projects. Hence, influence targets with high power distance tend to view the

influence attempts by powerful minority influence agents as legitimate and credible. Since their normative beliefs about appropriate behavior are not violated, influence targets with high power distance beliefs, when faced with a powerful minority influence agent, pay greater attention to the message, and hence engage in greater divergent thinking on the issue.

When an influence agent has low status, we predict the opposite response compared to those above. Since individuals with high power distance values regard less powerful minority influence agents as less legitimate, they focus on negative evaluation of the minority influence agent, are distracted by the influence behavior, and experience less divergent thinking related to the issue. We reverse our prediction for those with low power distance. Here, individuals view less powerful minority influence agents as confident and independent (Nemeth & Wachtler, 1974; Nemeth et al., 1977), and respected (Wolf, 1979). These positive attitudes lead to greater attention to the minority message. In summary, we postulate a cross-interaction between the status of the minority agent and the power distance of the influence target, relative to originality.

Proposition 4: *When exposed to minority influence agents with high organizational status, those with a high power distance cultural orientation will exhibit greater originality than those with a low power distance cultural orientation. At the same time, those with a low power distance cultural orientation will exhibit greater originality than those with a high power distance cultural orientation when exposed to minority influence agents with low organizational status.*

Minority Influence and Uncertainty Avoidance

Hofstede (1984) defined uncertainty avoidance as discomfort with situations where the outcome is uncertain, and operationalized the construct as willingness to take risks. At one extreme, those with low uncertainty avoidance are comfortable with ambiguous situations; at the other extreme, those with high uncertainty avoidance value certainty, security, and structure. Pelto's (1968) concept of tightness is theoretically relevant to the uncertainty avoidance construct. A tight culture requires members to conform to norms, while a loose culture allows greater latitude in behavior. This contrast parallels the distinction between those with high and low uncertainty avoidance. In other words, individuals with a high need for certainty possess subjective norms that reinforce conformity to conventions and avoiding the unknown. On the other hand, individuals with a low need for certainty hold subjective norms that being more adventurous and open to novel experiences is appropriate.

In the next two sections, we describe our predictions regarding uncertainty avoidance, and suggest that culture will have a greater effect for persuasion than originality. Figure 13.2C illustrates our predictions.

Uncertainty avoidance, conformity norms, and persuasion

Based on the above definition of uncertainty avoidance, we propose that individuals with high uncertainty avoidance (or tight culture) are less likely to adopt the minority position publicly because they possess subjective norms that characterize appropriate behavior as conforming to conventional views and adhering to the majority position. This is consistent with research on uncertainty orientation (as another form of individual difference) which demonstrates that those who value certainty stay with the familiar and predictable (Sorrentino, Bobocel, Gitta, Olson, & Hewitt, 1988). On the other hand, individuals with low uncertainty avoidance (loose culture) have greater latitude to deviate from the majority position because their subjective norms view the adoption of unconventional opinions as acceptable and, at times, desirable. Hence, they are more likely to agree publicly with the minority position.

Proposition 5: *When exposed to minority influence, those with a high uncertainty avoidance cultural orientation will experience less persuasion than those with a low uncertainty avoidance cultural orientation.*

Uncertainty avoidance, divergent thinking, and originality

For originality and uncertainty avoidance, we propose a similar interaction compared to that described above for persuasion. Individuals with low uncertainty avoidance beliefs are more receptive towards the minority influence agent because they embrace ambiguity and view the risk-taking behavior of the minority influence agent as congruent with their subjective norms. Hence, we propose that influence targets with low uncertainty avoidance are less distracted by the behavior of the minority influence agent (because it is consistent with their values), pay greater attention to the content of the minority message, and consequently experience more divergent thinking and demonstrate greater originality.

Conversely, people with high uncertainty avoidance cultural values view risk taking and the introduction of uncertainty as inappropriate behavior. They are likely to channel greater attention to the source of the nonnormative social behavior in attempts to understand the motives of the minority influence agent. As a result, they engage in less divergent thinking targeted at the issue and more divergent thinking directed at the source. Hence, they exhibit less originality.

Proposition 6: *When exposed to minority influence, those with a high uncertainty avoidance cultural orientation will exhibit less originality than those with a low uncertainty avoidance cultural orientation.*

Minority Influence and Masculinity–Femininity

Hofstede defined masculinity–femininity as "what, in a given environment, is deemed suitable for members of one sex rather than the other" (1984, p. 190). Masculinity–femininity is also an index of sex-role differentiation. In this chapter, we adopt Hofstede's (1984) conceptualization of masculinity–femininity as a bipolar construct and view masculinity and femininity as the two ends of a continuum. Those high in masculinity believe firmly in gender-based roles where men and women are assigned different tasks, rights, and privileges, and are subject to different rules of conduct (Spence & Helmreich, 1978). Paralleling this division of labor, men tend to develop independence, self-reliance, and other instrumental skills; women, on the other hand, usually develop nurturant and expressive characteristics. In contrast, those high in femininity view gender roles as fluid and flexible. They favor equality and believe that the roles of men and women are not fixed. Instead, each individual develops his or her own set of characteristic behaviors. A person who is high in femininity puts less emphasis on gender-role differentiation than a person who is low in femininity (i.e., high in masculinity) (e.g., Hofstede & Associates, 1998, p. 103).

In theorizing about the role of masculinity–femininity cultural values, we focus on the gender of the minority influence agent. We predict that the gender of the minority influence agent will interact with the degree of masculinity–femininity of the influence target and that the effect will be stronger for persuasion compared to originality. These predictions are illustrated in Figure 13.2D.

Masculinity–femininity, conformity norms, and persuasion

Those with a masculinity cultural orientation believe that it is appropriate for men to occupy dominant, powerful positions where they routinely attempt to influence others (Spence & Helmreich, 1978). These individuals hold subjective norms that specify gender-role differences, resulting in stereotypical expectations for men and women. This perspective is consistent with social role theory (Eagly, 1987), which asserts that men and women are socialized to exhibit different gender-specific role behavior. Within this framework, agential behaviors such as assertive attempts to persuade others are more appropriate for males and less appropriate for females (Eagly & Wood, 1991). Thus, we propose that those with a masculinity cultural orientation will be more open to influence or public persuasion when the minority influence agent is male (compared to female) because this behavior conforms to their subjective norms.

On the other hand, individuals with a feminine cultural orientation (i.e., low masculinity) view gender roles as flexible. They emphasize the community and the collective (Curtis, Grabb, & Baer, 1992; Rothschild & Whitt, 1986) and rotate leadership roles from person to person without regard for traditional gender-role stereotypes. This more fluid approach to roles and behavior is based on the absence of rigid gender-role norms. Thus, those with a femininity cultural orientation should be equally influenced by male and female minority influence agents since their subjective norms suggest that attempting to persuade others is equally appropriate behavior for males and females.

In summary, we posit that the gender of the minority influence agent will influence persuasion for those with masculinity cultural values but not for those with femininity cultural values.

Proposition 7: *Those with a masculinity cultural orientation will exhibit greater persuasion when exposed to male minority influence agents than when they are exposed to female minority influence agents. At the same time, those with a femininity cultural orientation will exhibit equal persuasion when exposed to male and female minority influence agents.*

Masculinity–femininity, divergent thinking, and originality

As with the persuasion outcome, we propose that the gender of the minority influence agent is important to those with a masculinity cultural orientation but not to those with a femininity orientation. Those who are high in masculinity possess subjective norms that men should be more independent, dominant, aggressive, and rational than women (Spence & Helmreich, 1978). Since they perceive the role of a minority influence agent to be appropriate for a male and not for a female, a female minority influence agent violates their normative beliefs, and triggers negative source evaluation. This negative evaluation shifts attention away from issue-relevant thoughts and toward assessment of the source. As such, less divergent thinking is aimed at the issue, resulting in less originality.

We also suggest that the gender of the minority influence agent will be less salient to those who are high in femininity (i.e., low masculinity). Since individuals with high femininity are flexible in their views of the roles of men and women, the gender of the minority influence agent should be less likely to trigger evaluation of the source. Hence, we do not expect divergent thinking to differ according to the gender of the influence agent for those with femininity subjective norms.

Proposition 8: Those with a masculinity cultural orientation will exhibit greater originality when exposed to male minority influence agents than when they are exposed to female minority influence agents. At the same time, those with a femininity cultural orientation will exhibit equal originality when exposed to male and female minority influence agents.

Conclusion

The globalization of businesses, diversification of the workforce, and the increasing use of productive conflict in organizations provide practical impetus for research on minority influence to include the role of cultural differences. We propose that culture can affect the minority influence process in two ways: first, by affecting the manner and/or frequency in which the minority influence agent expresses dissenting views; second, by affecting the reactions of the minority influence target when he or she is exposed to dissenting views. Our chapter highlights the role of culture from the minority influence target's perspective, and in particular, focuses on how public persuasion and originality of subsequent ideas can be affected by cultural values. Adopting Hofstede's (1984) four cultural dimensions, we presented eight propositions suggesting that individualism–collectivism, power distance, uncertainty avoidance, and masculinity–femininity moderate the effect of minority influence on persuasion and originality. We base our arguments on the rationale that culture is one basis for the formation of subjective norms about appropriate behavior, and that judgments of appropriateness affect individuals' public conformity (persuasion) and private divergent thinking (originality) in response to minority influence.

To recapitulate, we propose that collectivists are less likely to adopt the minority position publicly and will exhibit less originality than individualists. With regard to power distance, we posit that status of the minority influence agent enhances persuasion for those with high and low power distance, albeit in different magnitudes. However, influence targets with high power distance beliefs demonstrate greater originality (than low power distance influence targets) when interacting with a high status minority influence agent, but exhibit less originality (than low power distance influence targets) when the minority influence agent has low status. We also contend that influence targets with high uncertainty avoidance are less likely to adopt the minority position publicly, and generate less original solutions when compared to influence targets who possess low uncertainty avoidance beliefs. Finally, we argue that the gender of the minority influence agent affects the degree of persuasion and originality for individuals with high masculinity, but that it will have no effect for individuals with low masculinity (i.e., high femininity individuals).

Our propositions suggest contrasting moderating effects of culture on the minority influence outcomes of persuasion and originality. These initial steps toward developing a cultural model of minority influence should add value to research in two important ways. First, we can enhance the predictive power of minority influence models by considering the role of culture. Second, we can assess the generalizability of the minority influence model in a variety of cultural settings. In conclusion, we recommend empirical examination of our proposed model. Such research could provide valuable practical insight regarding persuasion and originality. In this time of globalization and diversity, such research can enhance managers' sensitivity to the cultural idiosyncracies of their employees and heighten awareness that psychological processes can be influenced by cultural characteristics (Fiske et al., 1998).

NOTE

We thank Nanne De Vries, Carsten De Dreu, and all participants at the Amsterdam Minority Influence Conference for their helpful suggestions on an earlier version of this paper.

REFERENCES

Amason, A. (1996). Distinguishing the effects of functional and dysfunctional conflict on strategic decision making: Resolving a paradox for top management teams. *Academy of Management Journal, 39*, 123–148.

Bandura, A. (1986). *Social foundations of thoughts and action: A social cognitive theory.* Englewood Cliffs, NJ: Prentice-Hall.

Bochner, S., & Hesketh, B. (1994). Power distance, individualism/collectivism, and job-related attitudes in a culturally diverse work group. *Journal of Cross-Cultural Psychology, 25*(2), 233–257.

Bohner, G., Erb, H-P., Reinhard, M-A., & Frank, E. (1996). Distinctiveness across topics in minority and majority influence: An attributional analysis and preliminary data. *British Journal of Social Psychology, 35*, 27–46.

Bond, M. H., & Smith, P. B. (1996a). Cross cultural social and organizational psychology. *Annual Review of Psychology, 47*, 205–235.

Bond, R., & Smith, P. B. (1996b). Culture and conformity: A meta-analysis of studies using Asch's (1952b, 1956) line judgment task. *Psychological Bulletin, 119*, 111–137.

Butera, F., Mugny, G., Legrenzi, P., & Pérez, J. A. (1996). Majority and minority influence, task representation and inductive reasoning. *British Journal of Social Psychology, 35*, 123–136.

Chan, D. K. S., Gelfand, M. J., Triandis, H. C., & Tzeng, O. (1996). Tightness–looseness revisited: Some preliminary analyses in Japan and the United States. *International Journal of Psychology, 31*, 1–12.

Chatman, J. A., & Barsade, S. G. (1995). Personality, organizational culture, and cooperation: Evidence from a business simulation. *Administrative Science Quarterly, 40*, 423–443.

Chen, C. C., Chen, X. P., & Meindl, J. R. (1998). How can cooperation be fostered? The cultural effects of individualism–collectivism *Academy of Management Review, 23*, 285–304.

Cialdini, R. B., & Trost, M. R. (1998). Social influence: Social norms, conformity, and compliance. In D. T. Gilbert, S. T. Fiske, & G. Lindzey (Eds.), *The handbook of social psychology* (4th ed., Vol. 2, pp. 151–192). Boston, MA: McGraw Hill.

Curtis, J. E., Grabb, E. G., & Baer, D. E. (1992). Voluntary association membership in fifteen countries: A comparative analysis. *American Sociological Review, 57*, 139–152.

David, B., & Turner, J. C. (1996). Studies in self-categorization and minority conversion: Is being a member of the out-group an advantage? *British Journal of Social Psychology, 35*, 179–199.

De Dreu, C. K. W., & de Vries, N. (1996). Differential processing and attitude change following majority versus minority arguments. *British Journal of Social Psychology, 35*, 77–90.

De Dreu, C. K. W., & Van de Vliert, E. (1997). *Using conflict in organizations.* Thousand Oaks, CA: Sage.

Eagly, A. H. (1987). *Sex differences in social behavior: A social-role interpretation.* Hillsdale, NJ: Erlbaum.

Eagly, A. H., & Chaiken, S. (1998). Attitude structure and function. In D. T. Gilbert, S. T. Fiske, & G. Lindzey (Eds.), *The handbook of social psychology* (4th ed., Vol. 1, pp. 269–322). Boston, MA: McGraw Hill.

Eagly, A. H., & Wood, W. (1991). Explaining sex differences in social behavior: A meta-analytic perspective. *Personality and Social Psychology Bulletin, 17,* 306–315.

Earley, P. C. (1993). East meets west meets mideast: Further explorations of collectivistic and individualistic work groups. *Academy of Management Journal, 36,* 319–348.

Earley, P. C., & Gibson, C. B. (1998). Taking stock in our progress on individualism–collectivism: 100 years of solidarity and community. *Journal of Management, 24,* 265–304.

Farh, J. L., Earley, P. C., & Lin, S. C. (1997). Impetus for action: A cultural analysis of justice and organizational citizenship behavior in Chinese Society. *Administrative Science Quarterly, 42,* 421–444.

Fishbein, M., & Ajzen, I. (1975). *Belief, attitude, intention, and behavior: An introduction to theory and research.* Reading, MA: Addison–Wesley.

Fiske, S. T., Kitayama, S., Markus, H. R., & Nisbett, R. E. (1998). The cultural matrix of social psychology. In D. T. Gilbert, S. T. Fiske, & G. Lindzey (Eds.), *The handbook of social psychology* (4th ed., Vol. 2, pp. 915–981). Boston, MA: McGraw Hill.

Fiske, S. T., & Taylor, S. E. (1991). *Social cognition* (2nd ed.). New York: McGraw Hill.

Graham, J. L. (1983). Brazilian, Japanese, and American business negotiations. *Journal of International Business Studies, 14,* 47–61.

Granrose, C. S., & Oskamp, S. (1997). *Cross-cultural work groups.* Thousand Oaks, CA: Sage.

Hofstede, G. (1984). *Culture's consequences: International differences in work-related values.* Beverly Hills, CA: Sage.

Hofstede, G. (1991). *Cultures and organizations: Software of the mind.* New York: McGraw Hill.

Hofstede, G., & Associates. (1998). *Masculinity and femininity: The taboo dimension of national cultures.* Thousand Oaks, CA: Sage Publications.

Jehn, K. A. (1995). A multimethod examination of the benefits and detriments of intragroup conflict. *Administrative Science Quarterly, 40,* 256–282.

Jehn, K. A. (1997). A qualitative analysis of conflict types and dimensions in organizational groups. *Administrative Science Quarterly, 42,* 530–557.

Kluckhohn, C. (1954). *Culture and behavior.* New York: Free Press.

Latané, B., & Wolf, S. (1981). The social impact of majorities and minorities. *Psychological Review, 88,* 438–453.

Markus, H. R., & Kitayama, S. (1991). Culture and the self: Implications for cognitions, emotion, and motivation. *Psychological Review, 98,* 224–253.

Maass, A., Volpato, C., & Mucchi-Faina, A. (1996). Social influence and the verifiability of the issue under discussion: Attitudinal versus objective items. *British Journal of Social Psychology, 35,* 15–26.

Martin, R. (1996). Minority influence and argument generation. *British Journal of Social Psychology, 35,* 91–103.

Milgram, S. (1961). Nationality and conformity. *Scientific American, 205*(6), 45–51.

Moscovici, S. (1976). *Social influence and social change.* New York: Academic Press.

Moscovici, S. (1980). Toward a theory of conversion behavior. In L. Berkowitz (Ed.), *Advances in experimental social psychology* (Vol. 13, pp. 209–242). San Diego, CA: Academic Press.

Moscovici, S., & Lage, E. (1976). Studies in social influence III: Majority versus minority influence in a group. *European Journal of Social Psychology, 6,* 149–174.

Moscovici, S., Lage, E., & Naffrechoux, M. (1969). Influence of a consistent minority on the responses of a majority in a color perception task. *Sociometry, 32,* 365–379.

Mugny, G. (1980). *The power of minorities.* London: Academic Press.

Nemeth, C. J. (1986). Differential contributions of majority and minority influence. *Psychological Review, 93,* 23–32.

Nemeth, C. J., & Chiles, C. (1988). Modelling courage: The role of dissent in fostering independence. *European Journal of Psychology, 18,* 275–280.

Nemeth, C. J., & Kwan, J. (1985). Originality of word associations as a function of majority vs minority. *Social Psychology Quarterly, 48,* 277–282.

Nemeth, C. J., & Kwan, J. (1987). Minority influence, divergent thinking and detection of correct solutions. *Journal of Applied Social Psychology, 17,* 788–799.

Nemeth, C. J., Mosier, J., & Chiles, C. (1992). When convergent thought improves performance: Majority versus minority influence. *Personality and Social Psychology Bulletin, 18,* 139–144.

Nemeth, C. J., Swedlund, M., & Kanki, B. (1974). Patterning of the minority's responses and their influence on the majority. *European Journal of Social Psychology, 4:* 53–64.

Nemeth, C. J., & Wachtler, J. (1974). Creating perceptions of consistency and confidence: A necessary condition for minority influence. *Sociometry, 37,* 529–540.

Nemeth, C. J., & Wachtler, J. (1983). Creative problem solving as a result of majority vs minority influence. *European Journal of Social Psychology, 13,* 45–55.

Nemeth, C. J., Wachtler, J., & Endicott, J. (1977). Increasing the size of the minority: Some gains and some losses. *European Journal of Social Psychology, 1,* 11–23.

Peabody, D. (1985). *National characteristics.* Cambridge, UK: Cambridge University Press.

Pelto, P. J. (1968). The difference between "tight" and "loose" societies. *Transactions* April: 37–40.

Petty, R. E., & Wegener, D. T. (1998). Attitude change: Multiple roles for persuasion variables. In D. T. Gilbert, S. T. Fiske, & G. Lindzey (Eds.), *The handbook of social psychology* (4th ed., Vol. 1, pp. 323–390). Boston, MA: McGraw Hill.

Rothschild, J., & Whitt, J. A. (1986). The cooperative workplace: Potentials and dilemmas of organizational democracy and participation. Cambridge, UK: Cambridge University Press.

Sanchez-Mazas, M. (1996). Minority influence under value conflict: The case of human rights and xenophobia. *British Journal of Social Psychology, 35*, 169–178.

Schweiger, D. M., Sandberg, W. R., & Rechner, P. L. (1989). Experiential effects of dialectical inquiry, devil's advocacy, and consensus approaches to strategic decision making. *Academy of Management Journal, 32*, 745–772.

Schwenk, C. R. (1990). Effects of devil's advocacy and dialectical inquiry on decision making: A meta-analysis. *Organizational Behavior and Human Decision Processes, 47*, 161–176.

Shane, S., Venkataraman, S., & MacMillan, I. (1995). Cultural differences in innovation championing strategies. *Journal of Management, 21*, 931–952.

Sorrentino, R. M., Bobocel, D. R., Gitta, M. Z., Olson, J. M., & Hewitt, E. C. (1988). Uncertainty orientation and persuasion: Individual differences in the effects of personal relevance on social judgments. *Journal of Personality and Social Psychology, 55*, 357–371.

Spence, J. T., & Helmreich, R. L. (1978). *Masculinity and femininity: Their psychological dimensions, correlates and antecedents.* Austin, TX: University of Texas Press.

Triandis, H. C. (1988). Cross-cultural contributions to theory. In M. H. Bond (Ed.), *The cross-cultural challenge to social psychology* (pp. 122–140). Newbury, CA: Sage.

Triandis, H. C. (1990). Cross cultural studies of individualism and collectivism. In J. Berman (Ed.), *Nebraska symposium on motivation* (pp. 41–133). Lincoln, NE: University of Nebraska Press.

Triandis, H. C. (1995). *Individualism and collectivism.* Boulder, CO: Westview Press.

Triandis, H. C., Bontempo, R., Villareal, M. J., Asai, M., & Lucca, N. (1988). Individualism and collectivism: Cross-cultural perspectives on self-ingroup relationships. *Journal of Personality and Social Psychology, 54*, 323–338.

Van Dyne, L., & Saavedra, R. (1996). A naturalistic minority influence experiment: Effects on divergent thinking, conflict and originality in work-groups. *British Journal of Social Psychology, 35*, 151–168.

Volpato, C., Maass, A., Mucchi-Faina, A., & Vitti, E. (1990). Minority influence and social categorization. *European Journal of Social Psychology, 20*, 119–132.

Wagner, J. A. III. (1995). Studies of individualism–collectivism: Effects on cooperation in groups. *Academy of Management Journal, 38*, 152–172.

Wolf, S. (1979). Behavioral style and group cohesiveness as sources of minority influence. *European Journal of Social Psychology, 9*, 381–395.

Author Index

Subject Index

acceptance, delayed 113
accountability, to constituency 235
affective consequences 12, 275
afterimage effect 8
afterimage paradigm 19–21, 33–5
afterimage studies 16, 19–28
  and perceptual artefact 26
  and suspicious participants 22, 27, 33
aptitude task 167
argument quality 66, 77
arguments, strong vs. weak 68, 76
arguments, valence of 107
Asch paradigm, reversed 3–4
attack–defend model of escalation 264
attitude
  –behavior models 287
  defined 287
  favorable and unfavorable 46
  prior 42
  -relevant information 42, 52
  see also influence
attributional
  analysis of persuasion 71–2, 75, 78
  reasoning 63
attributions 61–2
  dispositional 69
  and systematic processing 70
augmentation 71, 72, 74
  principle 71
  rule 69
authoritarianism 263

bargaining 246, 259
  representative 251
behavioral consistency 72, 82, 243
behavioral strategies 63, 84–5
behavioral style 3, 5, 7, 69, 201, 266–7, 274
  confident and consistent 99
  insufficiency of 210–11
beliefs
  focal vs. related 135
  prior 66, 70–3
  shared 114, 190
biased processing hypothesis 43, 45, 46, 49–54
biased scanning approach 146
biased systematic processing 52, 67
bureaucratic politics perspective 232
business negotiation 288

change
  delayed focal 130, 137
  see also influence
Christian doctrine 201, 222
Christian religion 221–3
coalition formation 241–2, 245, 246
cognitive dissonance 63, 107, 146, 148, 150
  and arousal state 63
cognitive effort 44
cognitive energy and stereotypes 47–8
cognitive load
  and effortful processing 81
  and strong vs. weak arguments 80